BLACK TUNA DIARIES

THE AUTOBIOGRAPHY OF ROBERT ELLIOT PLATSHORN

America's most written about marijuana smuggler...and longest serving federal prisoner for a non-violent marijuana offense.
Almost 30 years in federal prisons.

A special thanks to David Bienenstock Senior Editor at High Times magazine for all his help and encouragement.

The cover art was designed and provided by Murphy Green. Pre-publication technical assistance and layout files for the cover art were provided by Elise McDonough and the High Times art department. Thank you for all your hard work.

Author's Limited Edition
Unedited

Copyright 2007,2009 Robert Platshorn

All rights reserved. No part of this publication may be reproduced. stored in a retrieval system, or transmitted in any form or by any means, electronic, mechanical, photocopying, recording, or otherwise, without the permission of the publisher/author.

Library of Congress Control Number 2009933455
ISBN: 978-0-615-28780-5
Published by TV Publishing, West Palm Beach, Fl
Cover Design by Murphy Green

Printed in the United States of America

Copies of this Limited Edition of Black Tuna Diaries are only available through www.blacktunadiaries.com .
For discounts for educational or institutional bulk orders contact the publisher at www.tunaville@yahoo.com .

Formatting, Layout, and Proofing assistance
Provided by
Son of The Tuna

Dedication

For my pals Zev and Woody. When they were released from prison, they kept me in commissary funds. This made it possible for me to spend over a year writing this book rather than working in a prison factory or kitchen for twenty cents an hour to pay for toothpaste, deodorant, medicines, medical attention and a few snacks.

For Matt and Astrid who read each messy chapter banged out on a broken down prison typewriter and gave me encouragement to keep at it. Tom Noe my last prison roommate who read it all and liked it, despite being a Republican.

The entire staff at High Times magazine for all their help.

My wife Lynne, who since I was sixteen years old, has always been there for me and had a home for me when I was released after twenty-nine years in durance vile. And especially for my mom, dad, sisters Marilyn and Paula, my daughter Hope, and my first wife and dear friend Elen, none of whom survived my incarceration. I believe they would have loved every word. And for nephew Jon who helped me get back on my feet, his wife Jodie, son Mason...my daughter-in-law Leslie..who gave me two gorgeous granddaughters for whom this will be family history.

Black Tuna Diaries

Chapter 1
Death by Firing Squad

Everyone knows that a black cat has nine lives, but a Black Tuna only seven. Here is a true account of how I lost number two by firing squad in the jungles of Colombia.

Late 1977! The gun barrel painfully prodding the base of my spine was attached to an ancient M-1 carbine. A present from my Uncle Sam to the Colombian Army! Attached to the carbine was a short tan Indio in the uniform of the Colombian Army. He was effectively using the gun barrel to force me into the back of a rusting step van parked on a dirt trail near a clandestine airstrip, deep in the mountainous jungle of Colombia. It was over 100 degrees in the damp equatorial forest and it promised to be even hotter in the moldy interior of the truck. Crowded onto the 2 narrow benches with me were our loading crew, a dozen very large fierce Guarjiran Indians, and two pilots. The two pilots Capt. Beercan and Bo, an ex-NFL player called El Gigante, were captured with me and the Guarjirans on the nearby airstrip. The army, claiming they were not paid the customary "landing fees" was taking us to the nearby town of La Cienega to shoot us as a warning to others who might neglect their mordida. Our DC-3 and its cargo of 5000lbs. of the real legendary Santa Marta Gold, the most sought after marijuana in South America, was sitting on the airstrip guarded by a squad of Colombian soldiers. In truth we had paid our "landing fees," but the money had been misappropriated by the owners of the busy jungle air field. It was the rainy season and theirs was the only usable landing field on the Atlantic Coast. They would load four or five planes a day, but only pay mordida for two or three. It was our bad luck to be on the field when the army showed up to collect past due accounts. Held at gunpoint in the equatorial sun for over four hours with nothing to drink, we were already dehydrated. Climbing into the step van was like leaving a sauna for an oven. Being the last to climb in, I sat by the open rear doors. Capt. Beercan in the far dark corner was already asleep and El Gigante was in the middle of six large Guarjirans trying not to look scared. Me, I was stoned from handling and smoking 5000 lbs. of primo pot in the hot sun. To avoid thinking about

Black Tuna Diaries

the promised firing squad, I closed my eyes and asked myself, "self, how in the hell did you end up here?"

It was Hendela's fault. No doubt. You see, back in 1961 or 62, it was Hendela who first got me high. A bright and annoying child, Hendela is Robby's younger sister. She probably thought it would be hilarious to get me so wrecked that I wouldn't be able to pick up my mom at Berkowitz's ladies store on South St, where she was working, and drive her back to Atlantic City. We no longer owned the Cissy Shops on South St. My mom owned a small hotel in Atlantic City on Virginia Avenue. In the winter, in order to support herself and the hotel, she commuted 120 miles by bus each day to work at Berkowitz Ladies Coats & Suits, on South Street. If I wasn't away in school or on a road trip pitching blenders, I would always try to drive into Philly and drive my mom home, so that she didn't have to travel uptown to the bus terminal and take the long ride back to A.C.

I was an hour early when I hit South St. that Sunday in 1962. It was about 5 o'clock. The store closed at 6p.m. I decided to visit with Robert Jay. Mary and Sam were busy in the store with customers. I headed up to the fourth floor where we always hung out as kids. Hendela was propped on the sofa with a book, "Robby should be back soon". I walked over to the window to watch the traffic flowing in and out of the stores that lined both sides of the street. I was thinking about going across the street to Diamond's men's shop to look for a winter jacket. I figured I could still get a 25% "street discount" even though we had moved away four or five years ago.

"Hey Platch?" I really did despise that nick name. Hendela knew it and relished the sound of it. "Want to get high?"

Whoa! I turned from the window and took a good look. Hendela had grown up. When did that happen? Well, grown up or not, Hendela still liked to mess with my head. Of all her older brother's friends, I believe she got the most joy sticking pins in me. I, of course, loved Hendela, as I did all the ladies of the South St. Sisterhood (and secret sorority). I watched in semi-shock as she expertly rolled a fat doobie and told me

Black Tuna Diaries

what ass kicking pot it was. Okay! I had toked a few joints of Mexican ditch weed, but never gotten a serious buzz. At first, I demurred, saying it would be a waste as pot didn't do much for me. Hendela, of course, raised the stakes to a dare. Even at the age of 19 or 20, I was petrified that Sam or Mary might walk up the stairs and smell the roses, and figure I was corrupting their little angel. She already had it lit. Killer Colombian, you could smell the sweet pungent smoke a mile away. Oh well, in for a penny, in for a pound. She passed it over and that first toke almost took out my lungs. Tijuana Trash never did that! When I was able to breathe again I took another tentative toke or two and passed it back to the devil girl. Believing nothing much would happen, I went back to looking out the window. Soon I was lost in watching cars perform the incredible feat of parallel parking along the crowded street, while at the same time listening to the rush of blood pumping past the vicinity of my ear drums. Shit! I'd never make it down the stairs and past Sam and Mary, much less walk the entire block to Berky's and drive my mom home to A.C. I had to sit down before I fell down. My knees wobbled as I inched the four or five steps to the couch. Hendela was delighted with her handiwork. I was paralyzed and paranoid. Zombied out on the couch, unable to rise and hardly able to talk coherently.

I don't recall if Robby ever showed up. At 5 of six, I knew it was now or never. I had to go get my mom before she left for the bus station. Hendela, with a totally insincere show of concern, helped me to stand and watched me start down the steep stairway, holding on for dear life to the banister. Down three flights and out through the store, waving to Sam and The Mare, but saying nothing. It seemed like forever covering the block to Berky's. But by the time I arrived, I had pretty much pulled myself together. My mom still had a customer. The extra time spent in inane pleasantries with Berky Jr. sobered me up. It was an easy 60 mile drive on the new and thankfully empty Atlantic City Expressway, rocking to the sounds of the Beatles and the Supremes.

Maybe, it wasn't Hendela. It was Cool Hand Luke MC Cloud who put me in the pot business. Certainly he'd be the one responsible for my imminent demise by firing squad. Luke and I

Black Tuna Diaries

had worked together as pitchmen at fairs and home shows for many years. Luke got his moniker "Cool Hand" by demonstrating T-Fal nonstick frying pans while romancing the ladies in his audience. His blond good looks and soft southern accent charmed the girls and sold one hell of a lot of frying pans. Luke liked to work "low," that is, right down at eye level with his audience. I, on the other hand, whether demonstrating Vita Mix Blenders or T-Fal pans, love the "high pitch," i.e. I stood on a on a raised platform behind a high counter, well above the heads of my audience. With six spotlights on me, and a mirror overhead, I could hypnotize a crowd of 150 or 200 people at one time. Luke and I were two of the top grossing pitchmen in the country. But I digress. The year is 1976, late summer, at the Wisconsin state fair at West Alice, near Milwaukee. Luke now has his own T-shirt and souvenir concessions. He plans to run Christmas promotions in department stores in Philly and south Jersey. He knows that I own the Ice Cream Factory on South St. An ice cream and video game parlor, in the building that housed my wholesale ice cream and pushcart depot. Luke needed a place to keep his concession trailers and warehouse his Christmas merchandise. Since I closed my ice cream business in the winter, Luke wanted to sublet my depot. We struck a deal. "

By the way", says Mr. Cool Hand, "do you know anyone in Philly who can move some weight? I'm talking primo Colombian pot". Luke explained that in the "off season," in the winter, he was using his concession trucks to deliver pot for a big time smuggler in south Florida. Luke was looking to step up from delivery boy, to dealer (and eventually to squealer). "Let me think about it. We can talk more in a few days".

A couple of weeks earlier, before I left to work the fairs, Robby stopped by my office on South St. and told me about a friend who was wholesaling high end weed. It would be a simple matter for Robby and Luke to get together while Luke was using my depot in the weeks before Christmas. I was heading to Florida after the fairs, to reprise my college career with a view to law school at the University of Miami. Not being on the scene, if Robby and Luke were able to deal, I'd have to rely on them to thrown me a small commission. And so the

Black Tuna Diaries

first and last two members of the South Street Gang became pot dealers. Lukas MC Cloud would soon become an informer.

But as I think about it, it wasn't actually Luke the Puke who got us into the smuggling end of the business. For that I have to thank Capt. Crunch and his friend with two first names. Miles Norman or was it Norman Miles! By now its 1977. I'm living in the Spring Gardens section of old Miami, on the Seabold Canal. Capt. Crunch, a charter boat captain, and his mate Randy are temporarily unemployed and helping me restore an old 40 ft. Elco Sportsfisherman that I bought for 2,000 bucks from Tommy's Boatyard on the Miami River. I've got one bale of pot, left over from a few hundred pounds I brokered for a local Cuban river runner. I dole the pot out to Crunch and Randy to pay for parts and put a few bucks in their pockets. Crunch quickly figures out that I deal weight. Crunch decides to introduce me to a smuggler he worked with in the past. Miles Norman, or was it Norman Miles?

Miles was looking for someone to sell the small 1,500 lb. loads of Colombian weed the he was smuggling into the Everglades, in an old D-18 Beachcraft. A former partner had handled that end of the business, and now he needed an outlet. His mistake was to make Robby and I his partners, instead of just his customers.

He would prepare false expense accounts, to cheat us out of our end of the profits. We made less money as his partners, than we would have being brokers. We figured this out pretty quickly, but we decided to let Miles teach us the smuggling game.

My first adrenalin rush came, when Miles took me with him to a well known smugglers airstrip in the Everglades, called Grimy Gulch. Together we watched a D-18 Beachcraft, a small WWII era, twin radial engine plane, appear in the distance, hugging the tree tops until it was time to drop onto the dirt strip. A red pickup truck with a utility body like a plumber's truck, waited at the end of the airstrip for the load. The old plane taxied to the end of the runway, spun around, the door popped open and the pickup backed up to the opening. Less

Black Tuna Diaries

than three minutes later, the Beech was lifting off and Miles and I were leading Cowboy in the loaded truck through the maze of dirt trails leading back to Alligator Alley and the Tamiami Trail to Miami.

What a rush! We dropped the load off at Dr. Moe Keller's stash house to be weighed, then loaded into the vehicles provided by our customers from Philly, NY, Boston, Detroit and Chicago. Finally we returned to my house on the Seabold Canal and celebrated a successful mission. It wasn't such a rush a week later when we had to turn most of the money over to Miles to satisfy his phony expense claims. After the second trip, Miles, who was no dummy, could sense we were about to dissolve the partnership. That's when he made his second and final mistake in our "partnership". He invited Robby and I to join him in Barranquilla Colombia, for a meeting with his "connection". If that seemed too good to be true, it was. Miles said he would fly down first. Robby and I would follow, ostensibly on legitimate business for our auto auction. He insisted we not fly direct, but go via Bogotá, to shake off anyone tailing us. 007 stuff! Mostly a load of crap!

After spending a night in the most exclusive bordello in Bogotá, we flew to Barranquilla, and checked into the Del Prado Hotel to wait for Miles to contact us. The Del Prado is a gracious old world hotel, built around gardens and courtyards in the classic Spanish/Moorish style. The central courtyard has an outdoor restaurant, Olympic swimming pool, cabanas, and tennis courts.

We arrived there around noon. By 4 or 5 o'clock we realized that Miles wasn't going to show. Robby phoned his house in Ft. Lauderdale, to be told by his wife that Miles was back in Florida and sends his apologies for the "mix up" in timing. He left word we should fly back and meet him the next morning in Ft Lauderdale. Yeh right! Mr. Norman may have sent us on a wild goose chase, but geese ain't hard to find in a duck pond. We decided to stay a while and see what flew in.

Two prosperous looking gringos in their early 30s didn't go unnoticed for very long. We were up early the next morning

Black Tuna Diaries

having breakfast on the veranda overlooking the pool and tennis courts. By the time we were halfway through our breakfast of fresh fruits, huevos caballos, and tinto, Johnny, a Colombian about our own age, had walked over to our table, introduced himself, and joined us for coffee. His English was excellent, learned, he said, living five years in Detroit. He offered himself as a free tour guide, saying that after we got to know each other better, we might be able to talk about business opportunities in the import/export trade.

After breakfast we piled into his canary yellow Camaro, stopped to pick up his pal Roger, a street artist, and proceeded to explore Barranquilla and its environs. We ate at several good local restaurants, toked a little good herb, did the tourist thing and got to know each other well enough to talk business, at least in broad generalities. When we left Colombia the next day, it was clear that Johnny and Roger could get us a load of weed if called upon. Robby and I hinted that we might indeed be interested sometime in the near future. Johnny said we only had to ask the doorman at the Del Prado to call "Johnny with the Camaro". We left it at that and flew back to Miami. After one last 1400 lb. load with Miles, we dissolved the partnership and went our separate ways. We weren't quite ready to become smugglers. But Dr. Moe Keller would change all that in a hurry!

Dr. Morris Keller, podiatrist, professor, carnival concessioner, wanna be doper and eventually informer. We had met Moe when he was delivering small loads of weed for Luke MC Cloud. A bright likable upscale hippie, he had became a close friend. He spent a lot of time at my house and ate at my dinner table at least once or twice a week. Like the rest of us, Moe wanted no further dealing with Luke who had become a "Cocaine Cowboy". Dr. Keller was now an independent contractor offering warehouse and delivery services to south Florida pot purveyors. Mostly to me and Robby! We would pay Moe a flat fee per pound to warehouse our herb and load it into vehicles provided by our customers. Occasionally, Moe or his partner Carl Norwood would drive a load up north, for an additional fee. Moe had two friends who claimed to have been major smugglers of primo Colombian weed. So said Dr. Moe!

Black Tuna Diaries

And, according to Moe, these same two former herb haulers wished to resume their status in the drug trade. The only problem, they were broke, had no planes, no pilots, no boats, no crews. In fact, these big time purveyors of primo couldn't afford a plane ticket to Colombia to meet with their "connect". Moe proposed that if we could finance, transport, off load, warehouse and sell the promised primo, we could be full one third partners, with him and his two master smugglers. How very generous! Well, we were looking for a new supply and didn't quite have the confidence yet, to become smugglers.

Things began to fall into place. Robby was able to raise $150,000.00 front money from three of our customers, who were guaranteed a portion of the promised shipment. Finance and sales were taken care of. Offload and warehouse no problem! It would be a small plane load, less than a ton. Two people could handle it. The only missing piece was a plane and pilots. Now, I'm a pilot, but only a low time, single engine, non-instrument rated pilot. Not exactly qualified for a smuggling mission to Colombia! The man who was to become our third partner, Gene Myers, had the solution. Big Gene was already our customer. Buying small amounts, usually 60-200 lbs and taking it to the Tampa/St. Pete area, where he lived. He had been spending more and more time in Miami, trying to get close to Robby and I. Gene was a pilot with serious credentials. At one time a check ride pilot for Eastern Airlines, he told us the he had smuggled cigarettes from Panama, and claimed to know a bunch of pilots and aircraft operators not averse to doing a trip. That's how and when Gene became a full-one-third partner with Robby and I.

We fronted Moe and his two pot lords probably $25,000.00 of our customer's money, so they could return to Barranquilla in style. We spent another $50,000.00 of the front money to fix up a legendary DC-3 known as the Bad Ass, for its tail number BA 123. It turned out we couldn't use the Bad Ass because it was on the top of the DEA's hot list. Big surprise! In the end Gene arranged to do the trip with an Aero Commander, to be flown by its owner, with a copilot supplied by us. That took another $50,000.00 front and we hadn't brought in a seed yet.

Black Tuna Diaries

Moe's pals as best I can recall were Henry and Eddie. Henry lived in a tiny cardboard house, maybe in Hallandale. Threadbare carpets, dingy, with few lights. Not a good sign. I only got to see the place and meet Henry, because his partner Eddie had been in Barranquilla Colombia for three weeks, unsuccessfully trying to meet up with his connect, Tony the gangster. Robby and I were out of patience and running out of our customer's money. The Aero Commander guy was tired of standing by and threatening to back out. The copilot had lost his regular flying job because we had him on stand-by for three weeks. Moe had been feeding us bullshit stories, "pot being packaged," "check is in the mail," "one or two more days," "Little Eddie very ill, "bad water in Barranquilla". I finally convinced Moe that it was time for us to speak directly with one of his big time partners.

Meeting Henry in the shack in Hallandale convinced me that Moe's pals didn't have the credibility to produce a decent doobie, much less get someone to front them a load of primo weed on credit. I knew I would have to head for Barranquilla, if I wanted to salvage the trip. And so Robby, Bobby and Big Gene reluctantly got into the game.

Robby stayed behind to run the auction and coordinate. Gene had to be in Miami and Lauderdale to hold together the plane and pilots. We desperately needed a load of pot on credit. The best way to get it, we figured, was to make a flashy entrance down below. So Gene hooked me up with a chartered Lear Jet. Never been in one before. Lear 24, tiny but the ultimate flying machine, and beautiful. A fighter plane, with little wings like a rocket ship. It seemed to be flying while it sat on the ground. I knew one day I'd get to fly one. And so, I took the last $25,000.00 of our customers' money, to pay for the Lear and a splashy entrance into Barranquilla and I headed down to Colombia to find someone who would front us a load of weed on credit.

Thinking that I was flying out alone, I was more than a little surprised when Big Gene showed up with three huge bikers from his Outlaw Club in Tampa. They would accompany me to Barranquilla as part of the show, and then return to the states

Black Tuna Diaries

later in the day, leaving me to put together a load, before everything fell apart.

The two bikers sitting in the rear of the Lear could barely squeeze their leather clad bulk into the narrow fuselage. None of them had ever left the country before. So they sat silently trying to look stoic. There were complimentary beers and booze on the plane, but fortunately none of us was stupid enough to start drinking. That was fortunate, because at the end of the two hour flight, I found out that I was the only one on the plane carrying a passport. Now Colombia is a country that is very strict about visitors having a passport and a valid visa. I at least, had a passport. None of us had a visa. As we had hoped, our arrival in the Lear attracted plenty of attention, not all of it good. Having been there once before, I had a good idea where the head of the Colombian Customs had his office. I told Gene and the bikers to wait in the plane until I returned for them. I screwed up my huevos and casually strolled past five or six customs and police officers who had come out to watch the Lear disgorge its passengers. Luckily, the Commandante was in his officina. I deftly laid five one hundred dollar bills on the edge of his desk and explained that my friends had no passports but would be returning to the states in a few hours. They only wished to accompany me to the hotel for a brief business meeting. When I looked down the C notes had vanished. El Commandante made it clear that if my "associates" did not leave the country before the Commandante went home at five that evening, they would be "on their own" and subject to immediate arrest on the charge of illegal entry. I thanked him, assured him they would be gone in ample time and went to collect my little army.

Barranquilla Bob, the Baron of Barranquilla, Big Gene and the bikers gave me that name when I collected them from the plane and walked them past the customs officials and cops as if I owned the airport. No one but me could hear my knees knocking.

Waiting for us out front was Little Eddie, Moe's friend with all the excuses. Five feet nothing, pale as a ghost, soft as a marshmallow and scared out of his mind when he saw me

Black Tuna Diaries

emerge from the terminal with my brigade of bikers. That, of course, was the desired effect. During the 20 minute taxi ride to the Del Prado Hotel, Little Eddie told us his tales of woe.

The Del Prado looks like a movie set from "Casablanca". I marched up to the front desk and rented the Presidential Suite for an indefinite stay. Looking at my entourage, the staff at the front desk looked skeptical when I registered as the sole occupant of the suite. I tipped the doorman, who was waiting with my luggage, and quietly told him I needed to see Johnny with the yellow Camaro. He didn't think it would be a problem, and promised to deliver him to the Presidential Suite in half an hour. Johnny was the one person I had met on my first trip to Colombia that I felt I could trust. His close relationship with the Del Prado's doorman, the one person who knew everything that was going on in the hotel, would help me to quickly get to the bottom of all the bullshit surrounding Little Eddie. For a change my instincts were right.

Big Gene, the three Outlaws, Little Eddie and me, Barranquilla Bob, had just started in on the seafood tapas and cervesas delivered by room service, when there was another knock on the door of the suite. It was the doorman delivering Johnny. I tipped the doorman and shepherded Johnny into the bedroom where we could talk in private. He was as smart as I had remembered and had already figured out what the meeting was all about.

He told me that it was common knowledge among those in town who might be interested in such things, that Eddie had been waiting in the Del Prado for over a month to do a deal for a small planeload of yerba. It was also common knowledge that Eddie's connection, Tony the gangster, had no intention of fronting him so much as a seed. Tony hadn't visited the hotel or spoken to Eddie in two weeks. Johnny assured me that the doorman could verify all this, because Little Eddie had been pestering him for weeks to deliver a message to Tony. Eddie's deal was "dead and stinking". Eddie and his partners, Moe and Henry, had gone through the $25,000.00 front we gave them, and there would be nothing to show for it. Eddie didn't even have the cash to settle his hotel bill. If I hadn't

Black Tuna Diaries

shown up, he'd be in a Colombian jail, rotting until someone paid his debts. It was now or never! I told Johnny that I had an Aero Commander waiting to leave Miami. I needed 1500-2000 lbs. of top grade yerba and I needed it fronted to me. I was willing to stay behind in Colombia as a hostage until payment was made. Most important, I needed it fast, before everything fell apart. I made it clear to Johnny that the month lost waiting for Eddie's deal, put a serious strain on our resources. I liked Johnny and felt I could trust him with the truth. "Don't sweat it man. Everybody heard about your Lear Jet and your big bodyguards with no passports. I can bring someone here in an hour who will front you a good quality load. Besides everybody is dying to meet you, they think you must be crazy to come here like that".

I brought Johnny into the living room to meet the others, and to join us for a beer and tapas. I confronted Little Eddie with the story I had just heard. He admitted it may have been two weeks since he heard from Tony, but felt his deal could still fly. I told him to forget about it. I would arrange my own deal and let him help me so he could earn a few bucks, something he didn't really deserve after all the lies he had fed us and all of our cash he and his partners had taken under false pretenses. I gave him the option of a free ride home with Gene and the Outlaws in the Lear or he could stay and help me in whatever capacity was needed. To his credit, he chose the latter. Johnny left to get his connection, who would arrange an airfield and a load of grass on credit.

In less than an hour, Johnny reappeared with the "Chinaman". He wasn't really a Chinaman; in fact, I didn't think he even looked too much like one. Chino was a skinny, smiley faced Colombian, about my age, early thirties, wearing expensive jeans, casual shirt, and enough gold to be convincing. It turned out that Chino lived with his parents on a lovely tree lined street right around the corner from the hotel. I know this because I would live there for almost a week, sharing a bedroom with Chino's younger brother and eating at his family's table. For now it was getting late and I reminded Gene that he and his crew had to be back at the airport before the Commandante left at five o'clock. To his credit, he felt it was

Black Tuna Diaries

important for him and my "bodyguards" to stay until a deal had been made. He was confident I could get them back through the airport and onto the Lear. The bikers looked a little pale around the gills and I wasn't all that confident myself, but I agreed they should stay while I dealt with Chino. Gene and I were both hoping that should anything go wrong, the previous sight of him and my bodyguards would discourage anyone from messing with me.

It was now Monday evening; Chino promised he would have a load of top quality yerba, up to 2000 lbs., on a nearby jungle airfield by Saturday morning. It would cost us $60.00 a lb. which was high, but acceptable. I would stay as his "guest" until payment was received in full. Hand shake! Deal done...no more screwing around! Johnny looked me in the eyes and smiled. I know the deal was real. No more stalls or stories. Chino offered to take my crew back to the airport and see them safely through customs. He had a good connection there; it would only cost $200.00 to get them out. Things were looking up already. After paying for the Lear charter and Little Eddie's past due hotel bill, I had less than $19,000.00 left from the original $150,000.00 of our customer's front money. If this deal went south, I might as well stay in Colombia and pick coffee beans with Juan Valdez or swim with the pescados.

Believe this! I was not scared. I was confident that Gene would see that the Aero Commander, with our copilot aboard, would be in Aruba, ready to jump over to Colombia before Saturday morning. I was equally sure that come hell or high water, Robby would sell the load and deliver the money in record time to get me released. A million things could go wrong, but I just refused to think about them.

It took Johnny and Chino three days to iron out the details. By Thursday, Eddie, Johnny, Chino and I were in the resort town of El Rodedero, meeting with the three partners who would actually take the risk of fronting me a load and arranging an airfield and fuel for the return journey. Partner one was Chino's brother who for now I'll call Loco, for reasons that will become clear later in this account. Partner number two was Julio, whose family owned a hotel nearby and the third

Black Tuna Diaries

partner was the man who would be indicted, but never arrested, in the Black Tuna case, Raul Davila. All were in their thirties. Loco, clearly the city guy, didn't look too tough, but was quick to act the tough guy. Julio, thin, fierce, about 5'6", long dark hair, moved fast and took care of business. Raul, tall dark and silent, he came from a prominent family that pretty much ran things in that part of Colombia. All three carried big 45 caliber automatics and I don't think they were for show. I was eventually to become good friends with Julio and Raul, but distanced myself from Chino's brother.

Arrangements had been made to use a clandestine airstrip in the mountains above the town of La Cienega. We were at a small agricultural airfield below the lake, where Davila kept his Cessna 336, Push Pull, a two engine, fixed gear, high wing plane, with an engine in front to pull and one to push from the rear. Raul took us up in the 336 to show us the route to the mountain strip where the load would be waiting. Little Eddie's job would be to fly to Aruba, meet the Aero Commander and guide them to the airstrip. This was really a make-work job so that Eddie could earn enough to make up for the $25,000.00 front money he had blown, and maybe take home a few bucks for him and his two lying partners. A message to the pilots would have been sufficient. "Fly to La Cienega, the giant lake between Barranquilla and Santa Marta on the coast of Colombia. Turn inland to the town of La Cienega, on the edge of the lake. Fly over the tall church steeple on a certain heading, and in ten minutes after passing the church you can make radio contact, via short range CB radio". Anyone who could fly a plane could follow those instructions to a jungle strip so large, and at times, so busy, that we used to call it O'Hare south. This huge meadow was normally home to a herd of cows. When you made radio contact ten minutes out, two little kids on burros would chase the cows into the citrus groves bordering the field.

Speaking of kids on burros, the little agricultural field where Davila kept his Cessna had a narrow rutted 2000 ft. dirt runway. Before each takeoff, a little kid on a burro had to slowly ride up and down the runway carefully noting all the new ruts and potholes. He would then report to the departing pilot, who

Black Tuna Diaries

would attempt to avoid the worst of them by zigzagging during takeoff and landing. I flew the Push-Pull myself with Raul's pilot sitting in the right seat correcting my mistakes. First to La Cienega, then over the church steeple, and finally directly to the big meadow. Piece of cake! I circled a few times to make sure Eddie memorized the surrounding terrain and would have no problem finding "O'Hare South" when he returned in the twin engine Aero Commander.

Friday morning we put Little Eddie on a commercial flight to Aruba. He would meet up with the crew of the Aero Commander, for the short flight to the Colombian coast. Johnny, Chino, and I checked in at the Irotoma Hotel on the beach outside of El Rodedero, where we could monitor the trip. Friday night I was able to confirm by phone that Eddie, the plane and pilots, were on Aruba and ready to leave for Colombia in the morning. For the first time in over a month, things were going right. Jay appeared, to confirm he had delivered 1200 lbs. of super primo Santa Marta killer herb, to the air field. It was less weight than we wanted, but it was all that could be found on such short notice. It was early October, and the main harvest had just begun. Julio brought a sample of the merchandise. After two tokes, Johnny and I were so wrecked that we ordered everything on the room service menu. After weeks of disappointment and unrelenting tension, it really felt good to have everything smoothly falling into place.

Saturday, just after sunrise, Julio and Raul phoned to say they were leaving by jeep for "O'Hare South". Johnny, Chino, and I were eating breakfast on the patio of our Cabana and watching the sky for the Aero Commander. The pilots had been instructed to approach the Colombian coast at 10,000 feet. We never got to see them arrive, but two tension filled hours later, Raul and Julio showed up at the beach to confirm that the Aero Commander was loaded and headed for South Florida. The bad news was, while waiting for our plane to arrive, a small single engine Cessna 182 had landed, and the local Policia loaded it with 350 lbs. of our primo. The 850 lbs. in the Aero Commander would hardly cover the costs we had already incurred.

Black Tuna Diaries

It didn't matter! I knew Robby would hold out enough cash to pay for the load and gain my freedom. We were smugglers now, with a Colombian connection. Three of them! We could make our money back on the next load, and the one after, and the one after that. Well, at least that was the plan. I never actually planned to be in the back of an army step van, on my way to face a Colombian firing squad. But I get ahead of myself. I was taken to a small hotel in El Rodedero owned by Julio's family. It would be easier for them to keep an eye on me there until the $51,000.00 was deposited in a Miami bank to pay for the 850 lbs. at $60.00 a pound. Very late that night, I was able to reach Robby by phone. Everything went off without a hitch. The grass was put into our customer's vehicles and Robby had collected enough cash on the spot, to bail me out. I told him the bank manager would meet him Monday morning at a side entrance to the bank and relieve him of the agreed upon amount.

I spent a nervous Sunday fishing and water skiing with my hosts. My greatest fear was that Robby, who likes to sleep late, would miss his appointment at the bank. I had visions of being shot while Robby snored safely in his bed. Robby came through like a champ. By Monday afternoon I was on an Avianca flight for Miami.

I arrived at my house on 9th Court in Miami about 4p.m. The party was already in progress. Gene, Robby, the bikers who unloaded the plane, Ahmed Boob from the Fontainebleau Hotel, our customers from Philly and New York who had fronted us the money for the trip, Capt. Crunch, Randy, Moe Keller, Chip, and some ladies Boob had dragged out of his bar at the hotel. We celebrated the success of our first trip. The only problem was, having gone through the $150,000.00 fronted to us by our customers, paid $51,000.00 for the merchandise, paid for the pilots, the use of the plane, the unloading crew, and paid Little Eddie a stipend for being an unnecessary guide, we were about $50,000.00 in the hole. We had presold the load for $240.00 a pound. 850 lbs. The $204,000.00 wasn't enough to cover expenses and repay the three customers who had each fronted us $50,000.00 to get started on the deal. Robby promised them a substantial piece of our next load, at

Black Tuna Diaries

the same guaranteed price. It was clear; we had to do another trip soon. A bigger load at a better price. And to do this, trip we would have to borrow money again from our customers, and I would once again have to stay in Colombia as guarantee for payment.

Within two weeks Gene's friend Hal at Lauderdale Airport, located a long range DC-3 in Panama for sale for $55,000.00. It had the most powerful of the three engine options and Pan AM wings with long range fuel tanks. It was perfect for the Mission. Hal flew down, checked it out and bought it. The plane would remain in Panama until our pilots were ready to take it to Aruba, then on to Colombia. I headed back to Barranquilla to arrange for 5,000 lbs. of Santa Marta's best yerba to be put on the same jungle strip we had just used, as quickly as possible. This time I returned to Colombia as a proven "Miami Connection". Everybody wanted to do business with me. I decided to keep Johnny as my personal representative in Colombia. I knew he'd watch my back and give me good advice. The local pot shippers didn't want to pay him a commission, so I agreed to pay an extra two bucks a pound on every load, to be paid directly to Johnny. Now I had my own guy in Colombia.

Chino's brother, El Loco, got to me first and proposed I do business with him exclusively. Not a good idea! So I sent Johnny to Santa Marta to let Raul and Julio know I was back. I negotiated with the three of them for 5,000 lbs. of premium product at $35.00 a pound. Now, back in the late 70s, the price of pot in Colombia averaged $12.00 a pound. That was for commercial weed, packed with the branches and seed pockets undisturbed, in gunny sacks and odd sized boxes. We figured it was worth the extra price for premium smoke, packaged buds only, in our own uniform protective boxes. That proved to be the case. Our customers would line up to buy our superior product at $280.00 a lb. before they'd pay $180.00 a pound for the ditch weed the Cuban smugglers were bringing in by the shipload.

After three days, I returned to Miami, having been wined, dined, and taken to a jungle village where marijuana was

Black Tuna Diaries

dried, cleaned, and packed. Gene arranged for Captain Beercan, who he had smuggled cigarettes with in Panama, and Bo, an ex-NFL player who played on the same team as Gene, to be pilot and copilot. A week later I got word from down below that our cargo had been cut and was being moved down river to be packed and put on the airfield. We scraped together $10,000.00 expense money for fuel, repairs, hotel, and hookers, and sent Beercan and Bo off to Panama to fix up the DC-3 and head to Aruba. There they would wait for the word that the load was on the airfield.

The following week, our plane and pilots were in Aruba ready to jump, and I was on an Avianca flight to Barranquilla to bet my body on our ability to pull off another successful trip. I spent one night in the Del Prado in Barranquilla. The next morning Johnny and I drove up the coast to El Rodedero. I checked in to Irotoma and asked for cabina #7, the same one I occupied a month earlier. I put Johnny next door in Cabana #8. Word spreads quickly in that area. Within two hours Raul, his cousin Eduardo, and Julio were sitting with me on the patio of cabina #7 drinking cervezas and snacking on fresh crab and shrimp. The cabina and its patio were surrounded by jungle trees and foliage on three sides and faced a beautiful white sand beach. The view from my patio was a wide Caribbean cove that stretched from the mountains beyond Santa Marta, down past El Rodedero and halfway to La Cienega 15 miles up the coast. You could see the big freighters sailing into and out of the harbor at Santa Marta. Native fishermen in dugout canoes fishing with small sticks of dynamite, lighting the wicks from huge spliffs of marijuana they were smoking as they fished. A few speedboats, some pulling bikini clad South American beauties and even a couple of Sportsfisherman trolling the coast for sail, marlin and giant Dorado. If you look up the word paradise, you find Colombia's Caribbean Coast on the top of the list.

Raul explained that our merchandise was aboard a bungo up river on the Magdalena. Bungos are wooden boats and barges that move freight up and down the Magdalena River. Ours was waiting for a time when it would be safe to move its contraband cargo safely through the increased customs patrols on

Black Tuna Diaries

the river. Everyone assured me that the delay would only be for a few days. In the meantime, Raul would take me fishing in his 40 ft. Hatteras. Julio would take me for a tour of the coast in his tiger striped Donzi speedboat. In the evenings we'd take a culinary tour of the areas restaurants. Visit the local casino and end up partying with the local putas. Not a bad life for a hostage!

Every day or two, I'd phone to Miami and Aruba to let my partners and pilots know we would be ready to roll in a few more days. This dragged on for almost three interminable weeks, before we finally got word that our cargo had arrived in Santa Marta. It was being trucked up to the jungle airstrip. After a three week delay, my nerves, and those of my partners and pilots, were shot. The pilots had spent the last of their expense money. They couldn't pay their hotel bill or put fuel in the DC-3. I was broke, and Robby had no more of our customer's cash to send to me or the pilots in Aruba. It was time for action and I didn't have the price of a ticket to Aruba to bail out our plane and pilots, let alone the money to do so. Chino, my original Colombian Connection, had driven up from Barranquilla to have breakfast and spend the day with me. The time for bullshit was past. I told Chino the truth; I was so broke that I couldn't afford enough gas to get our DC-3 from Aruba to Colombia. Our "appointment" on the jungle strip, was for 10 am. the following day. Without a small miracle, we weren't going to be there. Without even a break in his smiley disposition, Chino went into my cabina to use the phone. An hour later we were in his dad's house in Barranquilla. His dad, a super guy who used to bring me books by Gabriel Garcia Marquez to teach me the history of his country, was waiting for us. He handed me a ticket to Aruba and $5000.00 in USA cash. He liked me and felt I was worth trusting. I felt like he had handed me a new lease on life. From hopeless to optimistic. I would pull off this trip and pay back Chino's dad. I was confident. Chino's father was not part of our "business", just a very good man who knew that if I couldn't fulfill my end of this deal, I might lose more than my investment.

Chino and Johnny drove me to the airport. Aero Condor had an island hopper that stopped in Aruba, before going on to

Black Tuna Diaries

Curacao, Bonaire, and points south. In Aruba I cleared customs and walked back out on the airfield looking for our DC-3. I had never seen it, didn't know what color it was painted, or even know the tail number. My new found luck seemed to be holding. After wandering around for 10 minutes, I spotted the only DC-3 on the field, parked by itself, in the customs area behind a chain link fence. With its red striping and big red "A" on the tail, the plane could pass, at a distance, for an Avianca plane. That would turn out to be a serious problem. I went into the little flight service office nearest the customs area and ordered a fuel truck. I wanted everything ready for an early departure in the morning. I went out to the plane to wait for the truck. I hadn't been this close to the legendary "Gooney Bird" since I was a paying passenger on a Southern Airways flight almost 20 years earlier. I opened the rear passenger door and walked slowly through the main cabin, which was bare except for two couches built into the forward walls, and reverently entered the cockpit. The DC-3 is a "tail dragger". That means it rests on a tail wheel with its nose in the air, as opposed to a modern tricycle gear plane which sits level resting on its nose wheel.

    I couldn't resist sitting in the pilot's seat, putting my left hand on the big ancient black yoke, and my right on the throttle quadrant, with its three sets of color coded levers. After flying little Cessnas and Pipers that sit only 2 ft. off the ground, it felt very strange to be sitting right up in the nose section maybe 20 feet above the ground. I was lost in a true flight of fancy when the fuel truck pulled up to my left wing. I slid open the small window by the Captain's seat, waived to the fuel truck driver, and hollered to "fill her up and check the oil and hydraulic fluids". By the time the old Gooney Bird was serviced, I had familiarized myself with most of the controls and instruments in the cockpit. I didn't know it at the time, but that would come in handy the next morning. The bill for 1100 gals. Of aviation gas and several gallons of aviation grade oil, landing fees, parking fees and airport tax came to just over $2,000.00. I paid up and advised the FBO that we'd be gone by 8am. We had an appointment in the Colombian jungle and I was determined to be there and on time.

Black Tuna Diaries

I taxied to the Holiday Inn where the pilots were staying. I checked in and paid for my room in advance and settled the bill for Beercan and Bo, which was almost a thousand bucks. I told the clerk we'd be leaving early and not to accept any more room service charges. I dropped my one small bag in my room and knocked on the door across the hall. Beercan and the normally fastidious Bo looked and smelled like they had crawled out of a cardboard box on skid row. In their underwear and squinting as if blinded by the late afternoon sun, Beercan 40, tall, gaunt, with a beer belly, and Bo, 34, 6'10", both appeared to be shocked to see me framed in their doorway. I didn't give them a chance to tell me their troubles.

"Here's the plan fellas. Here's two hundred bucks. Get yourselves cleaned up, maybe a shave and haircut, some fresh underwear and clean shirts. I'll pick you up at six-thirty, sport you to the best dinner on the island, we'll relax for a few hours in the hotel casino and at 6:30am, we meet for breakfast downstairs and leave for the airport. Your hotel is paid, but no more phone calls or room service. The Gooney Bird is fueled, serviced and ready. We depart this island at 8am. and must be on the field down below no later than 10a.m."

I left before anyone could raise an objection. I went back across to my room to shower and lay down for an hour before dinner. I've always been compulsive about being on time, not always an asset doing business in Latin America. At 6:30 I went back across the hall and knocked on the door. Bo answered. Neither pilot was ready so they agreed to meet me in the main dining room in 15 minutes. The Holiday Inn Aruba is a first class Casino Resort, with an excellent dining room. Beercan and Bo eventually showed up looking almost human. For the past week they had been broke and living on burgers from a nearby Burger King. We had a mini banquet, starting with cold crab and shrimp, followed by steak and lobster with fresh tropical fruit and cheese cake for dessert. While we ate and washed down our food with cold Becks, Bo and Beercan told me their sad story.

First they got stuck in Panama making minor repairs to the plane. When they flew out of Panama, they were sure they

Black Tuna Diaries

were being followed by the DEA. So they made an unscheduled stop in Haiti to shake off any surveillance. By the time they were in place on Aruba most of their $10,000 expense money was gone. After weeks of delay, they were broke, paranoid, and they had both contracted a painful and penicillin resistant crotch crud from the local ladies of the evening. Bo was anxious to get the job done and get back to the states for proper medical treatment. Beercan, on the other hand, had "bad vibes" as a result of all the delays. He wanted to dump the mission. In the nicest way possible, I made it clear to Beercan that he could be in the DC-3 at 8 a.m. when it left for Colombia, or he could walk back to Miami across 1000 miles of ocean. Bo, who was copilot, tried to appear neutral, but I knew he'd be at the airport in the morning. I was on borrowed money and desperate. One way or another, me and the DC-3 would be on our way to pick up a load of Santa Marta Gold at 8 am sharp.

Trying to lighten the mood, I shepherded the boys into the casino and gave them each a couple of hundred gambling money. By 11 o'clock we had all won a little money, which I exclaimed to be a very good omen for our mission. I walked the pilots to their room and told them I had already left a wake-up call for both our rooms for 5:45 am and would meet them for breakfast no later than 6:30 am.

I didn't sleep much that night. At 6:15 I knocked on the door across the hall. Bo stuck his head out and said they would meet me downstairs in a few minutes. I went down to the dinning room ordered coffee, fresh tropical fruit, and an order of pancakes with sausages. Bo showed up and ordered the same. We had almost finished without an appearance by Captain Beercan. Bo confessed that Beercan had gone back to the casino and stayed until he had lost every cent in his pocket. I took Bo's room key, went back up room and informed the sleepy Captain that in 15 minutes I was checking out of both of our rooms and leaving for the airport with Bo.

I went back to the coffee shop and ordered a thermos of black coffee, a bagel and cream cheese for Beercan, in the event he decided to join our little adventure. Just as Bo and I

Black Tuna Diaries

settled into the back seat of the taxi, the front door opened and Brooks, that's Beercan's real name, slid into the front seat looking and smelling like a denizen of the Expressway Hilton.

We had one final obstacle. The DC-3 had arrived on the island with two souls aboard. It was not licensed to carry passengers. The Dutch authorities were very strict about things like that. I would have to jump the fence and sneak aboard so the crew could report a departure with only "two souls aboard". If anything went wrong, I would disappear off the face of the earth without any record of my departure from Aruba. I was first aboard while Brooks and Bo filed a flight plan for Caracas, Venezuela. This would be canceled shortly after leaving Colombia with our load. Bo arrived and walked around the outside of the ancient airliner doing his preflight check. Through the little windows, I watched him remove the pitot covers, pull out the gust locks and the big pins that kept the landing gear from collapsing if the hydraulic fluid has leaked out.

Bo entered through the rear door of the ancient DC-3, proceeded uphill through the main cabin, and took his place in the copilot's chair on the right side of the cockpit. Without a word, he pulled out his checklist and, just like a real airline pilot, proceeded to preflight the cockpit, turning dials, flipping switches and checking gauges. I stood behind his seat watching and waiting for Brooks to take the Captain's seat on the left. It was the smell of stale booze and a freshly lit Marlboro that made me turn around. Captain Beercan was sprawled on one of the couches built into the front of the passenger cabin and told me "I don't really want to do this trip. It doesn't feel right. So, if we are going to Colombia, you are going to have to fly us there. For now I'm going back to sleep".

I've always been too stubborn or too stupid to turn down a challenge. I took the Captain's seat, closed my eyes, and gave the whole thing a minutes' thought. I had never flown anything bigger than a small Cessna. The only two engine plane I had flown was Raul's little Cessna Push-Pull. Because its engines were aligned in the front and back, it was more like flying a single engine plane than a real twin with the motors on

Black Tuna Diaries

the opposite wings. Doesn't matter! Gotta go! No choice! Bo knows how to manage the fuel and hydraulic systems. He knows the starting procedures. "Let's do it". Bo held the check list and read off the starting sequence. Fuel to the left engine, fill until you see it run out from under the cowling, throttle back to one quarter, mixture full rich, prop control forward. Okay left mag on, look out the little window and call "CLEAR". Hit the starter and watch the huge prop slowly begin to turn, after one or two revolutions, a cough and a puff of smoke, and then another, and another until the big radial engine caught and began to hum loudly.

The raw av. Gas that had poured out of the cowling caught fire and Bo reached over and added throttle until the speed of the prop put out the fire. Now I repeated the procedure on the right engine. I throttled back and let the radials warm until they purred like a pair of huge asthmatic panthers in a dark jungle. With my stomach in knots, but my heart bursting with the joy of being at the controls of the legendary old plane. I nodded to Bo, eased off the breaks, and reached over carefully adding power until we were taxiing off the parking ramp. Bo was on the radio getting clearance to taxi to the active runway. I listened on my headset following the ground controller's instructions and for the first time getting the feel of taxiing from high up in the nose of the Gooney Bird. By the time I reached the warm up pad at the end of the active runway, I was confident I could steer the big aircraft down the center of the runway for takeoff. I stood on the brake pedals while Bo ran up the engines, checked the pressures and temperatures, throttled back, and handed me back the plane. When I heard the flight controller say "DC-3 cleared for takeoff, I slid my heels off the brakes and pressed my quivering feet firmly on the rudder pedals, the only method of steering on takeoff roll. I rolled the large black trim wheel on the throttle quadrant from neutral to the takeoff position, held the yolk lightly with my thumb and first three fingers of my left hand and with Bo's hand next to mine holding props and mixture, my right hand gripped the throttles and smoothly pushed in full power for takeoff. It was only then I realized I had never flown a tail dragger. Every plane I'd flown had tricycle gear. All that was required was to lift the nose and let the plane fly off the runway. With a tail dragger you had to gain enough speed to lift

Black Tuna Diaries

the tail and then gain even more speed for liftoff. Just when I was about to push the yolk forward to lift the tail, it came up all by itself. By the time I located the ground speed indicator we had passed through eighty miles an hour and the wonderful old lady had left the ground so smoothly that I never felt a thing.

Raul had repeatedly emphasized the importance of approaching the Colombian coast at exactly 10,000 feet directly over the giant coastal lake at La Cienega. As we left Aruba I continued our climb out into a clear blue sky lightly punctuated with long wisps of clean white cirrus clouds. At 500 feet per minute it would take 20 minutes to reach our mandated altitude. It was one of those perfect Caribbean days. Intense azure sky above, vividly clear blue/green waters below. Steering west southwest, we should be able to see the coast of South America by the time we reached altitude. Hand flying the old DC-3 was so smooth and pleasurable I never once even considered engaging the autopilot. Happiness was feeling the not quite synchronized beat of the two big radial engines and knowing what the pilots of an earlier era experienced as they shepherded their passengers and freight in one of the tens of thousands of DC-3's that were the foundation of the world's air transport industry. Reality returned when Bo tapped the altimeter indicating we had arrived at 10,000 feet. I eased back the throttles and Bo once again adjusted the pitch of the props and the fuel mixture for max efficiency cruising. We couldn't see the coast of Colombia, but figured it would come into view any minute. After another 20 or 30 minutes we still couldn't see the coast of South America. How could we miss an entire continent? Embarrassed now, we began to check course, compass, maps, and our radio navigation equipment. None of which gave us any hint as to where we had gone wrong. We began to worry at the thought of missing our 10 a.m. rendezvous. After all, if we couldn't find South America, we had no chance of locating a remote jungle airfield.

Just as panic was setting in, Captain Beercan, , tapped me on the shoulder, and in a cloud of dragon breath and Marlboro smoke, told me to "get the hell out of my seat". I stood behind him not saying a word. He looked out of the cockpit windows

Black Tuna Diaries

to a view of nothing but sky and ocean. He looked at the compass, airspeed indicator, gave me a disgusted look, and turned due west. In less than five minutes we were approaching La Cienega on the coast of Colombia. A few minutes later we flew over the town, spotted our landmark steeple, and turned inland towards the mountains. Using CB radio we made contact with Raul in his Cessna and a few minutes later the little plane popped up a couple of miles in front of us to lead down to the giant meadow called Kennedy South. We had been warned that the lower end of the airstrip was too soft to land on. A sheet was in place to mark the end of the safe portion. Bo dropped the landing gear, while Brooks eased back the throttles and guided the old lady in for a flawless uphill landing. With barely a touch of brakes, he reversed directions at the top of the runway and cut the engines. For a moment we sat there frozen listening to the tic of the cooling radials and awed by the nearby Sierra Madres. An open flatbed truck with fuel drums and pumps pulled under our right wing. An even bigger flatbed backed up to our cabin door carrying our Santa Marta Gold.

Black Tuna Diaries

I was the first one to pop open the door and step out to be greeted by Raul and his cousin Eduardo. Julio was supervising a dozen Guajirans who were already refueling and loading the cargo on board. It was over 100° with no breeze to blow away the over sized mosquitoes that attacked by the dozens, with inch long stingers. It did no good to slap at them, there were too many. They would continue to swarm and puncture the entire time we were on the field. Within fifteen minutes the plane was refueled and the cargo was secured in the main cabin. Initially stacked toward the front of the cabin near the wings, for takeoff, the pot would be shifted further back after reaching altitude. This time it was Captain Beercan who did the preflight inspection. When he reached the left engine he stopped and stared at small black streaks on the cowling indicating an oil leak. Radial engines by their very nature leak oil from dried out or oil soaked gaskets. DC-3s always carried a large reservoir of oil. Bo and I saw no reason for concern. Beercan, with a sour "I told you so", look on his face and a cigarette in his mouth, declared, "We're going nowhere until the leak is fixed". Knowing that we'd be in danger of capture by the army, police or rebels if we remained there for more than another 15 or 20 minutes, Bo and I tried to argue with him. Tried to convince him that if the oil leak was bad enough to be a danger, we'd know it in time to land in Haiti to replenish the oil reserve. Brooks refused even to discuss it. Considering Bo and I had gotten lost trying to find South America, there was no way we were going to try to make it to Florida without the only one of us who had the experience to give us a good chance to get home with the load. Raul joined Bo and I, as Brooks sulked off by himself. "I can have a mechanic here in less than an hour. You guys take off the engine cowling and by that time I'll be back with an aircraft mechanic from Avianca in Barranquilla". Julio and Raul climbed into the Push-Pull and were off the ground in less than a third of the runway. Bo found a screw driver and pliers in our emergency tool kit. He and I climbed out on the left wing. The heat from the metal wing and the hot radial engine made a tough job even harder. Every screw had been wired in place so it wouldn't loosen from the vibration of the engines. Bo and I were soaked to the skin with perspiration by the time we handed down the cowling into the waiting hands of two big Guajirans on the bed of the fuel truck. Beercan had been no help at all. He was on the

Black Tuna Diaries

right hand edge of the field, talking animatedly to a kid on a donkey. The last time I had looked, I saw him handing over some cash. As soon as we climbed down off the wing, Raul's Cessna returned and was taxiing in our direction. I was desperately hoping they had thought to bring back something cold to drink. We were all beginning to dehydrate. No such luck. Raul and Julio brought over a youngster who looked about 16 and introduced him as a qualified mechanic who worked for Avianca Airlines.

Dressed in dirty dungarees and grease stained shirt, he didn't inspire confidence. I saw no mechanic's tool box. But sticking out from his back pockets, one screw driver, one long neck pliers, a folded sheet of gasket paper and a battered flashlight. In less than five minutes he had the lower cylinder head off and was looking up inside the cylinder with the weak yellow light of his old army flashlight. He identified the problem as a loose bolt up in the cylinder. He tightened it, cut a new seal from the sheet of gasket paper and remounted the cylinder head. The entire job hadn't taken 15 minutes. The young mechanic helped us wrestle the cowling back in place and re-wire the safety screws to hold it there. Now we were loaded, fueled, repaired, the trucks had been moved away, and I was shaking the mechanics hand and thanking him as we prepared to board and fly out of the equatorial jungle.

"Tranquillo. . .Tranquillo Hombres". . .this was repeated over and over. It took me a moment to figure out what was going on. The people around me all had their hands clasped on top of their heads. From behind the tail section of the DC-3, I could see Colombian soldiers emerging from the fruit groves on both sides of the airstrip. A dozen from each side, coming toward us with carbines at the ready, and shouting "Tranquillo. . .Tranquillo Hombres" which I quickly learned was universal Spanish idiom for, "Don't move and put up your hands". The Colombian soldiers, who were all indios of a much smaller stature than our Guajirans, very gingerly began to remove the big 45 caliber automatics that were stuck in the waist bands of everyone except for me, Bo and Brooks. The soldiers were clearly nervous, fearing that the Guajirans would live up to their reputation for violence and prefer a

Black Tuna Diaries

shootout to being disarmed. To my surprise, it wasn't the Guarjirans who refused to be disarmed; it was Raul's cousin Eduardo Davila who wouldn't give up his weapon. After much shouting and threats, the soldiers backed off and let him keep his shiny chrome 45 automatic. Now we all were standing around the plane with our hands on our heads, waiting for something to happen. But what? It was approaching noon. The equatorial sun was baking the open airstrip. The giant mosquitoes were draining our blood and our need for fluids was becoming dire. The tension was increasing. Some of the soldiers had shouldered their carbines and were trying to make conversation to lighten the mood. I was about to drop my hands to my side, when the soldiers began pointing down to the far end of the mile long airfield.

The far end of the runway was a mile downhill from where we were being held. I looked in that direction. I could just barely make out a figure dressed in green jungle camo. He had two Doberman on leashes in his left hand and a shiny silver automatic in the right. Walking slow and occasionally looking at us through binoculars hanging from his neck, it was clear he had no intention of joining our party until the situation had been completely defused. Once he was sure no one was about to start shooting, he picked up the pace, strutting like a little gamecock in front of the hen house. His jungle camo looked like it had just come from an expensive custom tailor. A sharp contrast to the mismatched and patched khakis worn by his soldiers. Obviously an officer, he was wearing the felt sombrero usually worn by cavalry officers. I'm not good about reading insignia, but I could hear the soldiers muttering something not too flattering about a cowardly "teniente", a lieutenant. I'm not sure if I ever found out his name, he wore no name tag on his blouse, but I quickly named him "Louie the Louse" or "Louie the Looter".

Things tensed up again when Louie reached the DC -3. The soldiers unslung their carbines and our hands went back on our heads. Beercan, Bo and I were put up against the plane and searched. Everything in our pockets was handed over to Louie, along with any jewelry we were wearing. The only thing returned was our empty wallets with I.D. and family photos.

Black Tuna Diaries

Louis the looter then boarded the plane and took everything of value from our luggage, leaving us only our passports. The dirt poor soldiers hadn't even thought to rob us, but the rich asshole in charge wiped us out. Lt. Louse spoke some English. He approached Brooks and said, "piloto, you pilot?" Brooks nodded. Not wanting to get too close to anyone as big as Bo, he pointed and asked the same question. Bo acknowledged he was a pilot. Now it was my turn, "El Hefe, you boss?"...."No senor....me el burro....poor worker....yo compasino solo". No way I was going to admit to being the boss. The boss would be a very valuable captive. I didn't think he bought my story, but he couldn't be sure. For the moment, he let it go and went over to where Julio and the two Davila cousins were being held. What ensued was a long loud argument in Spanish, mostly having to do with money. I couldn't understand much of it, but two things were clear. The Lt. was demanding a $2,000,000.00 bribe to release us and the plane. My people were not too politely, refusing and describing in detail, obscene acts performed by Louie's ancestors as they descended from the trees. It was just then that Louis noticed that Eduardo Davila still had his 45 automatic stuck in his belt. He immediately took a couple of steps back, cocked his big chrome 45, pointed it at Eduardo and demanded he drop his weapon. I think Louie went into shock when Eduardo took three large steps forward, stuck his chest right against the barrel of Louie's 45, and said what I took to be the Spanish equivalent of "Make my day.. .Touch my gun and I'll shove it so far up your coolu, you'll need a tree surgeon to get it out". Or something like that! Louis the Looter turned a very pale white. He backed off and went back to arguing about money. Ten minutes later Julio, both Davila, and their pilot climbed into the Push-Pull and were gone in less than a minute. "Oh shit! Wait for me! What's gonna happen now?" Nobody seemed to know.

After another 15 minutes of just standing in the awful heat with our hands on our heads and still nothing to drink, the Lt. decided to have a bit of sadistic sport at my expense. He said in effect, if I was only a worker, a burro, he wanted to see me unload the plane. I stared at him for a minute, thinking that a drink from the canteen on his belt would make the job a lot easier. He saw where I was looking and just laughed. Louis

Black Tuna Diaries

cocked his 45 again and waved me toward the door of the plane. I figured he'd be a lot more likely to shoot me than he would Eduardo Davila, so I started for the cabin. As I ascended the two or three steps to the hatchway, I could already feel the intense heat coming from the aluminum oven that was the DC-3's main cabin. One step inside, the sudden smell and potent miasma rising from 5000 lbs. of Colombia's best marijuana, was instantly stoning. The heat was pumping millions of molecules of THC into the stagnant air of the cabin.

There were more than 100 bales, 2 ft. x 2 ft. x 18 inches, weighting 45-55 lbs. each. Starting with the ones nearest the door, I toted them out one by one and piled them in stacks four high. Breathing more and more of the potent air every time I entered the fuselage. After a dozen bales, I no longer cared about Lt. Louis the Looter or his 45 Automatic. I quit toting bales and picked up a pack of Easy Wider rolling papers that the Lt. had pulled from my Valpak and tossed on the floor of the plane. Stepping over to the stacked bales on the airfield, I hooked up four of the large papers, tore open a corner of the top bale, took a handful of the sticky golden weed, shook out as many seeds as possible, and rolled a giant doobie the size of a Panatela. "Loco, loco" chorused the soldiers menacing with their carbines. But I noticed they were laughing. That was a good sign. Even better, Louis had walked off somewhere to find shade. My lighter was still in my shirt pocket. I flicked my Bic, took a deep drag and almost passed out on the spot. I leaned on the bales until the ground stopped moving. Then moving from soldier to soldier proffering the joint. I managed to get five or six of them to take a toke. Even as stoned as I was, I realized that playing the harmless fool was easing the tension and gaining me sympathy. I handed out business cards from South Florida Auto Auction, explaining in broken Spanish that if they came to Miami, I would get them any car they wanted and ship it to Colombia. A month later two of them showed up at my office and bought cars. True to my word, I bought and shipped them at my expense.

I don't know how long I stood by the bales and toked with the soldiers. It must have been over an hour when the asshole Lt. walked over to announce he would wait no longer for

Black Tuna Diaries

someone to return with the money. He was taking us down to the village of La Cienega to shoot us as an example to anyone who might consider not paying his "landing fees". Half the soldiers were left to guard the still loaded DC-3. The rest herded us together, through a banana grove, into the jungle and out onto a dirt road. That's how I came to be sitting in a sweltering step van with a dozen big Guarjirans and two pilots.

My mind returned to the present, when a soldier tapped me with the barrel of his gun. We were ordered out of the step van and told to push the rusty vehicle until it started. Starters didn't last long in the damp jungle. Pushing was the normal method of starting the engine. The step van had just started rolling down the dirt trail when I came to my senses. I wasn't going to aid and abet my own death. "Sientese, sientese, hermanos". I sat down in the middle of the trail and motioned for everyone else to do the same. Bo, Beercan, then the loading crew all got the idea. No amount of screaming by the Lt., or halfhearted threats by the soldiers, could get us on our feet. The soldiers wanted to wait for the cash. Louis the Looter wasn't all that anxious to push his luck by forcing his soldiers to shoot one of us.

My stalling tactics paid off. After 10 minutes an open jeep came flying up the jungle trail. Julio and Eduardo jumped out, each carrying a plastic shopping bag filled to the brim with neat bundles of Colombian cash. I had no idea at the time that it amounted only to about $40,000 U.S. The Lt. started to argue that it wasn't enough and he'd rather make an example of us, but quickly changed his mind when he looked around and saw a dozen armed soldiers eying the money. Not the bravest of men, he realized that if Julio, Eduardo, or the Guajirans loading crew didn't kill him, his own soldiers would. The money was paid and business was business.

Now it was late afternoon, too late to take off for our landing site at Punta Gorda Municipal Airport. Our financial arrangement with the airport manager dictated that we arrive after they closed down operations at 6 pm., but well before midnight, when the sound of a large twin engine plane would rouse the sheriff and everyone else living nearby. The runway

Black Tuna Diaries

lights could be operated by an approaching aircraft. We would tune to the correct radio frequency and click the mike button six times. Our plan was to arrive just after dark, about 8p.m., unload to trucks waiting between two large hangers, and then fly the DC-3 to a hanger at the Ft. Lauderdale Airport well before midnight. Timing was important. With no headwind, a DC-3 could fly a steady 150 mph. The 1200 mile trip would take no less than 8 hours and probably more like 10 or 12. Everything would have to be delayed until the next day.

We were taken to a nearby farmhouse where we could sit on the small shaded porch and slake our raging thirst, while we debated how to handle the delay, and to protect ourselves and the loaded aircraft. Fortunate for us, the caretaker family that lived in the one room farmhouse didn't offer us water. If they had, we might have drunk it, thereby insuring ourselves a severe case of amoebic dysentery. A quick and painful death or a long and painful recovery. What our host did was bring us, was a big basket of freshly picked oranges and grapefruits, grown in the orchards surrounding the airstrip. We must have looked like a bunch of savages, tearing at the warm fruit, squeezing the juice into our open mouths, then sucking the remaining moisture from the sweet meaty pulp. Captain Beercan was at the farmyard fence with the same compasino and burro that I had seen him with hours earlier, handing over the last of his cash. The compasino handed Brooks a white plastic bucket with about two quarts of what appeared to be beer. A big dirty hunk of ice floating on top. At no time did the Captain offer to share with his fellow captives. I had 5 or 6 large oranges and a couple of grapefruits, before I felt full. Bo finished all the fruit in the tall basket, maybe a dozen large oranges and half a dozen grapefruits, and then asked for more. He finished a second basket by himself while the family and our crew watched in amazement. "El Gigante", the giant, is what the farmer's kids called him. The former NFL player would forever be known on the coast of Colombia, as "El Gigante". When it seemed "El Gigante" had eaten everything in sight and was still hungry, the lady of the house sent her son up a nearby tree to retrieve a smoked monkey arm that was drying in the tropical sun. We were all in hysterics watching our big prissy pilot throw the hissy-fit of all hissy-fits when our hosts proudly presented him with their choicest provender. I can only hope

Black Tuna Diaries

they didn't understand his English as he showered all Colombians, and them in particular, with expletives heard only on ships far at sea and in NFL locker rooms; as he gave them explicit instructions on where to put the long black monkey arm with its tiny fingers. We were all in a pretty good mood when it was time to split up.

The soldiers and Guarjirans would stay and guard the plane and its load of marijuana. Bo and Brooks would be hidden for the night at a farmhouse a few miles away. I climbed into the jeep with Julio and Eduardo and headed for El Rodedero. There I could get on the phone to Miami and delay Gene and his crew of unloaders from occupying Punta Gorda Airport until the next night. It took more than an hour to set up a call to Robby. He would have to get a hold of Chip, who would then radio to Gene, who was already en route to the airport.

Finally, it was almost nine o'clock by the time I showered, dressed in clean clothes, and went down to a small restaurant on the beach for an excellent fresh seafood meal. Crab, shrimp, fish, lobster. Small plates of delicious foods washed down with ice cold bottles of local beer. By eleven, I was dead asleep in a second floor bedroom of the Imparador Hotel in El Rodedero.

It was just after 2 am when Julio's wife banged loudly on the door, to tell me I had 30 seconds to get dressed and be out of the room before the cops arrived. In a few seconds, I was out in the hall.

Irocima was frantic. "The police have been told that you are hiding in El Rodedero. They are downstairs and want to search the hotel. If they find you, with no entry stamp on your passport, it will be big trouble for all of us". She led me to a rear staircase, opened a locked linen closet, and pushed me in. "I'll be back for you when it's safe. Please don't make a sound". I put a couple of folded sheets on the small stool I found there and sat in the dark listening to footsteps moving up and down the corridor. Dead tired after my harrowing day up in the jungle, I was deathly afraid to fall asleep, knowing that as soon as I nodded off, I'd start snoring loud enough to be heard in

Black Tuna Diaries

the next village. When I'm overtired, I really cut logs. Of course the longer I sat awake in the dark, the more I needed to use the bathroom. It was probably the cramps in my stomach and the pressure on my bladder that kept me awake.

Six hours I sat motionless in that hot airless claustrophobic linen closet. Mercifully, a little after six am, a maid opened the door and motioned me to go down to the office. "Officina senor, Officina". I countered with "por favor nesicito el banjo". She pointed to an open guest room that was being made up. After a totally wonderful visit to the bathroom, I headed down to the small office where Julio, Raul and Johnny were having tinto and freshly baked breakfast rolls. Tinto is fresh roasted and ground Colombian coffee beans, boiled in a pot with unrefined cane sugar. No other breakfast coffee can compare. I was enjoying a second cup and beginning to feel half human. Raul and Julio had just come down from the airstrip. Raul was upset. He explained that, 'The army Lieutenant from yesterday, he told the Santa Marta police where to find you, and he called his friends in the Navy and told them where to find the pilots and the plane. We had to move the pilots around all night. Early this morning the Navy officer holding the DC-3 agreed to accept a check for $35,000.00. They also took some of the merchandise before they let your guys take off'.

I had hoped to leave with the plane, but now that was impossible. I had entered the country illegally on the DC-3. With no entry stamp on my passport, I couldn't stay around Santa Marta The police were already looking for me. Since I had originally agreed to stay in Colombia as a hostage for payment, we all thought it best if I went back to Barranquilla to stay with Chino's family.

With no traffic headed in that direction, we made it to Barranquilla in 45 minutes. Waiting for us was Chino's brother Loco. "We go to my house at Puerto Atlántico to wait for the money". I wasn't crazy about that idea. The last time I was there, Loco felt compelled to demonstrate his security system. He dialed a phone number, put the phone down, and five minutes later his friends and neighbors began arriving with Uzis, shotguns, sniper rifles, and the standard 45 Automatic.

Black Tuna Diaries

Of all the people I had met in Colombia, he was the only asshole who constantly tried to act the tough guy. I always suspected it was a case of "peanut dick" syndrome. Loco insisted I ride with him and only reluctantly agreed to let Johnny follow behind. It was the way he drove his BMW that convinced me he was Loco. Never less than 80 or 90 MPH up the narrow busy coast road that carried traffic to Cartagena. Talking and gesturing violently with his hands, every time we passed a church, cemetery, or roadside shrine, of which there were thousands, he would take both hands off the steering wheel to make the sign of the cross over his entire body. Being held captive on the jungle airfield didn't scare me nearly as badly as a ride in Loco's BMW.

It took less than 30 minutes to cover the 35 or 40 miles to Puerto Atlántico. A beautiful new development. Every mansion was more fabulous than the last, and most were built on individual cliffs overlooking the beach on a turbulent stretch of ocean. It was now just 10:30 am and I was desperate to phone Miami to alert Robby that our loaded DC-3 was its way home and likely to arrive earlier than planned. To my surprise, the call was put right through. Robby was in the garage apartment behind my house on the Seabold Canal in Miami. He had some bad news of his own to impart.

Because we hadn't been able to close the flight plan we filed in Aruba, the Dutch authorities were "searching for a missing DC-3, with two American pilots aboard, that failed to arrive at its destination in Caracas". That was on the six o'clock news last night. This morning all the Miami stations carried the story and announced that "Venezuelan and American Coast Guards had joined the search for two missing Americans in a DC-3 cargo plane, bound for Venezuela", that may have crashed. When I left the jungle farm and late the previous afternoon, Bo announced his intention to re board the plane to try radioing Aruba to cancel our flight plan. None of us thought it would be possible unless the DC-3 was airborne and flying at altitude. Robby told me my wife was frantic, believing the plane had crashed with me onboard. His last contact with Gene and the airfield crew was late yesterday. They had checked in to a motel near Punta Gorda, but didn't want to

Black Tuna Diaries

mention the name or phone number over the telephone. They were not monitoring the radio. In a pre cell phone era, there was no way to contact them, short of driving to Punta Gorda and checking motel parking lots for our trucks and cars. With the plane enroute, they had to be notified to move back onto the airport as soon as it closed at 6 pm. Chip had already left for Punta Gorda with the bad news that the plane was either lost or the subject of an intense search by the coast guards of three countries. Robby had to remain where he was, to try and hold things together in the event he heard from Gene or Chip. On top of everything else, my wife got on the phone, screaming that I had almost given her a heart attack and that if I wanted to stay married, I'd get my ass on the next flight for Miami. This is exactly what I had in mind!

There was a 12:30 pm. Aero Condor flight from Barranquilla that arrived in Miami by 2:30. I assured Robby that I was on my way. He would hang by the phone until one o'clock. If he hadn't heard from me, I was on my way. Then he could head for Punta Gorda to round up our crew. I had one last problem. Loco! He had been listening to my end of the conversation and apparently didn't like what he heard. He had his Uzi pointed at me to make it clear that I was going nowhere until the merchandise was paid for. A glance out the window told me that Johnny was waiting by the yellow Camaro. Loco was reaching for the phone to dial the alarm that would bring his armed posse. I stood between him and the phone. "If I don't leave right now for the airport, there will be no one to unload the plane, no one to pay for the load, and more importantly, my marriage will be over. I'm going to get into Johnny's car and try to get on the 12:30 flight to Miami. You can shoot me in the back, you can call your friends to shoot me, or you can get me a reservation and have your customs guy waiting to put a backdated entry stamp in my passport so I won't be arrested trying to leave the country illegally. Not waiting for an answer, I turned and crossed the room. Ten very uncomfortable steps to the front door.

No bullet in the back! Out the door and over to the car. Still no hail of bullets. We drove toward the gate expecting Loco's armed guard to try to stop us. The gate is open and no guard

Black Tuna Diaries

in sight. For most of the 40 minute trip, I kept looking for Loco's posse to appear in the rear view mirror. No one! The Customs officer met us at the front door of the terminal and took me to his office to fix my passport. He handed me a first class ticket and boarding pass, assuring me that my generous friend Loco would pay for everything. Too late! Loco had pulled a gun on me. I'd pay him for the herb, but never do business with him again.

We landed in Miami before 2:30. I was home by 3. Lynne met me at the door and after a serious hug; I got a serious reaming out for the scare. Robby had called her to let her know that the DC-3 was still sitting on the ground on the Colombian mountainside. At the same time, the six o'clock news announced the plane was missing and thought to have gone down. By morning, when he spoke to her, there had been so many .different accounts in the news; no one knew what to believe. In those days, international calls were difficult to place from Colombia. It sometimes took hours to get a line to the states. Since I wasn't originally expected to fly home with the load, it didn't occur to Robby to let Lynne know I had phoned with the change of plans. My excuse, was I didn't want to phone my home number from Colombia, except in the direst of emergencies. Robby was long gone, on his way to Punta Gorda to make sure Gene and his crew would be on the field when our load arrived.

Lynne took a good look at me and strongly suggested I go up to bed. She promised to wake me if anyone called. Although I had been sitting up all night in a little linen closet, after a really bad day in the jungle, I couldn't bring myself to go to bed. Bo and Captain Beercan were up in the pot laden DC-3 somewhere over the Bahamas by now, trying to evade the search planes of three countries. I had no doubt they were listening to all the chatter on the radios and trying to manage their fuel so they could remain offshore until dark, when they would be harder to identify in all the coastal air traffic. With no headwinds, a DC-3 flew 150 MPH and burned a hundred gallons of fuel per hour. Our DC-3 had "Pan Am" long distance wings that held 1450 gallons of usable fuel. By lowering their flying speed, they could lower the fuel consumption rate to

Black Tuna Diaries

maybe 80 gallons per hour and stretch out their flying time to 16 hours. There was nothing I could do to help. Radio contact would have been foolish , even if it was possible, which it wasn't. Brooks would not use his radio until he was over the field at Punta Gorda and ready to set down. That would be a two word code exchange to confirm the field was safe to use. Robby and Chip were both at Punta Gorda looking for Gene and his offload crew. There was nothing I could do to help, but stay by the phone and pass on any messages if I heard from Robby, Chip or Gene. I turned on the TV and stretched out on the couch. My two year old son climbed up to cuddle with me. I put my arms around him, and could feel his little heart beating strongly against my chest. It made me very happy to be home and alive.

At six, Lynne woke us to eat. The three of us sat on the floor eating from the low glass coffee table and watching the news. No mention of the missing DC-3. That had to be good news. My son and I were watching cartoons, when Chip called around 7 o'clock. Gene, and his crew, were hiding behind a hanger, waiting for the signal that the plane was on approach. Chip called again about 8:30, still no word from the plane. There was a lot of activity on the supposedly closed airfield and everyone was getting nervous. They would wait one more hour, then wrap it up, figuring the DC-3 was lost, captured, or had to ditch at sea. Nervous and depressed, I belted down a half glass of Glen Morangie and passed out again on the couch.

Next thing I knew it was 4 am. People were banging on my front door, ringing the doorbell and talking loud. Coming out of a deep alcohol induced sleep, I figured it was the cops, DEA, FBI, Customs and ATF, all come to bust me. With no place to run, I opened the door. Robby, Gene, Chip, Brooks and Bo! No cops! They had made it! The load was already in small trucks on its way to Philly, New York, Chicago and Detroit. The crew had come to bring me the news and open the bottle of Dom Perignon that was waiting in the fridge. There was also some very bad news, but that could wait a few minutes while we celebrated being alive, free, and hopefully solvent.

Black Tuna Diaries

After I refilled everyone's glass, we settled down around the sofas while Bo and Brooks told us what happened the previous night after I left them on the jungle airstrip. They had been taken to a small farmhouse a few miles from the field. At two in the morning, Julio appeared, only minutes ahead of a squad of Colombian sailors who had been alerted by Louis the Looter where to look for the crew of the stranded plane. Through most of the night the sailors chased Julio and the pilots through the jungle and up and down the side of the mountain. Shortly after dawn, Raul and Eduardo landed their Cessna on the strip and convinced the Navel officer guarding our loaded DC-3 to accept a check for $35,000.00 U.S. and allow the pilots to enter the aircraft and take off for the states. Taking a check wasn't the brightest thing that officer had ever done, but what was the Navy doing in the jungle in the first place? Alerted by radio in the get-a-way jeep, Julio drove the pilots onto the field. More bales had been unloaded and stacked with the ones I had been forced to unload the previous day. The pilots were ordered to leave the bales where they were, and to take off immediately. The local police were enroute to load a small plane that was expected at any minute. Load it with some of our herb! With barely enough time to remove the gust locks from the ailerons, rudder and elevator, they coaxed the cold damp old radial engines to life, doing their check list as they prepared to take off the heavily loaded Gooney Bird. Both pilots sat on the brakes while Beercan fed in full power. With the old lady straining to fly, they released the brakes to barrel down the runway. As the plane picked up speed Bo was almost ready to pull in full flaps to jerk the plane off the ground when the resident herd of cows, frightened by the screaming radials, hurtled out of the orange groves and ran full speed across the center of the runway. Not quite ready to fly, the loaded DC-3 managed to jump over the herd, stall back onto the runway, finish the take off run and barely clear the trees as they left the ground at the end of the runway. Scratching for altitude, Bo tried to raise the landing gear. Nothing happened! Try the backup systems! Nothing happened! It was then that they looked at each other in embarrassment. Neither had remembered to remove the safety pegs that kept the hydraulic landing gear from slowly loosing pressure and collapsing overnight. The gear couldn't retract until the pegs were removed. With the tall gear and big wheels

Black Tuna Diaries

hanging down, the added drag would use up their fuel supply long before they reached the coast of Florida. No choice, they had to turn around and land. Much to the surprise of everyone left on the field, Brooks landed, swung around for takeoff and kept the engines running while Bo jumped out, ran up to each landing gear, and pulled out the pegs. He was barely back in the plane when Brooks let go of the brakes and roared down the field, just ahead of a pickup truck full of local cops firing their carbines into the air.

Once airborne over the water they monitored the aviation radios. The first thing they heard was the Dutch Air force, flying out of Aruba, coordinating the search for a missing DC-3 that failed to close their flight plan. There were dozens of aircraft from three countries searching from the coast of South America to the western Bahamas. This is where Captain Beercan earned his pay. Trimming back to 60% power to stretch his flying time and fuel supply, he hid in the lowest cloud layers during the long slow trip home. Emerging after dark to fly up the Florida peninsula to Punta Gorda like a ghost plane spit out by the Bermuda Triangle.

The bad news! Brooks refused to get back in the empty plane and move it to the waiting hanger at the Ft. Lauderdale Airport. After two harrowing days, he wasn't going to tempt fate one more time. Deserting the DC-3 on the Punta Gorda field represented more than the loss of a $55,000.00 plane. It was a red flag that marked the trail back to the man who had bought the plane in Panama. A good friend of Gene's. Residue found in the plane, even after a thorough cleaning, would leave no doubt about what it was hauling. We would worry about that later. For now it was time to pay the pilots and crew, so they could scatter and lay low. Later that day Robby and I would take a suitcase of cash to a Miami bank to be forwarded to Colombia. Now we were real south Florida pot smugglers. Ready to plan our next mission.

Chapter 2
The South St Gang

Forget the Cheesewiz and the soft Italian bread. Heat the grill or heavy pan good and hot. Cover with oil. old-time South Philly steak joints used olive oil cut with soy bean oil to save money. While the oil heats, dice a medium sized onion. Sauté the onion until it begins to caramelize. Forget about the minute steak or chip steak or any kind of pre-made steak sandwich drek. Take very thin slices of raw beef. Almost any cut with some fat (not gristle) for flavor. If you lived in South Philly in the 1950's, you know the best steak sandwiches, were made with horse meat. You knew this because you often read in the Daily News, that some well known sandwich joint was fined and closed for a month for serving Trigger instead of Bossie. Put three or four slices of meat directly over the browning onions. After a minute or so, slide a spatula under the onions and flip .the entire thing. On top of this, put two very thin slices of domestic provolone cheese. Don't try to up-grade to imported provolone. It's too hard to slice; it doesn't melt well and doesn't have the smooth flavor of Wisconsin. In South Philly, Wisconsin provolone was the cheese for steaks, hoagies, and pizza. As soon as you put the cheese over the meat, split open half a loaf of fresh crisp, hard Italian bread. Tear out the center and put the shell over the meat, cheese and onions. In a few seconds the cheese is melted. Slide your spatula under the sandwich and lift it off the grill. A couple of slices of Italian cherry pepper is the authentic garnish.

I know that all of the above is true, because I grew up in South Philadelphia in the 1940's and 50's with fellow gang members, Robby Meinster and Cookie Baumholtz. We would hang out and play the pinball machine at Big Bill Londy's on 7th between South and Bainbridge St. From the age 6 to 12, we three and a few transient members of the South Street gang, would earn a few nickels, dimes, and quarters in the back room of Londy's, slicing onions, meat (Trigger had to be sliced and frozen before an inspector showed up) or working the grill until Petey the cook showed up. Pat's Steaks was more famous, but Londy's three locations served the best steak sandwiches. Steak sandwiches were born out of WWII when real steak was scarce and beef was rationed. Steak sandwiches were so popular that a new source of "steak" was needed. Big Bill Londy, who spent most of his time at the race track, was ahead of the field. In the 1950's and well into the 60s, there was a stable right on Bainbridge Street in Center City Philadelphia, that was rumored to be the source of "South Philly Steak", where horses were bred, fed, watered, and slaughtered and quartered without ever leaving the building.

We came from the old South Street. A street famous for it's clothing stores. Diamond's Paramount, Krass Brothers, and Silverman's Bridal Shop and Department Store. In a city of Blue Laws, it was the place to take the family to shop on Sunday. Families from hundreds of miles away came to spend the day. They filled the streets. Not just clothing! There was furniture, appliances, office supplies, and antiques.

You would stop for a hot roast beef sandwich at Cy' s, Londy' s for a steak sandwich or Kelem's for a real Jewish corn beef on fresh rye bread with the best liver or potato Knishes in the world, or the ultimate hot dog from Levis's. Quaker City Luggage sold Steamer trunks and duffel bags. Mom could be fitted for a real French corset or girdle at Rabinowitz Corsets. Fancy lingerie came from Manya Block or my Aunt Eva Lipschitz... The Jolly ladies made fat down filled pillows and quilts... if you were getting married, you wanted bedding from Jolly's. Toy's came from Mr. Paultin's. His narrow little shop was crammed to the ceiling with kids' dreams.

People wore hats in those days. Men's hats could be found at Dietz's or at the Stetson Store. Ladies millinery was created at Myrtles' wholesale and retail French Millinery. A Greek family could clean and block your hats, give you a first class shoeshine, and sell you a bag of hot fresh roasted peanuts. There were shoe stores for men, women, and children. My dad managed Goldman's Shoes at 2nd and South. Kid's clothes sere bought at Boy togs or my moms place the Cissy Shop for Girls (named for my sister). Whole families would stand on the sidewalk watch TV on tiny screens through window of the appliance shop or listen to music from speakers in front of the record store.

Every Philadelphian knew the famous South Street men's shops. Diamonds, Krass Bros, Harris Goodman, Speed Kagan, Al Berman, Joe Krass, and Big Hearted Jim's. Every lady wanted a coat or suit from Berkowitz or Paramount. Dresses from Robby's mom's store, Mary Meinster's and wedding dresses from Blue Bird Bridle and Silverman's were coveted. And the "barkers"! Men who stood out in front and described to passersby, the delights and the bargains to be found inside. Only a few stores still had barkers when I was growing up, but they were an important part of the atmosphere of old South Street. Many were Holocaust survivors with limited English. "Mrs. Please! Inside we got beautiful coats and suits. The best! And prices, special for you, you wouldn't believe! Come in let me show you. You don't have to buy nothing! Just take a look at what we got!" For the "South Street Gang", the barkers were often the targets of choice or maybe just opportunity. We would ride by on our bikes, blazing away with cap guns or water pistols. Our Favorite victim was "Mousy" a skinny little old man who barked for Weiss's Ladies Coats. Within minutes word of our bad behavior would reach our parents and part of our punishment would be to go back and apologize to "Mousy". This happened so often he would see us coming with our parents, and would disappear into the store to avoid the embarrassment of another confrontation. My uncle Al Beckman worked at Weiss's. When Mousy died, Uncle Al took his place as barker and Weiss's was off limits.

Today's South Street of clubs, restaurants, and boutiques, is nothing like the place where Robby and I grew up. We didn't realize it at the time, but the old South St. was also a bastion of Women's Lib. Probably half the businesses on South Street were built and run by the ladies of South Street. My dad went to work everyday at Goldman's Shoes and my mother Anny ran the Cissy Shop. Sammy Peanuts, Robby Meinster's dad, got up before dawn to distribute the Daily racing form, but Robby's mom, Mary (or as she was known and feared) "The Mare" , was in charge of Meinster's Dresses. No one could scare a kid into behaving, like my "Aunt" Eva Lipschitz who had a high class lingerie shop and in the summer ran the best boarding house in Atlantic City. If you grew up on South Street, it never entered your mind that men were in any way brighter or more capable than our moms.

This was during the 1940's and 50's when June Cleaver was expected to stay home and care for "the Beaver". Like everyone else I grew up with, both my parents worked seven days a week. Most days, our stores were open from 9am to 9pm. People worked a "normal 12 hour workday". Five day work weeks, 8 hour days, and housewife moms, were what we saw on TV. When I asked my Aunt Edith, who was from the Old Country about that, her reply was, "Feh, those things are only for the goyim". Jews were expected to work longer and harder, if they wanted an easier life for their kids. Big corporations like Ford, general Motors, and IBM didn't hire Jews in those days. Universities had a secret quota system to limit the number of Jewish students, no matter how high their grades and test scores. Hotels, Country Clubs, and even restaurants were often "Restricted NJA". We were taught that if Jews wanted a piece of the American dream; they had to create, build and own it, for themselves. No one was going to make it easy for us. No one knew this better than the fantastic ladies of South Street. Anny, Mary, Myrtle, Eva, Gerty and a dozen more.

Our South Street which ran from 2nd to 10th street, was a Jewish enclave in an Italian neighborhood, bordered on two sides by a black neighborhood. South Street, from 10th st. to 16th Street was a black shopping area, with many of the shops owned by middle class blacks. If you came from "the street", you were special. All the stores gave you a discount. No one had heard of a credit card, but South Street kids could say "Charge it to my mom or dad". Everyone knew who you were and who your parents were. From the age of five or six, just as we were about to sit down to eat, my mom would send me to Siegel's Bakery for a loaf of fresh baked rye or pumpernickel,. I don't recall ever taking money with me. It was the same if I went to Vallotti's for a loaf of Italian bread, Mr. Golden's for Jewish deli, or to Gerace's Italian grocery for a can of Madalia D'Oro, my mom's favorite coffee. And you were safe. Every store owner or salesperson was an "Aunt" or "Uncle. It never occurred to me that "Aunt Rose" and "Aunt Sally" were not actually my aunts. It wasn't till my early teen years that I began to sort out which of my aunts and uncles were actually related to me. Even at seven to eight years old, we could walk and play anywhere and know that we were looked after by every adult; Jewish, Italian, Irish or Black. In return we were expected to show everyone the same respect we gave our parents.

Particularly memorable was "Uncle Willie". A huge black man always immaculately dressed in bib overalls and a golf cap. We would see him early in the morning on our way to school. His business was washing the big display windows of the South St stores. But it was his afternoon job that made him special. He drove the horse and wagon that delivered fancy produce from the Washington Market. We didn't get to see many horses on South St, except in cowboy pictures, at the Model Movie Theater. On a summer's day when we were well behaved, Uncle Willie would let us ride on the wagon with him. He would tell us stories as we clip clopped slowly across the city, to far away exotic places like Strawberry Mansions and Rittenhouse Square.

Before the Black Tuna Gang, there was the "South Street Gang". It started when I was three years old, and for years we were the "terror" of South Street. The core members were me, Robby Meinster, and Cookie Baumholtz. Cookie was older than me by two years. His father owned the local real estate and insurance office. Robby was just over a year older than me. Robby and I each had an older and a younger sister. Cookie had two older brothers. The other members of our gang were at various times, Norman Spector, Pretty boy Levin, Tony Ordile, Alfred Maeola and Pedro Perez.

Tony one of our Italian "associates", lived on 8th street just off South. His dad, a carpenter, built our clubhouse in the communal "backyard" behind the deserted Roxy Theater. It was here we would hide out to play hooky or smoke the cigarettes we had stolen from our parents. We almost always got caught. The clubhouse was only three feet high, by four feet wide, by seven feet long. Someone would see smoke coming from the air vents and call Anthony's mother. She would call our parents and then she would holler in through the vent that our parents wanted us home immediately. We in turn would go stupidly silent and try to pretend that no one was in the clubhouse. This would last until Tony's father came home and threaten to wreck our hideout. When we finally gave up and staggered out reeking of cigarette smoke, he would slap a big padlock on the door. Often it would be weeks before he would take off the padlock and let us play inside again.

Having our gang headquarters in an inner city courtyard, behind a deserted theater, presented a world of possibilities for getting into trouble. With our toy bows and sharpened arrows, we were great hunters of Norway rats, and feral cats. As explorers, we would climb and travel over the neighborhood rooftops. We might, on a rainy day, screw up our courage and break into the haunted Roxy Theater to explore the projection booth with its huge old fashion projectors, or venture backstage and play with the props from the live stages shows of another era. Getting caught in the Roxy brought the ultimate humiliation. The cops would load us into the cop car or worse the Paddy Wagon, and deliver us a few hundred feet down the street to our parent's places of business. The haunted Roxy wasn't as half as scary as Anny or "the Mare" if you were delivered home in front of all the neighbors, by the cops. Every store owner and employee would be out in the street to witness our humiliation.

We had it all and didn't know it. The kids we saw on TV lived in nice houses in the suburbs. Mom stayed home and cooked wonderful meals. Kids got an allowance and they went downtown or to a real shopping center to buy things. No one in the South Street gang had heard of an allowance. When I asked the font of old word wisdom, Aunt Edith, she considered it for a minute and said, "Feh, allowance, it's only for the goyim! Jewish children earn what they need". And we did! From age four, If I needed a nickel for caps for my six shooter, or a dime for a new pea shooter and ammunition, I could "make boxes" or do some other chore in our store. Or I could present myself at almost any store on the block and do the same. For larger projects that required Quarters or even dollars, the Gang would shine shoes on the corner of 7th and South. We had a shoe shine box we kept at Cookie's house. Or we could take out an ice cream push cart from Mr. Schwartz. These activities didn't always produce the needed funds, but they often embarrassed our parents into paying up. And don't think that recycling is some new idea. The South Street Gang would "find" a wagon from somewhere and go store to store collecting cardboard boxes to sell to the junk lady for a penny a pound. A better recycling enterprise was collecting bottles. When you bought a soda, you left a 2 cent deposit on individual glass bottles and a 5 cent deposit on quart bottles. We would scour the neighborhood for bottles and take them to Morano's Italian deli, or my Uncle Meyer's grocery store, for a refund, If we couldn't find enough bottles, we might sneak behind Londy's and help ourselves to a few of the empty bottles stored there. As we got older and needed money for dates and clothes, we all found after school jobs somewhere on the "street".

And shopping centers? Feh, for the goyim! The best men's and ladies and children's stores in America were right outside our doors. Radios, TV, washing machines, and vacuum cleaners, came from across the street or down the block. Records, corsets, furniture, lamps, fabrics, handmade quilts and pillows, shoes for the whole family, bridal gowns and tuxedos, toys and hobby crafts, were within a two block walk. Our South Street from 2nd to 10th street had a Woolworth's, The Model Movie Theater, a doctor and optometrist. At Mr. Garr,s Dancing School our sisters learned tap and ballet, the boy's took tap and acrobat, and our parents could even learn ballroom dancing. There were three drugstores including a Nevins and a Sun ray Drugs. The famous Pat's Steaks never drew half the people that traveled to our neighborhood to eat a hot dog or fishcake or a "combination" at Levis's on 6th street just off South. Not only the best kosher hot dog in America, but the only place on earth to get a Champ Cherry soda or a custom built Chocolate soda with "extra syrup please". We had Siegel's bakery and Vallotti's Italian Bakery. Jewish delis and Italian groceries. Mr. Segal the butcher was also a "shocket", who would kill and clean for you, a kosher chicken. Around the corner on Lombard Street was our Synagogue B'nai Abraham, the third oldest in America. Across the street from the Synagogue was a real Jewish fish store where the carp and the whitefish swam around in a stone tank until they had cleaned themselves out enough to be made into geffilta fish at the hands of Aunt Edith and the old world bubbas. There were two first class kosher restaurants, a meat and a dairy restaurant, on 5th street off South, and the best Italian food came from the family owned places on 9th street near South. Snockey's and Joe Bookbinder's served the best seafood and everyone from Philadelphia and Jersey came to 4th street for bagels and lox from the "Famous". We even had two taverns. The Washington Inn and the Saloon. Back then, The Saloon was just that, a saloon, not a fancy restaurant. It had a "Ladies bar" in the back with a separate entrance. My Uncle Al Beckman, Sammy Peanuts, Nookie the Bookie, Segal the baker, and a handful of characters might be found behind the old fashioned swinging bar room doors. In those days" the Saloon" was owned by a big red dog named Sandy who lived on hot dogs that the kids brought him. Sandy was also the look out; he would lie in front of the swinging doors and bark a warning when he'd spot an irate wife. Like most South Street kids, Robby and I lived above our stores. Me at 641, and Robby first on the 500 block above Dr. Dubrow's the optician, and later on the 700 block above Mary Meinster's Dresses and Suits.

Don't get the idea that because our moms worked all day in the store, that they didn't know where we where and what we were up to at all times. Entering and leaving the house, meant trooping through the store. Even if your mom had a customer, she would stop and interrogate you as to where you were going, what you intended to do, and who else was going. On your return, there was no way to sneak past Anny or Mary without a recap of your activities. If you did something wrong, she already knew about it from the South Street telegraph, so there was no sense in trying to lie. In our world, the richer families had housewife moms and the poorer families had maids or housekeepers because mom had to go to work every day. On the one hand I can't imagine anyone being closer to their mother than I was, or for that matter, any of us in the South Street gang. But it's also true that I was raised by two very special black "Church Ladies".

From my birth to age five, it was Mrs. Georgia Brown. Short, plump, white haired, articulate and soft spoken. When she talked about god, there was no doubt that she knew him personally. She taught me about "please and thank you" and that everyone was to be respected. My favorite time as a small child was to sit with her as she ironed. She would feed me boiled cabbage, her favorite snack, and tell me wonderful stories about when she was a "little boy". Georgia retired when I was five and Miss Lulu Mac Fall took over running my life. Over six feet tall, almost bald, a mustache, and the biggest hands and feet I had ever seen. She must have been in her late fifties when she took custody of me and my sisters. Lulu had been a notorious drunk who occasionally showed up to clean our store. When Mrs. Georgia Brown retired, Lulu told my parents that if she could take over the housekeeping, she would never take another drink. She kept her promise.

From the age five until my bar Mitzvah at thirteen, I was her "boy". Simply put, if you messed with "her boy" Lulu would hunt you down and hurt you. She protected me from everyone, including my parents. If they raised a hand to give me a smack, they faced the prospect of having to get past Lulu. She was from the tobacco fields of North Carolina, and she taught me about collard greens and poke salad. She was a member of our family. To this day, I feel sad, because not long after she retired, and hearing that I had pneumonia, she got out of her own sickbed to sit at my bedside. A few days later she died of pneumonia. Her lungs had been destroyed by years of hard drinking and smoking Pall Malls. Her time at my beside must have finished the job. Somewhere, in a box of old photos, is the most wonderful picture of Miss Lulu Mac Fall, wearing her purple satin church dress, with her big black floppy brimmed church hat, and dancing with me at my bar Mitzvah. And another photo of her presiding at the table with the entire South Street Gang, Robby, Cookie, Norman, Anthony, Pretty Boy Levine, Pedro, Shaya, and Alfred.

Chapter 3
Return to Colombia

It took less than ten days to pay the Colombians for the marijuana we had smuggled into South Florida in the old DC-3. Considering I hadn't remained in Columbia as a hostage for payment, our partners there realized that we were serious businessmen who could be trusted to pay large sums without guarantees or coercion. They were anxious to grow the business and so invited Robby and I down to Santa Marta for a combination vacation and board meeting. Gene would remain in Miami, in a suite at the Fontainebleau Hotel, to continue collecting payments from our customers.

Two weeks after escaping a firing squad in the Columbian jungle and an irate EL Loco, who wanted to hold me hostage, I was headed back to Barranquilla as valued "Miami Connection". Bo, the ex NFL player who had flown copilot on the DC-3, Robby and I, flew down south in a husky Piper Navajo belonging to Gene's company, Land Air. The Navajo is a big eight passenger, twin engine aircraft. Docile, forgiving, easy to fly, this one had all the bells and whistles. Naturally, I usurped the left seat and relegated El Gigante to the copilot spot on my right. The DC-3 had been the first real twin engine plane I had ever flown, and I sure couldn't enter that one in my pilot's log book. Refusing to even turn on the autopilot, I logged about twelve hours of pilot-in-command time on the trip down and back.

As usual, I managed to give us all a butt pucker. After stopping at Porto Prince, Haiti, for fuel, I took off to the south, south west on a direct course for Santa Marta airport. Traveling at just over 200 mph and climbing at about 500 ft per minute, it would be a near thing to gain enough altitude to get over the twin peaks that were directly in our path in the nearby Dominican Republic. There was plenty of space to go between the mountains. The only problem, was the thick cloud layer covering more than half of the towering peaks. Long before we reached the mountains, we were flying blind in thick white cumulus clouds. I was stupidly confident that if weren't high enough to clear the top of the shorter peak on our right side, we were certainly on course to fly between the mountains. That's at least as smart as playing Russian Roulette with only one empty chamber. Both Robby and Bo threatened to drag me to the back of the plane and tie me up, if I didn't do a 180° out of those clouds and fly out to sea, away from the menacing Dominican peaks. Feeling dumber than a rock, I flew the rest of the way to Santa Marta Airport in my most sedate manor.

In the seventies, Santa Marta Airport was closed to international flights. Very few flights landed there. Perhaps one or two domestic flights a day! The field was almost deserted when I taxied over to a tie down near the small terminal. Raul was waiting with a customs officer from Barranquilla Airport, to put entry stamps in our passports. With Raul, were his cousin Eduardo and partner Julio. As we started walking towards the waiting van, Bo pulled Raul aside and inquired,

"The Columbian Lieutenant, the one who robbed us and wanted to shoot us, up on the airstrip, I'd like to pay him a visit."

Raul replied, "Senor Bo, I'm sorry, that Lieutenant isn't around here now."

"I'll wait. When do you think he'll be back?"

"He's been transferred, he's not coming back".

Bo turned and pointed to the plane. "I've got the Navajo and enough fuel to cross Colombia. Where was he transferred?"

"But Senor Bo, I'm afraid your Navajo doesn't go that high!"

By four or five o'clock we were checked in at the Hotel Irotoma. I was back in cabina 7; Robby was next door in number 8, and Bo in cabina 9. Robby and Bo had never been to Irotoma. They marveled at the lush jungle setting that began at the foot of the nearby Sierra Madres and surrounded the Cabinas. While a few feet in front, was a gorgeous white sand beach bordering the clear aqua waters of the Caribbean.

For two days we were wined and dined. Raul had a 42 ft Hatteras sports fisherman, and in the morning we trolled the azure waters in front of Santa Marta. We took the fish, mostly Dorado, back to the Irotoma where it was grilled, along with shrimp and lobster, at a small kiosko right on the beach. Darius, our always in attendance waiter, would serve the fish, with fresh fruit, melon, and ice cold cervezas Aguilar. Julio owned a huge speedboat. In the afternoon, he took us on excursions along the coast to an uninhabited beach cove, where he and Raul planned to develop a small private resort.

The morning after our arrival, Johnny and Chino showed up at 7 am to join us for breakfast on the patio of my cabina. Raul, Julio and Eduardo were already eating. As Darius served our huevos caballos and huevos pericos with tinto and melon, a troop of about 30 men in matching tee shirts and shorts trotted along the shore line. They stopped directly in front of our cabinas and began their calisthenics. It looked like a local army platoon, out for their morning exercise. After a while, they began passing around a soccer ball. Doing the kind of fancy ball drills Latin-American and European kids do in the streets and playgrounds. It was only when the troop was receding up the beach at a fast trot, that Chino informed me we had been watching Eduardo's professional soccer team, "Magdalena". Eduardo had arranged for their morning workout to be held at Irotoma for our entertainment. We were impressed!

Instead of traipsing around El Rodedero where the local authorities could get to know us and the under cover narcs could note our presence, our nightlife came to us on the beach. Darius, who seemed never to go off duty, would take the hotel van, go into town to bring back a small trio of musicians and a half dozen very beautiful young ladies from the local casa de putas. For the girls, a night away from the bordello was like a night off. They loved the chance to dance. eat, drink, smoke and party. Apparently, Bo lived up to his Columbian nickname. Forever more, the girls of the Santa Marta casa, would show up at Irotoma, knock on my door, and ask if they could see El Gigante."

On the third day, Robby, me, Johnny and Chino, drove to Barranquilla. We had a nice lunch at Chino's parent's house. The house where I had stayed while our first smuggling venture was being arranged. I was pleased to be able to return the $5,000.00 to Chino's dad. The money he had lent me to fly to Aruba and bail out our plane and crew. And I brought him several hard cover books on American and world politics that I knew he would enjoy. We had spent our evenings talking politics with him teaching me about Columbia and introducing me to the books of Gabriel Garcia Marquez. I had gifts for the rest of the family, all of whom had treated me more like a member of the family, than a customer or a hostage. I even brought an expensive set of chef's knives for the cook, who at every meal, had insisted on going out back to the meat rack to bring me a steak, that :looked like it was cut with a dull ax.

Next, was my final meeting with EL Loco, Chino's brother. Actually, it was a confrontation! Only afterwards, did I realize how dangerous a confrontation it had been.

Loco wanted to impress me with his wealth and power and I wanted him to pay my friend Johnny the commission that was promised him for putting the original deal together. It was Johnny who introduced me to Chino, and arranged our first small plane load. One of the reasons I had agreed to pay $60.00 a pound for the first small load, was to insure that Johnny received his $5.00 a pound. The $35.00 a pound I agreed to pay for the DC-3 load was still a very high price, and was to include Johnny's nickel. We had also agreed to an additional $10.00 per pound, to help cover the airfield ransoms.

Johnny had been given a token few hundred bucks, and then nothing but stalls and excuses. A deadly confrontation between Loco, who was acting as paymaster for the group, and Johnny who wasn't about to let anyone kick him to the curb, was looming. Loco wanted Johnny out of our business. Johnny was my friend. He watched my back! He was our representative in Columbia. Without him there would have been no business. I wasn't about to let him get pushed out and cheated by Loco. Of course, in those days, I had more guts than brains.

   Loco s office was in a condominium complex he was building in central Barranquilla. They were to be luxury pied- a-tiers. Tall, narrow, elaborately decorated buildings. Loco's office was on the ground floor of an almost completed structure. It was Friday afternoon, payday! The scene was staged to impress Robby and I. An orderly line of workmen stood patiently waiting to be paid by the hand of El Hefe himself. Seated behind a big desk, with an armed guard standing on either side, Loco was playing god. Not a very benevolent one! As each workman humbly approached to be paid, Loco would enumerate a litany of excuses to withhold some of the workman's pay. A missing or broken tool. A cracked board or a spilled can of paint. Any excuse to cheat a poor workman out of a few pesos. He may have thought he was impressing me with his power and business acumen, mostly, he was really pissing me off. Without machine gun toting body guards, he'd never have the courage to do what he was doing. On a one on one basis, he'd never face down Johnny, who may have been a poor street kid, but was more of a man, an honorable man, than Loco could ever be. For a guy who came from an honorable, nice family, Loco took a very wrong turn somewhere along the line. After, about 20 minutes, he told the remaining three or four craftsmen to come back in an hour, because he a very important meeting. That didn't do much to endear him to me. These men had been waiting hours to be paid. They wanted to go home to their families. After a brief greeting, we declined Loco's offer of scotch whiskey. I introduced him to Robby, and El Gigante.

   "I'm sorry we can't stay around and talk." I told him. " We're expected back in Santa Marta for dinner. Johnny wanted to stop by to pick the money you promised him"

   Loco didn't much care for that. "I'll take care of Johnny some other time. Let's have a drink. Maybe we can talk about some new business"

I knew the only way he wanted to take care of Johnny, was with a bullet in the back. Things were getting tense. I could see that Loco was trying to figure out if the four of us, me, Robby, Bo, and Johnny were armed. And he was no doubt wondering what his partners would do if he killed their newest, and at the time, best "Miami Connection". To end the stare down, I played my hole card.

"Look, I can understand if you're a little short of cash right now. I'm sure this construction job is very expensive. We brought a little extra cash to buy some nice jewelry for our wives. How about if we pay Johnny and you can repay us when you can spare the cash."

That had the desired effect. Trying not too successfully, to keep a smile on his face, Loco popped open the slim snake skin attaché case on the desk and tossed two slim, $10,000.00 bundles of hundred dollar bills, in the direction of Johnny.

"I already advanced this guy a few hundred dollars. That's plenty for him. There was no hurry for him to have the rest of the money."

Johnny had the good sense not to say what was on both our minds. Instead, I thanked Loco for his hospitality and promised to try to get back to Barranquilla to meet with him for a meal and a business talk. We literally backed out of the office. Ominously, the normally busy street outside Loco's building, was completely deserted. Even Ray Charles could see it was fear that cleared the sidewalks. We piled in to Johnny's yellow Camaro and with an eye on the rear view mirror, headed straight for Santa Marta. There we would be under the protection of Raul, Julio, and their crew of Guarjirans. The same Guarjirans who had been with Bo and me two weeks earlier, facing the threat of a firing squad on a remote jungle airstrip. My antics to save us from being taken down and shot in the town of La Cienega, and Bo's gigantic appetite for anything but monkey, had become legend along the Caribbean coast of Columbia. These big Guarjiran indios now looked out for me whenever I visited Columbia.

Later that day we settled down to talk business with our people in Santa Marta. It was now the height of the pot harvest. Warehouses were filling with first rate herb, freshly picked, dried and packed. Our .partners wanted to send larger shipments. Boatloads, 30,000 pounds at a time. Not huge amounts. Just nice select cargoes that could be easily transported in small Columbian fishing trawlers. Could we find boats and crews to offload the Trawlers? "No problem". Stryker Yacht Company would supply us with a couple of sports fishing boats and we already had the crew of our fishing team, "The Fishing Fools".

Our friends took us by jeep to a coastal village where their weed was being packed. We agreed to stick to the price of $35.00 a pound. Extremely high, for boatload quantities, but a bargain for cleanly packed buds. We also agreed on an "insurance policy" to mitigate losses for either side, in the event a load, or part of a load was busted, lost at sea, or ripped off. We would pay $50,000 to cover at least part of the Columbian loses and agree to accept another load to make up for the balance of the losses on both sides. It made good sense to protect each other financially. This part of our arrangement never came into play until we agreed to help Mark Phillips our boat supplier at Stryker Yachts, and his partner George Purvis Jr., secure a load from Columbia. But that would come later.

I arranged to return to Santa Marta when our friends had prepared our load and arranged for a trawler and crew to transport it to an off loading spot in the Bahamas. It would much safer to arrange map coordinates, radio frequencies, and time tables face to face. Later we would devise a phone code referring to the shipment of certain cars or trucks from our auction. This code would convey the times and places of future shipments, eliminating the need for frequent trips to Columbia. Sometimes, if a meeting was needed, friends or associates of our Columbian partners would meet with us in Miami, when they came over on a shopping trip. Additionally, we all agreed to explore avenues to expand our partnership into legitimate areas of commerce. Our friends were major growers of cotton, cattle & coffee. In addition to these, we also explored ventures into hardwoods and shipping.

Despite my pilotage, the trip home in the Navajo, was uneventful. Overall, except for our Barranquilla meeting with Loco, it was a pleasurable and successful trip. We had firmed up our business relationships and had a really good time. Once we eliminated Loco from the equation, the remainder of our people down south, we considered good friends. If El Loco remained a partner with our friends in Santa Marta, we never knew about it. We never met with him again. They knew he had tried more than once to monopolize our business, and may have dumped him as a partner. After paying pilots, drivers, unloading crews, airport managers, the DC-3, special radios, general expenses, travel, and paying off the marijuana, we were left with about a half million dollars in operating capital. We finally had some real bucks to work with. It would take almost all of it to finance our first 30,000 lb ocean smuggling venture. Robby ,Gene, and I, may have drawn 25 or 30 grand each for living expenses and a few toys, but the rest of that money went towards securing two tournament class sports fishing yachts, powerful radars, radios, safety equipment, crew and fuel expenses, and fishing trips to the Bahamas to establish a legitimate cover for our impending activities. We would gamble it all once again, to try for our first really big payday.

Black Tuna Diaries

Chapter 4
Criminal Depravities of the South St. Gang

I was four years old, Robby Meinster was five, and Cookie Baumholtz was six, when we organized our first criminal enterprise, The South St Gang! We were too young for sophisticated criminal activities. Not yet allowed to cross the street on our own, we had to depend on older siblings to reach the scene of our criminal objectives.

The Model Movie Theater and Woolworth's were the focus of the South Street Gang's disorganized crime. On any given Saturday, I would attach myself to my older sister Marilyn, for the two block trek to the Model, on South St between 4th and 5th. Once there, I'd "meet up" with Robby who had hitched a ride with his older sister Judy, and Cookie who would arrive with his older brothers Harold and Allen. The rest of our gang would filter in by ones and twos. Every kid in the neighborhood would show up at the Model on Saturday, without fail.

A double feature, five cartoons, two serials, a yo yo contest, and a lucky number drawing for dime store prizes! It was a weekly carnival and everyone was there. Hamburger Niremberg, with his sisters Elaine (who I had a crush on) and Barbra, Ruthy and Paul Goldstein, Freya and Leila Rabinowitz, Hannah and Annette Cohen, Norman and Hannah Spector, Rebeca Krass (who I later had a crush on), Pretty Boy Levin with one or two of his five sisters, and a couple of hundred kids from four to fourteen! The candy counter was continuous chaos! Hundreds of kids trying to load up before the first feature started.

At that age, we could only hide behind sister's skirts and watch, as the older kids would shake the popcorn machine to put a little extra into the small white bag from the ten cent dispenser. But we knew that in a few years, we would be old enough to shake extra popcorn from the machine ourselves. With enough popcorn, you could go up to the balcony where

Black Tuna Diaries

the older kids went to make-out, and you could toss cold stale popcorn down on the kids you didn't like.

The break in! Once we were old enough to travel the two blocks on our own, we planed to save the ten cent ticket price by B. and E.ing our way into the theater. Sort of! It went like this! One of the gang would buy a ticket, while the rest of us waited in the ally by the emergency exit doors. The inside man would casually sidle up to the fire door, and pop it open. Letting in not only our gang, but enough sunlight to blind half the theater and obscure the screen. This would cause a furor of whistles and catcalls. The usher/ ticket taker, Mr. Eddie, had witnessed the B&E from his post at the head of the isle, he would grab us one by one, toss us out, and bar us from the theater for a full week. After two unsuccessful attempts, we gave it up as a failed plan. Our first criminal enterprise an abject failure!

After a double feature, five cartoons, a newsreel, yo yo contest, and a drawing for prizes, you were pretty thirsty. Drinks weren't sold at the Model! That was probably a good thing, considering the popularity of throwing anything at hand from the balcony. If you saved a little of your candy money, you could get a nickel coke at Woolworth's lunch counter, next door the movie. Like most Woolworth's, this one had an entrance on two streets, South St and 5th St. Marilyn and Judy would treat us to fountain cokes and walk us through the store passing the candy and nut counter with its aromas, and the toy counters covered with colorful cheap toys that beckoned young hands to pick something up.

Perhaps theft would be the forte of the South St gang. We planned for the day when we would be old enough to escape the tethers of our older sisters. When the day arrived here's what we did. After leaving the Model Movie, Robby, Cook, and I slipped casually into the South St entrance of the Woolworth store. We strolled casually past the pistachio nuts and cotton candy, as we worked up our courage. The loot we had targeted was a ten cent plastic cap Bomb. An ugly green and yellow toy shaped like a real WWII bomb. You put a cap inside (do kids today know what a cap is?), tossed it high in the air,

Black Tuna Diaries

and when it hit the ground the cap exploded the bomb into two pieces. Since at five years old, I was the youngest, dumbest and slowest, I was drafted to pull off our first heist. Robby and Cookie would be the lookouts. It was a brilliant plan, subtle, and sophisticated. I would run as fast as I could past the candy counters, turn left for the toy department, grab a cap Bomb on the fly, and exit the 5th St side in full flight. If all went according to plan, Robby, Cookie and the rest of the gang would meet me in the alley half a block away, to celebrate our first heist.

With the loot clutched in my sweaty paw, I found myself out of breath, scared to death, and quite alone in the dark alley. Everyone else had gone home so they'd have an alibi when the shit hit the fan. As they knew it must! The reason no one had pursued me from the store, is that there was no need. Everyone that worked at Woolworth's and every other nearby store for that matter, knew who I was and that my mom had a children's store a block away. By the time I pushed open the door at 641 South St, Annie was standing by the register, with a quarter in her hand and steam coming out of her ears. I would be grounded for a month, but first I would have to take the quarter to Woolworths, pay for the Cap Bomb, which mom trashed, apologize for the theft, and I had damn well better bring back the fifteen cents change.

I regret to admit that six months later, I again let Cookie and Robby, (mostly Cookie), talk me into another attempt at the cap Bomb heist. Results! Two months no movies, and no going out after dinner to play! Worse! My aunt Edith, a serious old country Buba who managed to escape from Germany before most of her family disappeared into Hitler's ovens, lectured me for months on the dangers of eating or drinking thref from a place like Woolworth.

"Feh! It's only for the goyim!"

As a result, I was so traumatized; I didn't taste the delights at Woolworth's lunch counter until I was in college at the University of Miami, and operating my own demonstration concession in Woolworth's Lincoln Rd store on Miami

Black Tuna Diaries

Beach. In any case, that pretty much put an end to the South St Gang's career as major snatch and grab artists.

The only criminal career remaining for the South St Gang was extortion. That one, we were good at. Once a year! Each Halloween, armed with half bars of Ivory Soap, the South St Gang, would go "trick or treating". Every merchant for a three block radius, know that if he didn't come up with some serious candy, it was a soap curtain for his display windows.

Even better, was the "Shoe Shine Scam"! If we needed hard cash, especially in large amounts over a quarter, we'd drag out our shoe shine stand which was kept at Cookie Baumholtz's house, and set up for business on the N.E. corner of 7th and South. A stones throw from our family's stores. The objective wasn't necessarily to earn money by shining shoes. We knew it would cause sufficient embarrassment to our parents, so that they would pay us off, not to shine shoes. To this end we would tell our customers, that our folks sent us out to earn milk money for school, Depending on their mood at the time, our parents either paid or punished..

Sometime, when we were grounded and forbidden entre at the Model Movie, our sisters would give us an outing, by taking us somewhere "Educational". It was always a two stop trip! First stop, the Museum of Natural History. Where we would view the evolution of man in static diorama behind plate glass. What I recall, was mostly stuffed cavemen, cave ladies, and cave kids, in their natural habitat. It was the second stop on our "educational" tour that would become the favorite destination of the South St Gang on any rainy Saturday afternoon. The Franklin Institute! No place on earth was better designed to capture a child's mind. Our older sisters opened this fabulous world to us.

Philadelphia's Franklin Institute, with its Fels Planetarium, is such an extraordinary place, it can't be called a museum, or gallery, or any other name I can think of. It's a place where kids from four to ninety-four could touch, try, feel, play with, experiment and experience the wonders of our world. Foucault's Pendulum, ten stories high! Push it, make it move,

Black Tuna Diaries

watch what it does. Walk through a perfect model of a beating heart. Visit each chamber and see every vein and artery throbbing with life. Physics and chemistry exhibits you can set in motion! The first and best Planetarium in America, where you could take a guided tour of the heavens. But the best, the very best part, was the Hall of Transportation.

The Hall of Transportation was the neatest place in the whole world. Full size replicas of the Wright brother's first plane, Lindberg's Spirit of St Louis, and Amelia Earhart's famous Electra. You could climb on and explore full size trains of several types. There was even a huge steam locomotive. Kids could climb into the cab, open the throttle and it would travel up and back along a length of track. And you didn't even need to buy a ticket! Top that one Mickey, you big eared rodent! Except for a little lunch money, or a nickel for a big hot soft pretzel, a kid could spend the entire day, not run out of things to do and see and play with, and not spend a cent. I figure, if our sisters hadn't dragged us there a time or two, we might not have gotten the habit.

Once we were old enough to hike there on our own, we probably ended up there four or five times a year, maybe more. And we always stopped along the way, at the boring old Museum of Natural History.... because it was there. Once you had the Museum habit, it was hard to break. We even visited The Philadelphia Museum of Art, where Rocky ran the steps. My second favorite was The Atwater Kent Museum, on lower Market St. A maritime museum reflecting the glories of Philadelphia's waterfront in the days of the tall sailing ships. These were the terrible educational junkets forced on us young criminals, by our mean older sisters.

But it wasn't all bad. As we got older, aside from fights and shouting matches, older sisters came in handy. By the time I was twelve or thirteen, and starting to go to dances and parties, I had become an expert dancer. Thanks to my sister Marilyn, I could slow low dance, jitterbug, Mambo, and do the Cha Cha. It did of course, feel more than a little awkward practicing slow dancing with my older sister. On the other hand, boy was it worth it! I got to do a whole lot of up-close and very personal

Black Tuna Diaries

slow dancing with some very pretty "teenyboppers". I was a much sought after dance partner at an age when most guys didn't have the knack.

It was our sisters who took us to Cy's luncheonette for a hot roast beef sandwich with gravy and French fries, or to Levis's for a chocolate soda and a hot dog fishcake combination. If you've never had a Levis's combination, you haven't lived. Like Cheese steaks and hot pretzels, it's a Philadelphia thing. *A* fishcake is like a crab cake, only it's a delicious blend of fish, potato, and spices, sautéed to a golden brown. Mash one of these over a big fat all beef kosher hot dog on a steamed bun, slather it with bright golden mustard and your taste buds take off like the space shuttle on lift-off. On a summer's night at two a.m., the sidewalk would be jammed with people who had driven for miles to stuff themselves with Levis's combos, chocolate soda, or secret recipe Champ Cherry soda, served through a wide window that was open to the street.

Even as founding members of the South St Gang, Robby and I had to rely on our older sisters to take us to school when we started first grade, and to advise us about teachers and classes, when we reached Jr. High. By High School, sadly The South St Gang was no more. Cookie Baumholtz, who had rarely in his life left Center City Philadelphia, was attending Philadelphia Farm School, where according to him; he spent a great deal of time with his arm deep in a cow's asshole. I was in high school in Cherry Hill, NJ, and pursuing an acting career. I was appearing in an off-Broadway production of Tennessee Williams "The Garden District" at the Proscenium Theater, in the famous Academy of Music on Broad St in Philadelphia. The other guys, Pretty Boy Levin, Norman Specter, Alvin M., Tony 0, Pedro, all gone in different directions. The brilliant criminal organization that was the South St Gang, no longer existed, because the South St. where we grew up no longer existed! No longer a street of shops, where families lived and worked. It had become a street of boutique restaurants and New Wave entertainments. A few landmark businesses remained, but the families that made it a neighborhood were gone.

Black Tuna Diaries

Chapter 5
Fishing Fools

"The Fishing Fool", I didn't much care for that name, but without mentioning it beforehand, Captain Randy had it painted on the stern of our 44ft Stryker sports fisherman. He also had t-shirts made with the same name for our fishing team. I didn't much care for that either, but it was done and we were now, "The Fishing Fools". Had we not been instantly successful on the big game circuit, people would have just referred to us as the Fools. After the first few months on the tournament trail, Fishing Fool t-shirts were a hot item in tackle and souvenir shops all over the Bahamas and south Florida. To be truthful, I was in pig heaven. A fishing fanatic since the age of six or seven! I used to go flounder fishing with my uncle Meyer in Brigantine New Jersey. But I never had the kind of money it takes to go big game fishing. This was living a dream. And we were very, very, good at it. Thanks to Capt. Randy! In no time I acquired another nickname, "Billfish Bob". A little embarrassing, but I secretly loved it. I was accumulating too many names. Ray Jimenez, the obsequious asshole who worked at our auto auction, called me El Hefe, El Padron, and Don Roberto. Big Gene and his biker crew called me, Baron, The Baron of Barranquilla, and Barranquilla Bob. My ego didn't need that kind of stroking, but Billfish Bob I liked.

In order to off load the 30,000 lbs of marijuana that was coming by trawler from Santa Marta, we needed two good sized boats. Robby, who was always the class act of our ventures, phoned me at the office one day and asked me to meet him at a Pier Sixty Six in Ft. Lauderdale. He was waiting there with Mark Phillips from Stryker Yacht Company, to show me the Pacifier! The most beautiful 42 ft Rybovitch ever built. An older boat, with a fiberglass over wood hull, and exquisite woodwork interior, it did not have a single sharp edge or corner. The type of old world cabinetry, that's seen only in the most expensive kitchens in the mansions of the rich. Unlike the aluminum hulled Stryker, the Rybovitch is a high mainten-

Black Tuna Diaries

ance yacht. Few people can afford the upkeep, and the owner, was trading it in on a Stryker.

The Rybo was bargain priced and. Robby had already agreed a deal with Mark. Stryker Yachts had no dock space for the boat, and we hadn't yet taken over the Fontainebleau docks. The Rybo had to be moved right away to make room for the owner's new boat. We were taking it to our friend Howard's in Miami Shores. He had an unused deep water dock on the man made canal behind his house.

Howard joined us at Pier Sixty Six and was so awed by this exquisite gem of a boat that he refused to take the controls for the short trip to his dock. An experienced skilled helmsman, he was afraid he might damage this extraordinary old yacht. The honors fell to me. I climbed to the flying bridge and looked over the gauges and controls. I spun the helm and worked the single lever engine controls of the two turbo Cummins diesels. It was hard to believe that anything was attached to the wheel or levers, the movements were so light and friction free. I started the engines and let them idle while we checked all the gauges, switches, breakers, and disconnected the heavy cables that provided electric power at the dock. Much to the old owner's consternation, I took possession of the expensive custom dock lines and motored south on the intercostals. When we got to Howard's house, there was a fast incoming tide running crosswise to his boat slip. I asked Howard, who was much better at it, to back her between the poles, to the dock. He refused, fearing he'd scrape her hull on the mooring posts. Without a great deal of confidence, I gave it a try. The boat handled so well, I was able to back in between the poles, without even a bump, despite the fast moving current.

Now we had two of the nicest sports fishing boats in South Florida. The plan was to "legitimize" them by fishing a series of billfish tournaments. That way, our comings and goings would appear normal. It would be a couple of months before the Colombian trawler could be loaded with herb, and travel the 1500 mile circuitous route to our offload location in the Bahamas. In the mean time, I entered the Stryker in a series of

Black Tuna Diaries

light tackle, catch and release, billfish tournaments. The series started with the International Billfish Tournament in West Palm Beach Florida and each week moved south, until it finished in Key West seven weeks later. I didn't get to fish all seven tournaments, before we had to drop out, and head for the Bahamas to meet the trawler. I think we got as far as Islamorada or Marathon Key. Despite being the new guys among fifty or so experienced teams, we managed to secure trophy status in every competition we entered. Coming in second or third or catching the first, last, or largest fish of the contest. Our presence was always noted. And we had fun! The kind of fun a South St kid from Philly, dreams about.

First of all, you were required to fish with 12 lb test spinning tackle. You were fishing primarily for sailfish, which in the Atlantic would average 40-70l lbs. and would leap, twist, run and dive, powered by a whippy snakelike body and huge sail. You also caught White Marlin, which are bigger and stronger, maybe 70-120 lbs and Blue Marlin up to five or six hundred pounds. With only 12 lb test spinning tackle, angler skill, boat handling, and fish control during the release, were critical. This is stand-up fishing. No fighting chair! No one can touch a "hooked up" rod, except the official angler. His only aid was a lightweight belt with a Gimbel to rest the rod butt during the fight. These are live bait tournaments. Five or six rods are baited with live ballyhoo and placed in a Rocket Launcher, a six hole rod holder, placed where the fighting chair would normally be. Two lines trail far behind the boat off the tips of the outriggers, two lines slightly closer, from the middle of the outriggers. These four lines are designated "right long rigger, left long rigger, right short rigger and left short rigger. The final two lines are trolled directly behind the boat, not too far back and are called flat lines. The angler must be aware at all times, of the names and positions of every baited line. When the Captain or mate from his position on the flying bridge or tower, spots a billfish he will shout down to the angler "sail on the right long-rigger" or "white coming up on the left flat line". This cry produces a flood of adrenalin and a series of well rehearsed actions. The boat, which has been moving barely fast enough to keep the live ballyhoo from socializing with one another, picks up speed. This causes the billfish to become more aggressive. As soon as the fish tries to stun the

Black Tuna Diaries

bait with his bill, the angler grabs the rod from the Rocket Launcher and allows the line to free spool out from the reel.. This drops the now stunned bait fish into the hopefully gapping maw of the pursuing fish. Sailfish travel and feed in pods of four or five, and the angler, like it or not, might have two or even three fish hooked at the same time. The only help he can get from the mate, is to reel in and remove the rods that are not hooked up. This is to avoid tangled lines during the fight. Multiple hookups, more often than not, result in only one or none of the hooked fish, being landed and released. The angler's job is to keep the line taught, keep the fish's head up, and prevent him from diving. It would take much too long to tire a big game fish with 12 lb test line. The Captain backs the boat towards the running, jumping fish, as fast as he can, while the angler reels in line fast enough to keep the fish from turning or diving. If by some miracle, everyone does his job and the fish actually cooperates, the last and most important part belongs to the mate. Bear in mind, all. of this is watched by an official "observer", placed on the boat by the judges to determine if a fish has been properly caught and released, as opposed to merely hooked and lost.

   An official "Release" can only take place after the angler has brought the billfish to the side of the boat. Close enough for the heavier leader line to pass through the guide on the rod tip. The leader line keeps the abrasive and powerful bill from instantly severing the light line. Once the leader splice passes through the rod tip, the rest of the job belongs to the mate. The mate is the most important person in the cockpit. He prepares the baits, sharpens the hooks, baits the lines, and puts out the lines in their proper spot. When a fish is hooked, the mate leaps from his observation post on the fly bridge or tower and in less than a minute, has reeled in and removed the other five rods, so that the angler has a clear cockpit for the fight. Speed is imperative! The fish must be landed, and the baited lines returned to the water in order to be competitive. Now comes the insane part. The fish is brought to the boat "hot". It hasn't been fought to a standstill. Often it will turn and make another run under or away from the boat, and the fight begins all over again. To prevent this, the mate must "hot wire" the excited panicking sailfish. That means, with nothing but a pair of cotton work gloves to protect his hands he must

Black Tuna Diaries

quickly grab the leader and use it to pull the angry fish close enough to reach down and "bill" it. That is, to grab on to the rough bill of the trashing angry catch, and control the big fish long enough to remove the hook or flip it into the boat to remove the hook before releasing it, without harm.

The best "hot wire" guy I ever saw was Capt. Randy himself. A newly made Captain, who had mated for Captain Crunch for many years. Blond, rangy, a Vietnam vet, with a slight limp an in his mid thirties like the rest of us, except for Gene who was a bit older, Randy's limp was the result of a confrontation with a "hot" sailfish that flipped from his wet gloves and stuck his bill all the way through Randy's thigh. Marty, a Fishing Fool mate in training, usually switched places with the captain and let Randy perform the "hot wire", and release. The instant the sail or marlin was released, all the lines were rebaited, repositioned behind the boat, and the dance began anew. On a good day, this fire drill would take place ten or twelve times. According to Randy, the secret of our fishing success was, after putting out the baited lines, we would all gather on the flying bridge and share a doobie. When a second mate was needed, we'd bring along Gene's buddy, Captain Barry a.k.a., the stoner. Barry, a charter boat captain with his own boat in Ft Lauderdale, was always so wrecked on Quaaludes and coke, he could be counted on to hot wire and bill a seriously hot sailfish or Marlin. If you could get it close enough to grab, Barry would grab on to the bill. More than once, I had to snatch him by the back of his shorts or his ankles, to haul him back into the boat before a big fish could drag him out to sea. Once Barry grabbed on to a bill, he'd hang on for dear life until the fish dragged him over the horizon, or it was subdued and released. Barry was about 5'9", 170 lbs. dark hair combed forward and hair sprayed in a "Trump" flip to cover a mostly bald pate. Always fun to be around, Barry could be counted on to be too stoned to be counted on. This was often fun and entertaining, but would eventually result in the loss of a beautiful yacht loaded with Santa Marta Gold, and almost cost the lives of the crew. But that comes later.

The last member of the Fishing Fools was Captain Elm. Fiftyish, 6'4", 260 lbs, a big man with a full beard, like the

Black Tuna Diaries

Commodore from the Schweppes commercials! An experienced yacht master, he'd delivered big yachts all over world. Certainly the most experienced and competent seaman among us, Elm need money and wanted to become a smuggler. His yacht delivery business was on the wane. He first fished with us when we needed to fill out a five man crew to fish the Bimini/Cat Cay Giant Tuna Tournament.

   A word about fishing for giant tuna, because that's the genesis of the misnomer, given us by the DEA, "The Black Tuna Gang". In the spring of the year following our first successes at tournament fishing, and our first success smuggling by boat, we entered the Bimini/Cat Cay Tuna Tournament. The object, to catch a giant Bluefin Tuna. Operative word, "Bluefin"! The only species of tuna to attain the size and weight to be called giant tuna. A mature fish might be between 500 and 1500 lbs. Easily, the most powerful fish in the world. Once "hooked up", it's like trying to subdue a runaway freight train. Robby and I fished together on the 42 ft Rybovitch, Pacifier. It was the ultimate fishing trip for two guys from the "South St Gang". About a hundred and fifty of the world's most magnificent sports fishing yachts gathered for the tournament. Most were custom built by yacht builders like Rybovitch, Merit, Jim Smith, and Bob Garlington. Half docked and fished out of the exclusive private island of Cat Cay Club. The rest of us docked and fished from the various marinas on Bimini. Bimini, and its neighbor Cat Cay, are the nearest of the Bahamas to south Florida. Only 55 miles off shore, they are the favorite weekend destination for boaters from Miami to Palm Beach. A haven for rum runners during prohibition and a favorite fishing haunt of Papa Hemingway. Bimini was his "Island in the Sun". Only a block wide, and less than 3 miles long. Most of the action is on the north end in Alicetown. Brown's Hotel, The Blue Water Marina, and The Big Game Club, would fill to the last slot with million dollar Tuna Boats for the entire month of May. Our headquarters was the Blue Water. Our slots had been reserved for months. So as not to lose them, we had to make the crossing through a heavy storm. We arrived with two boats. The Pacifier, our 42ft Rybovitch which was designed and built to hunt and catch giant Bluefin, and the "Natures Way", a 54 ft Stryker Sportsfisherman, perfect for socializing, extra living quarters for our crews, and an un-

Black Tuna Diaries

planned fishing foray with a boatload of the most famous fishermen of the day.

We took rooms and an apartment at the Complete Angler. A huge Victorian Guest House, with the Islands most popular bar. Its walls covered with photographs of Hemingway, rum runners, docks piled with cases of scotch waiting for the rum runners, famous fishermen and record fish. If you were in the tournament, you ate dinner either in the Big Game Club, or the island's most popular restaurant, The Red Lion. If you weren't "off a boat", you could forget about ever getting a table in those two spots.

Our regular table was at the Red Lion, a spacious glorified fishing shack, owned and run by man everyone called Radio. We had a standing reservation, for a table for ten. All of the food was freshly pulled from the local waters and deliciously prepared by a kitchen full of Bimini ladies who heaped the plates and sent them out to the hungry fishing crews. The cold beer and drinks kept coming and by mid meal, "fishing stories" were being shouted across the dinning room by the fiercely competitive crews. Calcuttas or side bets, of thousands of dollars were wagered between the anglers, between the captains, and between the mates. Hundreds of thousands of dollars were bet on each day's fishing. First fish, biggest fish, most fish, last fish, were all the subjects of big bets.

At 5:30 am, when the first orange rays of sun, light the dark waters of the Caribbean night, the stately parade begins. Soon it will degenerate into a race for the best spots to wait for the daily migration of giant Bluefin. One by one the rumble of twin diesels precedes the graceful departure of another tuna boat. Each with its 40ft tuna tower, and outriggers, that will remain skyward and unused for the tuna season. Out of the harbor and through the dangerous narrow passage that guards the harbor's entrance. Once clear, the parade becomes a race south along the Bimini chain. A hundred boats out of Bimini, joined by another 50 or 75 flying out of the private club on Cat Cay. Within minutes, they have all stopped and are idling in a single line, maybe twenty feet apart, stern facing the shallow water of the Bahamian shelf. There the migrating giants will

Black Tuna Diaries

slid down in to deeper waters and begin to feed. A line of a hundred and fifty tuna boats, idling as the sun comes up, is not a sight ever forgotten.

Each boat has two men up in the tuna tower with powerful binoculars, searching the flats for the pods of four or five migrating leviathans, making their run for the safety of deep water. If a pod is spotted coming directly towards the stern of your boat, the spotter shouts down to the mate in the cockpit, who pulls out the single prepared bait from the ice chest. As the torpedo shaped shadows come off the shallow flats, only the three or four boats directly in their path begin to move ahead and gain speed. The angler dons the heavy harness and mounts the big fighting chair in the center of the cockpit. The thick stubby tuna rod is placed in the gimble between the angler's legs, the heavy reel loaded with 130 lb test waxed linen line is hooked to the anglers harness, and the angler braces his feet on the tilted footrest attached to the chair. The angler will only be able to gain purchase against the giant Bluefin, by using the strength of his entire body. Pushing with his legs and pulling with his back. The huge Finor reel has two gear ratios, 1 to 1, for keeping the tuna from sounding and 1 1/2 to 1 if the fish becomes cooperative. Normally a fishing reel is geared to retrieve line at 4 or 5 revolutions for each turn of the handle. With a giant tuna you're lucky to gain 6 inches with each pump of the rod.

As your boat runs ahead of the oncoming tuna, the mate tries to spot the largest of the pod and then drops the single bait, usually a large dead mackerel, into the water, and the angler free spools the reel until the mackerel is swimming directly in front of the giant Bluefin. Most often a hungry Barracuda will get to the bait first, and your run will be over. Most days a boat might be lucky to get 2 or 3 runs at a pod of tuna. But occasionally, on one of those rare perfect days, when everything and everyone is in perfect harmony, your chosen giant will eat. And your first thought will be, "I must have been insane to have harnessed myself to, this damn rod and reel".

Black Tuna Diaries

The second it feels the hook, 500-1000 lbs of powerful fish will head straight down for deep water. Your rod, as thick as a corn cob, is pulled down onto a pad protecting the transom, and bent almost in half. The line is screaming off the giant reel, despite the drag being set for over a hundred pounds of pressure. Two mates are positioned next to the fighting chair. One to pour buckets of water over the smoking reel and the straining angler. The other mate is controlling the chair, keeping it pointing in the direction of the fleeing fish. He is at all times, prepared to grab the angler, should the giant Bluefin jerk him right out of the chair. The angler is using all the strength of his lower body by pushing against the foot rest and all the strength of his upper body, by pulling with his back and arms. The object being to try and raise the rod tip a few inches, to regain a few inches of line. Push, lift, pump and reel. Over and over. Keep the fish coming towards the boat! If big Charlie can turn his head, even for a second, he'll be gone. Soon the muscles in your thighs begin to spasm. Your arms and back are screaming for relief and you don't think you've got another pump left in your whole body. That's when the mates begin to holler in your ears, "Don't stop! He's almost to the boat! Keep pumping! If you stop now you'll lose him. Looks really big. Might be a record. Keep pumping! Change gears NOW! He's coming toward the boat! Pump faster, keep the pressure on!" You know that if you stop, you'll let down the whole crew who may have worked for days, weeks, or even years to finally put you on a giant tuna. You find a second wind, flip the gear lever and increase the tempo. Push, lift, pump, and reel. Push, lift, pump, and reel. At last, one of the mates flips up the stern rail and opens the tuna door in the transom.

Without a door at water level in the stern, there would be no way to maneuver the giant fish into the boat. One mate grabs a marlin gaff to steer the fish towards the open door. The other mate using a longshoreman's hook, reaches out through the door and jerks the still swimming fish, into the cockpit as the Captain backs the boat until half the ocean comes through the tuna door along with the huge Bluefin. Only then, can the angler relinquish the rod and reel. A well placed tap with a bully club usually stops the dangerous thrashing of the stranded giant. You try to stand on shaky legs to stare at the mon-

Black Tuna Diaries

ster tuna. It is as long and tall as a Harley Davidson, and as fat as a VW Beetle.

I'll get ahead of myself and tell you about the fishing trip that engendered the name "The Black Tuna Gang". Bear in mind this was after the first time we had used boats, instead of airplanes to smuggle in a load of pot. The government's contention that we used Black Tuna medallions and radio codes as recognition signs is simply ridiculous. In any case this was the most amazing fishing trip ever.

Early May 1978, Robby and I, with our wives, made a storm tossed crossing from Junior's Bait and Tackle, near Government Cut in Miami, where we had fueled and loaded up on bait and supplies. We were on the Pacifier, a 42 ft Rybovitch, with Captain Randy and his mate Marty. What would have normally been a pleasant 2 hour trip, took more than four hours, before we reached our reserved slip at he Blue Water Marina on Bimini. A second boat in our entourage, the 54 ft Stryker, "The Natures Way"(another of Randy's chosen names I hated, because it sounded like a laxative, followed later that night. Leaving from Pier 66 in Lauderdale, crewed by Gene's buddy, Barry the stoner, and his friend Captain Elm, they didn't arrive until dawn the next day. We would all fish from the Pacifier. Robby and I would alternate as anglers. Randy would captain from the fly bridge, Barry and Elm would spot from the tower and Marty would mate in the cockpit, to be joined by Barry or Elm if a fish were hooked.

We spent one day on the island preparing baits and tackle before the opening day of the tournament. It was a big social event, with most of the famous big game fishermen from all over the world. Several experienced crewmen came on board the Pacifier looking for a berth. Mark Phillips, whose family owned Stryker Yachts, showed up at our dock with Captain Hook, the famous marlin hunter Ron Hamlin, the captain who would eventually capture the world record for Atlantic marlin. Ron was broke and desperate for a berth in the tournament. He was willing to sign on for a bunk, food, and small share of any prize money. Much more experienced than Marty, we took him on as first mate in the cockpit. Lastly, it's a tradition

Black Tuna Diaries

to take on a native captain who for the most part just rides along as Supercargo on the fly bridge. Our guy's wife owned the "Luncheonette". She prepared our lunch boxes. Mostly delicious lobster salad sandwiches on Bimini Bread, with sides of potato salad and coleslaw. The lunch bill for the eight of us averaged about $200.00 a day for almost the entire month of May, not including Becks Beer and the Pepsi we drank by the case.

The Giant tuna were late in making an appearance that year, very late. For over a week, a hundred and fifty expensive fishing boats, sat in a line several miles long, burning fuel for seven or eight hours, they're crews straining their eyes, looking for Bluefin Tuna that weren't there. Beginning at one or two in the afternoon, one by one, they would give up, rev their engines in a cloud of black smoke, and head for the dock. But not us. We were Fishing Fools! Randy would roll another doobie, and head in the opposite direction, south along the Bimini chain, to troll for whatever might be hungry. Since we carried no conventional trolling baits, only huge rigged mackerel and Ladyfish for Tuna, we would troll artificials. Artificial ballyhoo, squid and flying fish. Captain Hook would rig them up to swim behind the boat as we fast trolled the Bimini chain from Cat Cay, down past the cement quarry, and back again. And we caught fish. Barracuda, Wahoo, sail, a few stray Allison Tuna, and the odd hungry shark, On the third day of trolling we added one more mate, Peter Wright, the famous Captain who held most of the records for Pacific marlin over 1000 lb caught on light tackle. Peter was sitting at the dock on his old wooden Merit tuna boat, "Wooden Nickel". His charter anglers never showed up. He was prepaid and bored sitting at the dock. So he joined our happy, crowded, and well buzzed crew, to teach us a Pacific fishing technique that had never been tried on the Florida coast. But would quickly become popular following our well publicized successes.

We gave up on the giant tuna early that third morning. They weren't coming! A friend of ours had taken my Piper Cherokee Six and flown for 50 miles across the Bahama shelf without seeing a single tuna. Pacifier pulled out of the line of tuna hunters and headed south. In the cockpit, Captain Hook and

Black Tuna Diaries

Peter rigged hooks onto a half a dozen Kona Head teasers. In Florida, and along the Atlantic coast, Konas were used only as teasers. The big colorful wooden or fiberglass skirted plugs, were towed hookless, behind the boat to entice fish to rise from the depths and pursue the baited hooks on the other lines. The new lures were hooked up to six of our 30 lb trolling rods and put out in a precise spread of the type used by Pacific fishermen, in California, Hawaii, and Australia. Then came the biggest surprise, Ronnie and Peter told Captain Randy to troll the boat at 1800 rpms, almost double the normal trolling speed used by east coast captains. Peter explained that Pacific fishermen have to cover much longer distances to find the big billfish. They have to troll much faster! We all knew that most big game fish could sprint to over 60 mph and 1800 rpms was only a third of that, but no one was confident that they would feed at those speeds.

"Sail on the left short rigger", shouted Ron from up on the fly bridge. Robby slipped into stand-up belt, to fight the fish. Amazing! Three times the hungry sail flew to the fast moving Kona and whacked it hard with its bill. Robby put the reel in freespool, the lure went dead in the water and the sail ate. Marty, Ron, and I cleared the other lines. Robby had the leaping billfish under control in less than 5 minutes as Randy backed the Pacifier quickly towards the sail. Stoner Barry didn't even bother to grab the leader. As soon as Robby had the angry fish near the stern of the boat, Barry, reached over the transom, grabbed the bill with both hands and flipped it into cockpit. Everyone ran for cover as the enraged sailfish tried to impale anything or anyone it could reach. After watching the angry fish destroy a couple of hundred bucks worth of teak decking, we made Barry get the bully club and dance around the gyrating fish until he had a chance to tap it on the noggin.

"White up on the right flat line". My turn. A good sized White Marlin that weighed in at a hundred and twenty pounds. We had it in the boat in about 10 minutes. Captain Hook gaffed him and swam him in the tuna door. As soon as the lines were back in the water and Randy was passing down a fresh doobie from the bridge, the right short rigger line snapped out of its clip and the reel screamed as the line

Black Tuna Diaries

burned from the spool. Robby put the belt back on, jammed the rod butt into the gimble and locked down the reel. "Wahoo, it's a huge Wahoo". This one kept us busy chasing him around the ocean for almost a half hour. Finally Marty grabbed the leader and Hook hit him with the gaff up near the bow of the boat and walked him back to the cockpit. One more doobie, one more billfish. Nest it was Elm who shouted down from the tower, "Big Blue coming up on the left long rigger". He hit the lure with his bill and disappeared. "Now he's on the right long rigger", came another frantic shout from the tower. The husky Marlin whacked the lure twice, but didn't eat. It was my turn in the belt. I dropped the lure back, but the marlin had disappeared. "Speed up to 2000 rpms" Ronnie hollered up to the bridge. Pacifier picked up speed and in a few second the big Marlin surfaced, huge mouth gaping open and chasing the flat line that was nearest the boat. This time he ate as he came straight up out of the water so close to our stern, we felt the salt spray from the angry shake of his head. This one would go over 500 lbs, if we could land it. I locked up the reel and hit him as hard as I dared with only a 30 lb outfit. He felt the hook and took off toward the horizon. I was afraid he would strip all 300 yards of line from the reel. Randy had the boat in reverse and was chasing the fish as fast as he could. I began to regain line. Sixteen jumps, fishermen always count them, sixteen jumps and thirty minutes later, the fish was swimming at the stern of the Pacifier.

Marty had the leader, holding it gingerly, prepared to let it go should the monster Marlin decide to swim away. Barry had the flying gaff. This gaff has a detachable hook that's tied to a coil of heavy rope. If the fish runs, the mate just releases the gaff's hook with the fish still secured by the heavy rope. That is if the mate is someone other than crazy Barry! No way was he going to let that 500 lb. Marlin move away from the boat. Robby and Elm had to grab Barry's feet as the fish pulled him out over the transom. Captain Hook opened the tuna door. Robby and Elm pulling Barry by the legs, as Barry with a death grip on the gaff handle, pulled the giant Marlin through the opening while Randy backed down, taking in ocean and Marlin at the same time.

Black Tuna Diaries

Pacifier stopped at the fuel dock at Brown's Hotel, to fuel up and use the tall tournament scales to weigh our catch. There was already a crowd there. Many of the idle anglers and their crews had spotted the four catch flags flying from our out riggers and wandered over to see what we caught. As they stared at the massive Blue Marlin that almost filled the cockpit, Randy and Barry threw the big White on the dock for the Dockmaster to weigh. 120 lbs, big for an Atlantic White! The Wahoo was next, 85 lbs. A big one! Then the sail. 70 lbs. Huge for an Atlantic sail! Finally, the Dockmaster passed down the lifting tackle to hoist the Blue onto the scales. We were hoping it might be record on 30 lb tackle. 550 lbs. No record, but one hell of a fish to mount on the wall beside my swimming pool. Not another boat had put a fish on the scales all week. Our "Grand Slam" created as much jealousy, as it did interest. Many of the fishing teams came over to congratulate us and quite a few walked away grumbling about it being all about giant tuna, not billfish. That night at our regular table in the Red Lion, we tried to hold down our enthusiasm, so as not to engender more jealousy. Many of the crews looked unhappy at our arrival, and the conversation was subdued. It was going to get worse!

The giant Bluefin Tuna migration arrived the next day, and we caught two of them. Robby got the first of the tournament. Almost five hundred pounds. The giant was still wriggling on the teak deck when I hooked up with even bigger one that almost took me over the side and weighed in at just over six hundred and fifty pounds. A couple of other boats got tuna that day, but not many. No one on Bimini or Cat Cay caught a double. It was the name, "Fishing Fool", that was most heard on the tournament's radio frequency that day.

We slowly motored to the scales with our bow well out of the water and stern weighed down by over a thousand pounds of giant tuna that filled the Pacifier's cockpit. The smaller fish went onto the cleaning table to be filleted out and shared with all comers. Everyone in our crew took a nice size freezer pack, without making a dent in the giant carcass. Fifty or sixty people took portions. Many ate theirs raw on the spot, with just a squeeze of fresh picked island lime. As we were pushing

Black Tuna Diaries

and pulling the remaining fish up the street on a dolly, heading for the big freezer at he Big Game Club, an old drunk in expensive yachting outfit, stuck his dog-breath face next to mine and expressed what seemed to be the sentiment of many. He pointed to the huge dead tuna and said, "I've been coming here trying to catch one of those things for six years. You sons of bitches show up for the first time and get two of em. It just ain't right!"

Showered, and dressed in fresh jeans and our Fishing Fool t-shirts, we showed up at the Red Lion for dinner. The normal noisy banter died as we entered the room. Silence! We took seats and after a minute, half the restaurant gave us a polite round of applause. The other half just scowled. Two tunas weren't that big a deal and ours weren't in the thousand pound class that might win the tournament. So, what was going on? Radio, the Red Lion's owner, came over with a copy of the Fort Lauderdale paper. "Local fishing team, 'Fishing Fools catch a grand slam off Bimini". Considering our other business, the last thing we wanted was publicity. But there it was, with pictures of our fish, taken on the weigh-in dock, the night before.

The Challenge! The angler at the next table, whose obnoxious crew had been passing snide remarks about our "blind luck, and "hippie crew of potheads", stood up and offered a tongue-in-cheek sarcastic toast to our recent successes, then felt he had to add, "but of course they didn't really catch a grand slam. No swordfish!" Well that snobbish old drunk and his crew of well scrubbed Nazis finally got my goat. I leaned over and quietly asked Randy if we had a swordfish bait on board the Rybo or Stryker. "We've got one giant squid in the Natures Way's freezer and maybe one or two chem. lights in the tackle station". I told him "we're taking the Natures Way out tonight and we are going to get a Sword". I stood up and every head in the room turned in my direction.

"You are all invited to a Swordfish party aboard the 54 foot Stryker, Natures Way, docked at the Blue Water. We leave the dock at 8 pm and return when we put a Swordfish in the cockpit."

Black Tuna Diaries

Our crew had been out fishing since dawn, they groaned, and then brightened at the word party and the idea of shutting up the Yacht Club Nazis at the next table. Randy and Ron Hamlin took turns trying to warn me that no one had caught-a Swordfish off Bimini since before Hemingway left the Island. I reassured everyone at our table, "Don't worry, I have a plan". Of course I was half drunk and slightly delirious from being out in the tropical sun all day. Like everyone in the room, I knew perfectly well that there were no Swordfish to be found off Bimini.

As we left the Red Lion, I told Robby and Randy "the plan".

"Look, most of the people likely to show up will be hard core fishermen, that is, drunks, tokers and tooters. If we hitch up and run flat out for Miami, we can be at the Continental drop off in an hour. With any luck, we can boat a Sword and be back at the dock before midnight. Everyone will be partying too hard to even notice where we fished".

Robby and Captain Randy both thought I was nuts, "but what the hell!'.'"

Not surprisingly, none of the fishing Nazis showed up. We ended up with about thirty or thirty five people aboard. Ron Hamlin, Peter Wright, with his crew, which I think were his brother and sister, both well know charter captains in their own right, our crew, and an assortment of friends, fishermen and freeloaders.

It was a beautiful clear starlit Caribbean night. The heavy shouldered aluminum Stryker slid from its berth with a satisfying deep rumble from the twin twelve cylinder diesels. We motored out of the harbor and through the narrow passage between the sandbars. Randy had turned on the boat's stereo system. The tape deck was loaded with Blood Sweat and Tears, Chicago, Jefferson Airplane, Crosby Stills Nash and Young, and Three Dog Night. The Stryker's flying bridge could comfortably accommodate more than a dozen people and the deck level main salon likewise. In minutes the party was in full swing. I was just beginning to realize how tired everyone was

Black Tuna Diaries

and how early we would have to start the next day's fishing. I decided to change "the plan". In my beer addled brain, I was probably conceding defeat. Maybe! We were less than a mile offshore. I was standing behind Captain Randy, watching the depth finder. As we reach the Bahamian drop off, on the Bimini side, I told him,"set up a drift along the edge here and let's just put the squid down. Whatever happens, happens!

The quartz halogen Swordfish lights mounted in the tuna tower lit the cockpit and surrounding waters like bright sunlight. Randy left Peter at the helm. He and I descended to cockpit. Sticking up from the fighting chair rod holder was a fifty pound test outfit. A short boat rod with a gold sided Penn International reel loaded with 50 lb test Ande monofilament line. A half frozen squid, the size of a large t-shirt, was thawing in a bucket of seawater. Two big hooks inside the squid were attached to the line by a long wire leader. Directly above the leader was a quarter pound weight to take the bait deep, and inside the head of the squid, Randy had planted a chem light. Once broken, the Chem light would make the bait glow eerily deep below the surface of the warm moonlit ocean.

Randy bent the Chem light until the stick began to glow. He dropped the bait overboard and free spooled off about 200 feet of line. When he handed me the rod, I pulled off a few feet of line to check the drag, then stuck it back into the rod holder with the click engaged and the reel in free spool. I had climbed most of the way up the ladder to the fly bridge, and was reaching for the doobie in someone's hand, when we all heard the reel begin to scream, as line began peeling from the spool.

"Fish on" everyone on the bridge hollered at the same time, as I grabbed a quick toke and slid back down the ladder. Picking up the rod, I locked up the reel and took off the click. Raising the rod tip, I "hit" the fish once or twice to set the hook. Robby brought out the stand-up belt and buckled it around my waist. When a big fish is deep below the boat, there isn't much the captain or crew can do to help the angler. It was a long slow pump and retrieve fight. We didn't know what it was, we

Black Tuna Diaries

just knew it was big, very, very big. It never even entered my mind that it might have been a Swordfish, it wasn't!

After 20 or 30 minutes of hard work, I managed to drag the big fish to the surface. A Blue Shark! Maybe three hundred pounds and seven feet long. Lit up bright neon blue! Not too unusual if you were fishing off New Jersey or the North Carolina Coast, but not a fisherman among the thirty or so aboard, had ever seen or heard of one, in these warm southern waters. Captain Randy appeared with our shark gun and dispatched the big Blue Shark with a single neat shot to the head, before dragging it in through the tuna door. Everyone trooped out or down to the cockpit to gape at the bright blue oddity and then returned to their partying.

I reached into the shark's mouth with my fishing pliers to work the big hook from his jaw. It took me a moment to realize that the bait had slid up leader wire after the fish was hooked. The squid, the only one we had, was bitten almost in half, but not quite. It was still usable. My first thought was, "enough was enough". The seven foot blue shark was a serious prize. It was foolish to keep trying for a Sword Fish in a place where there were none. Robby and Randy wanted wrap it up and head for the barn to get some sleep. I said ,"lets just finish this drift. When we pass Cat Cay, we'll hitch up and run for home".

I was alone in the cockpit of the Stryker when I fired the half eaten squid back down deep below the boat. I didn't even have the patience to let out enough line. After maybe a hundred feet, I set the click, put the reel in free spool, and set the rod back in the rod holder on the fighting chair. I had had enough. Up at 5;30 am, out in the hot sun all day, fought a six hundred and fifty pound giant Bluefin Tuna, and dragged in an angry 300 lb Blue Shark. Now I was ready to relax with our guests for a while, then head for a bed. Once again, I climbed the ladder to the fly bridge. My feet felt like lead. As I neared the top of the ladder, the reel began screaming again as my line headed east for Miami. I looked up at Robby, who was up on fly bridge enjoying the party, "It's your turn". Robby just laughed, "You're the one who wanted to go night fishing. It's

Black Tuna Diaries

your fish". Everyone just laughed and pointed down at vibrating bent rod as the line continued to fly off the reel.

Back down the ladder! I reached down and flipped the lever that locked the reel in gear and disengaged the click mechanism. I just stood there watching the rod bend almost in half as some kind of big fish hooked itself. For a moment I just stood watching, unable to make up my mind if I wanted to fight this fish from the chair or standing on my own two feet on the deck. A stand-up fight would be harder, but quicker. I stuck the rod in the belt gimble below my waist and began to retrieve line. Pump the heavy rod up and down with my left hand, while reeling with my right. Using my back and stomach muscles to help pull the rod tip upright and then drop the tip so I could take in three or four turns of the reel. Almost the entire three hundred yards of line had been stripped from the reel before I had lifted it from the rod holder. Unlike the Blue Shark which had headed for the bottom, this critter surfaced and headed for the lights of Miami fifty miles away.

Peter Wright hollered from the bridge "It's a Sword, it looks like a Swordfish". All of a sudden I wasn't alone in the cockpit. Peter, Ron Hamlin, and Captain Elm were dragging the shark out of the way and clearing the cockpit so I could fight the huge gray hounding sword unobstructed. No messing around now, we were all business. Randy began to back the boat toward the fish allowing me to retrieve line as fast as I could crank, but not so fast that the line could go slack. Slack line, even for a few seconds, would allow the powerful fish to change directions and snap the 50 lb line like it was sewing thread. My right arm felt like I had retrieved a thousand feet of line by the time we had backed up to the thrashing billfish. "My god! It could go over 500 lbs", Ron Hamlin speculated as he grabbed for the flying gaff. The big fish was still "hot" and in no mood to be boated. He made another run for Miami and we followed. The next time he saw our transom, he went under the boat. We carefully pulled ahead and I pumped him up again. One look at Ron reaching over with the big gaff hook and Mr. Sword took off around the side and shot in front of the Stryker. I had to run to the bow to retrieve line. I kept the line taught as Randy slid the boat forward and I walked my tired

Black Tuna Diaries

fish back to the stern. Robby had come down and opened the tuna door. Captain Elm put on a glove and took a wrap on the leader wire, while Ronny and Barry the Stoner, used the gaffs to steer the monster Swordfish to the open tuna door. Randy waited for a wave to lift the fish, then backed down hard to bring the wave and fish in through the open door. Still "lit up" a bright green, what turned out to be a five hundred and fifty pound Sword Fish, flopped and twisted on the wet deck. Fortunately the cockpit of the 54 ft Stryker was big enough to run laps, because all 30 or 35 people aboard were standing on the deck gaping as Capt Randy who had come down from bridge, took the belaying pin and tapped the fish on the noggin to calm him down. I flopped down in the fighting chair, happy and totally exhausted. Now The Fishing Fools not only had a real Grand Slam, we had a rare three hundred pound Blue Shark as a bonus.

It was well past midnight when we entered the sleeping lagoon with our lights blazing and blinking, our siren and "Whoop Whoop" blasting, announcing over the loud hailer, that The Fishing Fools had landed the first Swordfish ever caught on rod and reel off Bimini since the days of Ernest Hemingway. We stopped at Brown's fuel dock to weigh our catch. Two hundred ninety pounds for the shark and five hundred fifty eight for the Sword. By the time we were back at our slip at The Blue Water Marina, half the crews on the island had come down to witness our catch.

The loud mouth fishing Nazis from the next table, never showed up at the Red Lion for dinner for the rest of the tournament. Within two weeks Bimini had a new fishing attraction. Charter boats from all over the Florida coast raced over for a shot at the new Swordfish grounds. A year or so later, the DEA located a newspaper photo of Robby and I with our giant Bluefin Tunas. Not knowing the difference between a Black fin Tuna that might weigh thirty pounds, and a Bluefin Tuna weighing six hundred pounds, they invented the legend of the "Black Tuna Gang".

If you visit their website, you can still see a photo of what they claim was a Black Tuna medallion, "that the gang mem-

Black Tuna Diaries

bers wore as a secret signal", so that they could recognize one another. Personally, I've always found it easier to recognize someone by looking at their face, rather than trying to check out their jewelry. The medallion was made for the Fishing Fools, to celebrate our "Grand Slam". The fish on the medallion, looks nothing like a Tuna, at least not to a fisherman, or for that that matter, to anyone who ever opened a can with Charlie on the label.

Black Tuna Diaries

Chapter 6
Death on Lombard Hill

Everyone knows a black cat has nine lives, but a Black Tuna has only seven. Here is the true story of how I lost the first of those seven lives.

At the age of eight or nine, I was the only member of the South St Gang, without a bicycle of his own. There was a perfectly good reason for that. We lived above our family's children's shop at 641 South St in center city Philadelphia. We had no place to keep a bike, without dragging it through a store full of customers. Of course to a bikeless city boy, that was not terribly mitigating. I finally got a bike of my own a few years later. Every time I wanted to take out or put away my red English Racer, I had to carry, not wheel it, through the store to the girls dressing room, knock on the door, carry it into the dressing room, raise the trapdoor to the basement, carry it down the stairs, return reversing the process, and close and lock the trapdoor.

But for years, if I wanted to ride with The South Street Gang, I had to endure the embarrassment of riding a rent-a-wreck hired from Bob's and Mable's Candy Store. Now if you attended grammar school at the MC Call School between 6th & 7th St's and Pine & Spruce St's, you would know that Bob's and Mabel's was a magical spot for neighborhood kids. Before and after school, what seemed like hundreds or maybe it was just dozens of grade schoolers, would jam into the tiny candy store, greedily peering into the glass cases and demanding, "Miss Mabel four Mary Janes, please", "gimme four red licorice and a penny taffy", "I want a superman tattoo and three cents worth of caramels" or "three soft pretzels for a nickel". At recess, morning and afternoon, Mr. Bob would setup his cart outside the schoolyard gate and sell the big warm soft pretzels he had just picked up from the bakery.

But, it was only a few us bikeless kids, who were forced to deal with that other enterprise, "Bob's Bike Rental". In a partially covered shed behind the candy store, were twelve or fif-

Black Tuna Diaries

teen beat-up bikes in various states of disrepair. Mismatched frames and fenders, hand painted any color found in the bottom of a leftover can of cheap paint. Patched tires, wheels, frames, and seats, hung from overhead nails. For 25 cents you could rent one of these humiliating rides.

The wreck that was to become my regular ride, was hand painted bright blue with paint left from some long forgotten Pepsi promotion. Its fenders badly dented and a sharp rusty piece of metal stuck up between the handle bars. The way I learned to ride a two wheeler, was to push "ole Pepsi", two blocks to the Star Garden playground at 6th and Lombard. To mount "ole Pepsi", I would have to stand on a raised section of dirt on the edge of the playground, I would sling one leg over the seat and wait for someone, usually my sister Marilyn, to appear and give me a push start. I would wobble around the concrete basketball court, until I fell or got tired. Mr. Bob's machines didn't come with training wheels. I was constantly on the lookout for some familiar face to beg, "gimme a push please".

Eventually I learned to ride just barely well enough to wobble around the neighborhood with the South St Gang. Of course I was forbidden to leave the immediate area, or to ride in the streets, with their heavy center city traffic. The most forbidden place for a South Streeter to bike ride was "Lumby Hill". The very, very steep hill, at the foot of Lombard St, down near the Delaware River. The steepest portion, being the two block that run from 2nd St, down past Front St and on down to Delaware Ave. Traffic flowed west, up the hill from the river. The street was cobblestone. Once launched down the hill over the cobblestones into the maw of oncoming commercial traffic from Delaware Ave, brakes were not an effective option. You picked up speed so fast, bouncing and flying through the air as each cobblestone acted as a miniature launching pad. Brakes had no effect, except to cause you to loose steering control.

So here I am, maybe 8 years old, the youngest and dumbest member of the South St Gang, Standing with one leg over the seat of "Ole Pepsi", five blocks from home, and looking down the steepest hill in Philadelphia. No way can I chicken out!

Black Tuna Diaries

Robby, Cookie, Norman, Anthony and Pedro, have already made one run right down the middle of "Lumby Hill". Oh, did I mention that it was necessary to avoid being trapped in the trolley tracks. You had to ride straight down the center of the street, between the tracks. This could obviously only be done when there was no oncoming traffic.

"All clear" shouted Pedro from the bottom of the hill. For the first and last time, I launched myself on "Ole Pepsi" down the center of Lombard Hill. By midway down the first block, I must have been doing 30 miles an hour. That's when I first heard Robby and Cookie Baumholtz,

"Platch, (I hated that name), Platch, lookout, lookout".

Of, course I first turned my head in the direction of the shouting. Big time mistake! By the time I faced forward again, it was too late. I was face to face with a huge red truck that had turned onto Lombard St from Front St. He was slowly coming up the hill and I was flying and bouncing over the cobblestones at over 30 miles, an hour, headed for his grill.

And then it was over! I returned to life lying in a soft pile of horseshit. It was the horseshit that had probably saved my life. Wait a minute you say. This was downtown Philly, where did the horse doo doos come from? It was Abbots Dairy at Front and Lombard St. They delivered by horse and wagon, to their accounts in center city, until the early 1950's.

According to Cookie, Robby, and Tony who had witnessed the whole thing from the top of the hill. I hit the truck, a 20 foot box body, so hard, that I flew over the entire length of the truck and landed in that nice fresh soft pile of warm manure. Realizing, I was probably dead, the truck driver used the call-box on the corner, to call the cops. It was several minutes later, surrounded by the milling terrified South St Gang, that the truck driver and a number of passers by, were much surprised to see me stir and rise to my knees.

"What happened?"

Black Tuna Diaries

"Oh man Platch" (I wish they wouldn't call me that) "we were sure you was a dead man. We saw you get kilt"! Everyone was talking at once. As the dizziness ebbed, I rose to my knees and thought,

"Oh shit, I'm in trouble! Five blocks from home, riding in the street, and on "Lumby Hill" no less!"

I wanted out of there as fast as possible. My chest hurt so badly, I could hardly breathe, but I inched over to pick up "Ole Pepsi". Forget it! Wrecked! Folded up like an accordion! Robby came over and dragged it onto to the sidewalk. I stood leaning against the callbox post on the corner of 2nd and Lombard. My insides shaking, my ears ringing, vision blurred, nauseous, and generally still having an out of body experience. But all I could think about was the look that would be on my mother's face, when she found out I was hit by a truck on Lombard Hill. Now, for sure, I'd never get a bike of my own! Never be allowed out to play for the rest of my life! That is, if I got to live that long!

What I wanted now, was to get home, look as if nothing had happened, and slip past my mom without her finding out about the accident. I can't recall ever being able, even with the help of Miss Lulu, to get over on my mom. .

"I'm OK, I'll walk home now". Everyone just stared at me as if it was my ghost talking.

Thank god for the cops who had just pulled up in the Paddy Wagon i.e. the older, larger version of a police van, named for the generations of Irish cops that drove them.

"Listen kid, we're just going to take you for a little ride over to the Pennsylvania Hospital so they can check you out. It'll only take a couple of minutes. Then we'll give you a ride home. Now just have a seat in the Paddy Wagon while we make out the accident report." Oh crap, I'm dead now. Everyone on South St will know what happened when the Paddy Wagon drops me off in front of the Cissy Shop.

© 2009 R. Platshorn

Black Tuna Diaries

It was while I was sitting on the bench seat by the open rear doors of the panel truck, that I noticed that my dungarees were slit open from the bottom of my right thigh, up to about an inch from my little fireman's equipment. Without the courage to look inside the long rip, I figured I was lucky it was only the pants that were cut open.

Robby was standing by the Paddy Wagon doors keeping me company. I showed him the rip. Pointing to a bent piece of metal sticking up on the roof of the truck above the rear doors he said "You probably did it when you flew over the truck".

After taking the truck driver's information, and statements from my co-conspirators, the cops closed Paddy Wagon's rear doors , got in the front, and headed for the Pennsylvania Hospital, at 9th and Spruce St. A place, as an accident prone kid, I was no stranger to.

A beautiful red brick colonial complex, it was Philadelphia's first hospital, organized by Ben Franklin before the Revolutionary War. Like the first fire dept., one of the many things that Franklin organized for his adopted home town.

We had almost reached the hospital entrance on Spruce St, when I finally got up the courage to gingerly spread open the rent in my jeans and saw that my thigh muscle was totally exposed. Not a drop of blood, but not an inch of skin remained covering the muscle, with its exposed veins, arteries, and yellow fat layer. The cop in the passenger seat saw me staring at the open wound. They recognized that shock was setting in.

"It's nothin kid. They'll just wash it out and sew it up. You was lucky! An inch higher and you'd a lost yer peepee. They'll sew you up and send you home in no time atall. You'll be fine."

The cop's banter helped to keep me from losing it altogether. And he was right. A few hours later, after they were sure the shock had passed, I was in my pop's Oldsmobile 98 for the short ride to 641 South St., a neighborhood legend, with seventeen stitches in my right thigh. Of course, with such a major

Black Tuna Diaries

wound, my parents showed just a tad more concern than anger. My dad even went out and got me a double-decker chocolate ice cream cone to eat while I waited for the doctors to release me.

A few months later, I finally got my red English Racer. But only with the express understanding that if I was ever seen anywhere in the vicinity of "Lumby Hill", the bike would be confiscated and I would be grounded until I was old enough to marry and have kids of my own. Of course my guardian angel, Miss Lulu Mac Fall, had a lot more to say about the matter while she fussed over my recovery.

Black Tuna Diaries

Chapter 7
Two Yachts-No Waiting

Back to the smuggling tale! I was fishing "catch and release" billfish tournaments on the 44-foot Stryker, Fishing Fool with Randy, Marty, and Barry the Stoner. We had started in West Palm Beach and worked our way south to Marathon in the keys, when the call came. It was Raul! A trawler loaded with 30,000 pounds of specially packaged Santa Marta primo, was ready to leave the coast of Columbia to rendezvous in the Bahamas in about 21 days. I withdrew from the tournament in Marathon and we headed for Miami.

We docked the Fool behind the south beach house where we planned to unload its precious cargo. The neighbors would get used to seeing the boat before we brought her back with a load. We also had an offload house further north on Miami Beach, for the second boat. When the time came, Stryker's boat yard would remove most of the interior of the 44 footer, so we could stow 7 or 8 tons of weed below deck and in the rear lazzerette, leaving the cockpit and main salon appearing normal. This would be done virtually the night before she sailed.

It had become obvious that the Pacifier was not suitable as a second hauler. It would be nearly impossible and a crime against the art of ship's joinery, to rip out the beautiful woodwork interior. Stryker quickly located another boat. A 53 foot Hatteras Yachtfish, the Miss Dorothy. They had just taken it in trade and it was in Bristol condition. A modern fiberglass boat, it would be simple to remove the below deck interior. We bought the Miss Dorothy and moved her to our north beach offload house, to put on a show of coming and going, for the benefit of the neighbors.

The next morning I flew to Barranquilla. My pal Johnny picked me up at the airport and drove me to Irotoma. I checked in to my usual, Cabina 7. Irotoma was the perfect meeting place. A very private, small resort, outside the town of

Black Tuna Diaries

El Rodedero! It had only about 18 Cabinas and a small restaurant. Located on the road outside of El Rodedero, it was patronized mainly by well to do South American families, who valued privacy. From now on, I would stay out of the cities and towns where I was likely to be spotted as a pot smuggler, at a time when pot smugglers were tripping over one another.

Things went unusually smooth for the next two days. My Colombian friends drove me up into the hills above Santa Marta to inspect the herb. The merchandise was very high quality. The buds had been stripped off the plants, carefully packed with only a light press that didn't crush the seeds, wrapped in plastic and burlap, and packed in sturdy cardboard boxes banded with heavy plastic strapping. Our merchandise should arrive in perfect condition! Raul, Julio and Johnny took me to the harbor to see the 70 ft trawler that was going to transport the cargo, and introduced me to the captain. Once on board, we agreed on "Hole in the Wall" off the southern tip of Great Abaco, as our primary offload spot. We decided on radio frequencies and radar protocol. Upon spotting each other on radar, both boats would do a prearranged series of turning maneuvers for positive identification. We exchanged call signs, and I described to the captain, my Cherokee Six airplane that I would fly to locate the trawler, a day out from the rendezvous. This would avoid our boats looking suspicious, hanging around for days near Hole in the Wall, in anticipation of the trawlers' arrival. Seventy-two hours after leaving Miami, I was back at my desk at the South Florida Auto Auction.

The following day Raul confirmed the trawler was enroute. We would wait 12 or 13days. If the trawler remained on schedule, our boats would go the Stryker boatyard to be stripped and have their waterlines raised. A day or two later they would leave for Bimini, clear Bahamian customs, and fish for a few days before heading to Chub Cay in the Berry Islands. There they would wait for word to make the final 70 mile night-run to "Hole in the Wall"..

Randy would captain the Fishing Fool and my neighbor, Captain Tico would master the Miss Dorothy, and Gene would supply the boat crews from his Outlaw Club near Tampa.

Black Tuna Diaries

Everyone on the boats would be properly dressed or uniformed, as would be expected of the crew of an expensive fishing yacht.

A week or so later, word came from down south that the trawler was making very good time. She would arrive off the Bahamas several days ahead of schedule. Randy rushed the Fishing Fool to Stryker's yard to have the below decks interior removed and the water line raised. The work could only be done in secret late at night. It took four nights to finish the job, much longer than we had planned for. Now there wouldn't be time to strip out the Miss Dorothy. She was a big boat and we would use her "as is". That turned out to be a big mistake, as your about to find out..

Big Gene summoned the crewmen from Tampa, dressed them as sailors, and gave them a quick course in rope handling and yacht protocol. Two weeks worth of provisions, food, water, filters, belts, mechanical and electrical spares, an extra set of radios, and a second radar unit, all had to be brought aboard and stowed or installed. This was our first boat mission, but we were well aware, that everything that could possibly breakdown would breakdown. It turned out that most of the redundancy would be needed. Lastly, the Fishing Fool and Miss Dorothy would stop at Junior's Bait and Tackle near Government Cut on Miami Beach. There, they would fuel and pick up enough bait to appear a normal fishing excursion. Robby and I were both there to see them off, after paying for over a thousand gallons of diesel, a few hundred bucks worth of bait, and handing Randy and Tico ten thousand dollars each, expense and emergency money. The two big yachts left for Bimini, to clear Bahamian Customs, dock at the Blue Water Marina, as we normally did, and fish for a few days. I would fly over, contact them by radio, and tell them when it was time to leave for Chub Cay.

Two days later, Raul phoned from Columbia to the auto auction and asked if I could find two or three Ford pickup trucks for his farm near Santa Marta. That was the signal that the trawler would reach Great Abaco in two or three days. A

Black Tuna Diaries

simple code, but safe, even if he had to leave a message with an employee. It was time for me to fly! Adrenalin time!

For my last birthday, Big Gene had given me a 10 year old Piper Cherokee Six. A husky six seat, single engine, fixed gear (non-retractable) airplane. I fueled up and took off from Pompano Airport, for the 60 mile trip to Bimini. It was late afternoon. I had a good idea where they would be fishing and had no trouble locating Dorothy and the Fool from the air. I buzzed the boats, within a minute; both captains were talking to me on the tiny marine radio I secretly carried in my briefcase. They told me that the fishing had been good. Both boats had landed several sailfish and a White Marlin. I told them to leave the fish in the freezer at the Blue Water and to head out in the morning. I would fly on ahead and serve as their "fish spotter".

I flew on to Chub Cay in the Bahamas' Berry Islands group. The entire island belongs to the exclusive Chub Cay Club, but they had a small hotel and restaurant for visitors and guests. Mark Phillips of Stryker Yachts had arranged for me to have guest status at the club. I circled the island three times to signal for the club jeep to pick me up on the 5000 foot black top landing strip, about a mile from the hotel and marina..

I tied down the plane and pulled out my Valpak just as the jeep pulled up. They were expecting me! The jeep, driven by the club manager, took me directly to my bungalow on the club's beautiful harbor lagoon.

I had a pleasant diner of shrimp, conch and fried Grouper, with a bottle of ice-cold Becks beer. There were maybe two dozen guests on the island. Fortunately, none that I knew. After dinner I walked around the harbor looking at the expensive yachts. Mostly serious sports fishing boats! I had a small brandy at the bar and was in bed before eleven.

Knowing Dorothy and the Fool would not arrive at Chub until late afternoon, I slept until 8; 30 in the morning. The dinning room was already deserted by the time I went in for breakfast. Most of the visiting fishermen had left the dock an hour ago. Dressed in cutoffs and a Fishing Fool T-shirt, I

Black Tuna Diaries

looked like a fisherman who had missed the boat. The waitress came over and offered to make me a plate of Bimini Bread French toast, and a piece of leftover ham. French toast made from Bimini Bread, is almost as good as French toast made from Jewish challah. The only other diner was the club's Dockmaster. Just the person I need to see!

"Mind if I join you for breakfast?" A big round-faced Bahamian, he flashed me a broad smile and gestured to the empty chair opposite his own. On an island like Chub Cay, the Dockmaster was king. He told you if you could dock, where you could dock and how long you could stay there. He controlled your access to electricity, fresh water, fuel, provisions and repairs. In other words, all the necessities of life for a visiting boater!

After slipping him a hundred dollar bill, I told him that two boats, part of my fishing team, would arrive later that afternoon. They would only be there for a few hours before leaving for a night fishing expedition to Tongue of The Ocean, a popular fishing destination in the Berry Islands. "I'll be flying out this morning in my plane to do some fish spotting and check out some areas we'd like to fish. If the Miss Dorothy and the Fishing Fool arrive before I'm back, please give them a place to tie up where they can catch a few hours sleep before they have to cast off and any thing they need. It can all go on my bill." Additionally, I told him that in about a half hour I'd need 40 gallons of nice clean marine gas to take with me out to the airstrip. Chub Cay had no aviation fuel, and I didn't want to expose my presence at Marsh Harbor on Great Abaco, to take on fuel. Marine gas worked fine as long as I was careful to strain it through a thick wad of cheesecloth which I always kept in my plane. Then I'd check it for moisture by draining a cup from the check valve under the wing. "No problem! I have my boy fill de jerry cans and put dem in de jeep. You be ready to go in plenty time." I thanked him and slipped him another C-note for good measure.

By 10 o'clock I was sitting in the cockpit of the big Piper single engine plane, running up the 260 horsepower engine, checking the magnetos, the instruments, and wiggling the con-

Black Tuna Diaries

trols to make sure I had removed all the gust locks. I reached over the throttle quadrant and pushed the mixture control to full rich for take off. Next, I pushed the prop control for full pitch. I eased off the brakes and pushed the throttle to the firewall. Before I was halfway down the runway, the speed indicator passed through 70 miles an hour and the Cherokee Six wanted to fly. I climbed to 2000 feet and headed for Hole in the Wall, on the southern tip of Great Abaco. My plan was to back track the planned course of the trawler until I found her.

Easy as pie! This time! I found her in less than an hour, only about 70 miles out from our rendezvous spot at Hole in the Wall. I dropped down to circle the boat. In less than a minute, the captain was talking to me on the marine radio frequency we had agreed upon when we met in Columbia. "Ola, senor, my crew will be ready to fish by midnight; over"

That was all he needed to say. "Two boats will join you to fish over." That was all I needed to say! The trawler captain stepped out of the pilothouse, looked up at me and waved. I flew by, a few feet off his port side and waggled my wings before climbing out and heading back to Chub.

Instead of landing on Chub, I flew east from the island looking for Miss Dorothy and the Fishing Fool. Things would never again be this easy. Around noon, 30 miles out from the harbor at Chub, I spotted the two sports fishermen, with the Stryker in the lead. When I heard them both click on to our channel, I kept the message short. "I checked out the fishing and it looks good for tonight. Before you sail, I'll buy you the best dinner on the island. Over" I flew back to Chub, circled the harbor to signal the jeep to pick me up and landed on the long blacktop strip.

By 12; 30 pm., I was back on the ground and enjoying my favorite island lunch, a lobster salad sandwich on Bimini Bread and a Becks. After lunch I went into the Club office and placed a call to Robby via radio phone. "Hi. We're going fishing tonight and we'll probably be home by tomorrow night." And Robby replied," Sounds good. I'll see you when you get back. If anything comes up, Ill try to reach you at the Club before

Black Tuna Diaries

you leave in the morning." As it should be, our conversation was short and circumspect.

The harbor at Chub Cay is almost completely surrounded by land, only a long narrow S shaped channel giving entrance from the ocean. Guarding that entrance is a huge rock fishermen call Mama Rhoda. Over the years, many a fishing trip came to an early and tragic end, when a distracted captain, especially on a night crossing, neglected to slow down to look for Mama Rhoda. I was sitting on a shaded-bench near the guest-docks opposite the harbor entrance, when I spotted the tops of two sets of tall outriggers approaching the outer entrance to the harbor. I watched them navigate the sharp turns until the Stryker emerged into the open lagoon, followed close behind by the 53 foot Hatteras, Miss Dorothy. I had arranged with the Dockmaster for both boats to tie up for a few hours at the guest docks near the dinning hall. I watched in wonder as the two biker crews in mariner's mufti, handled the docking lines.

Captain Tico was dressed in his captain's khaki's with epaulets, peaked captain's cap and Captain Randy, ever the fishing captain, in khaki shorts, 'Fishing Fool" T-shirt, and long-billed baseball cap. Their crews were smartly dressed in shorts, and T-shirts with the name of their respective yachts on the back. The two boats docking at the same time looked like a well rehearsed ballet, until the captains ordered the spring lines out. Not one of the big burley bikers had the foggiest idea that a spring line was to be set parallel to the side of the ship, so the boat could rise or fall with the tide, without drifting away from the dock. I could see that the six Outlaws didn't like standing there looking like dummies. So I walked over to the Fishing Fool to lend a hand. They watched as I took a line that was tied to the bow and secured it to a dock cleat towards the stern, then took a stern line and tied it to a forward dock cleat. The Dorothy's crew followed suit. With both craft secured, the two crews went into the Club's Commissary for cold drinks, souvenirs, and seasick pills.

Riding the waves turned out to be a bit more tummy turning, than cruising the highway on a Harley. To their credit, not one of the green gilled crewmen complained. Randy, Tico and I

Black Tuna Diaries

met in the main salon of the Miss Dorothy. They described their fishing show in front of Bimini. The last thing they had expected was to catch so many billfish. Normally, the fish would have been released, but Gene's bikers, being novice anglers, insisted on keeping their catch to be stuffed and mounted. The problem was, the fish were too big for the onboard freezers, so they were now sitting in the big walk-in freezer at the Blue Water Marina on Bimini. Randy wanted to pick them up on the return trip, figuring, if they were later stopped by customs; the sight of the big billfish lying in the cockpit would provide excellent cover. Well, maybe! But I wasn't happy about a boat loaded with marijuana, stopping even briefly, in the busy Bimini harbor. Especially, since the DEA was known to watch boats and photograph them as they left the island harbor. Randy argued that since they had just left Bimini for a "short fishing trip", no one would think it odd if they stopped back for a minute, to pick up their trophies. Not quite convinced, I gave in and got back to the business at hand.

I described the trawler to both captains and finalized our plans. Miss Dorothy, being the larger and slower boat, would come alongside the trawler and load first. That proved to be a mistake as I would learn to my regret the next morning. We went over the radar protocols, the radio frequencies and our call sign, which was Fishing Fool, not Black Tuna, as alleged by the DEA. The only radio talk would be about fishing and there wouldn't be much of that. The plan was, to rendezvous with the Colombian trawler around midnight, take on a fifteen tons of primo herb, then to cover the 150 miles back to Miami so as to arrive around 5 pm, when hundreds of boaters would be returning through the harbor entrances. The Fishing Fool would enter through Government Cut at South Beach, and the big Hatteras would steam in through Haulover Cut, to the North Miami Beach location. Everyone was on the same page. Time to eat!

I had arranged for an early dinner in the guest dinning hall. Conch salad, fresh caught Dorado, dipped in buttermilk batter and fried, conch fritters, black-eyed peas, greens, and bread pudding made from Bimini Bread. Milk, iced tea, soda, and wa-

Black Tuna Diaries

ter were served, beer and whiskey were not. Everyone had agreed, no booze or drugs of any type until the mission was over. It was just after 6 pm, when the two yachts took in their lines and disappeared around the first turn of the twisting harbor entrance.

I woke at dawn, planning to fly out, locate the boats, confirm they were loaded and safely on their way home. I slipped into my Britannia bell bottoms, the jeans of the 70's, and a "Chicago" T-shirt. When I opened my cottage door, the sight that greeted me, made me forget all about eating breakfast. Fifty feet away, tied to the fuel dock, with her generator humming loudly, was Miss Dorothy. What the hell! She was obviously loaded. No, make that overloaded! She was slightly down by the bow, and her waterline was nowhere to be seen. My heart was pounding in my chest. Nausea and shortness of breath set-in as I envisioned everyone on the island waking to the sight of a 53 foot Hatteras Yachtfisherman loaded to the gunnels with marijuana. If that wasn't bad enough, as I approached the starboard bow, I could see that the bow rail had been crushed. The fore deck was badly damaged and beginning to separate from the hull. If you looked closely you could just make out the cargo stashed in the fore cabin. Despite the trawler covering her side with old tires, Miss Dorothy had rubbed and bumped violently while taking on her load, until her cap mold separated from her hull.

Captain Tico in a fresh well pressed uniform appeared on deck. "Find the Dockmaster. I need diesel fuel, 200 gallons more, to make it home with this load." Being overloaded and low in the water, the big fat Hatteras was sucking fuel like a starving pig. Rather than tell him what I was thinking, which wasn't very nice, I wanted him fueled and gone as fast as possible.

The Dockmaster was just starting to eat his breakfast when I sat down at his table uninvited. Five, one hundred dollar bills disappeared under his napkin, as I quickly came to the point. "The boat on your fuel dock needs two hundred gallons of diesel and needs to be gone very quickly." He looked at me with a sly and avaricious grin. "I see dat craft when I get up

Black Tuna Diaries

dis morning, but my fuel dock open at 6; 30. Dat another 20 minutes from now." I counted out another five one hundred dollar bills and the Dockmaster was out the door before I put my wallet back in my pocket. I swiped a piece of French toast from his plate, took his untouched cup of black coffee from the table, and walked back on to the dock. One of Gene's Outlaw crewmen, perfectly attired in khaki shorts and Miss Dorothy T-shirt, was waiting in the cockpit for the fuel hose as the Dockmaster passed it down. Neither Tico nor the mate gave any indication that this was anything but a normal fuel up. Another mate was trying to seal the bow with duct tape and plastic sheeting, where the deck was separating from the hull. If she took water through the opening, the cargo would get soaked and the added weight would pull the bow under the on-coming waves. Instead of just his half of the cargo, Tico had insisted on taking on two thirds of the load. All of it had hurriedly been loaded into the salon and forward staterooms. I took him aside and made him promise to move as many bales as possible to the rear lazzerette under the cockpit deck, as soon as they were out of sight of the island. That should make her ride higher in front, and lessen the chance of her sinking.

By 6:30, when the island guests began moving around, the Hatteras was fueled, hurriedly patched, and on her way past Moma Rhoda. I would stay on Chub until after lunch, then fly out to check on the progress of the two boats. Then, if all was well, I would make a quick landing on Bimini, to phone Robby and confirm that both boats were enroute and on schedule.

About one o'clock in the afternoon, I climbed into the cockpit of the Cherokee Six, and took off westward for Bimini. The weather was gray, with occasional light showers. The ceiling was down to 2000 feet and lowering. Staying under the cloud layer, I was already down to 800 feet when I spotted Miss Dorothy making good time about 12 miles east of the Bimini chain. She was pushing a lot of water, but if she continued to waddle home at full throttle, she would pass through Haulover Cut 5:30 or 6 pm, with the bulk of the returning fishing fleet. I dropped down and flew by the flying bridge to see if Tico wanted to talk. His thumbs-up gesture told me he didn't need to break radio silence.

Black Tuna Diaries

I circled the harbor at Bimini. Randy had the Fool tied to the seawall near Brown's fuel dock. The 44 Stryker, with her raised waterline and less than 8000 pounds of weed onboard, looked normal, sitting by the seawall. Four frozen sailfish and a White Marlin lay on the cockpit deck. But I still had visions of some DEA or US Customs agent walking past and somehow sniffing our fragrant cargo. Randy, in command of the faster and more nimble boat, had arrived on Bimini by 9 am. Wanting to wait until 2 or 3 pm before running the last 50 miles, he tied-up at Brown's where he knew there would be little foot or boat traffic until much later in the afternoon. I landed and took the ferry over to Alicetown on the main island. Avoiding the customs shed, I walked the short distance to Brown's, where I found Randy and two of his crew drinking cokes in the deserted bar..

We discussed the worsening weather. It would provide good cover for his return to the states. He assured me, that even if the visibility were obscured by rain and fog, he'd have no problem navigating Government Cut by radar. As added cover, flying from the tall outriggers, would be, five catch flags, signaling to the rest of the fleet, that he was returning from fishing with four Sails and a Marlin. The fish would be in plain sight in the open cockpit.

I informed him that Tico, with a busted bow and badly overloaded, was, as we spoke, passing the island on his way to Miami. The Captain's were to be paid at the rate of. $10.00 a pound. Randy was pissed off that Tico had grabbed most of the load. I assured him that I intended to see that he was paid for half of the total load, regardless of Tico's apparent avarice, which now endangered the entire operation. Feeling the urgency of the hour, I urged Randy and crew out the door and onto the idling Stryker. I threw off their dock lines and waved as they left the harbor.

Once back in the bar I slipped Julian Brown a twenty, for a quick call to the states. In those days, before cell phones, there were only five or six phones on the island. One of which, was in the bar at Brown's Hotel. The operator up at the radio shack surprised me by putting my call right through, instead

Black Tuna Diaries

of the usual, "I call you back when we have Miami on de line". I gave Robby the good news. "Fishing was great, both boats will be home in time for dinner. One problem, the Hatteras bumped the dock pretty hard, the bow rail is crumpled and sticking way up above the deck." Then, Robby gave me the bad news.

"We won't be able to use the north house for a welcome home party. I'll explain when you get here. Tell your neighbor to dock at Art's house, it's not far from where he is heading. Chip and Howard, are both out looking for him to give him the news." I told Robby I'd try my best, but with the deteriorating weather and low cloud, I doubted if I could find Tico and the Dorothy again.

As I preflighted the Cherokee Six, a pilot who had just arrived, warned me against going up. The ceiling was down to 200 feet and lowering. The front was moving west toward Miami, bringing more rain and fog. I thanked him, but said that a family emergency, made me decide to race the front to the Florida coast. I knew in my heart, this was the wrong thing to do. There was almost no chance that I would find Tico in the lowering fog. If he didn't see me, he wasn't likely to break radio silence, and I didn't want to fill the airwaves with his call sign, alerting every law enforcement agency with a scanner, that something was amiss. Not being instrument rated, meant that I would have to fly by visual rules, and it was already below visual minimums. I just couldn't sit there doing nothing, so like a dummy with a death wish, I took to the sky.

Even down at 200 feet, my head was almost touching the clouds. I flew east for a few minutes to see if Tico had already passed the island. Facing east, I could see the oncoming cloud layer, already at sea level. I turned and headed for Miami, racing the lowering clouds. I was on a direct course for Haulover, hoping to spot the big Hatteras which should be on course for the same inlet. By the time I was 10 or 12 miles from Miami, I was down below 100 feet, the cloud and fog pressing me lower and lower. The sea seemed crowded with boats racing for home, barely ahead of the deteriorating weather. Most were large sports fishermen, any one of which

Black Tuna Diaries

could have been the Miss Dorothy. From the air, most boats look alike. I tried once or twice to raise her on the radio. I figured, even if I couldn't see him, Tico should be able to see me. No luck! I was now down to 50 feet off the water. I could barely make out the bottoms of the tall hotels and condos that lined the shore. With no idea what I was going to do, or where I was going to land, I headed back out to sea and put the Cherokee into a wide circle as I tried to climb through the fog and rain. Suddenly at 2,500 feet, I broke out into bright sunshine. I could see everything but the earth. I was low on fuel and running out of time. I had to get on the ground, if I was to be any help diverting the heavily loaded yacht away from what might be an ambush..

There was no way I could find an airport or let down through the clouds without an instrument rating I.D. number that I could cite to Miami Air Traffic Control for flight guidance to a nearby runway. Or was there? I reached own into my map box and pulled out my logbook. I found what I was looking for, the tail number from a Cessna 172 I had rented for refresher training, at a flight school at New Tamiami Airport, over a year ago. Using the Cessna's tail number, I radioed Miami Traffic Control and declared a "student emergency". I claimed to be a student pilot, low on fuel and unfamiliar with instrument flight. What happened next was amazing.

"Turn on your transponder and set it to squawk 1260, so I can identify your location" came the welcome voice of a friendly air traffic controller. Fortunately, I had a transponder with an encoding altimeter. Traffic control would be able see my location and my altitude. I flipped the switch from standby to on, and set the numbers to 1260.

"Good job student. I see you at 2,500 feet heading north. Please turn left to 270 degrees and follow my instructions. There is no need to respond. Now drop down gradually to 1,500 feet." I dropped into the cloud layer and was completely blind. "You're doing great Cessna. Now turn left again to 190°, throttle back to 90 miles an hour and continue your descent to 800 feet." As I descended to the southwest, the weather began to clear and directly ahead of me was a long wide

Black Tuna Diaries

runway, "Cessna student, you should now be able to see runway 19 Right. at West Miami Airport. Continue your descent for a straight in approach. When you are on the ground, please park your aircraft and wait for the FAA representative. He will help you file the necessary emergency report.

Safely on the ground, I took the first turnoff and parked on a nearby deserted apron. If I waited for the FAA guy, I would be in a world of trouble. Unless he was Ray Charles, he would figure out pretty quickly that I wasn't flying a little high wing Cessna 172. The Piper Cherokee Six is a husky low wing six seater. Then there was the matter of using a false tail number to declare an illegal "student emergency". The weather was clearing. I had just enough fuel to reach New Tamiami Airport in south Miami. If I was spotted on radar, I would look like the little Cessna going home.

I made sure that my transponder was turned off, and without saying a word to Traffic Control, I took off and boogied for south Miami. Once in the air, I used the marine radio in my briefcase, to raise Gene, who was monitoring the operation in Captain Crunch's radio van to let him know that I was enroute to New Tamiami and would grab a taxi to "The Hotel".

"The Hotel" of course was the famous Hotel Fontainebleau, on Miami Beach, where thanks to the owners valet, Ahmed Boob, we based our smuggling and distribution operations. At the time the world's largest hotel, with 1300 rooms and 100 suites, no one would ever be able to locate us in the hotel, unless we wanted to be found. With it's miles of underground parking and service corridors, we could move around and reappear in any part of the hotel, without using public elevators or hallways. Because we owned and operated the barbershop and yacht club at the hotel, our presence there was unremarkable.

In any case, New Tamiami Airport had two parallel east/west runways. The false tail number I used to declare a student emergency, belonged to a Cessna owned by Burnside-Ott, based on the east end of the left hand runway. I landed on the

Black Tuna Diaries

right hand runway, taxied to the west end and hangared my Piper at an FBO owned by a friend of Big Gene. Instead of a cab, Gene's friend drove me directly to the hotel.

Ahmed Boob was waiting in the lobby. A short bone thin, hawk nosed, dark complected Moroccan, Boob was a combination, meeter, greeter, host, dealer, concierge and pimp. Most times Boob was either coked up or luded out. He was in short, a Miamian of the 70's. Only occasionally, he could be found at his restaurant,"Boob's Steak House", located in the hotel lobby. After his usual greeting of a big hug and a couple of very sloppy wet Moroccan man-kisses, he informed me that Robby and Gene were up in Penthouse A, and that he was sending me up a steak and a Caesar Salad from Boob's. Realizing that I hadn't had a bite since swiping a piece of French toast from the Dock master's plate at 6 am on Chub Cay, I was all of a sudden famished. I went through the kitchen of Boob's and took the service elevator up to the Penthouse floor. Anyone following would have seen me go into the restaurant and disappear.

Robby and Gene were eating in the dinning room when I let myself into the suite with a key supplied by Boob. I joined them at the table, drinking one of Gene's Pepsi's and gnawing on a piece of garlic bread until my dinner arrived a few minutes later. The good news was, Randy was already docked behind the south beach house on San Marino Island. The bad news was, no one had found Tico on the Miss Dorothy. As far as we knew he was still waddling home, headed for the North Bay house that was no longer safe. The problem , according to Robby, was the real estate agent. Our "in-house" real estate guy, Larry Richter, a big shot at the Keys Co., had to involve another Keys Realtor who had the listing for that house. The other Realtor, turned out to be someone I met twenty years earlier, when I was 13 years old and spending the summer with my uncle Buddy, on 15th St on Miami Beach. The Realtor, Marcy the Yenta, was married to a local doctor, and the two of them lived in the same apartment building as my uncle. Dr Bernie and Marcy, the queen of all yentas, were best friends with my uncle and visited our apartment almost every day. I didn't think she remembered me. My last name is different

Black Tuna Diaries

from my uncle's, but I was never comfortable with the idea that she could identify me if anything went wrong. As a cover story, I had told her that the house would be used as a movie location. That was a big mistake! To fill her insatiable need for fresh gossip the Yenta queen would stop by almost daily, trying to see who and what was being filmed. One of Gene's guys had spotted her this morning, parked nearby, on the side of the road. Docking and unloading there was out of the question. Robby, had arranged to use a waterfront home belonging to a good friend of ours, a local doctor. The family living there had agreed to leave immediately, for an all expense paid fortnight in Hawaii. Now someone had to intercept Tico and guide him to the new location. Chip, with a marine radio and a powerful signal light, was pretending to be fishing in the fog and rain on the jetty at the entrance to Haulover Cut. Our friend Howard was doing the same thing from his boat, in the bay not far from the Yenta's house. No one had seen a sign of Tico or the heavily loaded Miss Dorothy. Captain Crunch was monitoring Customs, DEA, Coast Guard, and Marine Patrol radio frequencies. Not one word about the Hatteras.

It was now after 6 o'clock. I was beginning to fear the Miss Dorothy may have begun taking on water through her damaged fore deck. It wouldn't take long for incoming waves and rain to soak the bales of marijuana stored in the forward cabin. The added weight would drive the bow of the yacht under the oncoming sea and she'd go "down by the bow" to the bottom of the Atlantic Ocean. Too nervous to wait around the hotel for word of the boat, Robby and I took his car and drove to Tico's original destination, the house of Marcy the Yenta. We figured, if he wasn't at the bottom of the ocean or under arrest, and. if Chip and Howard had managed to miss the passing of a 53 foot yacht with a 40 foot high tuna tower, Miss Dorothy would likely appear at the original designated rendezvous. Bingo! Just as we approached the house, we could see the overloaded sports fisherman, looking like a felony in progress as she emerged from the fog. Tico was preparing to back the crippled yacht into the dock behind the house. Robby, who had made arrangements for the alternate offload site, told me to take his car and meet him at the new offload house. He jumped out of the car, ran to the Miss Dorothy, and leaped aboard before she could even stop. Someone had to guide

Black Tuna Diaries

Tico to the new offload site. It was still foggy. I had trouble finding the house, not being able to see the street signs or numbers. I didn't envy Robby riding the waddling overloaded, crippled boat, with its busted deck and twisted bow rail sticking up in the air. I finally reached the doctors house. One of Gene's unloading crew let me in. I went through the house and out through the sliding glass doors in the living room to the dock, 15 or 20 feet behind the house. In a few minutes, I could see Miss Dorothy's running lights as she turned into the deep canal behind the house. The rain and fog was the only thing that kept the whole world from spotting the waterborne felony. Tico eased her alongside the dock. Robby came on deck and tossed me the stern line from the cockpit, while one of the crew jumped off with the bow line. Five minutes later we were all in the living room checking out a bale of Santa Marta Gold. Absolutely gorgeous! We stuck it in a suitcase to bring back to the hotel, to show it to our customers, as they arrived to make their deals.

Offloading could only be safely done during the darkest hours of the night, when hopefully; the neighbors would be abed. Much to our chagrin, it took almost a full week to safely remove the 350 bales that made up the Dorothy's almost 17,000 pound load. Before leaving the house, Robby told Tico to remove the busted bow rail and try to cover the damaged deck with coiled ropes and rubber bumpers. We could only pray that no one thought it odd that the Hatteras had no visible waterline when she arrived and would have a normal waterline a week later.

Randy's arrival and unloading at the San Marino house went much smoother. In 72 hours, the 160 bales, about 8000 pounds, were unloaded and moved through the garage into vans and trucks that were disguised as local delivery and repair vehicles. They would leave the house a few hours apart during daylight hours, when these vehicles wouldn't attract attention. By the fourth day, the house was cleaned out and the Fishing Fool was back in Stryker's boatyard being remodeled and getting a new interior. We used the San Marino house as a guest house for a couple of months, then gave the keys back to Larry Richter and told him to terminate the lease.

Black Tuna Diaries

A year later, Richter rented the same San Marino house to Tico, who was bringing in his own 30,000 lb load of weed. Tico tried to sell that load to Robby and I. It wasn't very good pot and Robby turned it down. At the time, I warned Tico, that his regular buyer, Rodney a.k.a. "The Hillbilly", would undoubtedly pull a big yellow Ryder truck up to the house in the middle of the night, to remove the merchandise. It was his M.O! I told Tico that if he allowed that to happen, it would only be minutes before half the neighbors on the little island, called the police. Sho nuff! Rodney pulls up in a Ryder at midnight. A neighbor out walking his dog calls the cops. The joint is busted! Guess who was ultimately convicted as the owners of that 30,000 lbs of Tico's crappy ditch weed. Yup, Robby and Bobby! Richter turned informer and testified about the original lease, but forgot to mention to the jury, that Robby and Bobby terminated that lease months before, or that he subsequently rented the house to Tico. The only other evidence that connected us to San Marino was a old list, in Robby's handwriting, of cars to be sold at our auction. The DEA had black-bagged it from a drawer of our old fashioned roll top desk at South Florida Auto Auction.

During the two week unloading of Miss Dorothy, one of the resident Outlaws left a pan of bacon cooking on the stove and damn near burned down the house trying to put out the grease fire with tap water. Thank god none of the neighbor saw the smoke and called the fire department. Bales of buds were piled in every room of the house. Let me tell you, it takes serious huevos to stay in a house full of pot for two days, let alone two weeks. Anyone coming to the door might spell disaster. Mailman, meter reader, delivery person, landlord, salesman, workman, neighbor, or worst of all a Jehovah's Witness. Anyone with a sense of smell might drop the dime and the jig is up. By by biker dudes! Well, nothing went wrong. Well, almost nothing! The last 5,000 pounds were removed from the doctor's house and turned over to Moe Keller to warehouse and eventually deliver to our customers. Keller and his partner Carl Norwood, ran their own stash house and distribution business. They charged us $5.00 a pound for storage and an additional $5.00 for delivery.

Black Tuna Diaries

Without our permission, Moe sent 2,000 pounds of our herb to his own customer in Philadelphia. Now, if everything would have gone smoothly, Moe would have paid us for the goods and it would have been OK. But according to Moe's partner, the truck and merchandise are hijacked when he stopped at a gas station in Philly. To me and Robby, this story doesn't smell all that kosher, but we can't prove otherwise. It wasn't the first time Moe tried to put a move on us. So we decide to just take our loss and say goodbye to Dr Morris Keller. Within days his partner Carl Norwood leaves town bag and baggage, probably with a bunch of our cash. A few months later Moe gets busted trying to get into the cocaine business. After about 3 seconds of tough questioning by the DEA, he decides to become an informer, offers and testify against the infamous Black Tunas, Robby and Bobby.

After everyone and everything was paid for, we added our profit to the few bucks that remained from the DC-3 load after financing the boats; we had almost $3,000,000 bucks. A million for each of the three equal partners, Robby, Bobby, and Gene. This was the zenith of our fortunes, as you shall see. And speaking of boats! We never actually owned the boats that we used for smuggling. We loaned Stryker Yacht Corp the money to buy the boats. They loaned us the boats. We paid for dockage, maintenance, and repairs. We smuggled and fished on the boats. Stryker sold the boats at a considerable profit, and repaid our financing. Not quite! They beat us out of almost every cent we loaned them. You see, as soon as Stryker had title to the yachts, they "floor planned" them. That is, they mortgaged the boat titles to their bank. So! When the boats were sold, it was the bank that got the money, not the Tuna dummies. Think that was dumb? Wait! The one boat we kept for our selves, the beautiful Rybovitch, the Pacifier. Robby loaned it to Captain Crunch to fish and charter. Yup...you got it! Never saw the boat again!

Black Tuna Diaries

Chapter 8
On The Boardwalk of Atlantic City

For reasons neither relevant nor interesting, I attended five different high schools, in three different cities. Although I always had an after school job of some sort, my main objective was to study and pursue an acting career. I studied acting and took dance, music, and art courses at the Settlement School in South Philadelphia. Two of the high schools I attended, Miami Beach High and South Philly High had excellent drama courses. The high spots of my high school years were directing and M.C.ing the annual talent show at South Philly High, featuring a dozen well know South Philadelphia talents like Chubby Checker, and Fabian, and co-staring with the now famous attorney Neil Sonnet, in the Miami Beach High, production of "Dracula".

Finally, my last year of high was at Cherry Hill High, in Cherry Hill New Jersey. I rarely made it to school that year, because I was commuting to Philadelphia every night to co-star in an off Broadway production of Tennessee Williams "The Garden District" at the Proscenium Theater in the Academy of Music. After close to a year run, we closed the show a month or so before I was to graduate high school. The good news was, we were booked to reopen the play in Atlantic City the beginning of July, for a two month run.

My mom had bought the old Clearfield Hotel on Virginia Ave in Atlantic City two months earlier. When I joined her there after graduation, she had a dozen rooms rented for the summer, to a crew of pitchmen who worked on the Boardwalk. When it turned out that our show would never reopen in Atlantic City, for reasons mainly financial, it was only natural that I apply my acting talents to earning some bucks for college by becoming a pitchman on the boardwalk of Atlantic City. The pitchmen living at the Clearfield were earning $500-$1,000 a week in commissions. They pitched blenders or kitchen gadgets to the big crowds that would gather in front of the open storefronts at Pennsylvania Ave and at St James Ave,

Black Tuna Diaries

on the boardwalk. This was 1960, and that was a lot of money. A hell of a lot more than I was likely to be paid for acting, unless I became a star. For those who have never been to the boardwalk, or to a state or county fair, and have never attended a home or boat show, or never saw a real pitchman in action at the mall, think TV, people like Ron Popiel, or Chef Crowley with his garnishing book. All of whom I've worked with over the years. Or the current king of the TV pitchmen, Billy Mays (Oxiclean, Hercules Hook, Simonize,etc).

Confident to a fault, I presented my 17 year old self to Ron Popiel's cousins, the Morris brothers, at the Blender Queen "joint" at Pennsylvania and the Boardwalk. Archie Morris gave me a 20 page, 45 minute health lecture script to memorize. "Kid learn this pitch, hang around and watch the pitchmen, when you're ready I'll let you make a couple of pitches. I think you're too young to make the health pitch and sell forty dollar liquefiers, but who knows, I been wrong before."

Four days, later, at midnight on a Saturday night, I made my debut. Slim, dark curly hair wearing a short clinic gown open at the neck, I looked like the popular TV doctor, Ben Casey. Standing under a half dozen spotlights on a high platform, I quickly had a couple of hundred late night revelers standing transfixed, as I railed against processed foods and used the Blender Queen to turn fresh vegetables in a "strawberry milkshake, made with no strawberries and no milk." I didn't sell anything that night. No one ever did on the midnight pitch! But I did prove myself able to gather and hold a huge crowd of passersby for almost an hour. The next day, I began working the day shift with Jules Lasky, the man who wrote the script I had studied. By the end of the summer, I was consistently selling as many blenders on each pitch, as anyone else.

In the fall I went out on a route of fairs and home shows, working with one of the legendary pitchmen, Joe Magee, "The Fiddling Farmer from Tennessee". Joe claimed to have acquired that moniker when he played with Gene Autry's band, "The Sons of The Pioneers". From 1960 until 1977, full-time, part-time, or just occasionally, I was a Pitchman! Fairs, home shows, department stores, a dozen different TV commercials,

Black Tuna Diaries

and two Worlds Fairs. Most of that time, I was either in college or building my own businesses like The Ice Cream Factory in Philadelphia, or The Dynamic Reading Institutes in England, Holland, and Germany. But I always tried to at least keep my hand in as a Pitchman.

My most memorable pitch ? The Knitters, definitely the Knitters. Still 1960. The fall! The Allentown Pa County Fair. My first fair, my first pitch. Joe Magee, in his mid fifties, thinning gray hair, 5'7"tall, pale white, the red rimmed pale blue eyes of an alcoholic. Dressed in his usual dressy gray business suit. And me, a mature seventeen almost eighteen years old, five foot ten, dark curly hair, 165 lbs, in dress slacks and my Ben Casey doctor's smock. We've set up the "joint" in one of the exhibition buildings. Now to understand what goes on in the pitch business, you have to understand the argot.

l explain as I go. Many of these same terms are used in the carnival business, the circus, and by showmen in most branches of entertainment. The most used term is "joint", and it has several meanings aside from something good to smoke. The item being demonstrated, i.e. "The joint I work is the Vita Mix Blender". The stand on which I work, i.e. "I was up on the joint making a pitch. The place where I work. i.e. "The blender joint is in the Home Show building."

The next most important term is Tip, meaning audience, crowd , or any group. You can bally a Tip. That means, do or say something to attract enough attention to gather a crowd. Then you set the Tip. You promise to show, or give the Tip something, in order to anchor their attention. At the conclusion of your pitch, you turn the Tip, by getting them to buy something. Lastly you "sherry the Tip". You get rid of them, so you can bally a new tip.

The blender joint is a large horseshoe shaped counter, four feet tall. The base is usually matte black and the countertop white Formica. In the center, is the riser, another white Formica box eight inches tall and on that riser, sits the big shiny stainless steel Vita Mix blender that I'm about to demonstrate. On either side of the riser, anchored to the countertop,

Black Tuna Diaries

is a pole four feet tall. Near the top of each pole are four spotlights or floodlights that light the pitchman and his item. Often, suspended across the top of the poles, a mirror usually 4ft x 2 ft, that allows everyone in the tip to see down into the blender or onto the counter.

Now: Its about 9am on Monday, the opening day of the fair. Only a few people are drifting through the building. Being a JCL (Johnny come lately), I'm obliged to make the first pitch of the day. Magee is seated near the back of the booth at the little table we use to write up the sales. He is drinking coffee and enjoying a Pall Mall, while I struggle in futility to bally a tip in the near empty building. In my white clinic gown with the microphone around my neck, I am lining up various ingredients on the counter and promising to make and serve, free ice cream to all comers. Magee is laughing because I'm mostly talking to myself. Next thing I know, two dozen smiling well dressed people walk right up to the joint. Then three dozen more. By the time I'm ready to set the tip and make the pitch, I've got close to a hundred people crowding the counter, staring intently up at the mirror and hanging on my every word. Most seem between 20 and 40 years old, and look like good solid country folk. Blenders are a family item, and this crowd looks like a solid group of prime prospects.

A good pitchman performs a sort of mass hypnotism. The spot lights, the rhythms of his speech, his hand and body movements, all serve to assure the tip that they are happy and welcome. Often the pitchman begins to ask a series of rhetorical questions. "Wouldn't you like to wake up every morning with more pep and energy?" If the audience begins to nod in agreement at each question, and raise their hands when asked, you know you have them. Never before or since, had I worked a more positive, responsive audience. They smiled, nodded, and raised their hands in all the right places. I looked over at Joe Magee who smiled and gave me the thumbs up. I had visions of selling 1fifteen or twenty machines on my first pitch of the fair. I had been told not to expect to sell more than that many blenders a day, for the first few days. The big sales would come near the end of the week, when the crowds are

Black Tuna Diaries

really large. Looking at the smiling faces in my Tip, there was no way I could sell less than 10 machines.

Back in those days, I think the commission was ten bucks a unit. The crowd's reaction invigorated me. I used all my powerful health stories and stretched the pitch from 45 minutes to an hour, to maximize potential. As I made the "turn" and told the tip how easy it was to own a Vita Mix, "not for the regular price of $79.95, but for the special opening day discount price of $39.95. Cash, check, or lay-a-way". I laid out two trays of small soufflé cups and poured samples of the "strawberry milkshake", which was made from cabbage, carrots, celery, beets, banana, whole wheat, raw sugar, and an egg with the shell. I then directed everyone's attention to the table in the corner where Mr. Magee would be glad to write up their orders, after they tasted the drink.

I lifted the first cup to my lips and wished everyone "To your good health", and smacked my lips as I swallowed the pretty pink liquid. I placed the two trays on the outer corners of the stand where everyone could all help themselves before moving to the sales table.

As soon as they had all sampled the drink and carefully placed their empty cups in the trash, A woman who had been standing in the back of the Tip, raised a bright silver whistle to her lips and blew two sharp, loud blasts. In a trice, everyone lined up in the aisle, holding hands by twos. One more blast on the silver whistle and they smiled at me, and in unison said, "thank you" and happily shuffled off to see the fair.

I stood there with my mouth open, trying to figure out why no one had rushed over to the table to buy a machine. I knew something was peculiar, but hadn't quite figured it out. Magee sat there drinking his vodka spiked coffee, puffing a tall Pall, and trying hard not to burst out laughing.

"Sit down kid. Take a load off your feet. That big Tip you just pitched to were all knitters from the local home. They bring em to the fair on opening day every year. It's their big outing."

Black Tuna Diaries

I looked at Joe. "Knitters"?

So he explained! "It's a carnie term for nutters. People who sit around the "home" and knit all day".

Magee knew from the get-go, that I was pitching my heart out to a Tip of "Knitters".

"That's OK kid. It was a very nice thing you did, entertaining em for an hour. They'll be talking about you for weeks."

Working with Magee was an education. He was the only pitchman I ever met who had also been a carnie. He knew every "gaff" (secret trick) on every show and game on the midway. Each night as we walked through the midway on our way out of the fairgrounds, Joe would explain to me, why the basketballs failed to go through the bushel basket hoops, or why the milk bottles didn't fall when hit with a softball. He taught me about "flat joints", and "PC joints". That is "flat out" thieving games and games that always paid out a PC or percentage in prizes. He used to tell me how much money he used to take in as a "ballyman", making "openings" on the different midway shows.

One night as we were leaving the fairgrounds, we stopped in front of the "Wall of Death". One of the most exciting shows on the midway, where crazy motorcycle jockeys put on a thrill show as they rode their ancient motorcycles in circles around the steep circular wall of the drome.

"I know you think I'm full of shit kid. Watch, I'll show you the biggest opening this show ever had."

Joe was already half drunk and I knew better than to try to stop him. I figured they would never let him waste show time on the crowded midway. He went up on the platform in front of the drome. A rider was just getting on an old 1927 Indian motorcycle, perched on stationary rollers. The Frontman was tapping the mike to test the volume. Seeing Magee climb onto the stage, the Frontman and rider were about to call a "Hey

Black Tuna Diaries

Rube" (fight) when Joe held up the one thousand dollar bill he carried in his wallet and told the two men they could keep the grand if he couldn't fill the motor drome with one pitch. Warily, the rider got on and revved his ancient bike. He began to ride on the stationary rollers while Magee made the pitch. The Frontman gave Joe the microphone, but stayed close enough to grab it back, if Joe turned out to be some sort of a Wackadoodle.

It had been fifteen years since Magee had made a Wall of Death" pitch! I can't imagine how he remembered all the stories, patter, promises and lies, about "What you'll see on the inside". But in less than 10 minutes he had the joint so packed, there wasn't an inch of room on the viewing platform above the drome. Even I paid to see the death defying riders on the "Wall of Death".

The biggest pitch I ever made? 1962. The Seattle Worlds Fair. I was selling Vita Mix blenders. We had a huge booth in the exhibition area under the grandstand. Billy Graham had brought his Crusade to The Worlds Fair for ten days and filled the grandstands twice a day. Our exhibition area would be deserted until he finished his show.

I always waited for his "blow off", to bally my Tip. Now, I'm a pretty good mimic! That goes back to my acting school days when I would practice copying peoples accent's, gestures, and speech rhythms. Graham's Midwestern speech patterns, and karate hand gestures, were a cinch to emulate. I played to his tip. I even quoted the good book when I talked about the "Staff of Life" and the "fruit of the vine". The crowds ate it up. They pointed and whispered to one another, "a young Billy Graham". And I sold twenty-five or thirty machines on every pitch.

On the last Saturday of the Crusade, following the afternoon show, I had almost four hundred people jammed in front of my stand. The huge crow of watchers blocked the wide aisle, and overflowed into the Colonel Sanders booth across the aisle. I had my act down pat and the tip was hypnotized. When I made the "turn" almost no one turned to leave. Six of us began writ-

Black Tuna Diaries

ing up the orders. An hour later I attached a carrying handle to the last machine in our inventory and sat down to count the sales slips. If there were fifty slips, it would break the record for a live pitch (as opposed to a TV pitch). When I hit 50, there was still a pile uncounted, and a few people were drifting back to place orders. When the last slip was counted I had set a new record, more than doubling the old. I had sold ninety-nine Vita Mixes.

With an ego inflated to the size of the Goodyear blimp, I asked all my coworkers to "Please check your pockets. Somebody has to have one more order, so I can make it an even hundred. I won't recount all the nasty sarcastic remarks, but no more orders were found. I was ready to give up on the century mark and settle for ninety-nine, when a man walked up with his family, handed me a sawbuck. "Here's a deposit. Send me one of those machines, C.O.D.". If that record has ever been bested, I've yet to hear about it.

In my twenties, 5'11", 175 lbs, standing under the spotlights on the blender joint, and pulsing my deepest smoothest voice through the tiny Sony mike on my collar, it was usually no problem finding female company in any town in the English speaking world. But easily the funniest encounter took place behind the curtains, in the stockroom area of the Vita Mix booth, in the Home Building at the Ohio State Fair, in Columbus Ohio.

Probably 1965 or 1966! Some time before I moved to London, which was 1967. I recall I was late arriving on the fairgrounds. I had driven all night from the Wisconsin State Fair, which had closed the previous night. My working partner in Ohio that year was Frank Fitzgerald. Nice guy, a few years older than me, a shorter version of Liberace, only Frank loved the ladies. So much so, that instead of hiring a mature local lady to help us in the booth and to write up the orders, he had hired a top-heavy teen who had just graduated high school. Blond, blue eyed, zaftig, maybe five foot one, and recently married to her very jealous high school sweetheart. Frank was shamelessly firing away, but "Dolly" wasn't giving him any play. Pretty, but not my type, I was polite, but standoffish.

Black Tuna Diaries

The joint was all set up when I arrived. The background behind the stand was the standard blue exhibition curtains, over which we hung our signs and displays. Behind the curtains, was our stockroom and a place to rest between pitches. Frank had bought a reclining lounge chair, so that whoever wasn't up on the joint making a pitch could relax or catch a nap. Since I hadn't been there to help set up, I volunteered to make the first pitch, figuring I'd get it over with and catch a nap. Dolly probably had never seen me work before, because for the entire forty-five minute pitch, she never took her eyes off me. I got lucky and sold a couple of Vita Mixes on that first pitch. While Frank and Dolly wrote up the orders, I went behind curtains, flopped on the lounge chair and conked out.

I must have slept for a half hour or so. As I woke, I could hear Frank, who was up on the joint, telling the whole grain wheat story. I was intensely excited, and figured I must have been having a vivid wet dream. When I opened my eyes, I discovered I wasn't dreaming. The hot wet mouth in my dreams was Dolly. When she saw that I was awake, she stood, straddled the lounge chair, lifted her short skirt, pulled aside her soaked panties, and without giving me a chance to remove my pants, impaled herself. In full flood, she proceeded to ride me like a Quarter Horse in a ladies barrel race.

"OH yes, Oh God, Don't cum yet". The louder she got, the louder Frank cranked up the sound system to cover her screams. Finally at the finish line, she flopped down on me, damn near suffocating under her king sized pillows. After she had finished telling me how much better it was than any sex she had had with her jealous, quick on the trigger, husband, she stood up and jammed her hand between her legs to hold back the flood.

I looked around for a towel, paper towel or Kleenex. No way could I zip up without something to sop up the sticky fluids about to rundown onto my slacks. Nothing! Not even a cleaning rag! Dolly was standing stark still holding back the flood and I was waddling about, trying not to ruin my good slacks. Remembering that there was a box of Man-sized Kleenex sitting on the back of the counter top, I carefully waddled to the

© 2009 R. Platshorn

Black Tuna Diaries

curtains that separated us from Frank's audience, and slid my arm through, gingerly feeling around for the tissue box, while trying not to let the Tip see what was going on. Frank, to his credit, figured it out, and without breaking the rhythm of his pitch, handed me a huge fistful of tissues.

"Here, come again!" he boomed over the public address system.

Talk about one-liners, I was laughing so hard, I damn near fell out through the curtains.

The New York Worlds Fair, 1964-65! What sticks out most in my mind, is Scotty, the world's most audacious thief. Scotty, a Glaswegian "smudge worker". A "smudge worker" takes pictures with a camera that has no film, back before digital, when all cameras actually needed film. Scotty would walk the fairgrounds photographing visitors with his 35mm SLR filmless camera. He'd hand out business cards that identified him as the "Official Photographer" of the Worlds Fair. He'd convince visitors to buy and pay for, "a set of official souvenir photos of your family at the fair". Scotty even gave them an official Worlds Fair receipt. Of course no photos ever arrived! It's a British scam, not often seen in the U.S.

That was by day! By night, Scotty was a thief, a booster. Anything at the fair, Scotty could deliver, for the right price. Horses, cars furniture, jewelry, clothing, entire displays, beds, sofas, desks, pianos, or anything else on the grounds. To move the big stuff, he needed help. Who better than the Boy Scouts? Troops of Boy Scouts from all over the world were camped on the fairgrounds for an International Scout Jamboree. Scotty would approach a scoutmaster, identify himself as an exhibitor, and beg some help to move a few heavy items from his booth. The scoutmaster and his troop would follow Scotty to booth to be robbed, and proceed to carry the items in question out the gate to Scotty's waiting truck. Who would question a troop of uniformed Boy Scouts? When he was finally caught, it was hushed up to protect the scouts, and Scotty was quietly asked to leave the country. Years later he visited me at my offices in London, took me to dinner at the Victoria Sporting

Black Tuna Diaries

Club, and taught me a "little kitchen system" for winning at roulette. He always won enough money to pay the dinner check.

Over almost twenty years in the business, all of the items I pitched were legitimate and functional. The Vita Mix Blender, T-FAL Non-stick pans, the Zyliss Vice, even Popiel's Dial-a-Matic slicer, were all "K joints", that is Kosher, they all worked. But on occasion, I would make TV pitches for Ron Popiel's uncle, Nat Morris, a.k.a. N.K. Morris Mfg, or Judy Jewel Inc, or Remington Electric, located in Neptune N.J., near Asbury Park. That was a different story! Uncle Nat was a dapper former auctioneer and pitchman, who as a matter of principle, refused to manufacture anything that might possibly work. He would go to any lengths to knockoff a good item and re-engineer it so that there was absolutely no chance anyone might be able to make it work. He made Hula Hoops that wouldn't spin, choppers that didn't chop, graters that couldn't grate, slicers that would only slice fingers, and sun glasses that made you dizzy when you put them on.

I think it was 1963, when uncle Nat phoned and insisted I come to his factory to view his new "blockbuster bonanza" items. The Remington Electric Toothbrush and the Remington Electric Knife! Electric knives and toothbrushes were new to the market and a hot item. But, they were expensive, thirty or forty bucks each. Uncle Nat had wasted no time putting together cheap knockoff to retail for five or six dollars.

At the time I was working at Channel 17 in Philadelphia, writing copy and helping to produce several live shows. I also had a little side business, buying unsold commercial time and running commercials that I had written, produced, and performed, marketing my own line of promotional products.

It was late October, Asbury Park seemed deserted and gray. Uncle Nat's "factory" was the sole tenant in an old brick warehouse. An ancient office area with windowed partitions and a dimly lit room the size of an aircraft hanger, with a few jury rigged machines and dozens of long bare wooden tables. Uncle Nat's main source of production, were three or four

Black Tuna Diaries

dozen Puerto Rican ladies, heavily dressed against the lack of heat, gathered around the long tables gluing, assembling and packaging Nat's products. Uncle Nat, in his 60's, short, always well dressed in sport jacket and tie, with a leprechaun's smile, would walk the factory floor dispensing a little tap on the tush to his favorites. I doubt it was ever taken as other than a compliment, judging by the giggles and the" Oh, Tio Nat", that frequently echoed in the cold dim cavern. Nat always wore a sporty hat with a brim. He had several different ones stashed around the factory, and would switch them as he took you around the factory floor.

When I arrived that day, he greeted me like a lost son. Clearly he was about to lay some sort of serious pitch on me.

"Kid, this Christmas, the two biggest bonanzas will be the electric knife and the electric toothbrush. The ones on the market, sell for anywhere from $29.95-$49.95." He held up two cellophane windowed boxes, each the size of a shirt box.

"This is the Remington Electric Toothbrush. It comes with four different color brushes. Retail $5.99. And this is the Remington Electric Knife. Comes with two blades. A French knife and a serrated bread knife. Retail $7.99. Kid, at these prices, these things will be the biggest Christmas bonanza in the history of the pitch business. Let me show you the TV commercial I made for the toothbrush."

He had already setup a projector in his office. I hit the lights and he rolled the spot. It was a dreadful 60 second spot, shot in his family's bathroom. Featuring his daughter-in-law and grandkids. But, at six bucks the thing would probably fly off the shelves. I flipped on the lights. I didn't want to tell him how bad the film was, considering it was his family doing the acting, so I changed the subject before he could ask.

"Not bad!" I lied. "How about the electric knife? Let me see the knife commercial."

Black Tuna Diaries

He looked at me and smiled, "That's where you come in. I want you to do the knife spot. If you do that for me, I'll ship you enough merchandise on credit, to spring a Christmas promotion, and I'll give you the X (exclusive) for the entire Philly and South Jersey area."

Something didn't smell right! Nat's son Arnold is generally considered one of the best "knife workers" in the business. Years later his cousin Ron Popiel used Arnold to make the TV pitch for Ron's gazillion piece knife set. Why wasn't uncle Nat using son Arnold to do the spot? Then I recalled they didn't exactly get along with one another. If Arnold did a successful TV commercial, Nat might have to give him a share of the business, something he had always refused to do.

Nat took me out to the factory floor, to show how the things were made. Both the toothbrush and knife used the same vibrating handle. Nat told me he had gotten a kind of special deal on a million Chinese dildos for five cents apiece. He had replaced the business end, with a plastic collar that could hold a toothbrush or knife blade. Voila! Instant electric knife or toothbrush. The only problem....the handle vibrated, but the blade or brush was stationary. A Nat Morris Special!

The only reason I finally agreed to write, produce, and perform the TV spot, was the fact the uncle Nat had actually spent a few bucks for decent quality super-sharp, knife blades . Even without the "electric", "you could cut a cow in half with this knife. And that's no bull". So after making Nat assure me that I wouldn't go directly to jail for selling "Remington" products made in the N.K. Norris factory, I agreed to make the commercials and provide him copies for use by anyone else crazy enough to sell his drek.

When I create ads, TV spots, or radio commercials, my experience as a pitchman tells me to keep it simple. Simple demonstration commercials out sells even the most expensive agency produced extravaganzas. Demonstrate it, tell people why they need it, and why they need to buy it now, then tell them how to buy it. Do that well and you will sell!

Black Tuna Diaries

The pitch for the electric knife is exactly the same, as the pitch for the Ginzu Knife, the Frozen Food Knife, the Glass Knife, or Ron Popiel's Gazillion Piece Knife Set. I got Uncle Nat pay for a couple of one and two minute spots in my Channel 17's afternoon movie. The movie show was done live with a host, which was common in those days. I did commercials live in our studio during the commercial breaks. First a two minute spot and on the next break, a shorter one minute version. That way, zero production costs! I would only pay for a few copies of the tapes.

After practicing with the different blades, I came to the conclusion that the Remington Electric Knife cut better, if it wasn't turned on. I could cut the food more easily with the heavy D cell batteries removed from the handle. I set up two long banquet tables in the studio. Covered them with a nice table cloth, and lined up from right to left across the table, the foods I was going to cut. Italian bread, Ham, Rye bread, roast beef, eggplant, cheese, a packet of frozen spinach, and most important, a ripe tomato. Wearing a microphone, I would move down the table cutting the various items as I made my pitch. Several knives, without batteries, were laid out next to the appropriate foods. Everything went smooth as glass. I got both spots on tape, on the first try. The host and the studio crew applauded the easy one try job. After thanking the crew, I told them the groceries on the table, were free lunch. I even had mustard, mayo, and cold sodas for the crew. After the meat, cheese, and tomato, I had cut were gone, one of my camera men picked up one of the knives to slice some more.

"Hey! How do you turn this thing on? Wait a minute, there's no batteries in this thing." He gave me a seriously suspicious look.

The answer came quickly to my tongue. "Imagine, if it cut that good without the batteries, how great it would cut if it was turned on. Besides, if I turned it on, the humming noise would screw up the sound recording."

Black Tuna Diaries

The sound engineer looked over at me. "You know, you're right. Thanks man! You're a real professional! Not many people would have thought of that."

A few months later I left Channel 17, to work for Vita Mix at the New York Worlds Fair. When the fair was over, Ron Popiel's cousin Archie asked me to go to Puerto Rico to set up and promote, a water ice factory for Marino's Italian Ices. The company was enjoying great success in New York City, but could not get off the ground in San Juan.

Marino's was not my only project in Puerto Rico. I ran TV and merchandising promotions in all the Sears and Woolworth's stores on the Island. Some of the products I promoted were Popiel's Dial-a-Matic, Popiel's Pocket Fisherman and London Air No Run hosiery.

I did not find San Juan to be the friendliest place to live and work. My fondest memory of the island is the short film I produced for the movie Theaters, to advertise Marino's Italian Ices.

We had Marino's Italian Ices in supermarkets, but the product was new to the island and people didn't know what it was. It wasn't selling! So I had two dozen pushcarts built. I knew if people tried it, they'd like it, and would buy it in the supermarkets.

To promote street sales, I produced a short film to be shown in the movie Theaters. I had been running our Popiel commercials on Channel 18, the English language station. In return for doing the newscasts and some production work for the station, they would allow me use their facilities to produce my water ice commercial. The station, like most everything else in San Juan, is on the edge of a barrio. A poor neighborhood!

I rolled two cameras out the front door and pointed them toward the barrio. Down the street came one of my pushcarts. The vendor dressed in immaculate white.

Black Tuna Diaries

"Helados de fruta! Helados de fruta!" the vendor sang out.

From the nearest house came a Paula Abdul look-a-like, in a tight, skimpy, low cut, bright red dress. In a second, three small grubby kids run up and grab on to her dress, pulling and tugging.

'Mami, Mami! Helados de fruta! Helados de fruta! Por favor! Por favor!"

In the next scene, we see the grubby urchins smiling brightly as they slurp the paper cups of brightly colored ices clutched one hand, and continue to hold on to Mami's red dress with the other. The camera pans up the tightly stretched well filled dress, until we, see Mami's voluptuous mouth slowly descend over a small scoop of pink sherbet.

The first time Archie and I went to a San Juan movie house to see our spot, all the men in the audience whistled, cheered and clapped until the projectionist reran my commercial. Twice! It didn't matter if they ran it backwards or forwards, the lady in the red dress sold one hell of a lot of helados de fruta.

Black Tuna Diaries

Chapter 9
Starring Robert Redford and Donald Trump

You'd think that after the near disaster with the real estate lady from hell, Marcy the Yenta, I would have learned my lesson about using a phony film story as a cover for a smuggling operation. Wrong! It once again, just seemed the perfect cover story. "We're making a movie". Good lord that could cover anything from property rental to the actual unloading of our boats. Stick a few magnetic signs on the side of a few vans and trucks, put up some big lights and reflectors, rent a professional movie camera, and you could unload a ship in broad daylight at Donald Trump's Castle in Atlantic City. And that's precisely what we intended to do. At least that was Plan B. Plan A, was to unload 30,000 pounds of wonderful wacky weed at a private marina on the Jersey coast, far south of Atlantic City. The owner, a friend of Robby's, claimed that his marina could accommodate a fifty or hundred foot yacht. Another lie was, that his boatlift could haul out boats that size and they could be unloaded directly into our trucks in the dead of night, when no one was around. Sounds perfect!

After we had successfully landed 25,000 pounds from two sports fishermen at two waterfront houses in Miami, we figured it would be a good idea to change our modus operandi. Why not the Jersey shore? Robby and I both had grown up spending most of our summers in places like Atlantic City, Cape May, Wildwood, and Asbury Park. Robby's friend offering us the use of his marina, for a substantial fee, clinched the deal. We were Jersey bound. Our buyers from Philly and New York loved the idea. They could avoid the risky 1200 miles drive, moving the weed from South Florida to their home markets. If we were changing our offload locations, it also seemed a good idea to change our transports. Guys were often caught, because they used the same boats or planes over and over again. Instead of two sports fishermen, why not bring the entire load in on one large luxury Yacht? We contacted our friends at Stryker Yachts.

Black Tuna Diaries

A week later, Mark Phillips phoned from Annapolis Maryland. He claimed to have located the perfect vessel. A 110 foot Elco, built for the US Navy as an A.S.R, Air Sea Rescue, in 1946. The ship was yacht finished at the Elco factory, when the Navy canceled all their contracts at the end of WWII. An exceptionally sleek and beautiful design, the yacht appeared to be flying over the water, even when tied to the dock. According to Mark, she was in Bristol condition. The owner was only asking $110,000.00 because, back in the 1970s, no one wanted an older wooden boat. The nostalgia craze that would make those old yachts worth millions had not yet begun.

I flew to Annapolis. The boat was beautiful, inside and out. The only disappointment was the power. The original four 16 cylinder Rolls Royce aircraft engines, had been removed and replaced by a pair of 6 cylinder Jimmies, (G.M diesels). Instead of getting up on plane and flying across the water at 40 knots, she could barely cruise along at a stately 10 miles per hour. Oh well! I loaned Mark the money to buy the Elco, told him to change the name to "Senator", in hopes that no one would mess with a boat with that name, and ordered her bottom cleaned, hoping to pick up an extra knot or two of speed.

While Gene and Robby arranged for a captain, crew, and some updated radar and radios, I flew down to Santa Marta to secure the yerba and agree a rendezvous point off the Jersey coast. Fortunately, Raul had a coastal marine chart that matched one I had back in Miami. All we had to do was to agree on a spot in the open ocean, just over a hundred miles from the south Jersey shore. Not wanting to write down the coordinates in case I was searched by Columbian or US customs, I took out a photo of my three year old son, and put three very small pin holes in the picture. If I lined up two of the pinholes with predetermined spots on the map shore line, the third hole would fall on the spot at sea where we would rendezvous. The pinholes were virtually invisible, but to be extra safe I put the picture between two others in my wallet. Pretty damn clever right? Wrong!

Our Columbian partner Johnny drove me back to Barranquilla Airport to catch the afternoon Avianca flight to Miami.

Black Tuna Diaries

Clearing customs out of Barranquilla Airport in those days meant passing your passport along a table where five or six different officials examined your entrance stamps and applied your exit stamps. It could be a nervous tense time as your papers slowly passed from hand to hand.., customs, police, DAS, the secret police, especially if your passport was decorated with entry and exit stamps from previous trips. Even though I had the South Florida Auto Auction as a legitimate business cover, I always breathed easier after my papers were back in my hand. This could usually be speeded up by placing a generous donation between the pages. Once past the customs table there was one last hurdle. Before you could board your flight, you had to pass through a small booth, women on one side, men on the other, where you would be subject to one last search by members of the army. Usually, the soldiers were indios from the interior. They could sniff out the lingering odor of almost any drug know to man. While they stood close to pat search, their olfactory senses registered the entire culinary and pharmaceutical history of your visit. In my case there was nothing to smell, so they made me remove my wallet for examination. I could have avoided the search by handing over a fifty dollar bill when I entered the booth, but I foolishly thought that I was clean enough to walk right through.

Never underestimate these underpaid soldiers and their need for money. First the one with my wallet checked the cash compartment. Maybe a hundred or a hundred and fifty bucks! My real bankroll was in the bottom of my socks. Next he looked behind the lining in the bill compartment. Not exactly a secret compartment. The only thing hidden there was my birth certificate. Then he began removing the credit cards and photos from the plastic windows. The first two compartments held my credit cards and my business cards, but the third held two photos of my wife, with the picture of my son nestled between them. The recognition was instant, despite the fact that the three pin holes were virtually invisible; the soldier held the little picture up to the light and triumphantly announced, "mapa, mapa". Oh crap! I've got to get out of here! I reached for my wallet on the table, pulled out all the cash, kept twenty for cab fare, and split the rest between the two soldiers. Without waiting for permission, I scooped up my possessions and boarded my flight. The absence of a bayonet or

Black Tuna Diaries

bullet between my shoulder blades indicated that the mordida was acceptable.

In less than a week, a call came from Columbia to South Florida Auto Auction, requesting thirty recapped tractor tires, to be delivered in three weeks. Thirty thousand pounds of premium buds was enroute and would be off the Jersey coast in three weeks or less. Again, a simple, but safe, code! The clock was running and there was much to be done. Gene had arranged a backup boat in case the 110 foot Senator proved unreliable. The backup, the 54 ft Stryker Sportsfisherman, Natures Way, could take most of the load, if the big boat crapped out on us. A week later Captain Randy and crew left south Florida, for south jersey in the Stryker. Gene had also arranged a captain for the big yacht. It was, Captain Elm, who looked like the bewhiskered commander, from the Schweppes commercials, and a member of our Fishing Fool team at the Bimini Tuna Tournament. Elm was a licensed and experienced Yacht master, who owned his own yacht delivery business in Ft Lauderdale. Unfortunately, his designated First Mate was Barry the Stoner. A good friend of Gene, who spent most of his waking hours wrecked out of his mind. Pot, coke, Ludes, or booze! Barry didn't discriminate. Also joining the crew, were a couple of Gene's bikers from St Pete. The Senator needed a completely updated radar, radio, and electronics package. To save time, the new equipment would be flown to New Jersey and installed when the ship arrived at the end of its shakedown cruise. By then, we would know what else needed to be repaired or replaced and it could all be done at one time, while she sat in her new "home port". Great planning but!

The crews were dispatched with the usual ten thousand dollars expense money, for food, fuel, and emergency repairs. Now that I think of it, I do not recall ever getting any of that cash back, from any of our trips. Gene flew Captain Elm and his motley crew to Maryland, in his Piper Navajo, so that they could pickup the 110 footer and start up the coast for New Jersey. Then he flew back, to Miami and picked up Robby, me, Mark Phillips, his electrician, and the new radios, radars and electronics. We flew into Bader Field, just outside of Atlantic City. That's the field where I had learned to fly. Robby's family

Black Tuna Diaries

had a house in Atlantic City and my dad had a small shoe store on Atlantic Ave. But, my mom no longer had the Clearfield Hotel, and I had not spent much time there in the past four or five years. With the advent of gambling, the town was changing fast.

After spending an afternoon with friends and family, Robby and I headed south to checkout the marina we hoped to use to offload 30,000 pounds of Santa Marta's finest. That's where we hit the wall....hard! It wasn't going to work. It was a big busy marina full of small boats. 15 ft boats, 19 ft boats, 21 ft boats, there was even a small 26 ft cabin cruiser. But, not a single craft of 30 feet or over. Not a Sportsfisherman or yacht. Nor could one have entered the marina if anyone cared to try. It was simply too shallow, much too shallow. The only place a larger boat could reach was the outer seawall that protected the shallow water marina. Entering the marina and going to the boatlift was out of the question. Unloading 600 bales of Robby and Bobby's High Quality Herb, on the outer seawall, and schlepping it a block and a half to a truck on dry land, was not even to be contemplated. What to do, what to do? The 54 ft Stryker and the 110 ft, Elco were on their way. We needed to move the entire operation, and only had a few days to do it. Our customers had already parked their trucks and vans nearby. They did not know when the load would be landed, only that the vehicles would be loaded and their drivers told where to pick them up, after the fact. The marina owner had been given an advance payment and was vacationing somewhere in Alaska with his family, so that he could deny any knowledge of our operation.

Robby and I were in the marina restaurant trying to figure a new plan. The restaurant faced the boat basin and we were able to watch the coming and goings through the large picture windows. That's how we were able to spot Randy steaming in from the ocean channel and churning up the muddy bottom a hundred feet short of the seawall. The 54 foot Stryker, with a name that sounded like a laxative, "Nature's Way", barely made it to the seawall without going aground. Tossing a twenty on the table, we ran out across the parking lot and down the seawall. Hoping to keep the marina employees away,

Black Tuna Diaries

Robby and I caught the dock lines and secured Nature's Way to the seawall cleats and bollards. Randy had already realized that it would be impossible to enter the shallow basin with a loaded boat. Standing on the flying bridge, he described his seven day journey from Lauderdale to south Jersey. The boat had performed well, and with the addition of long range radar and backup radios, would be perfect for the mission. We told Randy to stay where he was for the next day or two until we could find a new base of operations. Most important he was to keep a visual watch and monitor the radio for the arrival of the yacht Senator, due to arrive anytime in the next twelve hours. He had to advise Captain Elm, to find the nearest deep water marina and wait for word of our new location. He was to do this by radio. If Elm somehow managed to get the 110 footer near the seawall where Randy was docked, he would likely need a skyhook and giant crane to get her out.

Robby and I returned to Atlantic City determined to find somewhere to unload one or both of the yachts. That night, Robby had dinner with his family and I took my dad to dinner to the only place the locals went for good seafood, "Doc's". The next morning, driving a rental, I picked up Robby, and we started our search for the right kind of place or places to unload one or two large yachts brimming with bales of Bobby's best Boo. Atlantic City is on Absecon Island. Starting from the Inlet, we drove along the bay side, through Absecon, Atlantic City, Ventnor, Margate, and Longport, all the way to the southern entrance to the "Back Bay". We were hoping to find and rent the same type of large private house on the water, we had used in south Florida. But the few private homes with decent size docks were not for rent. In those days, very few people in that area kept big yachts or large sports fishing boats, behind their homes. The nearest good big game fishing was out in the Baltimore Canyons, 70 miles away. Too far for most boaters! Local fishing was in the bays and inlets for flounder, sea bass, and mackerel. Small boats 15-21 feet made up the majority of local craft. Finding a place where our boats would not look out of place was beginning to look like an impossible job. If there was one person in all of Atlantic City who would know where we could unload 30,000 lbs of marijuana, it was Archie Morris. Archie was perhaps the most famous of the board walk "Pitchmen". For years, I worked for Archie and his

Black Tuna Diaries

brother Ruby, pitching Vita Mix blenders and Popiel kitchen gadgets, at their two boardwalk locations. Archie, who was built like Jackie Gleason, was a tumaulter. Archie could walk out on the empty boardwalk in the middle of December and gather a huge crowd willing to stand in the freezing wind to watch him make his "Pitch". Arch knew everyone in town, and every one knew Archie.

We found him in the National Kitchen Products office above the Pennsylvania Ave store.

"Kid, my god, its good to see ya. It's been five or six years, at least! Are you ready to go back to work? Ruby and I got some great shows and fairs for you to work. You were the best blender worker I ever saw."

I thanked him for the offer, and told him why I was in Atlantic City. I showed him a picture of the 110 footer and described the 54 ft Stryker. Then I told him what I was willing to pay for a safe place to unload one or both of our yachts. His eyes lit up! Not just for the money, Archie loved the excitement, the adventure and the challenge. More important, he was a "fixer", He knew every corrupt cop and politician in Atlantic City. Of course, back then, that was pretty much all of them. Archie leaned back in his chair, closed his eyes for a few seconds and then flew out of the chair heading for the door.

"Incredible, just incredible! I know just what you need. Come on, come with me. You got a car kid? Follow me to the Atlantic City Marina.

Back in the car, I looked at Robby. "When did Atlantic City get a marina?" He explained that Donald Trump made it part of his deal to redevelop the seedy slum area at the south end of the island. He agreed to build the Trump Castle, if the city paid for a public marina in his front yard. The slum was gone. In its place were a brand new marina. To our delight, there were quite a few visiting boats of a respectable size. Boats from New York, Virginia, Maryland and best of all, Florida.

Black Tuna Diaries

Within minutes, Archie had the Dockmaster and a local politician who happened to be having a drink at the marina, assure me that, under the guise of filming a smuggling story, we could dock and offload without worry or interference. Well, one step at a time! It was certainly a good place to dock the boats until mission time. I slipped the Dockmaster and the Alderman a grand each and reserved two of the largest slips in the marina. Robby, Archie and I went into the coffee shop.

"Listen, Arch", I said, "there is no way we are going to be able to offload six or seven bales of pot at a public marina, in full view of the hotel without someone figuring out what we are really up to, Even if the "Donald" himself, comes out to supervise".

"Listen kid". That had been Archie's standard form of address to me since I started working for him and his brother Ruby when I was 17 years old. "Listen kid, right now Donald Trump is in so much financial trouble, that I can guarantee, for the right figure, maybe a million, or maybe even half a million, he'd come out here with his entire construction crew and unload the damn ship himself. I swear to god kid! If you want, I'll introduce you to him, and you can ask him yourself. He's desperate for cash."

"Forget about it Arch", Robby told him, "It won't work! It would take a dozen men at least twelve hours of steady humping, in front of god and the world, to unload and schlep that many bales from way out on the end of the dock to a big truck a block away on the parking lot."

"You're right kid", Archie said, now calling both of us kid, "give me a couple of minutes and I'll come up with some place private, where you can unload at your leisure".

Archie dug into the piece of Apple pie in front of him, sipped his ice tea, and in less than a minute, his eyes lit up and he got that serious look on his face he always got when he was promoting someone for something.

Black Tuna Diaries

"I got it!" he smacked his forehead. "There's an old deserted fish cannery on the west side of the bay near Summers Point. I know the owner. For a few grand, he'll give you the keys and a short lease. You can drive a truck right up to the dock there and unload over a few days, with out attracting attention. The only thing I'm not sure of is if the water way is deep enough for your boats. The place has been empty for years and the channels silt up pretty quick in back bay."

We agreed that before Archie contacted the Realtor we'd send Randy and the 54 ft Stryker on a test run.

"I know an even better place you can use for your big yacht"

Archie was in full promotional mode now. "Kid, do you remember the old Atlantic City Tuna Club? The place where all those rich guys would bring their expensive fishing boats, to fish for tunas a couple of weeks a year. Big fence around the place to keep the riffraff out. Total privacy, kid, you could unload the Queen Mary at that joint and no one would see a thing! The club went bankrupt years ago, and its up for sale. I can probably rent it for you for a week or two. The only person there is a caretaker with his wife and daughter. You can give em some bread and a free hotel suite at Bally's for two weeks. Use your phony movie production story."

That sounded perfect. Robby and I both remembered the mysterious club, with the tall fence.

"Get it for us Arch. That's the perfect spot" Robby told him.

"Okay, but wait!". Now Archie sounded like the great pitchman he was. "I'll get you the Tuna Club. But there's one more spot you might want for a backup. Bobby Jones just bought a brand new townhouse on the water in Margate. In an emergency, you could park your smaller boat behind his house and bring the shit right in through his living room. Bobby has a lot of money now. He owns that famous gay club in Philly and his animal acts are making big dough. You're an old friend. He might do for you."

Black Tuna Diaries

I knew just what to do. Bobby Jones was a partner in the best hair dressing salon on the Jersey coast. I used to go in after hours, when the ladies had gone, and Bobby's partner would cut and style my hair. I'd arrange for Robby and I to get our hair cut. Bobby Jones always arrived to pickup his partner at closing time.

We went back out to the marina. I confirmed to the Dockmaster that my boats would arrive later that day or sometime the following afternoon. Archie split to arrange the Tuna Club rental and Robby and I headed south to where Randy was docked, to let him know he was to move to the Atlantic City Marina. Hopefully, Elm on the yacht Senator would be nearby.

We drove south out of Atlantic City and thirty minutes later pulled into the parking lot of the marina where we had left Captain Randy and his crew on the Natures Way. We went on board to find Mark Phillips and his technician installing the new 60 mile radar and new set of radios and antennas. Randy was on the fly bridge taking down the old antennas. Using an old chart, I pointed out to Randy where to find the new Atlantic City Marina. It was still early in the day and we wanted him to move Nature's Way before dark. The electronics installations could continue as they traveled up the coast. Too many people were strolling out on the seawall to gawk at the huge Stryker Sportsfisherman. It stuck out like an elephant in a herd of Shetland ponies.

"By the way," Robby asked, "where did Elm dock the Senator?"

Randy looked surprised at the question. "He never showed up. I slept up on the fly bridge with the radios on all night. But he didn't show or try to make contact."

The Senator should have arrived even before Nature's Way. Now we had good cause for concern. If there was a mechanical problem, Capt. Elm would have phoned Gene, who was coordinating the operation at our headquarters in the Fontainebleau. Gene would have had no trouble relaying the message. No! Robby and I both had the same thought. These as-

Black Tuna Diaries

sholes, that is Elm, Barry the Stoner, and Gene's crew, were docked somewhere between Annapolis, where they picked up the Senator, and the Jersey coast where they should have appeared twenty-four hours ago. Our Fear was, that they were partying aboard the 110 ft luxury yacht. That was best case scenario. Worst case, the local police had scooped them up after getting a tip that coke, pot and Ludes, were being freely dispensed at a non-stop party aboard a visiting yacht. Boy did we ever get it right!

The clock was ticking. The Columbian trawler was steaming up the coast of the United States, with a load of "This Bud's for you". We had to locate the Senator, redirect her to her new birth in AC and get the new electronics installed before it was mission time. We checked with Gene in Florida, to be sure there were no messages from Elm. Nada! Then we headed for Bader Field on the outskirts of Atlantic City. Five years earlier, I learned to fly at their flight school. Knowing that it's not possible to rent an aircraft without a check ride and extensive insurance forms, I booked a two hour "refresher lesson" in a Cessna 172. With Robby riding along as a sightseer in the back seat. I took off to the south, flying a mile or so off shore. I told the instructor that I wanted to fly south hoping to spot a friend sailing north in his yacht. That time of year it was still too cold for the summer boaters. With little traffic along the coast, it turned out to be easy to spot the Senator just as she was passing south of Cape May.

I dropped down to fifty feet or so above the waves and circled the pilot house to get Elm's attention. Without my marine radio, the only way to communicate was to try to drop a message onto the sun deck that ran the length of the ship from the pilot house to the stern rail. Talk about a stupid idea. Airplanes and old slow yachts travel at very different speeds. The Senator could only make about ten or twelve miles an hour. Depending on the speed of the wind, a Cessna 172 could slow to fifty-five or sixty miles an hour before it stalled and fell out of the sky. Add a choppy sea and gusting cold wind, and you have the makings of a very funny movie.

Black Tuna Diaries

First, I discovered that no one on the plane had pencil, pen or paper. Good start! Next, I couldn't find anything heavy enough to weight the note so it wouldn't blow away. After a frantic search, we finally found an old lipstick in the map compartment and two pieces of Styrofoam that housed a flare gun.

I turned over the controls to the instructor. "Slowdown and fly as low over the top deck as possible"

I wrote a short message on one of the Styrofoam shells, telling Captain Elm to go directly to the Atlantic City Marina.

The pilot was getting noticeably uncomfortable with what was going on. I took two one hundred dollar bills, from my pocket, and stuck them in his shirt.

"It's important to get that boat to Atlantic City as soon as possible. We'll be filming it this week at the Atlantic City Marina".

He bought the story! The pilot dropped down to about twenty feet above the top deck of the Senator, pulled in full flaps, and slowed to just above stall speed. As we approached from astern, I popped open my door just wide enough to reach out with my Styrofoam missile, and let it go. We watched through the rear window as the Styrofoam fluttered to the edge of the long sun deck and fell into the sea. Only one last piece of foam! Last chance to redirect the yacht! As we lined up behind the yacht for another try, I saw Elm pop out of the pilot house and begin shedding his clothes. This time when I dropped the foam block, it landed squarely on the rear of the sun deck. Then bounced twice, before going over the stern rail and disappearing in the ships wake. Captain Elm, naked, ran the length of the deck launching himself into the freezing Atlantic with a perfect Swan Dive from the two story high rear deck. Whoever was in the control room slowed and turned the boat. I saw Barry the Stoner appear on the lower deck to hook the dive ladder over the side. A minute later Captain Elm climbed aboard waving the hunk of Styrofoam. Buck naked and dripping in the cold wind, he smiled up at us, and gave the thumbs up.

Black Tuna Diaries

We had had a very busy day. But things were coming together. Both boats were headed to A.C. We had three potential unloading sites, and it was barely four o'clock when we landed back at Bader Field. Robby dropped me at my dad's shoe store on north Atlantic Ave. I knew he was two months behind in the rent and it was easy to see that the shelves were half empty. He had almost no inventory for the approaching summer tourist season. Although he was past retirement age, I knew he needed that little store, to keep him going. He and I had regrettably, never been close. That was my fault. Now I just wanted to help him stay on his feet. There was a customer sitting on one of the few mismatched chairs in the store. I found Joe in the tiny stockroom in the rear, futilely searching for something to sell to his only customer of the day. I tapped him on his shoulder. When he turned around and saw me, I handed him an envelope, One hundred, hundred dollar bills.

Ten grand would pay his back rent and provide enough cash to fill his shelves with cheap sandals and pumps for his tourist clientèle. I felt good knowing that my dad would have his shoe store for at least one more season. Maybe it was prescience. I only saw my dad one more time after that trip to Atlantic City. He visited me in the penitentiary at Lewisburg Pennsylvania, shortly before he died of cancer. On his deathbed in a Philadelphia hospice, he begged to see me. But there was no way I would be granted a deathbed visit, even with a slew of armed escorts, despite it being the policy of the Bureau of Prisons to grant deathbed or funeral escorted trips. I couldn't handle the tears that came to my dad's eyes when he saw what was in the envelope. I kissed him and claiming I was already late for a meeting with Archie, I fled the store.

To clear my head I walked the two long blocks to the boardwalk, planning to stroll south watching the ocean for the Yacht Senator as she steamed north for the inlet. I was almost to convention hall when I spotted Archie coming out of the Boardwalk auction house where he sometimes worked ballying tips (gathering crowds) for the auctioneers.

"Hey kid!" he waved me over to the railing facing the beach. "The Tuna Club is all set. Tomorrow morning we go over

Black Tuna Diaries

there and I introduce you to the caretaker". Just then he looked out to sea, and low and behold, the Senator was steaming past, less than a mile off shore. "Jesus kid! That's one hell of a ship! I love it! You're gonna load that baby with pot and dance back through the inlet like you're making a movie. I love it!"

Archie drove me to the marina. I gave him a tour of the big Stryker which was already sitting in her slip. A few minutes later, Captain Elm and his crew secured the 110 foot Senator to the outer Tee at the end of the dock. I took Archie aboard and watched him ooh and ah as I took him through the vast salon, the four master suites, two kitchens, captains and crews' quarters, laundry, and two dinning areas.

The following morning Archie joined me for an early breakfast in my suite at the Boardwalk Holiday Inn. Robby would join us at the Tuna Club and Randy had taken the Stryker to check out the depth of the water route to the abandoned fish cannery. After that, he would swing by the Tuna Club, to check the channels at the entrance to the basin. In the privacy of the hotel, I gave Archie twenty-five thousand bucks in cash to cover the ten grand rental for our Tuna Club "film location", five grand to the Realtor, and ten g's for the local constabulary, to supply security for the "filming".

Located on a dead-end street on Back Bay, The Atlantic City Tuna Club was headquartered in an elegant old wooden mansion, hidden behind a high wooden fence. Long past its glory days, it sat deserted, except for the caretaker and his family, waiting for the wrecker's ball. The docks still stood in decent condition. It appeared the perfect setup. The caretaker was a pleasant sandy haired Scot, with a five year old son and a pretty young wife. He had already been told that he would have to vacate the club for a few days while the film crew setup and broke down the equipment. I gave him two thousand dollars for the inconvenience and a fully paid suite at Bally's Casino. He agreed to leave by the next afternoon.

"By the way, he asked. "Who's in this movie, anyone I'd recognize?"

Black Tuna Diaries

I thought about it for a instant and made a very bad decision. "Listen, you can't tell a soul. This is a Robert Redford film. If word gets out that Redford is filming here, we'll be mobbed."

He swore not to tell a soul, but had one last question. "What is the film about?" Oh God I hated telling lies on top of lies, it always comes back to haunt. Of course, only one story that made sense.

"Its a smuggling film. Redford plays a yacht captain working under cover for the feds. They are going to land a load of smuggled marijuana and then the feds are going to follow the trucks to the headquarters of the smuggling ring. I can't tell you any more, but please, please, don't repeat what I've told you. Redford would fire me in a second if he found out I let anyone know the story line."

Phew! Now that, at least is a lie I'll have no problem remembering! Mercifully, Randy came around the sharp turn in the waterway. The 54 ft Sportsfisherman had to backup once to negotiate the bend. Oh crap! Could the 110 footer get into the basin? The caretaker left to help his wife pack and I jumped aboard the idling boat to speak to Randy. In short, He said that the cannery was a bust. Neither boat would be able to pass through the shallow channel leading to the dock. But he was confident that Captain Elm would be able to spin the Senator on its axis to gain entrance to the private docks of the Tuna Club. Good enough! Robby appeared, looked around and came aboard Natures Way. We agreed on the Tuna Club as primary offload, with possibly Bobby Jones' townhouse as an emergency backup.

Archie took off and Robby and I drove to the Atlantic City Marina to make final plans. Once aboard the yacht Senator, we found Chip, who had driven up from Miami, with the film company signs on the sides of our van. He and a couple of "Chip's Army" nerds were having breakfast on the fantail patio. Perfect! I could send him to Philly in the van to rent lights, reflectors and an Airoflex camera, so we would look like a real film crew. Mark Phillips appeared with his electrician

Black Tuna Diaries

to complete the installation of the new radar and radios in both boats. To speed things along, Robby had one of Chip's guys help with the installations. Lastly, in the privacy of the pilot house, we asked Elm why he was almost 48 hours late reaching New Jersey. Surprise! They had stopped to party. What the hell! A big luxury yacht was a chick magnet! They stopped at the new Baltimore Harbor, and in half an hour, Barry the Stoner had a dozen chics luded out and dancing on the top deck. Great way to attract attention! It wasn't until the following morning that Elm discovered two of the chics were runaways, and refused to leave the boat. It took him another day to trick the two teenyboppers to go ashore to pickup some things at a nearby drugstore. As soon as they were gone, Elm castoff the lines and beat a hasty retreat for the open ocean. Crap! Crap! Crap! Now we could only hold our breath and pray that no one showed up with the cops.

For two days all went well. Nature's Way and the yacht Senator got their new radar and radios. Both yachts were checked from bow to stern and sea trialled. Chip had the "film company" van loaded with lights, reflectors, boom mikes, and a big Airoflex movie camera. I was finally able to arrange after hours hair cuts at the beauty salon owned by Bobby Jones and his partner.

Sure enough Bobby arrived to pick up his partner and invited us for a drink at their new townhouse. About 5'll", husky, blond and butch. Bobby Jones was in his early thirties. Many years earlier he had taught me how to ride a horse. In those days he was high school drop out, hustling pony rides and renting barn-shy nags on the Atlantic City beach. Now he was a world famous animal trainer. He owned a couple of well known gay clubs. Belle, Bobby's favorite beach nag, was now the star of his Diving Horse Show at the Steel Pier. I don't know how old that horse was, but she was no young Philly when I used to pay two bucks an hour to ride her up and down the beach in the early winter mornings, ten years earlier.

Bobby's townhouse was a gem. Built on a seawall with half a dozen others, each had its own patio and dock on the Back Bay. The problem was that the townhouses, patios and docks,

Black Tuna Diaries

were side by side. There was no way we could unload a couple of hundred bales of Boo, without half of Atlantic City's gay community cheering us on from their town house patios. Just to give Bobby a little scare. I told him that I might have to leave the loaded Sportsfisherman tied to his dock for a few days while I looked for a place to unload her. He moaned, groaned, and begged me not to do it. Not wanting to let him off the hook right away, I promised to use his place only as a last resort, but he shouldn't be surprised, if he woke up one morning to see a 54 foot Sportsfisherman, backing up to his rear patio. I even promised to make bail for him and his partner if they were busted with the loaded boat. Of course I had no intention of using his place, but it was fun to put him on for a while.

The next morning, Raul called from Columbia. "You can ship me the big van on the late flight tomorrow night. Oh, and please include a dozen warm jackets and some long underwear for the workers here."

It wasn't hard to figure out that the rendezvous would be the following night and the trawler's crew was freezing out on the cold ocean without any warm clothing. Simple codes worked best. I called Robby at his parent's house, to tell him to pick me up a.s.a.p. It was time to go to work.

We stopped at a Army Navy store on Atlantic Ave. Twelve extra large heavy parkas, twenty-four sets of long johns, two dozen flannel shirts, and half a gross of sweat socks, one size fits all! That should keep the Columbian crew warm until they were back in warm waters. It was a chilly morning and our entire crew was in the warm main salon of the 110 ft Senator. The big yacht looked at home dominating the beautiful new marina in front of Trump's Castle. It was really tempting to take Archie's suggestion, and offer the Donald big a million bucks to offload the yacht where she stood. But not tempting enough! Robby and I schlepped the warm clothing on board. We told Captains Randy and Elm to fill their fuel tanks and take on enough food and water to last several days. Also to get a bunch of steaks and pork chops as a present for the poor freezing Columbian "fishermen". Chip was to set up the port-

Black Tuna Diaries

able marine radios in my suite on the top floor of the Holiday Inn. The height there and clear view of the ocean would greatly increase the range of the radios.

Later, we stopped by the auction house and met with Archie. He gave us the keys to the Atlantic City Tuna Club, a rental agreement, and a filming permit from the mayor, allowing our company to make, within the city limits, a feature film staring Robert Redford and Donald Trump.

The Senator, cast off at 6am the following morning. She needed eighteen hours to travel the hundred miles to her midnight rendezvous with the Columbian trawler. The Stryker, a much faster boat, would leave a few hours later, but not travel all the way to the rendezvous unless the Senator broke down and radioed for backup. If all went according to plan, the Senator, with thirty thousand pounds of primo aboard, would come dancing through the Atlantic City Inlet, at sundown the following day. Of, course, if you are a smuggler, no matter how good the planning, you know that nothing ever goes according to plan.

By noon we were back at the Atlantic City Tuna Club, where Chip and his "film crew", were setting up the lights and reflectors for the next days' "shoot". Thinking we had the place to ourselves, imagine our surprise, when we were joined on the dock by the ginger haired caretaker , his wife and young son.

"I thought you were going to move your family to the suite at Bally's this morning?" I asked him while trying not to show my acute annoyance.

He shrugged as if in defeat. "My wife is a huge Redford fan. She refuses to leave until she gets to see him in person. She promises to stay in the background and not say a word, but she refuses to leave until she sees him! I'm really sorry, but I can't reason with her".

Black Tuna Diaries

Oh crap! Now we have the same stupid problem we had in Miami, when Marcy the Yenta refused to stop visiting our "movie set", in hopes of seeing Robert Redford. That's the last time Redford will ever star in one of my lies. I looked over at the caretaker's wife. She had that look of a woman prepared for combat. I decided to leave it to Archie, one of America's truly great con men and promoters, to convince her to vacate the premises. Knowing Archie, I had no doubt he would promise to bring Redford to their suite for dinner and get him to babysit their son. I left Chip and his crew to finish setting up.

Robby dropped me back at the boardwalk. Now came the worst part, the waiting. Love the action, hate the wait! I called Arch and told him about the caretaker's wife.

"Don't worry kid. I'll have her gone before morning. Trust me."

Trusting Archie Morris wasn't always the smartest move, but considering the consequences, I was pretty sure he'd take care of business. I ordered dinner from room service. As soon as the waiter was gone, I brought out the marine radios from the closet and connected them to the antennas Chip had hidden behind the drapery of the ocean view window. Neither yacht would break radio silence unless something went wrong or to briefly report success with the phrase "Lovely cruise, returning to port."

I doubt I slept much that night. By six am I was getting anxious. Senator should have been loaded and heading back to port. I hadn't heard a word from either craft. At seven sharp, the phone rang in my suite. It was Raul in Santa Marta. He was in constant contact with the trawler via short wave radio.

Trying to be as discrete as possible, he was clearly upset as he told me, "My fishing boat saw your fishing boat on radar last night, but when they tried to get together, your fishing boat ran away."

© 2009 R. Platshorn

Black Tuna Diaries

I wanted more details, but not over the phone. I just asked him what he wanted to do now.

"It's too cold to fish up north; my boat is headed back south. Why don't you get someone to meet them at our old fishing place in four on five days?"

There was really nothing to think about. "Count on it. " And I hung up.

My mind was already working on a way to move the entire operation back to south Florida within 72 hours. At the same time, I was pissed off, wondering what went wrong. Just then Nature's Way broke radio silence to report both yachts homeward bound. I called and woke Robby.

"Meet me here for breakfast. We have big problems and a lot of work to do."

Black Tuna Diaries

Chapter 10
The House of Rothschild and the Bloomsbury Ghost

It's 1967! My dad is running my sandwich joint and water ski school at Bayshore's in Somers Point, New Jersey. I'm on the road again, pitching the Vita Mix at the Wisconsin and Ohio state fairs, The Eastern States Exposition in Springfield Mass., and the best little six day fair in America, The Bloomsburg Pa. County Fair. It was my best fair season ever! When it was over, I probably had six or seven grand in 1967 bucks! Lynne, who I had been with since we were sixteen and would marry nine years later, had just graduated N.Y.U. and was working in London for the Theater Division of J. Arthur Rank. I missed her; I really, really missed her! Things had not been good between us for the last three years and I hoped that after a few months separation, she might be pleased with a surprise visit. So....Next stop, London! A three week holiday that turned into a three year odyssey.

Lynne was sharing a flat with three attractive young women in a posh area of Victoria. Two of them were engaged to newly graduated lawyers. One, a young solicitor, Victor Blank, would go on to become one of London's leading developers and financiers. The other, Andrew Greystoke, a young barrister newly installed in chambers at Gray's Inn, was England's youngest Q.C. (Queen's Counsel). He would go on to direct a major investment bank in New York.

Victor and Andrew had been looking for a working partner to develop the first speed reading schools in the UK and Europe. They had a pile of material on how to do it, but no idea of how to start and promote a new business. Despite a brief romantic short jaunt to Paris together, Lynne was seriously involved with someone else and keeping me at arms length. I got involved in the speed reading venture so that I could stick around to pick up the pieces if her current relationship fell apart.

Black Tuna Diaries

By the time I had been in London for three weeks, I had a tiny office at 212 The Strand, with a hand written sign on the door that said, "Dynamic Reading Ltd." I had gotten really lucky and found a young genius, to oversee the academics. Michael Fortesque, a graduate student at the London School of Economics! Using material Andrew had collected when he was a student at Berkley, Michael was able to teach himself Dynamic Reading, and then train five or six others to teach the course. In the meantime, I sat in my little cubbyhole office, at the top of a narrow winding staircase, with only an old manual typewriter and a few cheap art supplies, writing ads, press releases, class schedules and budgets for money I didn't have. The entire capital of Dynamic Reading Ltd was £400. The pound was worth $2.40, so we are talking about a total capital of $ 940.00. That had to pay the office rent, my salary, Fortesque's salary, rent for a hotel room to hold classes, the printing of books and manuals needed for training teachers and teaching classes. The trick would be to start signing up students a.s.a.p.

The course normally took eight weeks to teach. Michael taught himself Dynamic Reading in two weeks and trained the teachers in another three or four. I had opened our office near the end of December, 1967, and by mid March we were ready to begin teaching classes. My goal was to fill four or five classes of twenty to thirty students, at tuition of £40 each. Using only a three line classified ad in the "Times", and a few pieces of sales literature I had produced on my ancient manual typewriter, we received a total of twenty-two enrollments. Not good! I needed a new plan. One that would fill our classes before the financial roof fell in.

Okay! I'm a pitchman. All I should need is people and a place to make my pitch. With no money, but plenty of guts and conversation, I booked a big meeting room at the Savoy Hotel on the Strand. I announced a press conference and public demonstration of Dynamic Reading. The press and public were invited to test our system and our teachers. They could bring any type of book to the demonstration. Three of our newly trained teachers would sit at a table on the podium and read at super speed, while I made the pitch. After twenty

Black Tuna Diaries

minutes, the demonstrators would summarize what they had read, and the books' owners could question them on the contents. Then, provided everything went smoothly, I would finish my pitch, and "turn the tip", that is, get them to enroll on the spot.

All this was a big risk. None of us had ever attempted to do anything like a public demonstration. I had a few ideas for a pitch, but mostly, I had to wing it. Would our teachers really be able to read an entire book or most of a book and be able to describe it in detail? There wasn't much choice. I could think of no other way to overcome British skepticism, and get people to shell out what was a hell of a lot of dough for 1967 London. The public consensus was that Dynamic Reading was probably some Yank fraud.

The problem was finding enough money to advertise the demonstration. I could write copy and send out press releases. Curiosity, free food, and an open bar would bring in the press. I figured, if I could fill six hundred seats, I should be able to sell over a hundred courses. That meant a few large well written ads, in at least two major London newspapers. Those ads were expensive and we were broke! The £400 and all the tuition money we had collected were long gone. In the advertising world, if you don't have an established track record, i.e. "media credit", then you must pay for your ads in advance. However, advertising agencies have media credit. If I could convince a small ad agency that Dynamic Reading Ltd was a substantial company, I would be able to use their credit for our launch.

I had no idea of the consequences, if my scheme bombed. Someone recommended a tiny agency, Broad Advertising. They needed my business as badly as I needed their credit line. I waited until the very last minute to contact them and have them place the ads. There would not be time for credit checks! I laid a heavy story on them about my media deals in the States. The entire time, I was frightened and very uncomfortable. I hated the idea of rolling the dice with someone else's money. I was afraid that the loss could ruin the small ad

Black Tuna Diaries

agency, and the two very nice talented people who constituted most of the agency's staff.

I booked the Savoy auditorium for three demonstrations on the same day. An early one for the press and public, so that the evening papers could carry the story, an afternoon demo for the London shoppers and tourists, and an early evening show for those headed home after work.

I think we had two hundred and fifty chairs set up for each demo. I don't know who was more nervous, the teachers who had never tried to demonstrate their new skill or me who had visions of being thrown in a Dickensian debtor's prison, when it was discovered that I couldn't pay for the ads and had already spent the student's enrollment fees to rent the hotel auditorium. If the demo bombed and I couldn't fill at least four classes, I was shit out of luck. I couldn't even flee the country. My return cheap fare ticket on Icelandic Airways had expired long ago. I didn't have enough money to buy another.

As the Brits say, "in for a penny, in for a pound". I had room service set up a free bar and buffet, and a small stage. On the stage was a long table where the "readers" would sit to race through the offered books, testing their speed and comprehension. The average reader can read light material at about 350 words per minute. A Dynamic Reader reads between 1500 wpm for difficult study material, up to 3000 wpm for light reading. All with enhanced comprehension! Now all I had to do was prove it in front of a large audience while I stood in front of the readers for twenty minutes, and pitched a pitch I was inventing as I spoke.

For the first demo, my best teachers were seated at the table behind me. Michael Fortesque! Early twenties, light hair and complexion, 6 ft, 170 lbs, studious demeanor, and wearing his standard rumpled green corduroy sports coat, white shirt and school tie. Khalid, A Pakistani part-timer, working on his Masters degree. And on my left was Astrid. A raven haired, twenty three year old Oxford graduate. Deep set haunting blue eyes with a striking face and a serious figure.

Black Tuna Diaries

By 10:30 am a few members of the public had drifted in and were removing the heavy coats and cardigans they wore against the gray damp cold of the London winter. Most of the seats were empty. My new teachers and staff outnumbered the audience. Then a chap comes in and introduces himself as a reporter for the Times, and then another from The Evening Standard, and one from the Guardian, then a TV crew from the BBC. By the time I looked up from meeting the members of the press and directing them to the free food and booze, the auditorium was full and people were standing in the aisles.

I stepped up on the stage to stand behind an old fashioned standing microphone. Seated behind me, from left to right were Michael, Khalid, and Astrid. I welcomed the press and the public and asked if anyone had brought a book to test our readers. At least thirty hands went up. I took one from the Times reporter, one from the BBC chap, and one from an elderly man who had arrived early and was seated in the front row. Our newspaper ads and press notices had invited attendees to bring books. Of course they brought the most obscure novels and text books they could find. There was no chance that our demonstrators had previously read them. Michael, whose field is languages, received a book on advanced mathematics. Khalid, an obscure 19th Century English novel, and Astrid had to demonstrate her newly acquired speed reading skills on a thick tome on Invertebrate Zoology.

I introduced the readers and explained that these people were themselves, newly trained in Dynamic Reading. They would read for twenty minutes, calculate their reading speed, followed by a précis of the material. At that point whoever had supplied the book, could question the reader. I flourished a big stopwatch, handed it to a lady in the front row, requesting she be the official timer.

"Please officially start our readers and at the twenty minute mark, please call, time over".

I went into my pitch. Explaining how a child learns to sound out each letter, then each word and at that point, stops learning to read.

Black Tuna Diaries

"That's the old way. It hasn't changed or progressed in 300 years. With Dynamic Reading, you'll learn to see larges areas of a page as if you are your looking at a picture or watching a film. Making it much easier to comprehend and retain."

For twenty minutes I pitched my heart out. Not even daring to peek behind me to see how the readers were doing. I didn't know where the words were coming from, but I had the audience mesmerized. "Time Over", shouted the nice lady with my stopwatch. I turned to the readers as they noted the number of pages they had read, the words per page, and calculated the words per minute. Wanting a strong first impression, I called on Michael. He had covered over 60 pages of a textbook on advanced mathematics theory. He had read at a rate of 1800 words per minute, more than 10 times faster then most people can read heavy study material. Fortunately, he had understood what he read and was able to give an excellent summary of an incomprehensible text. The book's donor was the chap from The Guardian. When I asked him if he like to question our reader, he admitted he had never read, nor could he possibly understand the book. He brought it for its obscurity and difficulty.

Khalid had read the entire novel. Three thousand words per minute! He gave a good review of the story and was questioned only briefly.

It was Astrid's turn. I had a feeling that the little old man who brought the book on Invertebrate Zoology, was, in fact the professor who had written it. He was! Astrid's speed, reading the study material was a blazing two thousand words per minute. Her précis was crisp and complete. The old professor, who had written the book, was smiling like a cherub as he rose from his seat to announce that he was the author, and wished to propose marriage to Astrid on the spot. The audience howled and clapped.

I had em! Time to "turn the tip". I recounted what had just taken place. Explained that classes met at various convenient times at the Savoy Hotel, once a week for eight weeks. I explained the different easy ways they could pay their tuition,

Black Tuna Diaries

and that there were only a limited number of slots available in the classes that would begin the following week. Then, the moment of truth! I pointed to the tables in the rear where enrollment applications and questions would be taken by our teachers, readers and staff. Truth time! My heart was doing the Mambo and I couldn't breath. Most of the audience stood, and looked at one another for a few seconds. It was Astrid's sweet old professor who started the parade to the tables.

"I say! I'll sign up if I can be in her class," he said as he pointed to Astrid.

Astrid stepped off the stage to collect the old dear, and lead him to the tables in the rear. After that, the staff was swamped with people clambering to enroll in our first classes. By the time all three demos were over, we had filled the first classes and taken reservations for places in the next several groups. With a new group to start each month, we were in business!

Four of the reporters who attended that first demo, signed up to take the course. That meant, that at the end of the eight week course, they would be reporting on the results. Judging by the success we had training the teachers, I knew we were in for another round of good publicity, and that turned out to be the case.

During the next few hectic days, Astrid, Michael, and I were interviewed by almost every newspaper, radio and TV news show in Great Britain.

It was right about that time, that Lynne invited me to the Royal Premier of "Romeo and Juliet". She was working in the PR department at Rank/Odeon, the theater division of the giant entertainment group, J. Arthur Rank. Considering she was having a hot and heavy affair with someone else at the time, I think the invitation was mostly a case of "have tux will travel". I owned two dinner jackets and was an exceptionally good dancer. She would be busy with her duties escorting a group of VIPs at the Royal Premier and the banquet that followed. I would be expected to be available as a dancing and dinning partner for several invited celebs, particularly, as I recall,

Black Tuna Diaries

Vanessa Redgrave whose new husband was elsewhere that night.

The Royal premier was at the largest and grandest of the Odeon theaters in London's West End. It was a major charity event, with The Queen, Prince Phillip, and the 14 year old Prince Charles, in attendance at the reception line. Beginning with Prince Charles, Prince Phillip, and then the Queen, all the attendees enjoyed a brief moment with each of the royals, as they passed through the reception line. Since I would be one of the last seated, I was relegated to the end of the reception line. That gave me more time to worry that I would not remember how I was to address each of the Royals.

It turned out to be a moot point when the reception line stopped moving. From where I waited at the back of the line, I was not able to see what the holdup was. At first there was laughter and then obvious annoyance from those waiting to meet the Royal Family. Lynne, was stewarding a group well ahead of me, she dropped back and whispered that because of the delay, the reception line would be cut short, in order that the film and the banquet could remain on schedule. She pointed me up the winding staircase to the Loge, where I would be escorted to my seat.

At the top of the staircase, I paused to look down at the reception line, and see what was holding things up. At the extreme right, was the Queen, who, even if she weren't tapping her foot impatiently, looked like she wished she could. To her left was Prince Phillip who was clearly scowling at his son. But the fourteen year old Prince Charlie was oblivious to it all . His hand was still firmly attached to that of Joan Collins, who had arrive ten minutes earlier in a glittering form hugging low cut silver gown. Slightly flushed and grinning from ear to ear, the Prince refused to relinquish the paw in question, until mum and dad both made clear their displeasure, by loudly clearing their throats. Even then, his goodbyes, took two more minutes. So thanks to Joan Collins and the horny young Charlie, I never got to greet the Queen.

Black Tuna Diaries

The second most embarrassing moment of my life, came at the banquet following the premier. This took place in the grand ballroom of a newly opened Rank hotel. I was seated at a round table that seated a dozen. There were celebrities at the table. I cannot recall who they were, but I recall that their presence added to my embarrassment. I'm pretty sure that Lynne was seated at a different table. You see, this was a formal banquet. The tables were set for full French silver service. There were more assorted forks, spoons, and odd looking knives, beside my plate, than I had ever seen in my life. Now, I had eaten in some of New York's fanciest eateries. Delmonico's, Four Seasons, Asti's, but I had no idea what to do with the two dozen pieces cutlery surrounding my plate.

If you are a Three Stooges fan, you have seen this scene before. Not only didn't I know what utensil to use with each of the seven or eight courses, I couldn't for the life of me figure why some of my courses were whisked away before I barely touched them and at other times everyone else was served a new courses and I was left with a mostly empty plate from the previous course. Around the middle of the meal, when everyone was enjoying the Beef Wellington, I was embarrassingly staring at my near empty pate plate. At last, someone sitting nearby took pity and solved the mystery of eating formal silver service, with three simple sentences.

She whispered in my ear. "Eat each course, with the outermost fork, knife and or spoon. The waiter is responsible for putting them in the proper order. If you are ready for the next course put your used utensils together or cross them on the right side of your plate, but if you aren't done, put your knife and fork on opposites sides of the plate and the waiter will know you wish to finish, before going on to the next course".

Thank heaven! I crossed my knife and fork. In a trice, my half eaten pate was gone and the Beef Wellington appeared. I do not recall much about the rest of the evening. I know I danced with several celebs.

Within a month or two of filling our first Dynamic Reading classes, I was looking for premises large enough for two big class rooms and generous office space. No more classes in rented hotel rooms! I could now move from the dingy little office at the top of the spiral stairway above the tobacconist at 212 The Strand. We received a small infusion of new capital from Sir John Drage. A bright and interesting wealthy investor in his late 50's. His father had received a knighthood for inventing the concept of "the HP" or Hire Purchase. The HP revolutionized retail buying in the UK. The owner of a chain of furniture stores just after WWII, he was the first to extend credit to families unable to pay in full. His innovation was so unique, that the nation adopted the Drage family name as a generic description for time payments. "I bought it on the Drage", was still a common expression in England.

I quickly found and moved into premises in a lovely old haunted 16th century house on Bloomsbury Square. We shared the building with a well known publisher of children's books, J. Robert Tyndal. Our offices and classes were on the first and second floor, and I later moved into a small flat up in the loft. Tyndal's offices were on the ground floor and his production department in the basement. Our classrooms and offices were built by Tora Andersen, Astrid's father. One of the finest craftsmen and drinking companions I have ever known.

More staff was hired and everyone worked hard filling the classes at our Bloomsbury school and running Dynamic Reading courses at BP, Shell Oil, Barclay's Bank, and a few other major companies. We were invited to conduct courses at Oxford, Cambridge, Edinburgh University, and had even been given a classroom in the House of Lords, in order to teach Dynamic Reading, to the members of both houses of the British Parliament. Within a year I had opened schools in Manchester and Birmingham, and was negotiating a franchise sale for Dynamic Reading schools to be established in Holland and Germany.

In the mean time, Lynne, who I had come to London the see in the first place, had moved to South Africa. Astrid and I became an item! I soon found out that Astrid was a Jewitch, that is, she was both Jewish and a witch. Now, I know a lot of men

Black Tuna Diaries

who think that isn't a terribly unusual combination, but Astrid actually has powers.

It was Astrid's presence and her powerful aura that probably caused the Bloomsbury Ghost to actively patrol the stairwells of our premises on Bloomsbury Square. Complaints from our teachers and students became an almost daily occurrence. Mysterious cobwebs would appear and disappear. Noises like the faint scream of a child. Aggressive air currents that would repeatedly brush against anyone alone on the stairwell. The English generally coexist comfortably with their ghosts! Indeed, having ones own ghost was a bit of a status symbol in a country with tens of thousands of ancient buildings. Our ghost was becoming a distraction. A daily subject of conversation! And this seemed to make our ghost even bolder and more aggressive. Something needed to be done before it got totally out of hand and someone was knocked down a flight of stairs by our frenzied spirit visitor. Astrid declared she would hold a séance in order to find out who was haunting our school and why. She explained that if we could find out why the ghost was attacking people on our stairwell, we might be able to get it to stop.

We needed a circle of five for the séance. Astrid picked a Saturday night when the moon would be full. She invited Michael Fortesque, his lady, and our PR guy, a former R.A.F. pilot, George Manly. With Astrid and me, we had the magic five. We gathered around a small table in my office. Astrid placed on the table, something like a homemade Ouija Board and an overturned glass. We joined hands over the glass as my Jewitch implored the haunt to speak. To identify itself, and tell us why it was causing chaos in our stairwell. After a moment the table began to shake. It rose up six inches from the floor and slammed back down several times. Astrid declared our spirit to be a naughty frightened child. She spoke to our ghost as one would to a scared child. The glass began to move. First in meaningless circles. Then in frantic misspelled words.

"Plagg.! All ded I"

Black Tuna Diaries

Astrid began to interpret, as the messages came faster and faster.

"These premises were a Crown Jeweler's. Maybe late 17th century. Garrick, that's this boy's name, lived here with his family. His father was a goldsmith and made jewelry for the Royal family. During one of London's worst plague summers, Garrick's entire family was wiped out by the black plague. His mother, his two little sisters, his uncle, and his father. Garrick, then only six, had to minister to his dying father. On his death bed, the father made Garrick promise to guard the gold and jewels that had been hidden beneath a secret panel. With his dying breath Garrick's father told the little boy the location of the hidden fortune, and made Garrick pledge to guard the secret until a family member would come to London to claim the treasure.

The morning after his father's death, the little boy went to the front door to find help to bury the bodies of his family. He found the front door had been boarded and nailed shut from the outside. He ran to the back door and found it sealed. He found an open window, but the shutters had been nailed shut. It was the custom in London during plague time, to seal the infected buildings from the outside. No one would be permitted to leave until the neighborhood was declared plague free. Garrick pounded at the shutters with his tiny fists, but no one would answer his cries. Although he wasn't sick with the plague, he was weak from lack of food; he'd hadn't eaten for days. Trapped in the house with no food, and the bodies of his parents and little sisters, he dragged himself to the stairwell, where the stench of the noisome corpses hadn't yet reached. Too weak to climb the stairs to his garret room, Garrick lay down to cry himself to sleep on the first floor landing. Mercifully, the little boy never awoke. Believing he had been murdered by the fearful passersby who refused to let him out of the house, he remained in the stairwell for over three hundred years guarding the family legacy, waiting for a relative to arrive to claim the treasure and free him of the pledge made at the deathbed of his father in our house on Bloomsbury Square."

Black Tuna Diaries

Well! Good story, but were five educated adults going to buy into that one. Okay! Five adults who had been drinking Glen Morangie single malt, and probably had toked a spliff of Paki hash before the séance. Thirty seconds later George was using an old screwdriver to pry up the floorboards of the garret where I. had my little flat. Nada! Next came the stairwell where Garrick kept his vigil. We tapped and tugged at each step. Then, we pulled off strips of the wainscoting to check for hidden panels. Nothing! We split-up to check the walls and floors in every room.. A blank! It only remained to break into our landlord's offices down stairs and checkout his walls and floors. So we B & E'd the joint, but still came up empty. Not so much as a lost earring!

At last we called off the hunt, vowing to pump our little ghost for the secret location, at our next séance. But our next attempt, elicited only table shaking and nonsense syllables, that Astrid could make no sense of. Curiously, Garrick settled down and only occasionally reminded us of his presence with the odd invisible cobweb or his icy breath on the back of an unsuspecting student's neck. Astrid and I would sometimes call to him or talk to him as we climbed the stairs after a night at the theater and a late supper in the West End. The only reward for these efforts was the faint tinkle of a naughty child's tittering laughter. A little research proved that our building had indeed been a crown jeweler's during one of London's worst plague years.

When I was a smuggler, my partner Gene dubbed me the Baron of Barranquilla, because I was been able to get him and three of his biker crew, in and out of Colombia, without passports or papers. But when I lived in London, I knew two real Barons. One was the annoying and supercilious Baron Von Putlich. The putz who managed to wreck our Dynamic Reading School in Cologne Germany after I stupidly appointed him the schools director.. The other Baron, was the Baron Evelyn de Rothschild, head of the British branch of the House of Rothschild.

By the end of 1969 Dynamic Reading had grown, primarily by self financed expansion and franchising, to three schools in

Black Tuna Diaries

England, a school in Holland and one in Germany. We had teachers running courses at Oxford, Cambridge, London University, Edinburgh University, several Red Brick Universities, The House of Lords, and at dozen large companies like BP and Shell Oil. It was around that time, Sir John Drage brought me an article about a marvelous new shorthand system, "Tee-Line Executive Shorthand". The revolutionary new system was being taught in one small school in Nottingham shire. What made it unique was that it could be learned by anyone in just a few weeks. Traditional shorthand systems like Gregg or Pitman took months or even years to learn and had a high failure rate.

Sir John I and traveled to the midlands to meet with James Hill, Tee-Line's inventor. We arranged with Hill to open a school in London and to promote his system world wide. We needed fresh capitol to expand Dynamic Reading Ltd and develop Tee-Line Executive Shorthand.

My barrister partner, Andrew Greystoke, although still a practicing QC, was working as part of an investment team at Rothschilde's. His investment team a group of young guns, in their late twenties, brought Dynamic Reading Ltd, into the fold at The House of Rothschilde on St Swivens Lane in the "City of London". The area of London known worldwide as the "City", is the financial district, located in one of London's oldest sections. Most famous of its streets is the banking center's Lombard St. But the place that excites the imagination is a tiny private Lane that few ever get to enter, St. Swivens Lane. Home of the most powerful and respected financial institution in the world. The merchant bank known as The House of Rothschilde.

As Chairman, Managing Director, and Dynamic Reading Ltd's largest stockholder, the decision to accept financing and thereby dilute my own stock holding was in my hands. It was the classic choice of owning a big piece of a smaller pie or a smaller piece of a much bigger pie. My original partners Andrew and Victor had arranged the deal at Rothschilde's. Sir John Drage indicated he was in favor, but would go along with my decision. I had met one of the investment team, Grant

Black Tuna Diaries

Manheim, at his flat in Victoria. He was as much hippie, as he was investment banker. I liked him instantly. He had rebelled against his family wealth by leaving home to live at a racing stable in hopes of becoming a jockey. Only when it became obvious he was growing much too large for the role did he returned to the fold. I also had had a meeting with William Courtould, another one of us in his twenties. He owned his own small investment firm, where he put to work a tiny portion of the vast Courtould fortune. William was more the traditional English banker. The only one of our group, more at home in the City uniform of pinstripe and bowler hat, than jeans and boots. He was a bit of an uptight conservative banker, trying to be one of our "new wave entrepreneurs/hippies"

The final decision whether or not to go forward with the financing deal would be made by both sides at a meeting in the boardroom at Rothschilde's St Swivens Lane, City of London W1.

I arrived by London taxi at 9:45 am for the 10 am meeting. St Swivens Lane is a single block cul-de-sac. The sole occupant is Rothschilde's Bank. Shockingly for London and doubly so for the City back in 1969, it was a modern steel and glass, six or seven story edifice. During the previous year, every bank, law office, and investment firm I'd visited was housed in the most ancient appearing premises available. This was based on the theory that older was somehow bettor. Even banks and law offices housed by default in post-war buildings, would construct their interiors with the oldest looking materials available, so as to resemble the office rooms of Ebenezer Scrooge. Rothschilde's was a daring bit of fresh air in a very stuffy London closet. I stepped from the square black London taxi and approached the double glass doors. Locked! I looked at my watch to see if I had not mistakenly arrived an hour earlier than intended. Nope! It took me just a second to realize that of course, Rothschilde, is a private merchant bank, not a public institution. It is in fact so private, that it is the first choice of companies seeking mergers or financing deals the require absolute secrecy.

Black Tuna Diaries

Before I could knock or look for a bell, the uniformed concierge opened the door and greeted me by name.

"Good morning Mr. Platshorn. You're a bit early for your meeting. I'll phone up to Mr. Greystoke and Mr. Manheim to let them know you've arrived"

I followed him to a small desk where he picked up the phone and a moment later relayed to me that;

"They are in a meeting. It should be over in a few minutes. In the meantime your welcome to have a seat in the reception hall or have a look around, but I must ask you not to leave the reception area without an escort".

He went back to his desk, where he had been ironing copies of the Times. A tradition amongst the wealthy and powerful, ironing the morning newspaper cures the ink, thereby preventing ink smudged fingers. The reception hall to the left of the entrance, was a large impressive marbled room with a few small benches. Above the tinted front glass wall, reaching up to the two story ceilings, was a magnificent mural, which ran almost completely around the huge hall, depicting the history of the Rothschilde. From the humble beginnings of the family founder in the 17 century, it followed the Rothschilde as they established themselves in Germany, France, and England. Looking from left to right , it was like seeing a movie. The financing of industries, providing the funds that financed the defeat of Napoleon Bonaparte. And much more! It was as I neared the end of the wrap around mural that I spotted what I thought was a flaw. All the Rothschilde depicted in the mural looked at least six feet tall and had exactly the same facial features. Male and female alike! The same pale blue veined complexion. The same narrow face, with a long thin French nose, bowed mouth and clear blue eyes. I looked back over the mural. Every face was the same. Damn, I wondered what those people really looked like.

Just then the elevator doors opened and out came Andrew and Grant. Both of them wearing jeans, no tie, and an open shirt. Sacrilege! No three piece pin stripe suite? Even I was

Black Tuna Diaries

wearing a pin stripe suit, with a waistcoat. We ascended to the top floor where there were several meeting rooms. They led me into a small conference roam where the tea lady was waiting to see if I wanted "tea or coffee with lovely little biscuits". When I had settled in, the boys excused themselves to finish with their meeting, promising to return in five minutes.

In those days I always carried a small tape recorder to dictate letters and memos that my secretary would transcribe when I returned to my office. It was a palm sized machine with a wrist cord to secure it on your hand. I had used it to answer my morning post, as I traveled from my office to the City and it was now in my attaché case. Turned off! Remember, this was 1969. There was no technology in use that could detect a tape recorder. Let alone one that wasn't even running. But, this was Rothschilde's, a place where secrets were kept, absolutely. Less than two minutes after I entered the room and placed my attaché case on the conference table, the concierge, knocked, entered, and asked with a fair amount of disdain,

"Excuse me Mr. Platshorn, do you by chance have a recording device ?"

It took me a second to figure out he was referring to the small dictation unit in my case. I opened the lid of my attaché and presented it to him to demonstrate that the recorder was not running. He reached into the case picking up the machine by the cord, as if it were a dead rat.

"I'm sorry sir. Recording devices are not permitted in the building. I'll have it for you when you're ready to leave."

I do not recall much of the meeting that followed. A deal was struck. Andrew's investment team at Rothschilde's would finance the expansion of our business. Bringing not only fresh funds, but worldwide business contacts and three hundred years of experience in helping to establish new industries. And of course, the immeasurable prestige of being associated with the House of Rothschilde.

Black Tuna Diaries

Andrew phoned down to the concierge that I would be descending on the lift. As I stepped out I was greeted by a tall distinguished gentleman who looked exactly like every face I had seen in the mural. To be sure, I looked over his shoulder at the painting. No doubt about it! He extended a long fingered pale hand.

"Mr. Platshorn? I'm Evelyn Rothschilde. I understand we may be helping your Dynamic Reading Company. I've heard nice things about you and wanted to welcome you to Rothschild's."

I shook his hand but couldn't quite think of what to say. The last thing I expected was to meet "The "Rothschilde". I kept glancing nervously over his shoulder at the faces in the mural.

"I see you've noticed the resemblances. Everyone does," he said as he pointed to the many male and female Rothschild's on the massive mural. "The fact is, until the late:19th century, our family, like most other well off Europeans, tended to marry cousins, often first cousins. After a while we began to notice that a limited gene pool didn't often produce the brightest progeny, so we discontinued the practice. However the family resemblances or maybe its the family curse, remains in tact".

The concierge appeared with our topcoats. He helped the Baron put his on and then did the same for me. And then, the Baron invited me to ride with him.

"Mr. Platshorn, I understand that you're returning to you offices on Great Portland Street. I'm on my way to Central London. Why don't you ride with me and we can chat."

I finally found my voice. "Thank you, I'd appreciate that.".. .As we headed out the door, it dawned on me that this was no chance meeting. He had timed his own exit so that we would meet.

Black Tuna Diaries

As we stepped outside I looked around for his chauffeured Rolls or maybe a Bentley. Instead, one of the four small minicabs parked a few feet away, pulled up to the curb. Evelyn Rothschilde opened the door, ushered me into the back seat, and slid in beside me. He was laughing at my confusion and obvious disappointment.

"You were expecting a Rolls Royce, weren't you? Most would!"

I nodded, not knowing what to say that wouldn't sound rude or presumptuous.

He went on. "I leave the Rolls at home in the country. Minicabs do much better getting about in London traffic. It actually costs less to keep four minis permanently stationed at our front door, for our associates and clients, than to keep a car and chauffeur on call for myself."

I don't recall much else about the ride to Great Portland St. Evelyn Rothschilde was quite charming as he politely questioned me.

"I've told you a bit about myself and my family . Now why don't you tell me a bit about Robert Platshorn."

I had no doubt that he had a dossier on Robert Elliot Platshorn. I answered his queries simply and honestly.

Over the next year, I would occasionally visit St Swivens Lane for meetings with my investment team. Once, as I was arriving and he was leaving, I again met Evelyn Rothschilde. He greeted me by name and asked about our progress. What can I say?. A very nice Baron, as Barons go!

Tee-Line Executive Shorthand! Now that there was a few thousand pounds in the kitty, I was able to do what I enjoyed most and was best at. Developing and promoting a new business! Dynamic Reading was doing well. Ruining it on a day to day basis was better done by the managers. Tee-Line Execut-

Black Tuna Diaries

ive Shorthand was an exciting and challenging new project, but would turn out to a disaster for this nearly British Bobby.

John Drage had brought me a tiny article from one of the provincial newspapers. It lauded a revolutionary new shorthand system that was so easily learned, a school child could master it in a few weeks and a bright adult, in a single weekend seminar. The system's inventor, James Hill, an "Unqualified (degreeless) teacher", was successfully teaching Tee-Line to middle school students in Nottingham shire. To appreciate how revolutionary this was, you have to understand that back in 1969, shorthand was still the major skill needed by secretaries and anyone wanting to record information in real time. There were two systems taught in high schools and secretarial schools around the world. Gregg and Pitman! In high schools it took two years to become proficient in either system. They were so difficult to master, that both systems had a near 90% dropout or failure rate in inner city schools. If Tee-Line lived up to its promise, it could change the teaching of shorthand worldwide, opening opportunities for inner city girls normally not qualified for high paying executive secretarial positions. It was an exciting prospect!

John arranged for us to meet with James Hill, at his home in Nottingham shire. While I must confess, I never once experienced a real "London Fog" (except by raincoat) in the entire 3½ years I lived there, I soon found that Nottinghamers dwelt in perpetual, miserable, unrelenting wet gray fog. How did Robinhood ever see what he was shooting at in the Sherwood Forrest? It was no wonder the Sheriff of Nottingham could never find him. In any case after a morning train ride, on which Sir John and I enjoyed a traditional British Rail breakfast of kippers and eggs, our taxi driver managed somehow, without the aid of radar, to locate the tiny cardboard cottage wherein dwelt James Hill and his evil wife. He was a soft fiftyish little balding white haired gent, with twinkly blue eyes and a natural enthusiasm for his chosen field and life in general. She, was a tiny sour faced black haired harridan who trusted no one and hated everyone. She spoke with an unintelligible midlands accent that grated on your nerves..

Black Tuna Diaries

Over tea in his dark dingy little sitting room, he told me a tiny lie that was lead to the demise of my little English business empire. I asked him if he had sold the rights to publish textbooks and to teach Tee-Line. His reply was a definitive "NO". He brought out a tiny booklet of perhaps twenty-five pages that contained all the basics of his revolutionary system. Heinemann, one of the largest educational publishers in the world had, a year ago, paid Hill the magnanimous. sum of £50 for the right to publish this little pamphlet which sold for five shillings, on the rare occasions, that it sold at all. Heinemann had never paid Hill a shilling of royalties. They had never promoted the system and Hill assured us that they owned no further rights to his system. As it turned out, Hill was lying and we were buying!

Taking Hill at his word that he still owned all the rights, we struck a deal to form a company for the promotion and development of Tee-Line Executive Shorthand. Hill, who as an unqualified teacher, never earned much above £16 a week, was to be a company director at £50 a week, and would own 25% of the company stock. I would open Tee-Line Institutes in London and other major European cities, train teachers to run seminars for major European companies, and arrange for the establishment and promotion of the system in the U.S., Europe, and the rest of the English speaking world. I had even stupidly agreed to hire Hill's wife and son as over-paid teachers at the first London school.

We shook hands on the deal and agreed to exchange informal letters of understanding. Based on Hill's assurances, I went ahead and arranged for a major publisher in New York, to pre-publish enough basic teaching manuals to run a test program in the New York school system. The woman in charge of shorthand education for New York loved Tee-Line and couldn't wait to begin teaching. She believed that Tee-line would make shorthand a viable subject again in inner city schools. Based on the test results, the publisher would then publish textbooks, teaching manuals, and promote the system nationwide.

I leased space for offices and classrooms in an expensive new, building near Dynamic Reading, in central London. I

Black Tuna Diaries

began spending a lot of money to build the classrooms, train new teachers, and advertise the "Revolutionary New System".

There was only one problem. James Hill, no longer owned the rights to his shorthand system. He had sold the entire kit and caboodle to Heinemann Publishing for £50 ($120.00) and a promise of a few pence in royalties on each of the 500 little booklets that had been published.. You see! That tiny pamphlet contained every symbol used in the system. Tee-Line was so simple that you could teach yourself shorthand using just the booklet. Since the entire system was in the pamphlet, Heinemann now owned the worldwide copyrights. Hill claimed he had been mislead and cheated. He told me that Heinemann assured him it was only the rights to a pamphlet to, "test the market", that he was selling. Right! Most of those booklets were never sold and were filling a closet in Hills cardboard cottage.

By the time I learned all of this, we were in too deep to turn back. I had made two trips to the states, trained a dozen teachers, opened the London School, and was already running weekend seminars for several London companies. We had spent a small fortune advertising the new system and held a successful press conference for the London opening. Hill's son, and wife Cruella, were collecting teaching salaries well above what they had ever dreamed of or deserved. They were both worthless as teachers. Now I was forced to go to Heinemann, hat in hand, to negotiate a division of rights, in a system I thought I already controlled. Not good! If this big international publisher was willing to screw poor old James Hill, what wouldn't they be willing to do to a twenty-six year old brash young American promoter. My only leverage was Hill's naive assertion that Heinemann had misrepresented to him, the meaning of the small print in the contract he never understood. Legally speaking I had epis.

My first meeting with the top executives at Heinemann took place at their impressive offices, at the close of the business day on a Friday. Just me and two of my counterparts. An informal get together to try and find mutual ground for negotiation. Heinemann's Managing Director and his personal assist-

Black Tuna Diaries

ant! The very Personal Assistant was a twenty something stunning redhead. They seated me in a low overstuffed easy chair in the Director's office, and served me whiskey after whiskey, with the statement, "week's over, time to relax". The entire meeting had been planned to get me lushed and pump me for my plans to develop Tee-Line. It almost worked. They got me swoozeled. But instead of waxing loquacious, I shut up, got up, and got out of there. I was learning the ground rules. They may have deliberately sounded like a bunch of poofs, but Heinemann's-Directors were playing serious hardball.

What followed was several weeks of meetings between our overprice publishing lawyers and Heinemann's overpriced publishing lawyers. These meetings were attended by at least three Directors of Heinemann, me, John Drage Andrew, Victor and Hill who dragged his wife along in an act of masochism. Heinemann, was now courting Hill like he was a new bride. At the same time they were whispering in Mrs. Hill's ear that I was nothing but a phony "Yank" who was out to rob poor James of his invention. This was coming from the people who robbed him of all of his copyrights, while I was paying the Hill family more money every month, then they had ever made in a year. And many times what Heinemann had paid James in total for the worldwide copyrights.

After six weeks of long meetings and very tough negotiations, we all finally agreed on how we would divide the rights and profits from what would be essentially my efforts to promote and develop Tee-Line. My partners Andrew and Victor had attended the last few meetings to help hammer out the final agreement. Final terms were agreed late in the afternoon on a Thursday, at the offices of our solicitors. We all agreed to meet the following day to vet the contracts that were to be dictated and typed overnight.

At 10am we met again and went over the long and complicated contracts.. A few changes, a few corrections, and it only remained to type a final set for signature by all parties. We broke for lunch agreeing to meet for a final reading and signing at 2 pm. Nothing I had ever done in business had been anywhere as difficult as wringing this deal from Heinemann,

Black Tuna Diaries

and at the same time from the now over confident and demanding Hill family. The six of us, Mr. and Mrs. Hill, Victor Blank, Andrew Greystoke, John Drage, and me, had a victory lunch at a nearby expensive restaurant, while the gaggle of lawyers ate in the office so they could supervise the final production of our agreement.

At 2 pm we reconvened at the large conference table in the offices of our attorneys. For some reason, instead of relief at reaching a difficult deal, there was a great deal of tension in the room. We began the reading and vetting of the final contract. Heinemann's Managing Director and his team were wearing poker faces that seemed to be hiding something. James Hill, had a sad and guilty look, and Cruella Hill had the usual mad at the world expression on her face. I think everyone in the room knew something was wrong. The pages of our agreement arrived from the typing pool, three or four at a time. Every paragraph had to carefully read and then initialed by all parties. By 4pm. we were maybe half finished. That's when Mrs. MC Nasty grabbed her husband by the collar, pulled him up out of his chair and announced in her almost incomprehensible midlands accent;

"Its tea time. I want a proper "cuppa". James and I are going out for our tea."

It was instantly and chillingly clear to me that the Hills would not be returning to the table. The deal was over! Had it been tea she really wanted, they would never have left the conference room. Every London firm had a "tea lady", either on staff, or in the building, who would have appeared at about this time with freshly brewed tea, biscuits (cookies), scones, or tea cakes. We waited almost an hour, making small talk, having our own tea, and pretending or in my case, hoping that the Hills would return. At five o'clock Victor, Andrew, and John Drage went in search of James and Cruella. A check of every restaurant and tea shop in the area proved futile. The Hills were gone! Probably back to Nottingham, to hide out in Sherwood Forrest.

Black Tuna Diaries

Two days later James Hill, unbeknown to his spouse, sneaked back to London, apologized, and privately told me the whole story. Heinemann had secretly met several times with the Hills to torpedo the deal so that they could retain world rights to Tee-Line. They convinced Mrs. Hill that I was out to steal the system from them. Heinemann being a worldwide publishing house, could do a much better job promoting the system, all the Hills had to do was to "dump the Yank" and Heinemann would take good care of them. Hill was ashamed of himself for backing out on a deal after he had given his word. He claimed it was pressure from his wife and worthless son that had forced him to act dishonorably. Even more dishonorable of course, were Heinemann's Directors who had orchestrated a very expensive farce and had never for a second negotiated in good faith. They had not only stolen the world rights to Tee-Line for £50 and a handful of lies to poor old James, they had shown me that at the ripe old age of twenty-six, I was very much still wet behind the ears.

I don't remember exactly what they had promised to do for the Hill family in return for "dumping the Yank", but what they delivered was NOTHING. .EPIS..UNGOTZ NADA..EMPTY BOX.!

I severed all ties with the Hills. Folded the Tee-Line school, took thousands of pounds in loses and had to tell our New York publishers that I couldn't deliver the rights to the system for the U.S.. After a year of hard work by me, my directors, and my team at Rothschilde's, to be called a Yankee thief and see all our efforts go down the drain, took the heart out of me. My only satisfaction came a few months later. James, I regret to say suffered a heart attack and died. His son and widow tried over and over again to meet with me and offer me whatever rights in Tee-Line they mistakenly believed that they owned, and on any terms I wanted to offer them. Each time I was given a message requesting a meeting with the widow Hill, it gave me immense satisfaction tearing it into small pieces or burning it in the big ashtray on my desk. Was I biting off my nose to spite my face? Nope ! Heinemann owned Tee-Line. Lock, stock and barrel! Without James to testify that he had been cheated by Heinemann, there was naught could be

Black Tuna Diaries

done. Heinemann never had any intention of investing in the new system. In a rare moment of candor, one of their Directors told me in confidence that they wanted to own the rights in the event that the system "somehow caught on".

The only good thing to result from my efforts, was that several inner city New York schools continued to teach Tee-Line with great success, using the temporary text books I had originally authorized. My decision to resign my position at Dynamic Reading and return to the states wasn't motivated by any one single factor. My time in England took place during the Harold Wilson government. The economy was a disaster. Young well educated people were leaving in droves. The "Brain Drain"! Taxes and currency restrictions made expanding a business almost impossible. Strikes were a daily occurrence and the "Irish Troubles" were just ramping up in Belfast. Our manager in Germany, the Baron Von Putlich, had single handedly wrecked our German company, by firing the entire staff, including his fiancé, who had gotten him the job in the first place. This nut job believed all the jobs would be done better if he did them all himself. That included the teacher's, receptionist, secretary, and janitor's jobs. In addition, we had taken on the promotion of a new programmed system for teaching languages. The Spanish government was going to use it to teach their grammar school teachers, to teach English as a second language. Then, they delayed the start of the program for a year. Now I had nothing new to hold my interest. Lastly, a personal matter in the states tipped the scales and as usual, it involved Lynne.. I resigned, gave up my stock, threw one hell of a going away party, and bid my sweet Jewitch farewell, before I got on the brand new QE-2, and sailed to New York with only a few thousand bucks to show for my three and a half year odyssey.

Black Tuna Diaries

Chapter 11
Quick Catch that Colombian!

While waiting for Robby, I ordered breakfast and big pot of coffee. Next, I phoned Gene in Miami, to let him know we needed a plane to pick us up and bring us back to Miami before the day was over. It was now Monday morning. We had to have our boats in position at "Hole in the Wall", off the southern tip of Great Abaco, by Friday or Saturday night at the latest. The trawler loaded with thirty thousand pounds marijuana, had already been at sea for a month. They were low on fuel, water, and food. It was highly unlikely they would hang around in the well patrolled waters off Great Abaco, while we organized and dispatched a couple of off-load boats. Oh! Did I mention that after two weeks on the cold Atlantic Ocean, without warm clothing or cabin heat, all twelve Colombians on board were severely ill with flue and several may have developed pneumonia?

Robby, being smarter and much more, realistic than me, declared immediately, that the Senator and the Natures Way couldn't possibly make it back to the Bahamas in time to rendezvous with the trawler. The Colombian trawler could only make ten or eleven knots, but she had been steaming south since Sunday night. Our boats would be back in the Atlantic City Marina by Monday night. Realistically, they wouldn't be able to leave for the Bahamas until Tuesday morning. I might be able too reach them by radio, but giving them new instructions over the public airwaves didn't seem a swift notion. Nevertheless, I stubbornly wanted to try and race our boats down the coast and have them in Bahamian waters by the end of the week.

"Are you frakking nuts", Robby declared, with great disgust. "The Senator is slower then the damn trawler, and Natures Way, will have to come into port at least twice for fuel just to make it to Florida. That trawler will dump her bales in the ocean and be halfway to Santa Marta before either of our boats reaches Hole in the Wall." I knew he was right, but giv-

Black Tuna Diaries

ing in gracefully isn't one of my great virtues. That assumes of course, that I have any great virtues!

I looked down at the cold remains of my Eggs Benedict, thought about it for a second. Then I stood up to make my pitch.

"Look man. You're probably right, but it's worth a try! If it looks like they won't make it, they can dock at the nearest marina and Gene can pick them up in one of Bernie Little's Lear Jets. In the meantime, we have Mark Phillips prepare our two fast Sportsfisherman, Miss Dorothy and the Fishing Fool, just in case."

We both knew my idea sucked, but Robby took the path of least resistance. He shrugged and went along.

I phoned Archie and told him to cancel all arrangements. I also asked him if he would please go to the Tuna Club and tell Chip to pack up the bogus film equipment and come to the hotel. Robby used the other phone in the suite to call Mark at Stryker, and tell him we needed our other two boats ready to go, no later than Friday morning.

Robby put down the phone and gave me the bad news. Mark says that "Fishing Fool" is in dry dock being remodeled. No way can she be the water by Friday! "Miss Dorothy" is also in dry dock having her front deck laminated back onto the hull and a new bow rail put on. He thinks she might be ready by the end of the week. In the meantime he'll try to line up two other boats, just in case! If two more boats were needed, it would take most of our remaining cash, to buy and outfit them. We didn't like the idea, but at that time we were still stupid enough to trust Mark's family to repay us for the boats after they were sold, so we foolishly agreed to let Mark line up two more boats. When Chip arrived, Robby gave him a bunch of bucks with instructions to return the rented movie equipment to the company in Philadelphia. After that, he was to boogie with his "Army", back to Miami, to set up the off-load stash houses. With no new locations, we would have to try to use San Marino and the doctor's house again. Oh boy! Not a great

Black Tuna Diaries

idea! That was precisely what we wanted to avoid, when we moved our operation to Atlantic City.

Lastly, we had to notify our customers to pickup their empty trucks, vans, and campers, and get them headed for Miami.

I packed my stuff, checked out of the hotel, and with Robby, drove to the Atlantic City Marina.

Nature's Way was backing into her slip, as we got out of the car. We were alone with an exhausted Captain Randy on the fly bridge as he related the events of the night before.

Using radar, he was able to trail a few miles behind Captain Elm on the Senator. They both had the Colombian trawler on their radar screens. When the Senator was within five miles of the rendezvous, the trawler executed his "S" turn for recognition. Instead of following suit? Elm turned the Senator around and steamed for home. Randy heard the Colombian trying to talk to the Senator on the radio. But Elm refused to answer. Randy, who was only along as a backup, in the event the Senator broke down, headed full tilt for the trawler. The trawler captain must have figured it was a trap and Nature's Way, a patrol boat. He turned south and steamed away, refusing to even acknowledge Randy's radio hail of our prearranged call sign, "Pescados Grande". When Randy caught up to the fleeing yacht, Elm told him via loud hailer, that he believed the Colombian trawler to be a disguised Coast Guard cutter laying a trap. Robby and I looked at each other with the same thought. Elm and Barry the stoner must gone paranoid on blow and pills, and then convinced each other they were walking into a trap.

Barry, a close pal of our partner Gene, should never have been aboard. Despite Gene's assurances that Barry could be trusted to stay off the blow and Ludes, I should have known better. Barry was a likable guy. The fact that he was constantly stoned didn't seem to affect his ability to function physically, but we later learned much to our detriment, that once under stress, Barry become totally paranoid. He coped by shutting down and going to sleep. This almost cost several

Black Tuna Diaries

people their lives when Gene insisted Barry sail on the "Presidential" several months later. As a member of our fishing team, The Fishing Fools, Barry was invaluable, he would hot wire and bill an angry Marlin in mid, leap, and flip him into the boat before the fish ever realized he was no longer in the water. But on a mission, he was a serious liability. Yet Gene insisted he be included, despite the misgivings expressed by Robby and I. In the back of my mind, I always believed that Gene didn't completely trust Robby and I. So he planted Barry The Stoner as his personal spy.

We were running low on cash, just managing to scrape up $5,000.00 in expense money for Randy and Elm for their dash back down the coast. It made no sense to wait for the Senator to arrive back in AC. It would have led to a confrontation with Barry and Elm that was better avoided for the nonce. We left instructions with Randy that both boat crews were to get a night's rest and be on their way south by first light on Tuesday. The object was to reach Bahamian waters by early Friday. If, for any reason they weren't going to make it in time, they were to dock at the nearest marina and call for Gene to fly them back to Miami, where another boat would be ready and waiting to make the run for Hole in The Wall. Both Captains were to phone from fuel stops or via the marine operator on VHF radio, twice each day to report their progress or receive a change in plans.

It was almost 6pm when we pulled up to the general aviation terminal at Bader Field. The two tone brown Lear 24 belonging to Bernie Little's charter service was already on the parking ramp. We unloaded our bags from the car trunk and Robby returned the car to the little Hertz substation at the terminal. By nine we were both back home in Miami.

The next morning, not without difficulty, I woke Robby at seven, and we headed up to Lauderdale. Mark Phillips was waiting for us at the Striker boatyard. As he had warned, The Fishing Fool, was striped to the bare hull, and would, never be ready to go by the end of the week. Miss Dorothy, the 53ft Hatteras Yachtfisherman, was a different story. Her fore deck had been relaminated to the hull. All she needed was a bit of

Black Tuna Diaries

paint to cover the repair, and a new bow rail. It was Tuesday morning. We told Mark the Miss Dorothy had to be ready to leave the yard for sea trials and provisioning by the next afternoon. Mark, in turn, told us he needed $20,000.00 toward the yard bill for labor and parts for Dorothy and the Fishing Fool.

Now, Mark and his dad Herb Phillips had wonderful, according to them, news. The Big Glo II, the nicest and fastest 44ft Striker on the water, was for sale. With her Mercedes Benz. diesels, she could outrun every boat in the Striker fleet. The owners wanted a quick sale. If we would lend them another $200,000.00, Striker would buy the boat, we would use her for one mission, and Striker would sell the boat and repay our $200,000.00.

If you've been keeping score of where our money went, you know that this would make two 44ft Strikers, one 54ft Striker, a 53ft Hatteras, a 42 ft Rybovitch, and the 1110 ft Senator, that the Phillips family had bought with our money, but unbeknown to us had immediately mortgaged to their bank. No way would we ever be repaid when the boats were sold! However, at that time we were still stupid and trusting. We ok'd the deal. At least the Big Glo II wouldn't need new electronics before she could sail on a mission. Her last owners had rigged her to the max.

Wednesday was auction day, at South Florida Auto Auction. I was up on the auction block auctioning off the cars in English and broken Spanish. The two high priced auctioneers who worked for us refused to try and auction in Spanish, despite the fact that most of the Miami car dealers were Cuban. Hour for hour, I could outsell both of those overpaid bigoted rednecks. Robby's job was to circulate among the dealers and try to convince them to sell their cars for a reasonable bid. That morning Randy called from North Carolina. One transmission had burned out a disc. It could never be repaired in time, so he was going to leave the Nature's Way with Striker's North Carolina dealer, George Purvis. Gene was already in the air, on his way to scoop up the crew and bring them back to Miami.

Black Tuna Diaries

At six am on Thursday morning Captain Elm phoned me from a marina on the coast of Georgia. One of his little six cylinder GM diesels had thrown a rod. His race was over. By ten am one of Bernie Little's jets had picked up Elm with his crew and deposited them in, Ft Lauderdale. They went directly to Striker's yard, where they boarded Miss Dorothy and steamed out for a sea trial. Our bill for the three Lear charters would be over $15,000.00 bucks. Gene, whose aviation company, Land Air, was a tenant at Bernie Little's charter building in the Tampa-St Pete airport, had arranged a "deadhead" charter rate. We could travel out and back to almost anywhere in North America for $5,000.00. Even back then, that was about half the normal charter rate for a Lear Jet.

As a last resort backup, Captain Tico agreed to take the 42" Rybovitch, Pacifier and pick up a load, if needed. We figured Pacifier could only carry seven or eight thousand pounds, but on short notice, it was better than nothing. She was still tied up behind Howard's house in North Miami. Unfortunately, an hour later, when Tico went to move the Pacifier to our docks at the Fontainebleau Hotel for provisioning, her engines refused to start. A few days later, the Cummins people informed us, that contaminated fuel, bought in the Bahamas, had created an algae farm in the fuel tanks, fuel lines, fuel pumps, and injectors.

Fortunately, by Thursday night, Miss Dorothy and The Big Glo II were fueled, provisioned, sea trialled, and ready to go. To maintain some semblance of security, both boats were moved to the private docks at the Fontainebleau. The crews were told to remain on board. No phone calls or outside communication of any sort! Robby and I brought them pizza and spaghetti from Sonny's on Miami Beach. After flying in and having to sea trial and provision the boats in a rush, the guys were ready to crash by nine o'clock. I slept; at the hotel to make sure both boats were on their way by six am.

This time they would steam directly for Hole in The Wall on Great Abaco. Only stopping briefly at Chub Cay to top their fuel tanks, before picking up their load and making a non-stop run for home. Assuming they met the trawler by 10pm Friday

Black Tuna Diaries

night, they could be loaded and on their way back before dawn on Saturday. If they ran hard, Miss Dorothy would steam through Government Cut headed for San Marino, and the Glo would dance through Haulover Cut, enroute to the doctor's house in North Miami at around five pm, alongside five or six hundred other south Florida boaters heading for the barn.

Robby and I worked at the auction most of Friday, trying to catch up on business after spending a wasted week in New Jersey. It was our wives that kept the place running when we were off on "other business". I spent Friday night at home with Lynne, my son and Charlie the Great Dane. Lynne made Orange Chicken with Rice Pilaf and asparagus. I was exhausted and fell asleep on the couch cuddled up with Lynne and my son, and Charlie's big head on top of the three of us. Next thing I knew, it was 5am and the phone was ringing. Raul in Colombia! Not happy!

"What happened? I thought you send two boats to fish with my boat. Only one of your boats show up, and now my boat has to dump half the fish, before she come home"

Oh crap! Some thing went wrong. "Listen, Raul! Two boats left here yesterday at the same time. One must have broken down. I won't know what happened until they get back tonight. I'll call you after ten tonight. It's too late to send another boat, even if I had one, which I don't! That's all I can do."

There was no sense waking Robby and I couldn't go back to sleep. So I made myself coffee, heated a bagel, and left a note for Lynne, that I would be back in a few hours and the three of us would have lunch together in the Grove.

With no traffic on 1-95 North, I made it to Lauderdale from Miami in twenty minutes. I had decided to annoy Gene and Captain Crunch, who were supposed to be monitoring the marine radios, in Captain Crunch's communications van. Gene loved hanging out with Crunch, shoveling blow, up his nose, and listening for radio traffic. The van was equipped to monitor marine, aviation, police, Coast Guard, DEA, Customs, Bahamian, Colombian, and extraterrestrial radio traffic.

Black Tuna Diaries

When I got to Lauderdale, I picked up a big bag of Dunkin Donuts and a thermos of hot coffee. I used our secret knock to gain entrance to Crunch's secret mobile communication center.

"Jesus, open a window or turn on a fan, it smells like a fart factory in there." The communication van, was actually a small R.V. about the size of a step van. In addition to Gene and Crunch, I found Chip inside messing with the radios. Pizza boxes, empty Pepsi cans, and a mirror with a razor blade decorated the small counter top by the tiny sink. In addition to overpowering miasma of van full of man-farts, Chip, who was not enamored of bathing or deodorants, exuded his own unique swamp gas. The van was parked on the parking lot of a bankrupt marina. With no one nearby, I was able to leave the door open for a little air exchange. I handed in the coffee and donuts and seated myself by the doorway. As they ate, I filled them in on my early morning call from Colombia. They had heard nothing from Elm or Randy. We didn't even know which boat was coming home loaded and which was returning empty, or was broke down somewhere in the Bahamas. Crunch told me that there was no radio traffic from any law enforcement or the Coast Guard that would indicate a drug bust or surveillance. There should be no problem sailing in through Haulover Cut at five o'clock along with a couple of thousand weekend boaters. I talked, it over with Gene and Chip. We agreed that whichever boat had "caught fish", should come in through Haulover and dock at the doctor's North Miami house. The San Marino house had been deserted for weeks. Any sudden activity on the quiet private island could attract the attention of the neighbors, especially the appearance of a strange yacht. The North Miami house was in a busy area and our comings and goings were less likely to be noticed. Best of all, the dock was very close to the back patio, making unloading easier and faster. This time, we could use the crews from both boats to unload the loaded boat. One or two nights should see the job done. Chip and his Army,' could remove the bales during the day, in vans marked, "Plumbing Repair" and "Electrical Contractor". We'd be done and out in forty-eight hours.

Black Tuna Diaries

Precisely at 9am. as planned, Randy's voice broke radio silence on the old shortwave set we used for long range talk.

"Shrimp boat "Kishmere" calling the "Little Tochas". Over! I've caught my limit and am homeward bound. Over!"

Crunch answered and told him to take his shrimp to pier two to unload. Randy would understand that meant the North Miami house. A minute later, Capt. Elm called in.

"Shrimp boat "N-Tokas" to Little Tochas. Over! I fished all night but never located the shrimp. Over!" Crunch told him to take his boat back to the boatyard.

The rest of the plan was simple. Chip would put the magnetic "Electrician" signs on the van and wait for Randy to dock at pier two, the North Miami location. Gene and Crunch would continue to toot, fart and monitor the radios until both yachts were safely docked. Then, Gene would pick up his guys from Miss Dorothy and take them to help with the unloading. That way, not only would we get unloaded much faster, but both boat crews would have a chance to earn a nice hunk of green for unloading. That would help makeup for the wasted fortnight on the New Jersey mission and the week spent on the race south to catch the Colombian trawler. Even Captain Elm and stoned out Barry, would be paid big bucks for totting bales. Like any other business, everyone has to be paid. It's only the bosses who must settle for whatever, if anything, is leftover. Or has to take the loss! If the rewards are potentially greater, so are the risks and expenses.

I stopped at Robby's house on the way home. I had to wake him up and wait until he made a pot of coffee before I could fill him in on my busy morning. He agreed with the plans. We arranged to meet at the North Miami house to check the load and find out why Elm came up empty again.

I drove home to pick up Lynne and my son. We spent the afternoon lunching and shopping in Coconut Grove. We stopped at "Shorty's" near the U of Miami, where Lynne and I had both

© 2009 R. Platshorn

Black Tuna Diaries

gone to school, and picked up the best ribs in south Florida. I once know a chef that worked at Shorty's for over a year, just for one opportunity to steal Shorty's secret recipe for BBQ sauce. It's that good!

By six thirty, Robby and I were standing on the dock in North Miami to catch the lines as Randy backed the Big Glo into her slip. Randy had no idea why Elm hadn't picked up his load. Randy estimated, correctly as it turned out, that he had about 16,000 aboard. The Glo had preformed flawlessly. He had kept track of the Hatteras on radar and was sure Elm hadn't broken down. He watched him approach the trawler and then leave and head home. I counted the bales while Robby checked several for quality and condition. It was even better than we had been promised. Now, I felt even worse about half the shipment being dumped in the open ocean.

Convinced that Elm had simply "chickened out", maybe for the second time, I thought it best not to confront him until I had more information. I would speak to Raul again later that night. I knew that Gene would question his biker crew in private, to find out what he could.

Gene arrived with the crew from Miss Dorothy, just as Robby and I were leaving. As soon as the neighbors were asleep, he would use both crews to unload the 16,000 lbs of primo weed. With any luck, two nights should see the job done. Chip's Army, a.k.a. the nerd brigade, would start moving the bales out of the house first thing in the morning. We needed to be finished and have the house cleaned up in 72 hrs, so the family could move back in.

We stopped at a pay phone on Biscayne Blvd. I placed a collect call to Colombia from "Dr Serucho". Raul was waiting for my call. He had spoken via short wave radio to the trawler. According to the captain, Randy led him to believe that only one boat was coming to "fish". When a second boat pulled along side, the Colombian crew, thinking it was a "pirate", ran the newcomer off with drawn guns.

Black Tuna Diaries

Because it was difficult to speak openly on the radio or over the phone, there was an awful lot of conjecture and unanswered questions. We would learn more after Gene had spoken to both crews and we met with Randy and Elm at Striker's boatyard the next afternoon.

Sunday Morning my son and I watched cartoons while Lynne laid out the lox, smoked white fish and bagels from Marshal Major's in Coral Gables. Robby showed up in time to eat Sunday brunch with us. Afterwards, we took his car and headed for Striker's yard in Ft Lauderdale.

The watchman let us in and told us that Captain Randy and some others had already arrived. Gene was standing on the dock in front of the Hatteras. The three of us took a walk around the boatyard to talk privately, before joining Elm and Randy. We needed to get things right because this meeting would determine who was to be paid and how much. During the course of the night and the morning, Gene had spoken to all six Outlaws and his pal Barry.

"Listen Baron", which is what he had been calling me ever since our trip to Barranquilla Colombia, "I spoke to both crews. My guys on the Glo said everything went smoothly. The Colombians came on board and did most of the work stowing the bales as they come off the trawler. Then Randy gave them the boxes of food and warm clothes from New Jersey. That was it! They pulled away and headed home. My guys on Miss Dorothy said they pulled alongside the trawler ten minutes after the Big Glo pulled away. All they know is the Colombian crew had guns and refused to off load the grass. Then they left! Elm chased them for a little while, but they refused to stop. No one is very happy about the possibility of missing a payday over something that wasn't their fault."

The three of us agreed that we would pay both crews. That meant that we would be paying double for transport and handling. There wasn't going to be a hell of a lot leftover for us after everything was paid for. It was still to be determined if we would have to pay our Colombian partners, for all or part of the 30,000 lbs that was onboard when the ship left South

Black Tuna Diaries

America. I told Gene what Raul told me the night before. Then we went aboard Miss Dorothy to meet with Randy and Elm.

The Hattie had a full bar with an electronic soda dispenser in the main salon. Elm was tending bar, pouring cokes for me, Robby and Gene. I repeated what I had told Gene. Randy recounted all the events of his rendezvous the trawler. He insisted he hadn't said anything that would give the trawler captain the impression that only one boat was to be loaded. He admitted that there had been some language difficulties, but didn't think that had caused the problem. He went on about how happy the Colombians were happy to get the food, medicine, and even the warm clothes that they no longer needed. Everything was fine when the Glo pulled away.

Captain Elm was visibly uncomfortable, but trying not to show it. He had tried twice to bring in a load, and came up empty. He was in desperate need of money. His yacht delivery business was on the rocks. He was living in his office at Pier 66 and was facing eviction for non payment of three months rent. He may also have been afraid, that Gene was going to take him for a "boat ride". One way! His story was no different than his crew's. He pulled alongside the trawler to be met by an armed crew that ordered him to leave. He said that he kept repeating the call sign "Pescados Grande" and anything else he could think of to convince the trawler captain that he was supposed to pick up half the load. Instead of passing down mooring lines, to the crew of Miss Dorothy, the Colombian captain started his engine, upped anchor, and boogied. Elm and his crew, had no choice, but to steam home empty.

One thing was clear, this time at least, it wasn't the fault of Elm or his crew, that they came away with nothing to show for their efforts. On the other hand, I was still in the dark and skeptical about what had happened off the coast of New Jersey. According to the captain of the trawler, the yacht Senator had simply turned tail and run. I was fairly sure that Elm and his paranoid first mate, Barry were probably coked up and that they had convinced each other it was a trap.

Black Tuna Diaries

Elm was very uncomfortable telling the story. He and Barry were together in the pilothouse for almost the entire trip. The weather was gray and windy. Six to eight foot seas, with patches of light fog. According to Elm, after using the yacht's long distance radar to locate what they believed to be the trawler, Elm began broadcasting the call sign and executing "S" turns to identify himself. The radar blip he believed was the Colombian, kept traveling toward him without "S" turns or radio contact. When they were less than five miles apart, unable to visually identify the trawler because of the patches of fog. They were convinced it was a trap. Elm maintained he was on the agreed radio frequency and using the correct call sign, but got no response. Convinced that the boat headed straight for them, couldn't possibly be the trawler, Elm and Barry decided to get out of Dodge as fast those GM diesels could move them.

"Was Barry stoned?" I felt I was asking the obvious, but Elm just looked at me and shrugged.

"How about you? Were you filling your nose with Barry's coke?"

I was pissed off! Letting my emotions dull my brain. All the frustration of having a carefully planned operation go off the tracks was coming out. All those weeks of work, the hundreds of thousand of dollars, all down the drain. Now; I made the mistake that almost got me beaten to a pulp.

"Or did you guys just chicken out and run?" Next thing I knew, I was laying on the deck and Gene, Robby, and Randy were trying without too much success to hold on to Elm long enough for me to get off the boat. I made it to the dock. A minute later, Robby came out.

"Are you crazy, calling him a chicken? He could kill you with his bare hands. Besides, we already decided to pay him and Barry. Why on earth would you want to antagonize someone who knows that much about our business? Now, if you have any brains at all, you'll give Gene a few minutes to get him

Black Tuna Diaries

calmed down, and then you will go in and apologize. Say it was a mental breakdown from the strain of the past few weeks."

I knew Robby was right. Calling Elm a coward or blaming it on the coke, would accomplish nothing. I didn't need to make enemies. I liked Elm and might want to call on his services in the future. I took a deep breath, went back on board, and hesitantly reentered the salon. Before I could begin the speech I had been mentally rehearsing, Elm stuck out his huge paw,

"I'm sorry I took a swing at you. No one ever called me a chicken before. I guess I lost it."

I don't really remember what kind of a bullshit pitch I laid on him, but a few minutes later we were hugging like long lost brothers. It just may have had something to do with the thirty-five grand "default pay" that Robby paid him on the spot. It was a great deal less than he expected to earn, had he successfully brought home the Senator loaded with herb, but it was a hell of a lot more than he was expecting under the circumstances. Probably more than he had ever earned at one time.

Captain Randy was to come to my house for dinner and to collect his money. Gene would take care of payroll for Barry and the two crews. Robby and I would take care of Chip and his hippie/nerd army, when they reported back to work as security guards at our South Florida Auto Auction. It was to be weeks before we were able to figure out if we had made or lost money on the 16,000 lbs of primo now sitting in the doctor's living room.

Black Tuna Diaries

Chapter 12
Death in the Bullring

Everyone knows that a black cat has nine lives, but a Black Tuna only seven. Here is the true story of how I lost my second life in the Bull Ring in Málaga Spain.

Before I take up the account of my life upon my return to the United States, I need to fill in a few blanks about my years living in London. That is, I got to see a great deal more than just London. I traveled frequently to our schools in Manchester, Birmingham, and Edinburgh. I visited the schools and universities where our teachers conducted courses. Oxford, Cambridge, and the redbrick Universities! On mainland Europe, I opened schools in Amsterdam on the famous canal street, Kloveniersbergval. One end of the street is the University district and the other end is the famous red light district, with its store front bordellos. Amsterdam was my favorite city in Europe. I kept a small flat there and even had an old Renault with a corrugated round roof that I drove around the country when I visited our classes in The Hague or Monikadam or traveled to the remarkable beaches at Zandvort. I tried to spend five days a month on mainland Europe. In Germany I regularly visited our Dynamisches Lessen Gmbh in Cologne located on the central Hannsaring Strassa. I spent a day or two there each month before driving or taking the train to Amsterdam.

But, like most Londoners, what I wanted most whenever I could get away, was sun shine. Gray skies and mist covered London year round, except of course during Wimbledon fortnight! So, each year, just before Easter, Dynamic Reading would shut down for two weeks, and Astrid and I would head for Spain. Sunshine, good food, beaches, and affordable hotels!

Our first holiday destination was Ibiza, in the Balearic Islands. This was 1968, years before Clifford Irving, and his bogus Howard Hughes biography turned that lovely sleepy

Black Tuna Diaries

little island into an international tourist trap. The smallest of the Balearic Islands off the coast of Spain, it is dwarfed by its better know sisters, Majorca and Minorca. With only two towns on the island, San Antonio Abad, a sleepy village with a few new tourist hotels, and Ibiza town, the old port city, Ibiza was still an agricultural community. I recall two examples of how undeveloped the island was back in the 1960's.

One morning I asked the concierge to arrange a fishing trip. I had in mind, a deep sea fishing charter. Astrid and I arrived at the waterfront to find ourselves helping our "Captain" to push his red and green sixteen foot rowboat off the beach, and into the bright blue Mediterranean Sea. Once on the water, I looked around our colorful little craft to see what type of fishing rods we'd be using. No rods! In an old bucket, were a dozen homemade hand lines. Each with six tiny hooks and a crude lead weight. After paying him the grand sum of sixty bucks, we were to have the privilege of assisting our captain to catch his daily quota of Sardines. After five hours in the hot sun, I had managed to hook two small sardines, using maybe ten sardines for bait. Astrid caught one sardine and a wicked sunburn.

I am not a beach person. I cannot sit still for very long. I need to be doing something. So when we heard there was going to be horse races as part of approaching Easter celebration, we dressed as we would for a day at Ascot and asked directions to the "race track". The race track turned out to be the crumbling remnants of an old Roman arena. All that was left of it was a small section of the original stands and an ancient half mile race track. The only remarkable feature of the track was a huge boulder, maybe eight feet long and four feet high, that sat in the center of the opposite side of the track. Most the attendees were local farmers and shopkeepers, out for a day of local competitions. These were to be cart races. Local farm horses pulling an assortment of small carts that ranged from homemade sulkies, to two wheeled farm carts with old car tires. Betting slips were issued in five peso denominations, equal to only a few pennies back in those days. I think I had two hundred tickets on the "feature race". The farmers were to race for four miles. Eight times around the small oval. The

Black Tuna Diaries

crowd of perhaps two thousand people, who had themselves arrived mostly by horseback or horse and buggy, were by this time well into their wine skins. The entire audience was buzzing with excitement as a dozen assorted carts lined up at a line drawn in the dirt.

There was nothing remarkable about the appearance of the cart or driver we had backed. The driver was of average height, thirtyish, dark hair and eyes. The cart was a two wheeled, car tired, flat bed vegetable wagon, about four by four. Clearly homemade, with traces made from a pair of saplings. Astrid being my Jewitch, could divine winners, and had picked this one assuring me it was a sure thing. With our two hundred betting tickets in hand, we were prepared to shout and cheer with the best of the noisy, wine besotted Ibethinkos.

With an ancient pistola, the town's Alcalde let loose the melee. Standing up, hollering to their horses and using an assortment of homemade whips, the drivers broke ranks in a blaze of dust. By the first turn our driver was well ahead. When, for the third time, he reached the boulder opposite the stands, he bad lapped the field. That's when he stopped , dismounted, and stepped behind the boulder to take a leak. He seemed in no hurry! By the time he as done and remounted, the competition was passing him by. Much to our consternation, he waited courteously till all the others had gone by, before rejoining the melee. Once out on the track, he took off like his horse had a passing gear. Smiling and waving to his screaming fans, he regained the lead by the sixth lap and was again ahead half a mile. And again he stopped by the rock, dismounted and stepped behind the boulder to relieve himself. And again the entire field went by before he climbed aboard and gave chase. With less than three-quarters of a mile to go he leisurely began passing the others , one by one, waving and tipping his cap as he went by. At the top of the home stretch, with three more carts to pass, he was already standing up to wave and bow to the crowd. He easily passed the last competitor just a few feet from the finish line. Somewhere I've got a picture of the winning cart parked beside the big boulder and our driver-'s head just visible above the rock. I think our two hundred winning tickets gave us a profit of eight bucks.

Black Tuna Diaries

Visiting Spain right before Easter has many advantages. The tourists, for the most part hadn't arrived yet. Waiters and shopkeepers have the time and inclination to be attentive and polite.. This is the time of year that the Monasteries and ancient Cathedrals hold Easter processions, often by torchlight late into the night. It is also an occasion for special bull fights. When even the smallest towns, will spend the money to bring in the best bulls and bull fighters for the Easter corrida. Ibiza was no exception.

This is where I saw my first bull fight. It was the concierge at our hotel who came to us and asked if we wanted tickets for the Easter corrida. He explained that we would get to see the famous red fighting bulls from the mainland at this special corrida. The featured matador who's name escapes me, was as famous as a pop star. Instead of a second matador, the corrida would feature, Los Hermanos Peralta. Two members of the famous family who for generations were know for their ability to perform the entire bullfight from the back of a charging Paso fino stallion. A very special kind of bullfight called, a " Jinete". Horses have a natural intense fear of bulls. The Peraltas fight from the backs of magnificently trained stallions, using only leg commands. Passing only inches from the charging bull they place the bandilarilles, use the cape, and finish with the traditional sword stroke. I might add, that if challenged, they fight equally well dismounted. My introduction to bullfighting couldn't have been more perfect. It was easy to understand how Hemingway became enamored with the pomp, and ceremony of the corrida. From the soulful wail of the first trumpet marking the beginning of the parade into the ring, to final dispatching of the last bull, it's a catharsis of human emotions.

The featured matador, barely five feet tall in his high-heeled pumps, strutted around the ring like a bantam rooster. Utterly fearless! Facing the monstrous red bulls, whose head and horns stood taller than him. Forcing the bull to lower his head to the cape, and then turning his back on the enraged animal and doffing his eared cap to the ladies in the stands and throwing them kisses. And the ladies! They screamed like teeny boppers at an Elvis concert and threw hankies, scarves,

Black Tuna Diaries

and panties into the bullring. The tiny torero practically had to make the bull kneel in order to place the final sword for a clean stroke to the heart. He dedicated each of his three bulls to different senorita or senora in the stands. The Peraltas were magnificent. Galloping into the ring! Racing in front of the charging bull as the rider leaned out of his ornate Spanish saddle to place the bandilarilles or wheeling around as the bull charged through the bright pink cape. It was a fabulous corrida.

A few years later, thanks in large part to Clifford Irving's best selling bogus biography of Howard Hughes,a and the criminal prosecution of Irving and his girlfriend, that followed, Ibiza caught the attention of the Jet Set. The cheap fare tourists followed and the charm was gone.

The following year, we took our holidays at one of the many coastal resorts in Andalucía on the mainland of Spain. Again it was the pre-Easter fortnight and the bulk of the European tourists hadn't yet appeared. After a day or two on the beach, I was looking for activity. First choice, fishing. This time I found a real, charter boat that offered shark fishing. It was a small cabin cruiser, with a motley assortment of rods and reels. I asked the captain what else they fished for in that area, and he told us there was nothing else. Sharks were the only sizable fish left on that part of the coast. If indeed there were any sharks, we never saw any sign of them. But, a day on the water ain't all bad, if you're a fisherman. Next I drove our rented Seat, a little box on wheels with a sewing machine engine, up the steep, cloud shrouded "road" barely clinging to the side of a very high mountain, to the ancient town of Rondo. Site of the arena where the Romans introduced bullfighting to Spain. It was a lovely little town and the old arena was still occasionally used for special bullfights. Now, the only thing more frightening than driving up a tall mountain through clouds, on a road with no guardrails, is driving back down the side of the mountain on a narrow road with no guardrails, at dusk through thick clouds. That night after a bath and change of underwear, we drove into town to a small nightclub to see a Flamenco troop. The club was practically empty. The "Troop", was two attractive couples, barely out of their teens and a young gui-

Black Tuna Diaries

tarist. Like most Flamenco dancers , they were "Gitano", gypsies. Surprisingly, they were excellent. It isn't easy to workup the enthusiasm to play and dance the wild Flamenco rhythms for a room full of empty tables. After the first set, Astrid and I slipped out the side door for a smoke and a toke. You have to remember it was 1970, and this was the Spain of the Caudillo Francisco Franco, and the Guardia Seville. The Guardia were the bad dudes with paten leather hats who passed for police. In those days, busting a doobie simply was not done. Except! By the Gitano!

As soon as we lit up, all five of the young Flamenco dancers peeked out the door to sample the pungent night air. A Moment later we were seven kindred souls catching a buzz in a dark alley in a little Spanish town.

An hour later the seven of us were jammed into a tiny car driving up another steep mountain road to a secret nightclub in a cave. A gathering place for Flamenco artists from all corners of Andalucía

Their car, a fairly new gray Renault, although larger than the Seat was not nearly big enough for seven adults. All five of our new friends were still in costume. If you have ever seen Flamenco, you know that heavy sweating is a major result of the performance. So, in a world where dry cleaning is at best an occasional luxury, the noisome miasma of perspiration, grease paint, perfume and smoke, was overpowering the seven of us jammed into a small five seat car.

Forty minutes later, we were seated in a genuinely cavernous nightclub built into the side of a mountain. The room was jammed. Maybe three hundred and fifty people! In the dim light and thick smoke from the heavy Spanish tobacco, it took me a few minutes to realize that most of the patrons were Flamenco dancers, still in costume. It was like New York's Birdland after midnight, where all the great jazz musicians would gather to jam. One troupe after another took the stage. Some were only one couple with a guitarist, others with a dozen dancers with several musicians. Like a battle of the bands, the dancers and the flamenco guitarists would vie for

Black Tuna Diaries

the applause of their peers. After all these years, I will not swear to it, but I'm sure I saw the famous Flamenco guitarist, Sebecas, bring down the house after a ten minute solo. The kids we came with may have been the youngest ones there, but they're routine was one of the most impressive, earning thunderous applause from the gathered Gitano.

It was full daylight by the time we arrived back at the small club in Marbella to pick up our car. Astrid and I were exhausted. I could barely muster the energy to drive the Seat the ten miles back to our hotel. Our new friends had insisted that we go to our hotel, freshen up, and rejoin them for a ferry ride to Algiers to shop for hash. But we were too tired and probably too scared.

Two days later, bored out of my mind, I proposed we rent a couple of horses and explore the villages in the hills surrounding the coast. At home in London, Astrid and I, one or two Sunday mornings each month, would ride on Hyde Park's "Rotten Row", where the Queen would often ride 'with her entourage. Everyone at our hotel thought it an odd request, wanting to rent horses and ride around the countryside. After several inquiries, the woman who fancied herself the social director said she knew a man with horses in nearby Estapona. An hour later after driving to Estapona and back, our social director informed me that her friend would arrive at our hotel, with horses, after the day's siesta.

Promptly at two, he arrived. A seventy year old Don Quixote! Five foot two, skinny with a little pot belly, bowed legs, and a twinkle in his eye. He was dressed in the traditional Spanish riders' garb of tight pants, short brown embroidered jacket, and round wide brimmed hat of heavy black felt. His three prize steeds, Roscinante times three! Spavined, swaybacked, knobby kneed, and sporting big Spanish saddles with huge tin stirrups that clattered and clanked as we rode the mountain paths. Despite my fears that the horses were near collapse, we were soon into foothills of Andalucía.

The first village we rode through, all the children came running out calling our guide by name. "Don Jose, Don Jose. Por

Black Tuna Diaries

Favor, por favor!". Leaving Astrid and I to watch, Don Jose stepped his old warhorse to the center of the cobblestone town square and put on a display of dressage riding as good as any show by the famous Lipizzaner horses. Our ancient mounts had once been parade horses at the main bullring in Málaga. Don Jose and his horses loved to put on a show. Astrid and I soon followed his lead and joined the show, letting our steeds show us the ropes.

Afterwards, we were invited to the villager's houses for snacks and homemade Sangria, a potent double fermented wine with added fruit and sugar. This became the pattern in each little village we visited. Just after six o'clock, we trotted into a small bullring owned by of Don Jose's brother, Don Miguel. Here the elderly former Toreador was training his son and several others in the skills of the bullring. Four or five young men were practicing with the cape. Neither Don Jose, his brother Don Miguel nor anyone else at this rural bullfight academy spoke a word of English. My Spanish, at that time was less than rudimentary. Mostly learned while I lived in Puerto Rico, it was not well understood in Spain. Astrid, spoke little Spanish at the time.

Don Jose introduced us to his brother, who immediately wanted to know if I knew his cousin who lived in Chicago. Lack of language skills is probably the main reason I found myself in the bull ring with cape in my hands and a small child with a sharp pair of horns in his hands, trying to gore me through the cape. Don Miguel had personally put the cape in my hands. The first surprise came when I almost dropped it. The entire bottom seam was lined with thirty pounds of lead weights. This prevents the cape being moved away from your body by the wind. If presented with a choice, El Toro will charge the man, not the cape. The imperative is to block the bull's vision with the cape. You do not move it away from the front of your body until the head of the bull is almost touching the cape.

We stayed the night and the next morning Don Miguel tutored Astrid and I on how to perform the basic passes of the corrida. At first our "bull" was the small speedy little boy hold-

Black Tuna Diaries

ing the sharp horns above his head. His great joy was successfully sticking one us with his horns. Next my new skills were tested against a wide set of horns mounted on a bicycle wheel with handles like a wheelbarrow. It was propelled by a son of Don Miguel, who could run and hook as fast as any bull. After a few hours practice, I could barely lift the lead lined cape to the top of my chest. It felt as if I had been weight lifting for hours without letup. When I went to rest, the old man called Astrid out into the ring and gave her an abbreviated version of what I had just gone through. Although we hadn't planned to stay away from our hotel overnight, it was again too late to head back down the mountain in the dark. We stayed another night and spent the next day again practicing with the heavy cape. I figured, if I ever found myself alone with an enraged bull and I just happened to have a large lead lined cape handy, I could use my skills to keep El Toro at bay while impressing anyone nearby. Years of acting and dance classes helped me to imitate the graceful moves of a real Matador. Something I would soon come to regret!

Before leaving the bullfight school, Don Jose and Don Miguel invited us to a fiesta, a Tentadero! His son and the other students were to show off their skills while testing the courage of this year's crop of fighting bulls. It was a big event and was traditionally held in the famous bull ring in the city of Málaga. Bear in mind all this communicating was in the most basic of broken Spanish. My broken Spanish! For the most part I understood what they were talking about, but not exactly what they were saying. The fiesta sounded like a good way to spend a day.

So, "Si, Mañana, Si fiesta", I said as we mounted up and headed back down to our hotel.

At five am the next morning, Don Jose was knocking at our hotel room door. "Fiesta, El Tentadero. Vaya, Vaya."

I looked at my watch and groaned. Then I tried to tell him that we would meet him at the fiesta in a few hours. He refused to move till I indicated we would dress and come right down.

Black Tuna Diaries

With only a brief stop for a big saucer of strong Spanish coffee, we piled into an antique VW bus that already held everyone we had met at Don Miguel's. Not knowing the proper attire for the occasion, Astrid wore a short skirt, high heels and blouse, and I wore a pair of dark slacks, open collar casual shirt, and a light sport jacket. Too tired to try to figure out what was being said, I just looked out of the window and nodded my head if anyone was speaking to me. Big mistake! Forty minutes later we were in a small chapel under the bullring in Málaga. Don Miguel, his son, and the other Toreros, knelt and offered prayers for the upcoming testing of the bulls. Astrid and I stood respectfully in the rear resisting everyone's imprecations to kneel and pray. It being futile trying to communicate that we were not Catholic and that Jews did not kneel to pray.

After a light breakfast of small meat pies and coffee at a cafe across the Street, the young Toreros headed for the dressing room under the bull ring to put on their costumes. I offered to wait with Astrid near the van, but was pulled along with the others, by Don Miguel. Once in the changing room, I was given a costume that looked like Don Jose's riding outfit. Tight brown embroidered straight legged trousers, an embroidered short jacket, and round brimmed black felt hat, the costume of a novice bull fighter. I figured, Okay! Maybe I'll get to ride one of Don Jose's nags into the bullring.

Never happened! Next thing I know, I've got a cape over my arm and I'm slowly walking into the bullring with the "other" Toreros. I still didn't get it! The music was playing and we were waving at the people in the half full stands of the immense arena. What the hell! Fiesta! When we arrived behind the barrier that kept the bulls out of the stands, Astrid was already there and wearing a wide brimmed hat like mine. There was a parade and show of horsemanship by Don Jose on a Paso fino that didn't look anything like the horses we had ridden. Then began the testing of the younger bulls!

To the delight of the crowds, the Toreros took turns capping the bulls. After each good pass, the band played, the audience clapped, and shouted O lay! O lay! Next, a small slightly

Black Tuna Diaries

knock-kneed bull with oddly askew horns was let into the ring. Several men from the crowd tried their hand with the cape, only to be chased from the ring by the angry little creature. Each time, the audience roared with laughter and booed the cowardly would-be Matador. Then Don Miguel put a cape in Astrid's hand and pointed her out into the ring.

High heels, short skirt, and big round hat! Without hesitation, she strutted out in front of cheering Spaniards. Just like at the little bullfight school; she opened her cape and called to the bull. "Toro"! "Toro"! The bull was confused for a moment. Then Astrid stamped her foot and shook her cape. That did it. The funny looking bull took off running and charged through her open cape. "O lay!" She spun and called again to the now enraged little bull. Again it charged at full tilt into her cape. The audience was on its feet. "O lay, O lay! O lay!" I was frantically trying to capture the action with our crappy little Kodak Instamatic. The Toreros reentered the ring to distract the bull as Astrid strode back to the barrier.

It was time to test a full grown bull to be used in this year's corridas. A huge black leviathan, with very long sharp horns, maybe two and a half feet from tip to tip, and weighing almost a ton, charged out of the dark tunnel angry and blinded momentarily by the sun. Each time he tossed his massive head, snot and saliva would streak his glossy black coat. The Toreros, the real ones, surrounded the bull at a respectful distance. One by one they stepped forward with their capes and called to the bull.

"Toro, aha Toro"

Every time he charged the cape and found nothing but air behind it, he got angrier and angrier, and each time he would shorten his charge, tossing his sharp horns left and right seeking a solid target. Twice he was able to hook the offending cape and toss it into the air. And each time the others would move in with their capes to distract the enraged animal until the unlucky bullfighter could reclaim his cape.

Black Tuna Diaries

Once all the young Matadors had taken a turn capping the bull, they backed up to the barriers and slid behind the safety wall as the featured Matador, Don Miguel's son entered the ring. He was the only one dressed in a full "suite of lights". At just over five feet tall, the bull's horns stood taller than the Matador. At a Tentadero there is no lance wielding Picador to sever the neck muscle of the bull. This would normally keep the bull's head down and lessen the danger of his hooking the Matador or the cape. For five minutes the bull charged true and the crowd cheered as the son of Don Miguel made pass after pass, even kneeling with his back to the bull, before calmly walking all the way across the arena, bowing to the audience and stepping behind the barrier where I was standing.

I was the first to shake his hand and congratulate him. Then he hugged me, handed me his cape and pointed to the bull standing quietly on the far side of the arena, perhaps 50 yards away. Don Jose and Don Miguel joined him in urging me to go out and take my turn capping the sweating, panting, pissed-off, animal. I wanted to demure, to find some excuse to stay safely behind the barrier, but lack of language and testosterone driven idiotic machismo, propelled me into the bullring. I could see the heads of the toreros behind the barriers around the ring, but none stepped out to help. With the heavy cape held high in front of me I ventured twenty feet from the barrier and called the bull; "

"Toro! Toro! Aha Toro!", He just stood there with his sides heaving, but never moved a muscle.

Hating the idea of moving further from the safety of the barrier, I moved another twenty feet towards the center of the arena.

"Toro, Toro, Aha, Toro!. This time he looked across at me, but didn't seem to see me. The longer I stayed in the bullring, the more I wanted to run. So! Okay.. .let's get this over with one way or another. I slowly walked to the center of the ring and then a little further towards El Toro.

Black Tuna Diaries

"Toro!" a little louder, "Toro , Aha Toro!".

This time he heard me and he was coming. Slowly at first, then at a trot. At thirty feet away he stopped to look me over and paw the dusty arena floor. I tried to see which barrier was closest, if I needed to flee for my life. I'm not a fast runner and knew I could never make it ahead of the bull, so I tightened my sphincter and extended the cape, inviting the charge I knew was coming. The massive black bull dropped his head and gathered his back legs to explode towards the bright gold and pink cape in my trembling hands. Wait, I told myself, wait till his head is almost to the cape before smoothly sliding it away to the right.

"O lay" The bull was past and turning back towards me, I spun and again hid my body behind the cape, just as he charged.

"O lay!" I led him to the left this time. Close enough to feel his super heated body pass against my own. My fear forgotten, traded for the cheers of the crowd, I tried a more difficult pass. With the bull's head in my cape, I spun leading him around my body in a full circle, before spinning away and lowering my cape to salute the audience.

"O lay, O lay, O lay, O lay!"

Out of the corner of my eye I could see the angry frustrated creature. He again began pawing the ground as the drying sweat and saliva painted white streaks against his panting inky hide. This time I planned to lead him in circles around my left side. Being right handed, this is more difficult and less natural. Oops! My ego outgrew my brain! As the bull exploded into the cape, my mind went blank. I couldn't figure out how to lead the bull and turn my body at the same time. Turning to the left just wasn't as instinctive as turning to the right. I hesitated for just an instant. That's all it took. The bull was under the cape and hooking his horns to the left. The tips just missed my back, but I could feel his head and then his entire length press hard against my back as he tried to spin back towards my exposed groin and stomach. I spun around trying to keep

Black Tuna Diaries

my back pressed against his body. I was covered with his acrid sweat as the circle of death got tighter and tighter. Then the mad bull broke away from me to his right and I had a split second to raise my cape. I took as deep breath trying to calm my nerves. As my vision cleared from dizzy fear driven red, I saw that all the Toreros had come out into the ring. Don Miguel's son had the bull's attention a few feet from where I stood on shaking legs. It took me a couple of seconds to figure out which way to run. Then I fled to the barrier where Don Miguel and Astrid stood watching.

Someone handed me a wineskin, which I emptied. I can only recall two thoughts as everyone clapped me on the back and congratulated me. The first was, if Astrid didn't get photos of my passes with the bull, I'd strangle her, and my other thought was,

"Torquemada would have climbed out of his grave and reconvened the Spanish Inquisition had he seen Jew and Jewitch being cheered and feted at the Easter celebration in the ancient bull ring in Málaga".

Black Tuna Diaries

Chapter 13
Frank Sinatra, Redd Foxx, and Jimmie the Weasel's Flying Bordello

"**Don't trust my cousin Scratch!**" Big Gene was staying at my house in the Spring Gardens section of Miami, when Scratch invited Robby and I to visit Las Vegas. At Gene's request, we had fronted his cousin Scratch a couple of bales of pot to take home to Vegas and sell. For Scratch, whose main source of income was as a racetrack tout, the sale of a hundred pounds of Colombian, represented a profit of about twenty-five thousand dollars. That's more than he could make at a month at the track. After two trips, he said he wanted to express his thanks, by inviting us to spend a week in Vegas. He had booked us into the best suites at Caesar's Palace as guests of the house. Gene refused to go, and advised Robby and I to do the same.

"I guarantee, my cousin Scratch is up to something. You can go if you really want, but be very, very careful. Scratch wants something." I was ready to take Gene's advice and forgo the trip, when Scratch made us an offer "we couldn't refuse". Like anyone who has ever been a guest in our home, Scratch knew of my wife's obsession with Sinatra and his music.

"By the way, I forgot to mention, Sinatra will do two shows at Caesar's that weekend. You'll have front row seats and I'll introduce Lynne to Frank after the show".

That did it! Lynne had the suitcases out before Scratch finished talking. The absolute joy on her face, made it "an offer I couldn't refuse". Scratch flew home to Vegas to prepare for our visit. Gene, reluctantly arranged a Lear jet to fly us out.

A few days later, the seven of us, Robby, Suzie, and their two daughters, and Lynne, Matt and I, stepped out of the small brown and tan jet on to a red carpet and a waiting Limo. Scratch was laying it on thick! The driver, a smiling, rough voiced ex-prize fighter, greeted us ,

Black Tuna Diaries

"I'm your driver Charlie. I'll be available to drive you any place you'd like to go while you're here. Scratch will meet you at Caesar's after you've had a chance to unpack." Charlie handed us two sets of room keys. " You are already registered. You can go directly to you suites."

He ushered us into the limo and gave us an insider's tour of the town as we made our way to Caesar's. Waiting to greet us as we entered the lobby, was the legendary heavyweight champion of the world, "The Brown Bomber", Joe Louis. While our kids were too young to know who he was, Robby and I were in awe of the giant figure who had always been "THE CHAMP", when we were growing up. To shake his hand, was better than meeting a movie star.

"I'm sorry I couldn't meet you at the airport. I had some business to take care of for Frank". It was Scratch on the phone and the implication was, that he was somehow a part of Sinatra's entourage. This proved to be the case.

"If you're settled in, meet me for drinks in the cocktail lounge next to the casino." Scratch had arranged for a nanny to take care of our kids. Lynne, Suzie, Robby and I trooped down to meet our host, who was waiting by the elevator. Vegas hotels are planned so that no matter where you are going, you have to go through the casino to get there. It was late afternoon, people were having drinks or getting ready for dinner and a show. The tables were half empty. I halted everyone at the first craps table we came to, and did something out of character. I took two grand cash, and dropped it the eleven.. One roll of the dice at seventeen to one, for thirty-four thousand bucks! I enjoy gambling, but only for entertainment. Fifty dollars a night, is my normal limit. If I lose fifty or a hundred bucks, I lose interest and quit. I don't know what prompted the extravagant gesture, but it turned out to be the only bet I made for the entire trip. The croupier slid the dice over to me. I picked them up shook them in my hand, blew on them like in the movies, and rolled em hard across the green felt. They bounce up, hit the dimpled rubber wall at the other end of the table, and landed. One came up a five, and the other a six.

Black Tuna Diaries

" EEE OOH Eleven! Winner eleven! Pay the lucky shooter on eleven" He passed me two stacks of five hundred dollar chips, and the rest in stacks of hundreds. I pulled off my bet, put aside $5,000 to pay for the Lear charter, tipped $100.00 each to the croupiers, and split the rest of the chips with Robby. We each then gave our wives $5,000.00 gambling and shopping money. With our pockets bulging with chips, Scratch led us to our table in the nearby cocktail lounge.

The cocktail waitresses all knew Scratch. They made a big fuss over our party. As soon as drinks and a plate of hot hors d'oeuvre were on the table, Scratch asked the ladies to excuse us for a minute. He led Robby and I to a nearby table where four well dressed, dark-suited guys, wise guys, as it turned out, were waiting to meet us.

"Robby and Bobby, I'd like you to meet some very "nice" people from New York. This is Sal, Tony, Vinnie, and John. This is Robby and Bobby, two good guys from Miami, who are "friends of ours".

Now it all was becoming clear. Gene was on the money! Scratch brought us to Vegas to pimp us to the mob. Robby and I are from South St in South Philadelphia. We were raised around wise guys in the era of Angelo Bruno. That was before Nicky Scarfo invaded the city and turned it to a war zone. Robby turned to me with the slightest of glances to indicate he had the same thought. We both knew that to most "made" guys, liked nothing better than having a couple of Jewish partners who were "big earners". Sal and company were our age, younger generation, wise guys, who wanted to get into the pot business. They ordered drinks, sent another round to our wives, and we talked for a few minutes ritually establishing mutual acquaintances from Philly, New York, and Miami. Then we exchanged phone numbers with a vague promise of a future meeting in New York or Miami. This turned out to be a pattern. Every place we went, there were "nice people" that Scratch wanted to introduce us to. "Nice people" from New York, Chicago, Detroit, Kansas City, and L.A.. They never let us pick up a check and our pile of chips that could be spent like cash anywhere in town, never seemed to diminish.

© 2009 R. Platshorn

Black Tuna Diaries

Our wives sunned by the pool, gambled, shopped and got the VIP treatment wherever they went. Our kids were entertained by a professional Nanny. And Robby and I were given the High Rollers tour, even though we stayed out of the casinos.

"Have you guys heard of Rancho Mirage?" Scratch was making a pitch to get located on the West Coast. "That's where Frank and his family live. A lot of big people are building homes there. It's by Palm Springs. Most of it is already sold out, but there's a chance you guys can pickup the last few lots to build a swim and cabana club."

We were riding in the limo on our way to a car dealership, to meet another of Scratch's "nice" friends. The man was a car dealer and land developer. Gene's cousin was trying to sell us on the idea of building a private cabana club at Sinatra's Rancho Mirage. He assured us that not only would Frank and the other residents join the club, he personally guaranteed that every major casino hotel in Las Vegas would lease several cabanas, for their high rollers that wanted to visit Palm Springs. There would also be the vig from high stakes card games played in private around the pool and clubhouse. If that weren't enough, Scratch had already told Lynne that we would be able to buy house a few doors from Frank's.. To make a short story even shorter, we plunked down ten G's for an option on the last ten contiguous lots in Ranch Mirage, at the ridiculously low price of ten grand a lot. What the hell! I think we paid for the option with the chips from Caesar's that had been bulging out pockets. Now we were hooked into a west coast operation. Gene was right. Scratch was making his move.

Sinatra showed up as promised for a special show at Caesar's on Saturday night. And as promised we were seated front and center. A lot of his voice was gone by that time, but his phrasing and magic was very much in tact. Later that night Scratch came up to our suite to pickup Lynne and take her down to meet Sinatra. She had made me promise to stay behind, in case Sinatra wanted to sweep her away for a night of love. I wasn't too concerned. He was rarely sober enough, and

Black Tuna Diaries

his wife Barbra never let him out of her sight. As I heard the story later. Frank was just leaving the Baccarat tables when Scratch brought Lynne over for an introduction. As he stepped out from the roped off area, Frank tripped over the base of one of the stanchions that held the velvet rope, and fell right into the arms of my wife. It took his Barbra five minutes to get Lynne to relinquish her death grip on "Old Blue Eyes."

"Don't tell Frank!" We heard that lament a hundred times. Every time one of Sinatra's entourage showed up at my door, begging for a blow, or a toke of the primo Tai Stick we brought with us on our jaunt. The entire "Rat Pack" was in town to see and be seen with Frank. Everybody knew that while it was OK for Frank and company to stumble through life in an alcoholic haze, if Sinatra found anyone tooting or toking, they would no longer be welcome to run with the Rat Pack. I won't name those who showed up to get high, suffice to say, the list of no-shows, would be much the shorter of the two lists.

It was Gene's cousin Scratch, who had whispered in everyone's ear that they could visit Robby and Bobby, any time they wanted to catch a buzz without Frank finding out. Back in the 70's it was a prestige thing for a smuggler to have only the best drugs. We smoked and gifted to our friends only the best Colombian, Hawaiian, or Thai Stick herb. If we did coke, it was "off the boat", uncut. Something almost unheard of at the time, especially on the west coast, where cocaine cost fifty percent more than it did in the east, and was rarely more than 30% pure. Much to our discomfort, well known actors, comedians, and Frank's buddies, showed up at all hours of the day and night for a taste. "Please!. Don't tell Frank!" It got so bad while we were visiting Palm Springs, the only way we could get any sleep at all, was to leave the front door to our suite unlocked and a pile of blow on the living room table. The couple of ounces we brought with us were quickly gone, and Scratch convinced us it would be beneficial to our image, if we sent the Lear back to Miami for more blow. This time we had Gene send us the kilo that Captain Tico had given me as a birthday present.

Black Tuna Diaries

Less hypocritical about his party drugs, was Redd Foxx. "Sanford and Son", was at the height of its popularity. Redd had a steady gig at The Sands, doing a once a week Sunday morning breakfast show that drew every celebrity and casino worker within a hundred miles. It was the place to be, when dawn broke over the desert. Naturally Scratch took us back stage. It was an hour before show time and Redd was with his entourage, which included most of the cast of his TV show. We met Grady, Aunt Ester, and Lamont. They were hanging out and catching a little buzz, so I opened my cigarette case and donated a couple of doobies. In a few minutes the sweet aroma of Thai weed filled the dressing room. Now mellowed out, Redd waved Robby and me to his make-up table.

"Pull up a chair, I want to show you something".

Redd pointed to two chairs nearby. He wiped off a hand mirror and put it on the table. He reached in his pocket, pulled out a "bullet", a little gadget that could hold and dispense up to two grams of cocaine, and unscrewed the bottom.

"Have you ever seen red cocaine?" He dumped about half a gram of bright red powder onto the mirror. "I cut it with a B vitamin called Core. That way, it's not only good , it's good for you." We both laughed and looked skeptically at our host.

"Go ahead, try it that pile is for you."

Not to be out classed, Robby brought out his silver razor blade and straw. When both of us had done a generous "one on one", Robby opened the antique acorn snuff bottle he wore on a chain around his neck, and dumped a gram of pure on the mirror.

"Try this Red", Robby told him, "its white, right, and uncut."

Redd started to wave it away, then changed his mind. He took half the blow and divided it into two fat lines. Our straw was too narrow for his Holland Tunnel airways, so Robby

Black Tuna Diaries

rolled up a C-note to the diameter of a fat pencil and handed it to Redd.

"Are you sure you want to do all that at one time?" Robby inquired.

Redd just laughed, lowered his head to the mirror, and made the two lines disappear like they had been inhaled by a Hoover.

"Oh my!", His eyes were watering and sweat was starting to pop out on his brow. He grabbed at his heart and cried, "Lucile ,I'm coming to join you!"

Half a gram of pure Peruvian flake had his heart pounding like a conga drum at a Voodoo ceremony. In an act of total surrender in the game of "Whose dope is better", he looked at Robby and said,

"Wanna Swap?" And he dumped the remainder of his Red toot on the mirror and reached for Robby's Acorn.

On Monday, we all piled back in the little Lear Jet and flew to Palm Springs California. Scratch was already there waiting to pick us up in Charlie's limo. Ostensibly, the purpose of our visit was to look at the ten lots we had optioned at Rancho Mirage and to make preliminary plans for a private swim club, to be underwritten by the big Las Vegas casinos. However, Scratch's real agenda was somewhat different.

On our second day in Palm Springs, Scratch asked Robby to have the Lear pilots meet us at the airport for a sight seeing flight. In the limo enroute, he explained that all the land around Palm Springs was laid out in a checkerboard pattern, with half the land being the property of the local Native Americans. Specifically, the Palm Springs Airport was on Indian land and was therefore controlled by the tribe. The purpose in telling the story, was to let us know that he could arrange to safely land and unload a plane, no matter what the cargo, if payment were made to certain parties. To confirm his story,

Black Tuna Diaries

Scratch introduced us to the head of airport security, who appeared to be a close friend.

Once through the airport, we were met at the hangar by Joey, another friend of Scratch. According to his business card, the man was an aircraft dealer. Scratch said he was a local "expert", who was going to show us the sights. We filed a flight plan for some local sightseeing, and took off across the desert. Once airborne Joey directed the pilots to a huge flat clear strip of desert, identified on our air maps as "Soggy Dry Lake". Our expert described it as the world's biggest natural landing strip. Used by the government and civilian companies for test flights and emergency landings. And much loved by smugglers bringing in marijuana from Mexico. He even had our pilots drop down and do a touch and go, to demonstrate how easy it was to land on the flat desert floor.

"You could land a loaded 747 here. In fact this is an emergency landing sight for the space shuttle." Joey informed us.

When he said that, I felt the icy fingers of Uncle Sam creeping up my spine. No way there weren't a gazillion sensors and cameras hidden in the featureless desert floor. And guess what! I was right. Three weeks later, the Lear was on charter, returning from the Bahamas with three senior IBM executives on board. They were detained, searched and the entire plane dismantled. The Customs officials let it be known that the search was a result of our little sightseeing tour over Soggy Dry Lake. But back to Palm Springs.

We never planned to set up a smuggling operation on the west coast, but events, mostly arranged by Gene's cousin, were carrying us along in that direction. The final piece fell into place the next day. Gene, who was still unhappy about our sojourn with his cousin, phoned Palm Springs to let us know that "Captain Rivers", our code name for Brooks Moore, was on his way to join us in the desert. He was bringing an Aussie pal, Duncan, who had been his flight engineer back when Brooks and Gene were smuggling cigarettes from South America in giant old four engine Lockheed Constellations.

© 2009 R. Platshorn

Black Tuna Diaries

"They will be in your neck of the woods, looking at Connies".

Since the day I met him, Brooks talked about doing back to back Connie trips from Colombia, then retiring from the smuggling business. A Constellation could carry over twenty thousand pounds of herb on each trip. I never took the idea too seriously, because a Connie required a third man in the cockpit. A highly trained and experienced "flight engineer", to operate the throttles, mixture controls, and navigation instruments! Although once the most popular trans Atlantic plane, Connies where no longer in service with any regular airline. The chance of finding a qualified and amenable flight engineer was almost nil. Or so I thought! Now...Up pops Duncan, the Aussie flight engineer who flew Connies with Brooks and Gene in the bad old days. Add Bo, who had been captured in Colombia with me, and we had a full crew to do the "dirty deed".

Gene had committed us to the deal by trusting Captain Rivers to bring out two hundred thousand dollars of our hard earned capital, to buy a flyable Lockheed Constellation. The Western desert is dotted with "aircraft graveyards". Gene was anxious for Robby and I to take charge of the cash while Brooks and Duncan combed through the available Connies. Brooks had already used some of our funds to buy himself old Piper Twin Comanche. A very fast small six seater, he had always wanted as personal transportation. Buying Brooks a $26,000.00 flying sports car was not supposed to be part of the deal.

Things were turning serious. So we sent our wives and kids back to Miami in the Lear. The next morning Brooks and Duncan picked us up in the Twin Comanche. This is one those aircraft usually referred to as "a pilot's plane". Meaning, unless you are a high time pilot who is both highly skilled and born with a rabbit's foot up your butt, this plane will kill you. Originally a very slick little single engine aircraft. Some crazy designer hung a second engine on it and then added a set of Ray Jay turbos so it could leap tall mountains in a single bound and fly faster than a speeding bullet. Oh, and the only source of heat in the cockpit was a tiny unit no bigger than a can of Sterno.

Black Tuna Diaries

So, the next morning, cramped, and freezing cold in the early mountain air, with Captain Rivers at the controls, we headed out to visit the desert bone yards. As we sped down the runway in the little devil plane, Brooks managed to engage the turbo on the left engine before the one on the right. The power surge on the port engine almost ground looped us into the concrete. The right turbo caught just barely in time to let us fly off as we careened off the runway.

The big bird bone yard was somewhere between Palm Springs and Las Vegas. It held a couple of hundred large aircraft. Many still had the colors and logos of the major airlines. Reminders of better days when these DC-3's, 4's, DC-6s, Constellations, Electras, and Boeing 707's represented the pride of the finest fleets in the world. The old beauties were parked in orderly rows, often showing their downward spiral by the remnants of multiple repaints as they passed down from airline, to charter outfit, and finally to freight hauler.

En route to the dozen or so majestic triple tailed Connies, I stopped to inspect a Lockheed Electra that looked brand new. America's first commercial turboprop airliner, it was the darling of the airlines, until a series of unexplained crashes, forced the premature retirement of the entire fleet. The fault was found and easily corrected, but the commercial airlines wanted no more of this graceful swift bird. This one had recently been in charter service. The interior, bright, clean, and ready for boarding. Sadly, it was unlikely anyone would ever board this lovely plane again. Brooks and Robby pulled me from the empty interior of the Electra.

"Don't even think about it! We came here to buy a Connie."

Robby knew what I had been thinking. We could buy the perfectly lovely bird that no one wanted, for practically anything we cared to pay. My mind was rationalizing the foolish act of buying one, as they dragged me away to a genuine awe inspiring sight for a lover of old radial engine planes. Constellations! A dozen of them in three orderly rows of four. Little Connies, Big Connies, and Super Connies! Gigantic four engine birds, designed to carry millions of passengers safely

Black Tuna Diaries

across the world's oceans. The huge triple tails appeared to be higher than a ten story building.

    Brooks and Duncan picked out a big Connie that had been a freight liner. Wide double doors for cargo, metal flooring with slots for the straps that held the palettes, and tracks to guide them along. It seemed a long walk from the rear stairs to the large three station cockpit. With Brooks in the Captain's seat and Duncan in the flight engineer's chair, they explained how the two of them could fly the Connie themselves, if no co-pilot were available. Using the APU, the Auxiliary Power Unit, they charged the electrical system. Now they lit up the maze of gauges, meters, and switches, to show me that all was in working order. Short of a test flight, which could only happen after a purchase deal was agreed; the giant aircraft appeared ready for duty.

    Neither Robby or I wanted to be identified as the buyer. Brooks and Duncan were posing as employees of a small freight hailer. Who was going to walk in with a briefcase full of greenbacks and make the purchase ? Eureka! Scratch's buddy, the airplane broker who showed us the desert aerodrome. For a small fee, he would provide the insulation to keep our faces out of the transaction. We all agreed, this was the best course of action.

    Next stop, back to Vegas to hookup with Scratch and Joey the broker. Brooks and I were just beginning to get comfortable with one another again, after our confrontation over finances, following our capture by the Colombian army. He knew it was his fault. We'd never have been captured, if he hadn't refused to get airborne as soon as we were loaded. In an effort to bury the hatchet, he offered to let me fly his little devil plane on the short flight to Las Vegas. I thought about our near disaster on the runway coming out of Palm Springs that morning and decided to take a pass. If the legendary Captain Rivers, who flew in the Reno Air Races every year, couldn't tame the Twin Comanche, Bobby Platshorn, low time pilot was sure to get us killed.

Black Tuna Diaries

As soon as we landed, Brooks opened the small luggage compartment and handed over the briefcase with the remainder of the cash that Gene had given him to buy the Connie. He was glad to be rid of the money. He was deathly afraid that his wife, The Redheaded Barracuda, would somehow find out he was carrying around all that cash. In which case she was bound to show up from wherever she had been hibernating, confiscate the briefcase, and spend every last cent on clothes and cocaine, before she disappeared again. It always amazed me to see Brooks, who never owned much more than the jeans he was wearing, with that go to hell sexy redheaded harridan in furs and designer clothes. She would only appear when Brooks had a big payday. As soon as the money was gone, she would vanish again with this admonition,

"It's been fun. Call me when you make some more money". Being broke meant bachelorhood for Brooks.

We spent the night at Caesar's. In the morning we hooked up with Scratch and the broker. Brooks and Duncan would go with the broker and Scratch to buy the plane and then move it to Palm Springs, where they could ready her for a mission to Colombia. With Gene's words, "Don't trust my cousin Scratch", making my hand tremble, I handed over the briefcase with the scratch, to Scratch. That afternoon the Lear returned to fly Robby and I home to Miami, where we would wait for word that the Connie was "mission ready". And wait! And wait! And wait!

"I told you not trust my cousin Scratch! Why didn't you or Robby hold the cash?"

Gene had been staying in the Mother-In-Law apartment above my garage and was now in my living room reading me the riot act. We had been back in Miami for two weeks. Not a word from Brooks or Duncan! They had done a Houdini! At least twice a day for the last ten days, we had phoned Scratch's house in Vegas, only to be told by his wife or kids, that he was "out of town." I was still trying to feebly maintain that I didn't believe Scratch would simply steal the loot and

Black Tuna Diaries

disappear. We had been quarreling about it since my return. Gene stomped out and went back to his nest above my garage.

Four am.! Doorbell, doorbell, banging on the door! Who the hell? Always fearing the worst, my body temperature dropped 20 degrees. I went down to the living room and peeked out on the porch. There was Scratch. With my briefcase! He looked like he hadn't slept since I left him, two weeks earlier. And, he hadn't! Cocaine and Demerol! He'd been flying on coke and Demerol since I left Vegas.

I sat him down on the sofa to try to get a coherent story out of him. First he opens the case and hands me "a present". A bottle of Merc, pharmaceutical cocaine, the champagne of cocaine. Next, he reaches in, and hands me forty G's.

"Here's what's left".

I just looked at him for a minute, trying to intuit what he meant. And then he tells me the story. Scratch never noticed that his cousin Gene had come in through the kitchen and was sitting in the adjacent dinning room, quietly listening to Scratch's paranoid babbling..

"I haven't slept in two weeks. I've been moving around trying to shake off the FBI and DEA. They've been tailing me since you left me the money. The broker got word from the Sheriff, that our deal was bugged. They were going to bust us as soon as we appeared with the cash to buy the plane. I told your pilots to disappear, and I've been on the lam ever since."

Something didn't sound quite right. So I asked the question, that I had feared to ask since he handed me the four remaining bundles of C notes.

"Scratch, what happened to the rest of the two hundred G's I gave you to buy the airplane?"

"I invested it for youse." He was grinning as though proud of himself.

Black Tuna Diaries

Then Scratch reached into my briefcase and came out with an official looking property deed and a hand full of photographs.

"You know prostitution is legal in Nevada?", he said, as he passed me two photos of a group of doublewide trailers parked together behind a sign advertising one of Nevada's more famous "chicken ranches".

"This place even has its own landing strip". He handed me a photo of the grass landing strip behind the "Ranch".

He saw I wasn't too enamored with the idea of pimping. Legal or illegal! So he passed me the deed.

"Listen this place is on twenty acres of prime road front property. It's gotta be worth more than the hundred and fifty G's I paid for the joint."

Gene had come into the room and was standing behind me.

"Don't even touch that deed. It's worthless. You could never operate that joint without a mob partner. It's been sold a half a dozen times and it always ends up back in the hands of the original mob guy who built the place."

"You must think I'm stupid!" Scratch was on the defensive and white with fright.. He looked like he would have shot Gene if he had a gun. Now he was almost screaming.

"I'm not stupid. I made a deal with Jimmy the Weasel. The fix is in! He's going to run the joint as our partner."

Gene was on his feet now, standing over his cousin.

"You're even dumber than I thought. You're probably the only connected guy in America, that doesn't know Jimmy the Weasel Frattiano, is a rat. Watch the newspapers, it'll be public knowledge in another day or two. Frattiano is going into the Witness Protection Program. You just made us partners

Black Tuna Diaries

with the biggest rat since Joe Valachi." Gene turned in disgust and went out the back door.

Scratch was ashen. "I don't believe it. No way is Frattiano a rat. He's the most powerful guy out west." He was putting the papers and pictures back in the briefcase. I grabbed the photo of the trailers, sign and airstrip. Scratch knew that his cousin Gene would never bullshit about a guy turning rat, unless it was true. He headed for my front door, and in a voice that could barely be heard said,

"Don't worry I'll get youse guys your money back...somehow."

That was the last I ever saw or heard from Scratch. Of course we never saw a cent of that money. Nor did we ever try and claim ownership of Jimmy the Weasel's fly-in Bordello.

For many years, lying in my lonely prison cell, I could always generate a smile, or sometimes a laugh, by remembering that photograph, and imagining myself landing an old Lockheed Constellation on that strip behind the whorehouse and all the girls running out to unload the plane. And of course, the victory party afterwards!

Black Tuna Diaries

Chapter 14
Back in the USA

Leaving London after more than three years wasn't easy. It was a vibrant city despite Harold Wilson's stifling and ineffective labor government. A city of contradictions! The "Brain Drain" was sending Britain's brightest and most ambitious to foreign shores where taxes weren't designed to make everyone equally poor and business was less regulated. Yet from the mid 1960's through much of the 70's England led the world of fashion and pop music. The Beatles, The Stones, Dave Clark Five, Petula Clark, and Britain's most famous export, The Mini Skirt!

Dynamic Reading Ltd and the Teeline center in London had almost a hundred employees, most of whom were also my friends. Backers and associates like Sir John Dradge, Andrew Greystoke, Victor Blank, William Courtould, Grant Manheim and Sally Broad who ran the little advertising agency that got Dynamic Reading started, were people who had put their trust in me and I didn't feel good about leaving to return home, but it was time to go.

Astrid and I threw one hell of a farewell party. Both floors of my mews house on Smallbrook Mews in Paddington were jammed with good friends. Twice that night Sally Broad's daughter informed me that a couple of The Stones had crashed the party. She pointed them out, but I was too involved with farewells to pay attention to celebrity party crashers, or maybe someone had invited them, I can't recall. The next morning I took the boat train to Southampton and boarded the Q.E.2 for its second voyage to New York.

A fisherman all my life, I had never been on an Ocean Liner. The good news was, the dinning room steward seated me at a table for two with an extraordinarily beautiful woman. The type that always gets to me, petite, dark hair, dark eyes, brilliant and bottomly! In short she reminded me of Lynne. I was attracted and the feeling was mutual. The bad news was, I was

Black Tuna Diaries

slightly seasick almost all of the time. And so was she. The English insistence on traveling the rougher North Atlantic route insured that our shipboard romance would never be consummated. Even after a romantic supper in the Captain's private dinning room, which neither of us was able to eat, we both repaired to our separate cabins rather than risk a mutual upheaval during seasick sex. After four days at sea, spent mostly in the ship's library, steam room, or anywhere without a view of the heaving North Atlantic, I was delighted to step ashore in Manhattan.

I've had the extreme good fortune to know a number of extraordinary women. None more so than the two I married. Elen Galanter and Lynne Romberg! I was sixteen when I met them both the same week, right after my family moved from South Street to Cherry Hill New Jersey. Elen claimed me when I walked in to a dance at the Jewish Community Center and Lynne enticed me to her table with a Chocolate Chip cookie, in the lunchroom at Cherry Hill High School. In neither case did I have or want, any say in the matter. Except for the first few weeks, I never tried dating both of them at the same time. It was more the case that periodically one or the other of them would dump or desert me and the timing always seemed right to go back to the other. Add to this happy situation, the fact that when I enrolled at Cherry Hill High, I was also appearing in Tennessee William's "Garden District" at the Academy of Music in Philadelphia. It was the Zenith of my acting career and I never lacked for female attention. In fact, I was once expelled from Cherry Hill High for having a brief affair with a substitute teacher who had seen me on stage in the role of the suave George Venable.

My intention was to keep my personal relationships out of this narrative. Both for brevity and because the people I love deserve privacy. Or maybe that's a load of BS and its just too difficult for me to deal with, because most of them died during the almost 29 years of my incarceration. So I'll try to give you the outline and get on with my story.

Most of my best friends have been women. My mother ran a business, raised three kids, ran a household, and still found

Black Tuna Diaries

the time to be my closest friend, confidant, and my biggest fan. She encouraged me to follow my heart and believed I could accomplish anything I set out to do. My sisters Marilyn and Paula were always there for me. More loving and supportive than competitive or combative. Like Elen and my beautiful daughter Hope, those three wonderful women departed this earth during my many years in prison, as did my dad, who I regret not being closer to during his lifetime. The pain of losing loved ones while your in prison is not something I'm capable of expressing in words, either printed or spoken. Of all the women mentioned here, there isn't one of them that I didn't speak to at least once a week while they lived, even from prison. Nuff said!

Shortly after arriving back in the USA, Elen and I were married and moved to Baltimore, where she managed a famous art gallery. I went to work as vice president of Lieba, a promotional jewelry and novelty marketing company. I might mention in passing that shortly after I moved to Baltimore and just before my wedding in Cherry Hill, N.J., Astrid showed up and prevailed upon the Lathams, who owned Lieba, and who she met when they visited me in London, to give her a job. Lieba was in the pitch business. At the time, I was making TV commercials, buying TV time, booking space at fairs and shows, and traveling the country setting up exhibits. Most of that time, Astrid and I were joined at the hip. Not a great way to start my marriage to Elen! I should have realized it from the start, when Astrid talked me into letting her stay in my Baltimore apartment until my wedding, when Elen would move down from Philadelphia. After all, I didn't really believe she intended to sleep on the tiny leather couch in my living room.

I'm a bit slow, but I finally realized I needed a new plan when I returned from my honeymoon in the Bahamas. I had to fly out the same day to set up exhibits at the Wisconsin State Fair. When I arrived to register at my hotel, the clerk just handed me the key and said that my wife had already registered. Even had she wanted to surprise me, there was no way possible that Elen could have beaten me to Wisconsin. I had taken a connecting flight when we returned from our honeymoon in Freeport. Plus, Elen had to start her new job the

Black Tuna Diaries

next day. No, it must have been one of our crew who just wanted to make sure the hotel didn't sell my room to someone else. Rooms are hard to find during fair week. So with no further thought, I took my key and headed for the room. Good thing there was no bellman with me. Because when I opened the door, Surprise! There was Astrid, in her best "go to hell" black nightgown, stretched out across the bare sheets of the king sized bed, her long black hair fanned out over the huge bed pillow. I'd like to say I had the willpower to toss her out. But after all, it was fair week, and rooms were hard to find. The best I could manage was, "don't you dare answer the phone".

For the little its worth, I had one hell of a guilt trip. I wanted to make a serious effort at a successful marriage. To break the pattern, I decided to go on the road with Elen. I had an idea for a business we could manage together. "The Collectors and Investors Art Show". I sold the concept as an attraction for high-end department stores. Over a thousand signed and numbered original prints. Picasso, Miro, Klee, Calder, and many more. Free lectures on collecting and investing three times a day. Each show would run for a week and move on to the next store. Elen would teach me about art and I would make the lecture/pitch. With Elen's good reputation and great contacts in the art world, I had no trouble pitching the idea to the art wholesalers. In no time I had almost two thousand valuable and some not so valuable, original prints on consignment. All I had to do was read a couple of books on art investing, work up a pitch on art collecting as a hot investment, and hit the road with Elen. I booked us into two well known high-end department stores in Texas. To advertise the show, I booked a saturation TV campaign to run for a week just prior to, and during each show. The agency I always used for TV promotions, Atwood Richards in New York, arranged an hour of studio time at a Maryland TV station so I could tape a thirty second and a sixty second commercial for each show. Since I wrote, directed, and performed the spots, I was able to finish taping in less than half an hour. I like to make simple commercials. So it was just me talking about the artists and showing a few slides of the more famous prints that would be on display for sale. I told the audience, where, when and invited them meet me in person at "The Collectors and Investors Art Show".

Black Tuna Diaries

The first show was a great success. Most of the best prints were sold in the first twenty-four hours. Three times a day I made my "lecture" and for the next two hours Elen and I would be writing up sales. The store executives loved us. We were generating traffic and bucks. But unhappily, after the first few days the excitement of starting a new business wore thin. Being on your feet for twelve hours a day in a busy department store is a killer. Each night the entire inventory had to be schlepped to a locked room for security. And each morning we had to schlep it all out again and rebuild the entire art show. Displays had to be remounted and inventory restored in the special display bins. Each of the almost two thousand prints was "matted in frames" and each was in its own heavy plastic protective folio. At the end of a long day on the selling floor, it was no joke having to take down, move and store an entire art gallery, knowing you had to put it all up again in the morning.

At the end of the first week, we loaded the entire show into a rented van and drove it to the next department store, a couple of hundred miles away. The store manager had heard about our success at the first store and greeted us like celebrities with a Champagne and Caviar show opening. But the blush was off the rose. We smiled and worked like good troopers through another very successful week. Without saying a word, we both knew this would be the last "Collectors and Investors Art Show". We were zombies by the time it was over. The tough part was canceling the rest of our shows. The word had gotten out that our promotion was a monster hit. Every high class department store in America was calling our office in Baltimore to book a show. It had been a great idea, just not a practical one. We couldn't just hire people and send them out with an art show. It took specialized knowledge and a real pitchman. The inventory was just too valuable to risk to someone who might not know or care how to handle it. We went back to Baltimore, shipped the remaining prints back to the vendors, settled up with Atwood Richards for the TV time, paid for the art work, and split with the Lathams who had financed the promotion. After the road expenses and the cost of building the displays, there was little money left in the pot to share. Elen and I were ready to move on.

Black Tuna Diaries

Elen's cousin, David Williams Wolkowsky, an architect from Philadelphia, had built and opened the first really trendy hotel at the southern end of Key West, Florida. The Pier House. He had also developed Pirates Ally and was largely responsible for the renaissance taking place on the Island. His grandfather had made enough money from the whorehouse concession during the construction of Henry Flagler's railroad, to buy much of the undeveloped land at that end of Key West. Then, beginning with small clothing store and later a clothing factory, he had built-up the lower end of Key West. David took that moribund property and developed the first new attractions in over fifty years. He invited us down for a visit. We came! We saw! We stayed!

After a week, I talked David into giving me the "waterfront concession". Boat rentals, water skiing, diving, fishing, a sailboat that did midnight sails, and a float plane that took tourists to Fort Jefferson, in the Dry Tortugas three times a day. Elen got a job as assistant to the president of the Chamber Of Commerce. We rented a tiny house and were living like a pair of happy hippies. I let my hair grow down below my shoulders. It was almost blond from the sun. I spent my days, teaching swimming and diving, taking people water skiing or fishing and trying to keep the couple of old boats and outboards in working order. With almost no capitol, I had very little equipment. If I had had a few decent boats, I probably could have made a pretty good living. As it was, I had to travel to New York and go out on the fairs to earn some bucks for some boats. I loved living in Key West. It was easy to see the explosive growth and exciting developments in store for the island. I wanted to buildup the business and start buying property, so that we could be part of that dynamic growth. I had plans for several new businesses.

The good news, Elen was pregnant. The bad news, she was diagnosed with diabetes and was uncomfortable in the heat of Key West. I thought she would get used to it. But that never happened. In the fall I went out on the fairs to work for Vita Mix to pump up our capitol. An old friend from Philly was staying at the house with Elen and taking care of my marina. A few days before I was to return to Key West, I phoned home and

Black Tuna Diaries

was told to call Elen at a number in New Jersey. When I reached her, she explained that she could not take the heat anymore and had moved us back to Cherry Hill. I was disappointed, but not upset. She was pregnant and having difficulties stabilizing her blood sugar. I understood and hid my disappointment.

Elen had been staying with her parents, waiting for me to join her before finding an apartment. With the start of gambling in Atlantic City, my mom had been able to sell the Clearfield Hotel and buy a smaller guest house, in Chelsea, a much nicer section of Atlantic City. It was late fall, my mom was living alone in the guest house and once again commuting to work, at Berkowitz Coats and Suits on South Street in Philly. In those days AC was a quiet, clean, almost empty, and very serene place to live in the off-season. Elen was having a difficult pregnancy complicated by the onset of her diabetes. I was back working as a pitchman for the Morris brothers at National Kitchen Products, based on the Boardwalk above the storefront where I had made my first pitch at age seventeen. I felt it would be best to move into one of my mom's vacant big sunny rooms until the baby was born. Elen could relax and enjoy the cool clean ocean air. I planned to stay at home with her for the last few months until the baby was born. We walked on the boardwalk and saw many movies.

To help fill my time, I took flying lessons at Bader Field. Despite a couple of narrow escapes, I loved flying little planes from the first time I touched the controls. Like Miami Beach, Atlantic City is on a long narrow island, only a few blocks wide. Bader Field is on a small peninsula just across the bay from the center of town. So close, that when the approach is from the east (the ocean side), you have to drop down between two tall beach front hotels. One of those, the old Ritz Carlton Hotel, had been converted into condos. One day I was returning from the practice area over the marshes north of Absecon. I was flying a tiny Cessna 150 and racing an incoming fog to the airfield. I passed the side of the Ritz at less than 200 feet off the ground. Maybe level with the 10th floor. As I looked out my right window to check my distance from the building, not forty feet away, looking right at me from her apartment win-

Black Tuna Diaries

dow, was my aunt Jean, who I hadn't seen in at least five years. In fact I had no idea she had a condo there. The last time I had seen her she was living on South ST in Philly, above Uncle Meyer's grocery store. Recognition was mutual and later that day I found her sitting in the sun on the boardwalk in front of the Ritz.

Our beautiful daughter Hope was born that winter and in the spring we moved back to Cherry Hill to be closer to her family, and to the doctors Elen needed to treat the onset of complications from her diabetes. I needed a business that would provide for us, so that I could stay at home with Elen and Hope. Ice cream parlors were back in vogue. So, I opened "The Ice Cream Factory". On South Street, of course!

The South Street Gang always kept coming home. South Street was in Renaissance and morphing from a shopping street of mainly clothing stores, to a trendy street of restaurants, boutiques and head shops. The Ice Cream Factory, directly across the street from the house where I had grown up, was a combination old-fashioned ice cream parlor and video arcade. The place in its last incarnation had been a men's hat store. Dark green carpet, dark wood paneling on the walls, and an old white paneled ceiling! Breyers Ice Cream supplied the freezers, Coke the soda fountain, and the vending machine king of Philadelphia, David Rosen, put in the Pongs and the few other video games that existed at the time. The tables, chairs, scoopers, cash register, and the rest of the equipment, I bought from Ricky Shear's Used Restaurant Supply Company. When I was a kid I used to ride to Hebrew school with Ricky's son, in the back of Ricky's old red Chevy pickup truck.

All of a sudden, after twenty years, I was back where I started and it was as if I had never left. Cookie Baumholtz still lived around the corner on 7th St and Robby's family was still up the block. Even Pretty Boy Levin was working nearby in center city and would sometimes drop by.

I had no funds left for decor. The ice cream parlor looked more like a funeral parlor, or at least an old hat store. I was thinking of finding someone in the neighborhood who I could

Black Tuna Diaries

pay a few bucks to paint the joint white. That's when my pitchman pal and street peddling partner Jerry Crowley showed up. He took one look at the place, asked me where the nearest hardware store was, and walked back out the door. Ten minutes later he reappeared with three gallons of paint, three wide brushes, and three paint rollers and pans. Twenty four hours later I had the brightest ice cream parlor in town. Tall wide alternating stripes of bright red, yellow, and white. Shazam! Instant fun place! Now the joint looked right, and business perked up. But not enough to make it interesting! I needed a way to make some serious dough so that I didn't have to spend half the year out on the road pitching blenders and nonstick frying pans.

I think it was my idea, but it might have been Jerry's, or even the Breyers salesman's. But I realized that to the best of my knowledge, no one had ever found a way to sell fresh dipped ice cream from a pushcart. The Breyers guy explained that if the temperature of bulk ice cream varies by more than four degrees, it will be either too hard or too soft to scoop onto a cone. What's more, different flavors require different temperatures. Look in the display case in any ice cream parlor. The chocolate and darker flavors, i.e., those with the highest sugar content, are always clustered at the end of the freezer nearest the compressor, the coldest part. This was a challenge. Jerry agreed with my assessment. If we could find a way to put fresh dipped Breyers ice cream on a real fresh baked Philadelphia sugar cone, and sell it on a busy downtown street, the vendor would probably need four arms to keep up with the demand.

First we had to test the theory. I asked the Breyers rep for the loan of a small old fashioned six hole ice cream freezer. The kind with the heavy black rubber doors on the top as opposed to one of the modern glass fronted display cases. He loved the idea and had the freezer there in less than two hours. He also brought over a ton of banners, signs and Breyers motif decorations. For couple of ex New York street peddlers, it was a piece of cake devising a dolly to wheel the small freezer around.

Black Tuna Diaries

We left the freezer plugged in overnight to get it as cold as possible, in hopes it would hold the ice cream long enough to test our theory. The next morning, I went out and bought fifty pounds of dry ice, just in case. My last twenty-five bucks went for a cheap colorful beach umbrella and a piece of plastic pipe to attach it to the "push cart". Always guided by the principle that, "a man with a van can always make a living", my current vehicle was an old beat up Econoline I bought from a rental company for a couple hundred bucks. Fortunately, leftover from our last peddling venture, was a plywood ramp we could use to roll the loaded freezer into and out of the van. It took a running start for the two of us to get the heavy old freezer up the ramp on the second or third try. Getting it down the without losing control was even more treacherous. It was close to noon when we finally had it set up on the busiest corner in downtown Philly, 15th and Chestnut St. We had jury rigged a container to rinse off the scoops between sales and had somehow gotten the umbrella to stand upright over the cart. I also remember giving Jerry the only box of sugar cones in the store, leaving me to sell plain cones or cups in the ice cream parlor.

"Give your tongue a sleigh ride!" was Jerry's sales cry.

He was inundated with customers from the first minute. I. took a picture of the scene and jumped back in the truck to head back to South St, to open the store for the day. I had no idea how it was going on the street. I had told Jerry that after things slowed down in the store, sometime after two or three, I would ask someone to watch the place while I took the van to pick him up. It wasn't even two o clock when Jerry pushed the jury rigged cart right through the front door. Oh crap! I figured either it was a bust or the cops had chased him off the street. Incredibly, he had pushed the awkward rig thirteen blocks over Philadelphia's cobblestone streets.

"What happened man? How come your back so early?"

He dropped into the nearest chair looking like someone who had just been dragged across the Sahara dessert. When he could speak, he looked up at me and said,

Black Tuna Diaries

"Robert, they almost killed me."

"What" I said. "Who almost killed you?"

"The tip, the customers! It never slowed down. First I dipped until my right arm went dead. Then I dipped till my left arm went dead. Then I switched back to my right arm. Then the ice cream started to melt. I ran out of sugar cones and I decided the joint was a bonanza, and it was time to get out of dodge. I was going to phone you for a pickup, but the customers chased me all over center city trying to get me to stop and make them a cone. I couldn't stop at a pay phone long enough to make the call, so I just pushed in."

He threw the ice cream smeared cash apron on the table. "I got no idea how much is in this thing, but I'll tell you this. You better find young strong vendors, maybe college kids or weight lifters, because at fifty cents a cone, you have no idea of how much physical effort is involved in dipping two hundred ice cream cones, in order to gross a C-note. I may never be able to lift my arms again. Oh, and if your arms hold up, you're still going to ruin your back bending over to scoop the ice cream."

We now knew two things. The idea was a winner, but an old freezer on wheels would never work well enough to rely on. Even with dry ice, the heavy freezer would not hold the ice cream at the needed temperature for much more than an hour. It was time to consult an expert, someone who actually knew what they were doing. A professional pushcart builder! New York City! Canal Street! The guys who build the hot dog carts for the New York streets!

The next day I hired Toni, who lived across the street in the house I grew up in, to take care of the ice cream parlor and video arcade. Jerry, by the way, was living in Bally Pa, and whenever he wasn't on the road or working in Atlantic City, he would drive into Philly and hangout and help out. We took my old van and drove ninety miles over the Jersey Turnpike into Manhattan. Once down on Canal St, Jerry directed me to a small storefront workshop where several people were building

Black Tuna Diaries

hot dog carts right out on the sidewalk. The owner, a huge well muscled old man in his late seventies was welding a stainless steel water tank onto a cart when we walked up. Jerry had explained that this man, a Russian Jew, was considered a genius designer of "mobile food dispensers", but spoke very little English, only Yiddish, Spanish, and Ladino. Well, I spoke no Russian, only a few words of Yiddish, my high school Spanish could get me a meal or a slap in the face, and I had never heard Ladino spoken. We had been smart enough to bring the makeshift ice cream freezer on wheels, with us in the van. We also had some empty three gallon ice cream tubs, the umbrella, and a scooper. With the help of one of his Puerto Rican craftsman, and an elaborate pantomime, we were able to communicate what we wanted. Additionally I had a rough drawing of an attractive stainless steel cart with a big umbrella in the center and a place to rinse the scoops. Also, I had written down the temperature range needed to hold the different flavors for dipping ice cream cones. I said I would buy twelve carts, if the first one worked.

The old man motioned for quiet, wrote a few figures on a piece of scrap lumber, then closed his eyes for a moment. When he opened them he was smiling.

"OK, eight hundred dollars! You come back eight days. Ready! Give me two hundred dollars now."

That was the extent of his English, but it was enough. I was still a little skeptical. No one had ever been able to build a cart that would do what we wanted. It was 1973, eight hundred bucks was a considerable sum, and I had spent everything I had to open the Ice Cream Factory. But, there was no doubt I was going to give it a shot. I had about a hundred and fifty in my pocket. Mostly sticky ice cream coated ones and fives that Jerry had collected on Chestnut St, the day before, and forty or fifty bucks of the ice cream parlor receipts from the previous day. The Old Russian looked at the crumpled stained bills as I counted them. He could see it was case money. When I reached a hundred he stopped me.

Black Tuna Diaries

"OK! Bring rest eight days". He shook my hand, shook Jerry's hand and went back to his welding.

Eight day later, by scraping together the store receipts and emptying the video games, I had the rest of the money. I had to stay in the store that day, so Jerry took the cash and my van, and hit the Turnpike. I was on pins and needles until he rolled up about dinner time. I motioned him to drive around to the big fenced in yard behind the store, were we could unload the cart and wheel it into the back room. It was a thing of beauty. A gleaming stainless steel work of art. Not too massive, a perfect size to hold eight flavors, two tubs of each flavor, with a special compartment for dry ice. It had four insulated doors in the top. Each door was wide enough to access two flavors. In the center a shaft to hold the huge green and white umbrellas that Breyers agreed to pay for. But could it actually hold forty-eight gallons of bulk ice cream at critical temperatures for six to eight hours in the hot summer sun? When Jerry showed me the how it was supposed to work, I figured I had wasted eight hundred bucks. It was so utterly simple, that I couldn't believe someone hadn't tried it before and failed.

The next morning still skeptical, I loaded twenty pounds of dry ice in the specially designed compartment, dropped in sixteen tubs of Breyers best flavors, two boxes of sugar cones, wax papers and napkins, two scoopers and a few gallons of clean water to rinse off the scoopers, Using the makeshift plywood ramps, Jerry and I carefully horsed the pretty ice cream cart, now decorated with Breyers signs and colorful photos, into the old Econoline. Once again we set it up at 15th & Chestnut St. We had a crowd as soon as we mounted the open umbrella. It was something new in the world! Eight flavors of Breyers Ice Cream, hand dipped onto freshly baked sugar cones, from a gleaming stainless steel "mobile food dispenser". A pretty as you please genuine damn pushcart. I took a few pictures, jumped back in the double parked van and headed back to South Street.

This time instead of waiting for Jerry to call for a pickup, I left Toni alone in the store and drove back to 15th and Chest-

Black Tuna Diaries

nut. Everywhere I looked there were smiling people licking ice cream cones. Vanilla, Cherry Vanilla, Mint Chocolate Chip, Butter Almond, Butter Pecan, Chocolate, Strawberry and Vanilla Fudge. As soon as he spotted the van Jerry gratefully lowered the umbrella and waved away the crowd.

"Don't worry, we'll be back tomorrow. And you can all scream for ice cream. But I got ta go!"

I jumped out of the double parked van, pulled out the heavy old ramps and together we managed to load the now mostly empty cart on the first try. As I pulled away from the curb, I could wait no longer.

"Well, did the temperature hold? Did everything work? Was it easier to scoop from the lower cart height? How was business?"

Jerry looked exhausted, but he was smiling.

"Whoa. Robert, slow down. You live in a hurry. You die in hurry. They bury you in a hurry. And they forget you in a hurry! Gimme a chance to catch my breath! I must have scoped three hundred ice cream cones." He lit a cigarette, leaned back and didn't say a word until we were almost back at South St.

"The cart worked perfectly. Its lower than that old freezer on wheels and much easier to reach in to scoop. I had no problem keeping the ice cream at a good temperature. In fact I was able to adjust the cold air flow over the tops of the flavors to compensate for all the hot air coming in through the open serving doors when I was busy. If the ice cream started to get too hard, I just had to drop the dry ice level to raise the temperature."

We were back at the Ice Cream Factory and unloaded by three. I flew up the stairs to my office to call New York and order the rest of the pushcarts. Lucky for me, it was the Russian's son who answered the phone. His English was functional.

Black Tuna Diaries

I told him that I wanted the rest of the carts as soon as possible. I would send him a two hundred dollar deposit on the next two carts and pay the balance when they were ready in two weeks. Do the same thing twice more and be able to take delivery and pay for the final five carts in mid July. He told me the next two carts would cost me an extra fifty bucks each to cover the cost of heavier hinges for the serving doors. I agreed. In fact with each order came a price increase, till the last five carts cost me twelve hundred dollars apiece. Even at that price, they paid for them selves in a few weeks.

The next morning, Mike, a junior at the University of Pennsylvania, showed up looking for a job selling ice cream on the street. He had seen Jerry on Chestnut St the day before, and gotten the address. He had decided on the spot that he wanted to spend his summer outdoors vending Breyers ice cream cones and talking to people on the street. That is, if he could earn enough to cover his books and rent at school. No problem! My vendors got to keep almost half of what they took in. Mike averaged close to a hundred and fifty a day gross, six days a week for the entire summer. Back in 1973, over four hundred take home pay for a college student was a serious bunch of money.

Things started going well. First I got the food concession for the Bicentennial Celebration at Independence Mall, Home of the Liberty Bell. This was a high class Sunday antique flea market held on the Mall. I put in two ice cream carts, a stand selling fresh made apple cider from a big wooden barrel, and a stand selling hot roast beef sandwiches on fresh baked Kaiser Rolls. Now I was working seven days a week, ten or twelve hours a day. The money began to roll in, but it was rolling right out again to pay for more and more equipment. I needed a huge lift gate truck to move the carts and catering equipment. A freezer truck to store and deliver ice cream to my vendors. Everything was being financed by each day's receipts. Two or three rainy days in a row would be disastrous. More than once, I wrote checks that I was counting on the next day's receipts to cover. Some how I always managed!

Black Tuna Diaries

Things were going so well, that by late June, I was offered the food concession at Playhouse In The Park, a fifteen hundred seat summer theater in Philadelphia's famous Fairmount Park. Each summer the playhouse brought in top stars in the hottest Broadway plays. I talked old Ricky Shear into giving me a two week credit line for a bunch of used hot dog steamers and the rest of the stuff I needed. Pepsi put in the soda dispensers and I managed to get week to week credit from my hot dog and bun suppliers. The candies and paper goods I bought each day from a "cash and carry" wholesaler. Lastly, one of my best sellers at the theater was hot fresh baked Philly soft pretzels.

Each day at about four I would drive deeper into south Philly to the Federal Pretzel Bakery. Located on a narrow alley of small brick homes, in an old Italian neighborhood. The bakery occupied two buildings with the ground floors opened into one moderately large room. Although I had a standing order for five hundred pretzels a day, the baker would wait until I arrived to start production. First he would go to the far left corner of the bakery and pull a rope hanging from the ceiling that started the amazing Rube Goldberg machine that produced the best soft pretzels in the world. A storage bin near the ceiling would open and pour flour into a mixing vat on the floor. At the same time a spigot opened and just the right amount of water flowed in, and the mixing arm began to slowly turn. Now the baker would go out the front door and ring the shiny brass bell that hung beside the door. In less than two minutes eight or ten tiny middle aged Italian ladies would leave their homes on the block and scurry to the bakery. Then the baker would start the conveyor belt. As the dough emerged long thin rope, the ladies would pinch off a strip about a foot long, drop it in a double loop on the conveyor exactly far enough apart so that the pretzels would attach to one another in a continuous strip, as the dough rose. Next it was conveyed through a jury rigged convection oven. Fifteen minutes later the ladies were back in their little houses and I was back in my van with five hundred hot pretzels that smelled so good, I ate one after another until I was back on South Street, loading food for the theater.

Black Tuna Diaries

How did I manage to run all these businesses and do so much of the work myself? Well, I had help. Lynne had returned to Cherry Hill. Her marriage to a radio executive in Ohio had broken up. It turned out that her husband was an abusive drunk who enjoyed beating her up. She was working as a time buyer at a Philadelphia advertising agency. She would frequently call or drop by The Ice Cream Factory, "just to say hello". Right! When I landed the concession at the playhouse, she offered to manage it for a split of the profits. I knew I could never find anyone more capable or trustworthy. I'm sure I knew, at least subconsciously, that it could wreck my marriage to Elen.

I kept my relationship with Lynne strictly business until my marriage began to breakup on its own. Thanks to her, the theater concession was a huge success. We grossed six or seven thousand dollars a week. This additional cash flow helped me pay off the small bank loan I had gotten to buy the last five pushcarts. And the theater was fun. Lynne would go out there when she finished work at the ad agency. I would pick up the supplies and join her there after all my vendors had turned in their receipts. If it was a good show, we would watch from a rear aisle seat until the first intermission. Sometimes Lynne would convince the stage manager to stretch the intermission an extra five minutes, giving us more time to sell hot dogs, soda, pretzels and candy.

Most of the shows where big hits and the atmosphere in the park was festive. As a frustrated actor and lifelong theater devotee, I loved being even a minor part of that world. We even got to cater the cast parties. I remember the party menu. Spicy steamed hard shell crabs, corn on the cob, Cole slaw and Lynne's fabulous homemade potato salad. The parties were held outdoors, late at night, after the last Saturday night performance. A keg of beer, comfortable chairs under the trees on the green carpet of Fairmount Park. Gene Barry, Moses Gunn, Jean Stapleton, Ursula Andres, and a dozen other stars kicked back and partied with us under the Philadelphia night sky.

Black Tuna Diaries

By late August, with a dozen pushcarts on the street in downtown Philadelphia, my Breyers' rep informed me that I was now the second largest distributor of Breyers Ice Cream, behind only the US Army. The president of Kraft Food Service Division was coming to Philadelphia to see my operation. Kraft Foods owned Breyers, at that time primarily a regional brand. Now Kraft was about to launch "Breyers All Natural Ice Cream", as a national brand and wanted my carts to introduce Breyers on the streets of major cities across the country.

He arrived a week later and spent the whole day watching the operation, talking to the vendors and chatting with the customers on the street as they licked their cones. Before the sun went down he had made up his mind that my carts where the perfect way to introduce Breyers as a national brand. He asked me to draw up a business plan for two cities, New York and Miami. He assured me that Kraft would provide all the financing and assistance necessary to be ready to open Miami that winter and New York, the following spring. Once again, like it had in England, visions of real wealth and success danced in my head. Having built the South Street operation, I had no difficulty drawing up a budget and business plan for each city. I would need four hundred thousand dollars to open four depots in Manhattan. For Miami, I figured I could cover downtown, the beaches, and the other business districts for a start up of a hundred and fifty thousand.

The president of the Food Service Division first took me to New York to see the world's largest ice cream factory, where Breyers, Sealtest, and dozen proprietary brands of ice cream were made. He was quick to point out the difference in the quality and cost of ingredients that were used to make the different brands. Breyers being all natural, was the most expensive to produce.

He assured me that the monies I had requested were not a problem. We next traveled together to Miami to arrange licenses. That's where everything once again hit the wall. I had no trouble with licensing in Philadelphia. I bought pushcart permits, and when the health inspector showed up at my depot, I only had one or two carts. The inspector told me the

Black Tuna Diaries

level of sanitation he expected and I complied without difficulty. First in Miami and then in New York, we were told there was existing licensing laws for carts selling prepackaged ice cream novelties like Popsicles and ice cream sandwiches. There were also regulations allowing trucks to sell soft ice cream. But no one had ever heard of anyone wanting to dip ice cream cones on the street. There were no health regulations dealing with it and no one wanted to go out on a limb to grant a licenses.

Kraft hired the best politically connected law firm in Miami to push through a regulation permitting us to operate. After a few weeks the law firm informed Kraft that it would take a year or more to get licensing in Florida. That didn't fit in with Kraft's plans to introduce Breyers in south Florida. The story was similar in New York. Kraft decided to drop the project and one more time my dreams did a crash and burn.

I carried on with the businesses, but a lot of the heart was taken out of me. My marriage to Elen collapsed through a self-fulfilling prophecy. Elen gained a lot of weight while she was pregnant with Hope, was unable to take it off. This destroyed her self esteem and with it her self confidence. She was certain that I would leave her for someone more attractive. Namely Lynne. The truth be told, I never even considered leaving her and Hope. I was building the business so that we could make go of our new family. But Elen would was so paranoid about her weight, that she would start the most awful screaming fights, insisting that she was sure I was about to leave her. Eventually she drove me out.

It was only a short drive from Cherry Hill Apartments to Cooper River Apartments where Lynne was living. My divorce was without acrimony and Elen had no problem with me seeing Hope as often as I pleased. In the end Elen and I were much better friends than we were a married couple. Both Elen and Hope, who was only twelve at the time, died during the first decade of my imprisonment. Hope of complications of her juvenile diabetes, and Elen after a long fight with diabetes and Lupus!

Black Tuna Diaries

Elen was generous during my prison years, and always accepted my weekly collect calls so that I could speak to her and Hope. When it was permitted, she sent me expensive Christmas packages and always kept me supplied with the latest books. After Hope's death, Elen and I spoke almost daily, until her own death a few years later. She was my friend!

Lynne and I finally married, and moved to Miami! I went back to the University of Miami to finish my undergraduate studies and go to law school. I was tired of fighting to establish new businesses, only to hit a wall, when it looked like things were about soar. As a top pitchman, I knew I could be a top attorney. There isn't a great deal of difference between the two. And that's how I came to be in Miami just in time for the Colombian Convoys, the marijuana madness, the wild world of wacky weed, in short, the swinging seventies!

Black Tuna Diaries

Chapter 15
Kidnapped at the Fontainbleau Hotel

Early 1978......I spent the day at our headquarters in the Presidential Suite of the Fontainebleau Hotel on Miami Beach. It was almost five when I phoned home to tell Lynne I was on my way. I took the elevator to the lobby, put the money I had collected from two of our Philadelphia customers into the hotel safe, and headed out the wide glass doors. The doorman waved and sent a valet to bring up the Ford E-350 van that was my ride. Coming up the entrance ramp, waving and calling my name was Rigaberto Santana. His older brother, Fello Santana, was a major marijuana smuggler; and a big shot from the CIA trained Cuban Brigade that invaded Cuba at Bay of Pigs. We had once brokered a big load of poor quality pot for Fello. I didn't much care for his macho tough guy demeanor and refused his recent offers to sell the cheap crappy weed he bought at bargain prices in Colombia. His younger brother Berto was likable, but I couldn't imagine what he wanted.

"Take a short ride with me. My brother wants to have a drink with you and talk about some business. It won't take long, and then I'll drive you back." He looked uncomfortable, besides I had no desire to discuss anything with Fello Santana

I shook his hand and smiled. "Look, it's almost dinner time I'm headed home, maybe some other time"

Berto looked around, opened his jacket and gestured to the ugly chromed .45 automatic tucked in his waist band.

"Its OK hermano, we just go to my brother's house for a short talk."

I didn't think he'd shoot me on the steps of the biggest hotel on Miami Beach, but I didn't want him or his brother's goons showing up at my house. I walked down the ramp and got into his BMW. The conversation on the short ride was awkward.

Black Tuna Diaries

Fifteen minutes later we turned onto a cul de sac in south Miami. All six houses on the horseshoe street belonged to members of Santana's family.

Fello's house was the big one in the center. We went through to the Olympic size indoor pool in the rear and circumnavigated to the long bar against the far wall. Complete with barstools, it looked like a private cocktail lounge. To the right was Fello's office. I could hear him on the phone arguing loudly in Spanish. When I heard him say "la subasta", the auction, I realized he was referring to me. Robby and I owned the South Florida Auto Auction. Sitting at the bar were six big Guajirans from the Rio Ocha area of Colombia. A couple of them looked familiar, but I was too distracted to think about it. I returned their smile, refused the drink Berto offered me and stood waiting for Fello to get off the phone. Then the light went on! These guys were the Colombians that had loaded my DC-3 with 5000 lbs of Santa Marta's best pot, on a jungle airstrip above Lake Cienaga, where we were all captured by the Colombian army, who wanted to take us to the nearest town to shoot us (see "Death by Firing Squad") A minute later all six of them were laughing, shaking my hand, and giving me hugs.

When Fello come out of his office and saw the happy reunion he looked confused. He didn't know anything about our DC-3 adventure and none of us were about to enlighten him. The Guajirans were supposed to be there to intimidate me, or that was his plan. He didn't like what he was seeing.

"Just tell me what's on your mind. I'm late for dinner." I was feeling braver now that I figured I had allies.

He put on his macho face.

"My yerba, forty thousand pounds lbs, its missing!. The entire shipment disappears from the behind my fish house in the Keys. Except for my people, you and your people were the only ones who knew where it was." He pointed to the Colombians. "These people come for their money. Now you and your partners have to pay. You stay here until they bring the money."

Black Tuna Diaries

Now I had the picture. The Colombian suppliers never trusted Santana. The Guajiran crew where there to collect from Fello, not from me.

A week earlier Fello had come to the hotel and offered to sell us the load suspiciously cheap. The yerba was sitting dockside behind his fish house in the lower Keys. All we had to do was get a couple of trucks and pick the stuff up. Yeah right! It was obvious he was afraid to bring it out of the keys himself. No doubt the load was under surveillance by the Coast Guard or DEA, or he would have brought it too Miami himself and gotten $50 more per pound, than he wanted from us. Two days later there was a very small article, buried in the Miami Herald local section, about a big load of marijuana that was busted by the Coast Guard, behind a fish house in the keys. Fello didn't want the Colombians to know he didn't have the cojonies to move the goods before it was busted, so he was selling wolf tickets, to pass the blame.

Problem solved. The rest was too easy. I picked up one of the two phones on the bar, asked Berto to put it on speaker phone and to translate for the Guajirans,. I got the number for the Coast Guard and dialed.

"This is Elliot Roberts. I'm with the Atlanta Journal. Could I please speak to your PR guy, Jim Dingfelter?" A moment later he was on the line. "Hi can I get some info on the load of marijuana you busted in the Keys a few days ago"

"Mr. Elliot, there aren't many details. Who ever unloaded it, ran away. We watched for three days. When no one showed up to claim it, we took it down to Key West to the confiscation compound. We didn't arrest anyone, because the fish house where we found it had been closed for months" I thanked him and hung up.

Now there were six .45 automatics on the bar and I knew they weren't there to scare me. Fello was trying to claim he didn't know anything about the bust. The Guajirans weren't buying his story. They told him they knew who I was, that we

Black Tuna Diaries

had been together in the jungle, I was their friend, and could get all the Yerba I wanted without putting up a penny.

Without another word, I gestured to Rigaberto and headed for the front door. It was no further business of mine. I have my doubts whether Fello ever paid the Colombians. A few months later a bomb went off in a hotel room in Coral Gables. Mr. Santana, a loose cannon who had always been at odds with other members of the Miami anti-Castro factions, was scattered in tiny bits across Coral Way.

A pity...couldn't happen to a nicer Fello!

Black Tuna Diaries

Chapter 16
A Promise Kept

I can clearly recall from the age of six, telling everyone on South St, including our next door neighbor Manya Block, my aunts Edith, Eva, Frenchy, and Katy, the entire Baumholtz family, at least two of the Meinster families, the Goldsteins and Cohens, that one day I would be rich and take my mom away on a big yacht. It was a recurring theme with me for many years. Of course, the standard reply from my aunt Edith was,

"Feh, that's only for goyim". Everyone else just smiled.

After the fiasco in Atlantic City, and the disappointment of only bringing in half the load when we finally caught up to the trawler in the Bahamas, Robby and I were seriously considering our retirement from the pot smuggling industry. By the time we paid off the two boat crews, the captains, the warehouse crew, the cost of the merchandise, a couple of hundred grand in expenses, and the cash we had loaned Stryker to buy the boats, we, the three partners, me, Robby, and Gene Myers, split about four hundred and fifty thousand dollars three ways, not all that much considering the risk, the months of planning and hard work under pressure, and the investment of past profits. Our cash position was still right around a million a piece. We figured that if all the boats were sold, we could almost double that figure. We had not yet discovered that Stryker had mortgaged the boats and we would never see a cent of that money. Robby and I were content to concentrate on building up our auto auction and to legitimize our Latin American connections. We looked into importing cotton, hard wood and coffee from Colombia. We exported cars and trucks to Colombia and Venezuela. Gene, instead of returning to Tampa, hung around Miami collecting the last of the monies due from our pot buyers and trying to convince Robby and I to get involved in smuggling trips with Captains Crunch and Tico. Eventually, it was Mark Phillips who came up with the deal we should have refused. Mark was making good money supplying us with the yachts we used to smuggle and fish the

Black Tuna Diaries

big game tournaments. He was also doing the same thing for a few other pot haulers like Donny Steinberg and Lyn Miser, who had copied our M.O. Mark wanted to be a pot smuggler! We should have known better. Mark was one of those nice guys who were not very good at anything but being a good guy. His marriage had fallen apart and he was being pushed out of the family business. We had fronted him a few bales of weed which he never seemed able to actually sell and pay for. A short light complected, elfin character, Mark was easy to like and hard to turn down. So when he told us he was forming a partnership with his prep school pal George Purvis Jr., scion of one of "the five families" of North Carolina, and that Purvis was in a position to send a steady stream of used cars from his family's Ford dealerships to our auto auction, we agreed to help with one trip to get them started.

Oy vey! Big mistake, as you will see.

But one very good thing came out of this ill fated arrangement. Mom got her yacht trip. Not a week after agreeing to a deal with Mark and his partner George Jr., Mark phoned to ask Robby, Gene and I, to meet him at Director's boat yard in Fort Lauderdale. He had found what we all agreed was the perfect vehicle for our venture. A 110 ft, yacht! Custom built in Nova Scotia for the president of a major shipping company. Classic, classy, but not showy. Reliable twin turbo Caterpillar engines, twin stabilizers, several generators, and excellent electronics. And a bargain! Because of her hard wood construction, in an age of fiberglass and steel, there were not many interested buyers. Even back in the late 1970's, a yacht that size, in excellent condition should have been worth over a million bucks. This one was going begging at two hundred and fifty thousand. We even figured we could make a nice profit on the boat when we were done with it. Yeh right!

We loaned Mark the money for the boat and his partner Purvis registered her in North Carolina, renamed the Presidential. It was still early summer. There would be no marijuana available in Colombia until harvest season in the fall. We moved the Presidential to our docks at the Fontainebleau Hotel. She would be available for charters, midnight sails; and convention

Black Tuna Diaries

meetings, until a load could be dispatched from South America. Captain Elm, the only captain we knew capable of handling a big luxury yacht, would be given one more opportunity for a big payday. In the meantime, he would captain any charters and captain my mom's long awaited yacht trip when we went over to fish the Bimini Native Fishing Tournament in late August.

Our fishing team, The Fishing Fools, was still a hot name on the island. After landing two giant Tunas and a Grand Slam of big game fish, including the first Swordfish caught on rod and reel since Hemingway's time, our Fishing Fool Tee Shirts remained the best seller in the island gift shops. Our fishing boat would be the fifty-four foot Stryker Sportsfisherman, Natures Way run by Captain Randy and his mate Marty. Captain Elm and Barry the Stoner would crew the Presidential. Traveling and staying on the yacht would be my mom, my wife and two year old son, my niece Shari who was seven, and my wife's twelve year old goddaughter Kim. We provisioned the galley and freezers with gourmet meats and assorted viands from the famous Epicure Market on Miami Beach. Robby and his family would stay in the apartment at the Blue Water Marina.

Our trip had a spooky start. Herb Phillips, Màrk1s dad and supposedly an experienced ship's master, insisted on captaining the Presidential over to Bimini. According to Mark, his dad, the owner of Stryker Yacht Corporation, wanted to captain the yacht on her smuggling mission. The company wasn't doing too well and Herb was eager to earn the potential three hundred thousand dollar captain's fee when we did the deed in the fall. The Bimini trip in August was a sort of audition. Activity generated by the pot business had been keeping Stryker afloat for the past year. Herb figured he might as well jump in with both feet.

We all boarded at our docks at the Fontainebleau. Herb Phillips at the helm, Elm and Barry the Stoner as crew. Lynne, my son, my Mom, Kim, Shari, me and Robby's family the passengers. For some reason I never understood, Captain Herb took us through the inland waterway to Fort Lauderdale, intending to make for the ocean at Port Everglades. Considering Govern-

Black Tuna Diaries

ment Cut was miles closer, and we had to pass by Haulover Cut enroute to Port Everglades, Captain Herb was making me paranoid. By traveling north to Port Everglades, he added ten miles to the ocean passage and ten more traveling up the intercoastals. If that wasn't sufficiently bazaar, when we reached Stryker's home waters near Lauderdale, Captain Herb managed to run us hard aground. So hard aground that we were forced to wait four hours for high tide and call for a tugboat to pull us off. He had grounded us on a well marked mud flat that even the greenest South Florida tyro mariner would have easily avoided. Of course Captain Phillips offered to pay the tug fee, which was substantial. I gratefully accepted, not yet knowing that Herb had borrowed enough money against our boats, to buy the damn tugboat company.

Somehow we made it to Bimini and were tied up at the end of the main dock at the Blue Water before dark. The embarrassed Captain Phillips begged pressing business and took the last Chalk flying boat back to the mainland. Elm would be our captain and host for the remainder of the trip. A charming host and excellent ship's cook, Captain Elm, assisted by an only slightly stoned Barry, made it a memorable fortnight. That is if you didn't count the two days Elm went missing.

Actually, that was a memorable event. I hadn't known that Captain Elm liked to go on a bender once or twice a year, and almost always when he was on Bimini. He was huge and looked like the Schweppes Commander with his full beard. Every bartender and waitress in Alicetown knew him and would try to cut him off before he got drunk enough to fight, which was his purpose in getting drunk. Once in his cups, he would offer to make the fight fair, by taking on every man, woman, and stray dog in the bar, all at the same time.

Once he was well and truly soused, the only place that would serve him was a small native bar in an old shack on the outskirts of town. They knew him and were prepared. Four men would arm themselves with lengths of two by fours and the contest would last until Elm was beaten bloody and out cold in the weeds behind the bar. That's where Barry and I found him, after he had gone ashore for a drink, thirty-six

Black Tuna Diaries

hours earlier. It took ten minutes with the garden hose to wake him up. He was so badly beaten, we had to take him to the local infirmary to get his wounds cleaned, stitched, and bandaged, before we could take him back to the Presidential.

The rest of the trip was perfect. The Bimini Native Tournament is more of a festival than a fishing contest. A never ending series of parties and prizes. Anything that swims in the sea was eligible to win a prize. Bill fish, bottom fish, big fish, small fish, ugly fish, and shell fish. Senior anglers, lady anglers, junior anglers, and baby anglers, every category offered a host of prizes. Beach parties and street dances. Daily award dinners and native pot luck lunches. My mom was wined and dined every night and had two of her grandchildren in attendance all day. Some days she fished with us and other she spent by the pool at the marina with the kids. My only regret is not spending a lot more time with her. She returned to Atlantic City and I was indicted a year later. Except for prison visits, I didn't get to see much of her before she died during my twelfth year of incarceration.

The Presidential and Nature's Way returned to our docks at the Fontainebleau Hotel. The Pres would remain there until early September when the Colombians dispatched a trawler with thirty-five thousand pounds of primo, to our rendezvous spot at Hole in the Wall, off Great Abaco in the Bahamas. Nature's Way would move to North Carolina, where the Purvis family had a Stryker dealership. The plan was to use her to offload the Presidential off the North Carolina coast, if it appeared too risky bringing in the entire load on the Presidential. At Mark Phillip's urging, Purvis had registered the Presidential in North Carolina. With the help of a senator he knew well, it was registered to a fictitious southern "Colonel", by the name of Roger Culpepper. That name, along with Knapp, was names used by Purvis, but later ascribed to me, when Purvis turned informer.

Often, late at night in my dark prison cell, listening to the snores, cries, screams and pleas for attention, from the surrounding cells, I would fight off the depression by remembering my mom and a promise kept.

Black Tuna Diaries

Chapter 17
Death over Walkers Cay

Everyone knows that a black cat has nine lives and a Black Tuna only seven. This is the true story of how I lost number three when the plane I was flying ran out of fuel two thousand feet over the Atlantic Ocean above Walker's Cay.

It was almost midnight on a pitch black moonless night. Robby and I were in his brown Mercedes 450 SLC barreling north on Route 95, heading for Pier 66 in Ft Lauderdale. We had a problem, a serious problem! Earlier that day, our partner Big Gene had switched crews on the yacht Presidential and had it moved from it's berth at the Fontainebleau Hotel, to the Pier 66 Marina in Ft Lauderdale. The Presidential, a 110 ft luxury Yacht was built in Nova Scotia for the president of Eastern Steamship Lines. She had twin turbo Cats, five generators, two bilge pump systems, air conditioning, and a host of sophisticated electronics. She needed an experienced crew.

With less than 24 hours before sailing on a "mission", Big Gene removed Capt Elm, an experienced yacht master, to replace him with a coastal shrimp boat crew from Tampa. Captain, mate and engineer! None of whom had ever been on a ship like the Presidential. The only crew member who had served aboard, was Gene's friend Barry, a stoner who couldn't stay sober enough to remember where he left his Quaaludes or coke stash. The Presidential was to cast off for Great Abaco in the Bahamas at first light. Robby and I were uncomfortable with the crew change. We were getting a bad feeling about the "mission", which was to meet a Colombian trawler at "Hole in The Wall" in the lee of the eastern tip of Great Abaco, and transfer 35,000 lbs of primo Santa Marta Gold to the big yacht. It was after midnight and we were racing the sunrise to reach the Presidential in time to inspect the ship from bow to stern and remove anything that could tie us to its ownership.

Black Tuna Diaries

We reached the marina after 1am and made our way to the end of the long pier where the large yachts were berthed. It seemed odd the Presidential did not show a single light. Normally a berthed yacht was lit like a Christmas tree. Robby and I both had thought to bring flashlights. We held them low and called out for permission to board. No reply! Thinking the crew might be spending the night ashore, we silently boarded directly into the main salon. Not wanting to attract attention from on shore, we began our search by flashlight. When we reached the dinning area, we found ourselves surrounded and held at gunpoint by the recently awakened crew. A crew we had never met, and hoped to avoid. Stoner Barry, the only one who could vouch for us, must have been passed out somewhere. We were in the embarrassing and dangerous position of having to explain our presence to a very jumpy crew of armed strangers.

No one wanted to turn on the lights for fear of attracting unwanted attention. Bobbing flashlights and pointed guns in a pitch dark ship's dinning room! Boy that will make the butt cheeks clinch tight. Eventually they got the message and figured out who we were. Not cops or hijackers!

Using only flashlights, we did a bow to stern inspection, finding only a few personal items left from a recent pleasure cruise. We wished them luck and fled before the sun was bright enough for the crew to get a good look at our faces. This had become Big Gene's mission to run. Robby and I wanted to stay as far away from this accident waiting to happen, as possible. Fat chance!

Twenty-four hours later, 5am., the phone is ringing and I have that awful cold feeling in my gut. It's Big Gene! He and Captain Crunch are in Crunch's communication van up in Lauderdale. They have been up all night staying in radio contact with our "mission". They are wired to the max!

"We've got a problem", Gene informs me, trying not to sound panicked.

Black Tuna Diaries

I'd been watching the weather reports. I was well aware it was foggy and kicking up a bit in the islands. Gene sounded panicky despite his feigned calm.

"I just lost contact with the Pres. They caught their fish, but started taking on water from the storm. Last thing I was able to understand was, the engine room was filling up and they couldn't get the pumps to work."

I told Gene to keep trying to contact the boat and get her location and condition. I told him I'd buy a pair of emergency pumps as soon as Sears opened. I asked him to meet me at the Pompano Airport, where I kept my Piper Cherokee Six. Then I called Chip, brought him up to speed and asked him to contact his guy at the helicopter service with a view to joining my search and rescue operation in the area of Great Abaco. Lastly, I called Robby. Still half asleep, he agreed to stay in Miami, to take care of business at our auto auction. He would also stay in touch with Gene and Crunch to try to keep them on the job, and off the blow.

It was almost noon by the time I was able to buy the pumps and make my way from Miami to the Pompano Airport. There was no sign of Gene. I finished loading the pumps and the emergency raft I had rented at the airport. Chip rolled up to my plane.

"My copter guy is out on charter, but I lined him up for a three day charter, starting tomorrow morning." he explained.

I told Chip I would fly out today and try to locate the Pres. "Then I'll hook-up with you at Marsh Harbor airport around noon tomorrow, when I fly in to refuel. I'll get word to Robby or Gene if I locate our guys. If you hear nothing, start searching as soon as you reach the area".

Chip helped me to preflight the big single engine Piper, and then headed back to the helicopter charter office to finalize arrangements. It was two o'clock when Gene finally showed. The weather was closing in and I was anxious to fly out. Gene had

Black Tuna Diaries

been a check-ride pilot for Eastern Airlines and was a lot more qualified to fly into bad weather. I had no instrument rating and could only legally fly by visual flight rules, VFR.

"You're insane" Gene told me. "Even if you could find them in this weather, you couldn't help them".

I told Gene that if we could locate the sinking yacht, we could land at Marsh Harbor, hire a boat and take them the emergency pumps.

"At worst" I told him, "we'll be ready when Chip arrives tomorrow with the chopper."

It was hard to believe. Gene refused to help. His pal Barry and the shrimp boat guys were his responsibility.

He looked at me as though I was nuts, and said, "I'll be in the radio van with Crunch. If I hear from the Pres or pick-up any law enforcement chatter about a beached yacht, I'll contact you by radio or if I can't reach you, I'll leave word for you at the Club on Walkers Cay."

Disappointed and more than a little scared, I climbed into the plane that Gene had given me for a birthday present and without even speaking to the tower, took off into the fog and cloud that was fast moving in from the east. The ceiling under the clouds was less than a hundred feet off the water feet, with the cloud tops at over two thousand feet.

Thinking and hoping that the Presidential might be limping toward Miami, I decided to begin my search about a hundred miles west of Great Abaco. I looked for a sunshine hole and climbed through the gray clouds to the bright blue sky above the cloud tops. At three thousand feet I eased back the prop, mixture and throttle settings for max cruise, and engaged the autopilot. Every now and then the sky below me would clear so I was able to figure out my position by identifying the islands below. In the briefcase on the seat next to me were two small radios of a type not usually found in aircraft. I hooked

Black Tuna Diaries

them to the small motorcycle battery in the case and switched them on, hoping to hear from Big Gene with good news. Nada! At three o clock I found another hole and dropped down to begin my search.

Because the Bahamas are on a shallow shelf in the ocean, any decent size craft must travel via the deep channels running through the flats. This limited the area I would have to search. If the Presidential was heading for Miami, I only had to follow the main channel to locate her. I started in the deep water area known as Tongue of the Ocean and flew a search pattern heading east toward Abaco. From the air, even down at a hundred feet, all boats look pretty much the same. I was constantly dropping down on the deck to identify any boat that looked promising. This burned an incredible amount of fuel. By four-thirty or so, I had to land at Marsh Harbor on Great Abaco, to refuel. I climbed out to stretch my legs and empty my bladder while the fuel truck filled my wing tanks. I hungout for a few minutes in the little snack bar listening to the pilots and natives, but heard no mention of a beached or distressed yacht.

When I paid for my fuel, the fuel truck driver asked me about the pumps and big green hoses filling the rear seats of my Cherokee Six. Mumbling something about draining a small swamp, I mounted up and took off for Hole in The Wall. My plan was to check the area, then fly down the Windward side of the island before flying on to Walkers Cay Club for a good meal and a comfortable bed.

Finding Hole in The Wail deserted, I headed north along the Ocean side of Abaco. Visibility was so poor, that even flying below a hundred feet, I could barely see the shore line. Halfway up the coast, I gave it up. A nice break in the cloud cover tempted me to climb above the slop and start towards Walkers. When I reached the cloud tops at 2,500 feet I checked my fuel gauge and was surprised to find that I had burned most of my fuel once again. Flying low level search patterns, to check out the coves along the island's coast had almost emptied my tanks. To make matters worse I could see

Black Tuna Diaries

streaks of fuel residue on my wings. The fuel truck driver hadn't tightened the fuel caps.

As I flew toward Walkers, I had to continually climb to stay above the clouds. This was before the days of GPS navigation. You navigated mainly by sight reference because the radio beacons called VOR and the newer LORAN system didn't cover much of the Bahamas. Once I reached the general area where I hoped Walkers Cay was somewhere below me, I put the Cherokee in a wide circle and started looking for a break in the cloud cover to show me the island.

Finally, after almost twenty minutes a small hole in the cover passed below me and I was just able to spot the southern edge of what I was pretty sure was Walkers Cay. That's when my engine began to sputter, telling me, I was about out of gas. I dove for the hole, but before I could get under the cloud cover, the hole closed and I was lost in the solid gray fog. I stayed on course for the island until I ran out of nerve when my altimeter indicated I was less than a hundred feet above the water. I hadn't recalibrated my altimeter since I left Miami. In bad weather, it wasn't likely to be very accurate. My engine was cutting out more often now and for longer periods of time. I was totally blind in all directions and knew that at any second I might fly into the radio tower on Walkers or smash into the ocean waves. I turned left trying to stay level, but losing power. Checking my instruments I saw that I was nose high, causing me to lose airspeed and increasing the danger of a stall. Decision time! I couldn't risk trying for the strip on Walkers. I might never find it in time. There was also the risk I could crash into the radio tower there, killing innocent people.

The greatest danger of going down in the water, is, a Cherokee Six is a fixed gear aircraft. The landing gear does not retract. A water landing would likely result in the plane flipping onto its back when it hit the water. I knew there were two small uninhabited islands on the west side of Walkers. I figured my best chance to survive, was to try to locate and land along the shore or between these islands.

Black Tuna Diaries

As I lost the last hundred feet of altitude I felt pretty sure that I was lined up with these little cays, even though I still couldn't see an inch beyond my cockpit. I finally emerged from the fog about fifty feet over the water and about four hundred feet from the edge of one of the small cays. At precisely that second my engine sputtered for the last time and quit. Dead silence! I glanced at my air speed indicator. Eighty miles an hour! Enough speed to stay airborne long enough to make the island.

Directly ahead of me, right at the tip of the tiny cay, was a black smooth patch that looked like the end of a boat ramp. My forward visibility ended at the start of the ramp. I decided to chance it and try to touch down on the boat ramp and hope that it led to a clearing or road long enough for me to stop my landing roll or at least slow down before I hit anything.

The wheels of my silent aircraft barely made it to the tiny patch of blacktop. I could see maybe ten or fifteen feet ahead. So far it looked clear. For no good reason I could think of, I managed to keep my feet off the break pedals and held the nose wheel off until it came down on its own. Through patch after patch of fog I rolled along the black tar, desperately wanting to press the break pedals and stop the coasting Cherokee. It finally rolled to a full stop. I sat there waiting for my legs to stop shaking and maybe crying a little bit in relief. After a few minutes I popped open the door and very carefully, slid weak legged off the wing and onto the road. Walking a few feet to the left, through the fog a small wooden building emerged. As I got closer I could just make out a sign over the door.

It said, "**WELCOME TO WALKERS CAY AIRPORT-BAHAMAS CUSTOMS**".

And that's the gods' honest truth!

Black Tuna Diaries

Chapter 18
Ambush on Abaco

Amazed to find myself still alive after running out of fuel two thousand feet over a fog shrouded Walkers Cay and somehow feeling my way down to a safe landing, I checked in with Bahamian Customs and made my way to the Club. Walkers Cay Club is the luxury resort and fisherman's paradise featured on the TV show "Walkers Cay Chronicles".

The Club's manager was already holding a message for me from Big Gene. There had been no radio contact with the missing yacht Presidential. Chip had managed to charter a chopper and would meet me at Marsh Harbor Airport noon tomorrow, to help search for the missing yacht and its hapless crew. Leaving my bag at the desk, I proceeded on shaky legs to the dinning room. I ordered a dinner I did not think I could hold down and a double Glen Morangie on the rocks. My system was so overloaded with fear generated adrenalin the malt whiskey put me down like a sledge hammer on a Lady Bug. I do not remember how I made it to my room.

I woke early still fully dressed and with a monster adrenalin hangover. A shower, three cups of black coffees, and a plate of kippers and eggs, got me on my feet. Back on the airstrip, I supervised the fueling of my big Piper. The sky was gray but the visibility was improving. The 260 horsepower Lycoming growled to life. I looked skyward for any incoming traffic, pushed the throttle to the firewall .and became a creature of the air.

Heading for Abaco, I flew at four hundred feet over the water and began searching once again for the lost yacht. By noon I was almost out of fuel. Still no sign of the Presidential! I dropped out of the sky and onto the runway at Marsh Harbor. As soon as I pulled onto the fuel pad, I spotted Chip's chartered helicopter parked nearby. I ordered fuel and went into the snack shack and joined Chip at a table in an empty corner. The charter pilot had gone into town looking for diesel

Black Tuna Diaries

fuel for the Bell Jet Ranger. The good news was, Chip had spotted the Presidential in a cove on the windward side of Great Abaco. I had flown past that cove three times without spotting her, because I was looking for a boat in the water, not a 110 foot yacht lying on its side on the beach. According to Chip there was no activity on the beach and no sign of the crew. He told me the charter pilot was getting suspicious and wanted to head back to Pompano as soon as he could find enough fuel.

I told Chip he had done great finding the Presidential and should return to Florida with the chopper. I would try to locate the crew and get them off the island before the authorities found them.

People used to tell me I was crazy, flying over the ocean in a single engine plane. My feeling was, the fewer moving parts, the less chance of something breaking. The big fixed gear, six seat, single engine Piper was my dream machine. A birthday present from Big Gene! Now I was flying low over the coves that dot the windward side of Abaco. Using the crude map that Chip had drawn on a paper napkin, it wasn't long before I spotted the beached yacht. Nothing I had ever seen looked quite as forlorn as that magnificent yacht lying on its side with only her stern poking out into the surf beyond the gray windswept beach. I flew low over the sand but could find no sign of our crew. There was some activity in the coves nearby and I feared it was the cops.

More anxious than ever to locate the crew and get them away, I flew up and down the road that ran along the shore line. As I approached a mangrove swamp a few miles to the north, Barry, who must have recognized my plane, popped up from the mangroves waving like a madman. As I circled only a few feet off the deck, three more crewmen appeared. All of them looking like mud covered swamp rats. Thirty-six hours hiding in a bug infested muddy mangrove swamp had already taken a toll. They all were badly sunburned, and their clothes were in tatters. It was clear they were desperate to be away.

Black Tuna Diaries

I circled out over the water to get a good look around the area. Seeing no one that appeared threatening, I lined up with the road, pulled in full flaps and dropped the last twenty feet onto the asphalt. Fortunately, my hand hadn't left the throttle, when I felt something brush my right wingtip. Realizing that the low winged Piper wouldn't clear the mangrove bushes lining the road, I jammed in the power. With flaps still extended, the big single engine plane leapt back into the sky. I could see the awful disappointment register on the faces of the crew as I flew by only a few feet off the road.

In my map compartment, I found the lipstick my wife had dropped on our last fishing trip. As large as possible and in reverse, I wrote on the cockpit window, "24 HOURS, HERE, BOAT". After two low slow passes, my crew signaled they understood.

I climbed out, searching for a hole in the cloud cover. I formed a plan as I popped out the gray clouds and into blue sky at four thousand feet, heading west for Bimini, an hours flying time away. Captain Randy was fishing a charter party on our forty-four foot Stryker, "Fishing Fool". My plan, if you could call it that, was to convince Randy to dump his charter party and run like hell for Abaco to rescue Barry and the crew before the DEA or Bahamian Police could locate them.

It was almost four in the afternoon when I dropped out of the clouds to fly low over the parade of million dollar battle wagons entering the harbor after a day of big game fishing. For once in my life, my timing was perfect. The "Fool" had just crossed the sandbar that guards the entrance to the inlet. The weather still sucked, so all the boats were coming in early. I dropped to the deck and buzzed the boat. Randy waved and lifted the microphone of his CB radio. My special briefcase with our portable radios was on the seat next to me. On a long prearranged frequency, I asked Capt Randy to meet me in the bar at Brown's Hotel. Brown's bar was usually deserted, and only a short walk from the Blue Water Marina where we docked our boats.

© 2009 R. Platshorn

Black Tuna Diaries

I landed on the long blacktop strip that runs from west to east on South Bimini. Managing to slow enough to make the first turnoff, I taxied left to the airport shack. I secured the Cherokee to a tie-down, and ferried over to the main island. Ignoring the customs office, I walked past the Complete Angler and into the nearly empty bar at Brown's.

Randy was having a Beck's, but I ordered a coke, knowing that I'd be back in the pilot's seat in less than an hour. It was evident from the start that Capt Randy wanted no part of my quixotic rescue mission. I played hard on his conscience about leaving his friend Barry and the rest of the crew stranded and in serious trouble. I told him they had been hiding in a mangrove swamp for two days without food or water and that a massive manhunt was to get underway when the weather cleared. To close the deal, I offered Randy fifty percent of anything we could salvage from the beached yacht. Randy caved! He admitted that the bad weather had discouraged his charter party. They were flying back to Miami in the morning. He finally agreed to fuel up and run for Chub, where we would meet and co-ordinate the last phase of the rescue, before running the last fifty miles to the ocean side of Great Abaco.

I had been on the ground for less than an hour, but I had to get to Chub Cay before dark. Night landings there were illegal and might draw the kind of attention I didn't need. It was already after five. I paid a fishing guide to ferry me over to the South island airstrip as fast as possible. I checked my fuel, oil, and did a quick preflight check. Three minutes later I was flying at two hundred feet over the water, heading for Chub Cay, a hundred miles east, in the Berry Islands.

Chub Cay was a private fishing club and small residential community made up exclusively of club members. As an invited guest of Stryker Yacht Company, I could stay at a guest cottage on the "visitors" side of the harbor. The light was beginning to fade as I buzzed the Club to summon the jeep that would pick me up on the runway. I was expected. By the time I had tied down, the club's driver and the island's lone Customs Officer had joined me for the short journey to the Marina view cottages.

Black Tuna Diaries

The visitor's enclave had about twenty rooms, a bar, a dining room, a canteen, and a small office with radio phone communications. I was the only guest in residence and so had the undivided attention of the small off season staff. I phoned Robby and told him to let Gene know where he could reach me. I told him I was "picking up the kids", and that Randy and I would bring them home the following day.

After dinner and a drink prepared for me in the empty chow hall, I rolled a doobie and sat by the water's edge watching the bigger fish chase the smaller fish around the lagoon. Exhaustion set in. I must have fallen asleep, because I dreamed that my Cherokee Six was a fighter plane. I was in a dogfight with a big two engine "Islander", belonging to the Bahamian government. There were a dozen Bahamian marines hanging out the windows and doors, firing machine guns. I was out of ammunition but kept diving directly in front of the Islander's cockpit trying desperately to force them to turn away from where my crew was hiding. Eventually they turned away fearing I was crazy enough to Kamikaze their ass. I landed unscathed to the cheers of my crew who had watched the skirmish from their hiding place in the mangrove swamp.

I never made it to my cottage. At first light I woke up still on the bench by the water. The first thing I saw was "Fishing Fool" tied to the fuel dock. Her generator running and her crew still asleep. I let them rest while I went inside and showered. I made coffee in my cottage, then went looking for the Dockmaster. After telling him that the "Fool" had run most of the night to get to Chub. I asked him to fuel the boat as quietly as possible while Capt. Randy and Marty slept. I also had him fill a dozen jerry cans with marine gasoline and send them to the airstrip to top off the tanks in my plane. There was no aviation fuel available at the Chub Cay airstrip.

I filled the plane myself, pouring the fuel through a thick wad of cheesecloth to filter out the dirt and moisture. By the time I got back to the marina, Randy and Marty were drinking coffee on the dock and looking for me. I took them into the, empty dining room. Finding no one in attendance, I went into

Black Tuna Diaries

the kitchen myself and rustled us up a couple of cheese and mushroom omelets with toasted Bimini raisin bread.

Randy and Marty had managed to get a few hours sleep. They were ready to leave for Abaco to pick up the crew of the Presidential. For an outrageous fee, I was able to rent an outboard dingy that might be needed to pluck our guys off the beach. Randy could tow it behind the Stryker and bring it back to Chub when they dropped off the crew.

Our plan was for Randy and Marty to appear to be trolling for marlin near the area where our guys were hiding. Just before noon, I would fly over the swamp, flush out the crew, and point them toward the incoming dingy. I could keep in touch with Randy by radio and change things as necessary.

A little after eleven, I flew out to finish what I had started three days ago. When I reached the windward side of Great Abaco, the "Fool" was right where I wanted her. I buzzed the boat and Marty climb down into the dingy. Barry and the crew of the Presidential had already spotted my plane and were heading for the water. Three minutes later they were safely onboard the Stryker heading out to sea. I circled low over the flying bridge. Barry was drinking from a big water bottle and talking animatedly to Captain Randy. A minute later Randy turned back toward Abaco.

Barry must have convinced him it was safe to try salvaging some of the thirty-five thousand pounds of primo Colombian weed still aboard the beached yacht. Shit! I didn't like the idea, but I had offered Randy salvage money and I knew the crew of the Pres wanted a payday. So I overflew the beached yacht and the cove several times. Seeing no danger, I circled overhead to keep watch.

Randy backed the Sportsfisherman within forty feet of the stern of the Presidential. Leaving Marty on the bridge to hold the boat in position, Barry and Randy slid over the transom and into the dingy. The tide was up and the stern of beached yacht stuck out into the serf. They tied off to the stern rail, climbed onto the slanting deck, and disappeared into the main

Black Tuna Diaries

salon. Thirty seconds later they came flying out of the cabin, tossed something into the dingy, scrambled aboard and fast as it could go, ran the dingy back to the "Fool". The two of them dove headfirst over the transom just as a dozen Bahamian marines emerged from the cabin of the Presidential and let loose a barrage of machine gun fire. At the same moment six more marines popped up in the nearby sand dunes and let loose with neat little Ingram submachine guns. Marty on the bridge of the big Stryker, pushed both throttles to the wall. The Stryker dug in, squatted deep in the water, kicking up mud, but did not move forward. She was digging their graves with her own propellers. To buy them some time I circled higher, then dove at full speed across the stern of Presidential and straight at the marines on the beach. The kamikaze run and the roar of my engine took them by surprise. They didn't know what to make of it. A second later they were firing up at me as I climbed away for another run. At a hundred feet I leveled out and looked down to see the "Fool" break loose of the mud, go completely airborne, and land flying over the water. The Bahamians, without a boat, had no way to give chase. So in anger and frustration, they emptied their weapons up at me and at the fleeing Stryker.

A brief radio check assured me that, miraculously, no one had been hit. I circled overhead until they cleared Abaco and were headed for Tongue of The Ocean and Chub Cay. I flew fast and low, wanting to get on the ground before the adrenaline shock set in again, leaving me a quivering mess. Twenty minutes later, I buzzed the Chub Cay harbor to alert the jeep driver to pick me up on the airstrip. In another minute, I was on the concrete airstrip taxiing to the tie down apron. The jeep pulled up next to the plane, but I just sat there unable to move. Little Mikey, a young resident who loved driving the jeep, tied down the Cherokee Six, giving me a little time to pull myself together. Somehow I crawled out onto the wing and lowered my feet to the ground. Mikey, was just fifteen and the son of a wealthy club member who lived on the island, helped me into the jeep. I looked over at my plane checking for bullet holes. Nothing ! What I didn't know , was that I was looking at my beloved Cherokee Six for the last time. I would never fly it or even see it again.

Black Tuna Diaries

As we bounced down the dirt trail to the harbor, Mikey was jabbering about urgent messages for me at the club office and begging me to tell him what was going on. At fifteen, he shouldn't be driving a jeep or living with a housekeeper alone on Chub, while his dad was off the island on business. He was a great kid, just desperate for a little respect and attention. I tried to discourage him from hanging with me, but with little else to do, he stuck to me like Gunga Din to Carey Grant.

The messages at the club told even more bad news. Big Gene, who was monitoring a bank of radio scanners in Crunch's com truck in Ft Lauderdale, left me a thinly coded message informing me that the Bahamian marines, Bahamian police, U.S. Customs and the DEA, were all actively in the hunt. They were seriously embarrassed, and pissed off, that we had managed to escape their Ambush on Abaco. They knew where we were and they were coming to get us!

Black Tuna Diaries

Chapter 19
Escape from Chub Cay/Robert Vesco's Secret

It was barely past noon and my day was already deep in the dumpster and headed for hell. I have been machine gunned over Great Abaco, and half the law enforcement agencies in North America are looking for me and the crews of the Yacht Presidential and the Fishing Fool. To top it off, I get a message from Robby that Mark Phillips and his partner George Purvis Jr. were on there way from North Carolina on the fifty-four foot Stryker, Nature's Way, to try to offload the thirty-five thousand pounds of Santa Mata Gold aboard the beached yacht now being used as a machine gun nest by the Bahamian marines.

One thing at a time! Nature's Way would have to stop to refuel at Walker's Cay, before making for Abaco and the beached Presidential. I couldn't risk using the Club's radiophone to send word not to proceed. At this point, it would be like sky writing our location for the world to see. There was a retired airline pilot, Rob Trotter, living on Chub who sometimes fly my plane to pickup guests or supplies for our fishing parties. I asked Mikey, our aspiring pirate, to see if Trotter would fly a message to Walkers Cay for a small fee. While I waited in the Club's small office, I outlined the situation on a piece of stationary and addressed it to Mark Phillips, aboard the Nature's Way. Trotter showed up a few minutes later, eager to do some flying. I gave him the keys to the Cherokee Six, the message, and some cash. I asked him to deliver the message personally to Mark Phillip, who he knew well. Then he was to refuel the plane and fly back to Chub. Hopefully my message should stop Mark from going anywhere near the well guarded yacht.

I settled down with a sandwich and a Becks, to wait for Capt Randy and the crew to arrive. I was on my favorite bench by the lagoon. It didn't take long before I was dozing in the sun, my body trying to recover from the morning's Ambush on Abaco. By 2:30 pm Mikey was shaking me awake. The Fishing

Black Tuna Diaries

Fool was passing the rock called Moma Rhoda that marked the beginning of the narrow twisting channel leading into the Chub Cay lagoon. At the same time Big Gene was on the radio phone demanding to talk to me. I told Mikey to get the keys to the fuel dock so Randy could refuel without wasting time trying to find the Dockmaster, who was often missing for hours at a time.

I went back into the visitor's office and slid behind the desk in the little phone room. I wasn't happy about talking over the airwaves while two governments were using all their resources trying to find and catch me. I tried to communicate this to Gene but he let me know that my location was no longer a secret. He and Capt Crunch were monitoring DEA, Customs, and Bahamian government frequencies. He said that I could expect the same marines we had I escaped earlier, to fly in to Chub Cay about four pm to scoop up me and the crews. They were coming armed and angry! I asked Gene to stay by the radios and I'd contact him from the air as soon as we were off the island.

When I walked out of the office, Randy was refueling the Fool. The four crewmen from the Presidential were following Mikey into the Canteen for food, drink, sunburn medication, soap, shampoo, and clean t-shirts and shorts. Randy and Marty had already checked the Fool for bullet holes. Nada! It didn't seem possible that eighteen Bahamian Marines with machine guns could manage to completely miss a forty-four ft Sportsfisherman and an airplane flying at sea level directly in front of them. At our trial, a year later, the Bahamian Chief Inspector swore that his men "had riddled da craft wit high caliber bullets". But he also swore to many other things that weren't exactly true.

I filled Randy and Marty in on what Gene had said. They were already planning to book as soon as the tanks were topped off. They made it clear they had no intention of taking the crew of the Presidential along with them. They figured that their only chance of getting safely back into the US, was straight up denial. No bullet holes, no rescued crewmen! A case of mistaken identity! It actually worked. US Customs

Black Tuna Diaries

went over the Fishing Fool for two hours looking for bullet holes, crewmen and dope, Nada! The Bahamians had informed them that the boat was riddled with bullet holes. That's what saved Randy and Marty from being arrested when they got home.

I was headed for the canteen and just happened to turn in time to see Randy hot footing it into the Dock master's office with a bale on his shoulder. He had had to desert the dingy, but managed to save the bale of Santa Marta Gold they had grabbed off the Pres, before the Bahamians sprung their trap. Well he deserved it! I just wanted one doobie so I could say that I had at least had a taste.

Barry the stoner was standing outside of the canteen. He wanted to give me his version of what happened to the Presidential and its load before the others had a chance to talk to me. His speech was slurred and I mistakenly put it down to three days hiding in a mangrove swamp. His story was, the yacht took on water from the rain and the waves. The so called engineer couldn't figure out how to turn on either of the two independent bilge pump systems. After screwing up the complicated electrical system, they sent Barry, who was the only one who had crewed the boat before, to get the pumps working. According to Barry it was too late. The engine room was swamped. All five generators were about to be submerged. Two diesel generators, one gas gen, and two generators on the big Caterpillar engines! None could be made to run the pumps. Something didn't sound right, but I let it go for the moment and gave Barry a key to my cottage, so he could shower and rest until my plane returned and we could flee the scene before the Bahamian Marines showed up.

I went into the canteen to find the three shrimpers eating everything in sight. I let them know that there was some urgency for them to be cleaned up and ready to leave within the hour. As I walked them to another cabin, they me told a very different story of what happened to the Presidential. According to the captain, when the ship started to take on water, Barry volunteered to go down to the engine room and start the pumps. An hour later the engineer went check on Barry and

Black Tuna Diaries

found him passed out snoring to beat the band, while the engine room had filled with water. The engineer tried to activate both of the pump systems, but not understanding the ships switching system, had no success. Barry was too stoned to help. When he couldn't get the pumps working, the shrimp boat mechanic tried the old sailors' trick of removing the exhaust hoses and letting the ship's forward momentum suck the water out of the rear exhaust ports. He told me that there was already so much water in the bilges; he couldn't get the clamps off the exhaust hoses. They were sinking and the only thing they could do, was to beach the ship.

I went back to the fuel dock to see off Randy and Marty. Mikey ran over with another message from Gene. My plane had been confiscated on Walker's Cay. Rob Trotter had been arrested and taken to Nassau. I couldn't ask Randy to take us off the island, because we would all surely be arrested before we reached Bimini.

I resolved to either steal a boat, which wasn't a great plan, because stolen boats are easy follow, or find another way to get my guys safely away from Chub Cay. I watched as the Fool disappeared through the narrow winding channel. Hearing a plane approach, I looked up and saw the government Islander circling for a landing. I yelled for the crew just as Mikey pulled up in the jeep. He drove us to a boathouse on the members side of the, island. I was not sanguine with the idea of being locked in a boat house while the authorities searched the island. It felt like we were caught and just waiting to be picked up. What choice did we have?

The boat house was actually a two car garage, housing an overturned twenty-six ft fishing boat, under which the five of us were supposed to hide if the Bahamian search parties got too close. It was at least a hundred and ten degrees in there, with the late afternoon sun beating down on the airless sealed garage. If we were trapped there more than an hour or so, dehydration and heat prostration would become a serious reality. There were no windows, only the locked garage door. Every time we heard noises, one of us would lie on the ground and try to look through the crack between the floor and the bottom

Black Tuna Diaries

of the garage door. Twice we heard voices and footsteps as the searchers tramped through the members area of twenty or twenty-five private homes. Once they were so close that we all actually crawled under the overturned fishing boat but quickly realized it was a ridiculous and futile idea. It was the first and only place for our hunters to look. After more than an hour in the extreme heat, the dark, and the heavy fumes from the paint and fiberglass resins stored there, we contemplated beating down the door, while we were still able. Fortunately it was almost dusk. If the Marines wanted to return to base on Nassau, they would have to leave Chub Cay immediately, to make the six pm deadline, after which Bahamian pilots refused to fly. A few minutes later we heard the Islander climb away from the nearby airstrip. All five of us were now lying on the ground trying to suck a breath of clean air from the crack under door when young Mikey arrived to free us from the sweltering garage.

In a few minutes we were sitting on the floor of the air conditioned canteen drinking cokes and waiting for the dizziness to pass. The club manager and the Dockmaster soon arrived to demand heavy bribes for leading the search parties on a wild goose chase. In the next fifteen minutes all seven Bahamians working at the Club had joined our group for cokes and bribes. Ten thousand bucks later, figuring that this might be our last night of freedom, I declared a celebration.

Steaks and lobsters were the only things in the Club's freezer, but what the hell! Beer was in good supply in the canteen and whiskey at the bar. Not many people were on the island at that time of year, so I invited all of them, members, guests, workers, and even the resident customs officer who had been hiding as far from the action as possible.

If you've ever visited an island like Chub or Walkers Cay, you know that everything cost three or four times the mainland price because it has to be transported by boat or plane from the US mainland. Maybe twenty people showed up for the party. My final bill at the commissary and the chow hall was over two thousand dollars. Steak, lobster, red beans and rice, beer, music and stories. The Bahamians described in hil-

Black Tuna Diaries

arious detail, how they led the Bahamian Marines on a futile search claiming that we all had left the island on the Fishing Fool. Barry and the crew of the Presidential told everyone about their three days hiding in the mangrove swamps on Abaco while waiting and hoping to be rescued. Then they told how were machine gunned at close range without being hit or the boat getting even one bullet hole.

The Bahamians were almost crippled with laughter picturing a squad of the fancy uniformed marines with Ingram sub-machine guns, unable to hit a forty-four ft yacht, a few feet in front of them. Lastly, I told the story of the search for the Presidential and my harrowing let down through the fog, after running out of fuel over Walkers Cay. During the festivities, I slid over to the deserted Club office, to speak to Gene by radio phone. He was still monitoring the radio traffic between the Bahamian and U.S. law enforcement agencies. He was adamant that we leave Chub before six am., when the Bahamians would return in force to arrest us.

They knew they had been snookered and weren't happy about it. Gene wanted me to "borrow" a boat and head for Florida a.s.a.p. The problem with Gene's plan was, there was only one boat in the marina at that time. A seventy ft custom mega yacht Sportsfisherman. I had already snuck aboard and spotted a Bearcat 250 scanner in the master bedroom. A sure sign that the boat belonged to a smuggler. Once reported missing, this yacht with its sixty ft tall tuna tower, would be easier to spot than a shvatza at a barmitzva. It was only eight pm., when on the second call, I told Gene that escape by boat was impossible. The easiest way off the island, would be for him to pick us up by plane, any time in the next ten hours. Gene was a qualified transport pilot who could fly anything with wings. He was part owner of a company that bought and sold used aircraft. At that moment in time, he had in his inventory, a Cessna 402, a Beachcraft Baron, a Piper Navajo Chieftain, and several other twin engine planes that could easily make it to Chub and transport all of us safely home.

All of a sudden, the tone of our conversation changed. Instead of concern, Gene was making excuses. It was a replay of

Black Tuna Diaries

two days ago, when I begged him help me search for his friend Barry, and the three crewmen he had put on the Presidential. Now his first excuse was, "no runway lights on the Chub Cay airstrip". I explained that with an almost full moon on a concrete strip, his landing lights would be sufficient. Additionally, when I heard him circle overhead, I would light the downwind end with the jeep headlights and the other end with a gasoline fire. Next he claimed that he had no hanger keys and so he wouldn't be able to roll out any of his aircraft. That excuse stunk all the way across two countries. I didn't want to hear any more weak excuses. I told, him that his friends and I would be waiting on the strip to light his landing. From midnight until the Bahamians came to arrest us at first light, we'd be there waiting for him.

Keeping my doubts to myself, I returned to the party and discreetly told the crew that Gene would pick us up on the airstrip sometime after midnight. I knew in my heart that he wasn't going to show. Everyone headed for the cottages to get a few hours rest before going out to the airstrip.

At five of twelve Mikey appeared club jeep to transport us to the runway. He brought along a hammer and nails so we could nail the customs officer's door shut to give him an excuse for not arresting our crew. There were two airplanes parked on the strip's apron. A Piper Seneca and an old Beech Queen Air. In my mind I was already figuring that I d "borrow "the Queen Air, if Gene didn't show up by the break of dawn. Using the fuel drains under the wings of the Seneca, we filled a five gallon can and drove it to the far end of the airstrip. Wanting the crew out of sight, it pained me to ask, but the only hiding place was the mangrove swamp running down the ocean side of the runway. I walked back to the jeep to ask Mikey who owned the Queen Air and if he could get a hold of a set of keys. Giving this kid a mission made him light up like a chandelier. He lit a joint, looked at me for a very long moment, trying to decide if he could trust me with Robert Vesco's secret. Vesco, the famous fugitive financier, had been expelled from the Bahamas at the request of the US government a couple of years earlier. Mikey told me that he still had a house on the island and used the Queen Air to fly from his refuge in Cuba to

Black Tuna Diaries

Chub Cay for meetings with the CIA and the other US agencies who were supposedly trying to arrest him. The big smuggler's yacht in the harbor also belonged to Mr. Vesco. He used it to transport pot from Cuba to the islands where it would be off loaded for shipment to south Florida. I assumed that at least part of the revenue would was used to finance CIA operations in the Caribbean. Vesco's pilot lived on Chub Cay. Mikey took the jeep and went to pick him up.

To make a long story short, for five grand, he would turn over the keys, if I promised to leave the plane at Sunair charters at Ft Lauderdale airport. He would pick it up there the next day. I paid up. Put the keys in my pocket for insurance, but still hoping that Gene would show up to fly us out.

Six times that night we heard an airplane overhead. Each time we emerged from the mangrove swamp and ran to the far end of the runway, poured a line of petrol across the concrete and lit it up, while at the other end Mikey sat in the jeep blinking his high beams. Pilots flying overhead must have wondered what was going on, as they flew over the island. I'm sure they realized something nefarious was taking place below. Somehow during the night, Barry, who swore he hadn't brought any drugs from the mainland and hadn't passed out stoned in the engine room of the Presidential, was Luded out of his mind and couldn't talk without slurring his words. He staggered over to the jeep trying to convince Mikey to raid the commissary and bring us out cokes and cupcakes. It didn't sound all that bad if you were too stupid or stoned to realize that without the jeep, we couldn't signal to Gene, if by some miracle he showed up. Barry reached into his shorts for some cash to bribe Mikey to make the run. Instead of cash he pulled out a half a dozen 714s, Quaaludes. There was no longer any need to deny he was stoned and had most likely been stoned in the engine room of the Presidential when it started sinking in the storm. He looked at the pills like he had never seen them before. With nothing more to say, he walked back into the mangroves and out of my sight.

The sky began to lighten in the east. It was time to leave. Gene wasn't coming! At least not in time to save us. I rounded

Black Tuna Diaries

up the guys, untied the ropes holding the Queen Air to the apron, removed the gust locks and pitot tube covers, and did a quick walk-around, before climbing into the left seat. I had never flown a Queen Air. In fact I had only a few hours flying twins of any sort. This Queen was ex-military, as was Vesco's pilot. It still had military switches and gauges which are very different from those found in civilian aircraft. The good news was, the start-up procedures were engraved on a small plaque fastened to the instrument panel. There was a similar plaque with the appropriate information next to most of the gauges and instruments. If you are not a pilot, take my word for this. No two planes of differing make or model, have the same systems. That is why you must take instruction and a check ride in every model you wish to fly. The Queen Air has geared engines, making it one of the more complicated piston twins. The only thing I knew about this plane before hand, was, that you could blow an engine by over boosting the power settings. The little military plaques at least gave me some idea of the parameters for systems settings. I waved to Mikey, and checked the gauges one last time. We rolled to the end of the runway, ran up the engines, checked the magnetos and oil pressure, pushed in full props, rich mixture, and fed in the throttles. Release the brakes, eat up some runway and climb into the sky.

At twenty-five hundred feet I eased back the power and leaned the mixture. Everything sounded good. The gauges were all in the green, so I let well enough alone and ceased fiddling with the instruments. I was headed due west toward the coast of Florida. It would be a short flight. I was thinking about looking for a map so I could set a more direct course for Ft Lauderdale International. There were no maps on board, so I just continued west trying to think up a plausible story for bringing five mud covered, mosquito bitten, sunburned, men with no I.D. of any kind, through U.S. Customs.

When I came out of my revelry, I was looking directly ahead at the unmistakable twin East-West runways of the Ft Lauderdale International Airport. Checking my radios for the first time, the little plaque told me that one radio was already set on the Ft Lauderdale tower frequency, and the other on ground control. I called the tower, reported that I was five

Black Tuna Diaries

miles out on short final for a straight in approach, going to the General Aviation Terminal for Customs check-in. With no one else in the pattern they cleared me for a straight-in on my requested runway. Drop the wheels and pull in some flaps or is it flaps first then wheels? No wonder I preferred fixed gear planes. Flaps, wheels, throttles back all the way, lightly kiss the runway, hold the nose wheel off and push hard on the brakes. Forgot to speak to ground control! Turned off at G.A. and parked on the right side of the terminal near the Sunair Charters office as I had promised.

There was a clip board with General Declaration forms in the map pocket. I filled one out for the five of us. As Pilot in Command, all I had to do was fill in a General Dec. and walk us through customs. I was counting on the fact that the two customs officers had been there all night and were ready to change shifts. As my sad looking crew marched past, I explained that we had been on an extended fishing trip and had been robbed of everything we owned, included our wallets with our I.D. They bought it! It wasn't that unusual, I gave the shrimp boat crew the remainder of my cash. Maybe two grand! When they looked at me like I had cheated them, I lost it. Told them they had fucked-up and they were lucky that I put my ass on the line to find and rescue them. Their friend Gene would have left them there to rot. To be fair to Gene, it turns out he did send a plane to pick us up. It arrived right after the Bahamian Marines! According to the pilots, Captain Beercan and Double Eagle, Ralph Slaughfter, they were armed and prepared to fight us free. Yeah Right!

I was about to get into a cab and head home when it occurred to me that Barry hadn't followed us out. I really didn't want to go back through customs to look for him. But I did. At first I figured he jumped the fence, rather than go through customs. I peeked in the Queen Air. There he was! Dead asleep. Once again luded to the eyeballs. I dragged him through the customs barrier as the inspectors looked on in sympathy, thinking he was sick. The last thing I did was drop the Queen Air keys at the desk at Sunair as promised. I was finally headed home to Lynne and my son. Burnt, broke and disgusted!

© 2009 R. Platshorn

Black Tuna Diaries

*Captain Beercan aka Captain Rivers, aka Brooks, was one of the most famous smuggling pilots of the 60s & 70s. Double Eagle was one of the founders of Soldier of Fortune Magazine.

Black Tuna Diaries

Chapter 20
Streets of New York

1966-1975! At times! Although the "Pitch" business paid for my college and served as my fall back, it was the streets of New York that provided me with a new bankroll or paid the bills when nothing else was generating cash for me. As a Vietnam era veteran, I was entitled to a New York City peddler's license that, in theory at least, allowed me to peddle various and sundry wares "on the East Side, West Side, or all around the town". It was my close friend in the pitch business, Jerry Crowley, or as he came to be known on TV, Chef Crowley, author of "The Fine Art of Garnish", the best selling garnishing book in the world, who taught me the "street game" and was my partner on "The Sidewalks of New York".

When most people think of a New York street peddler, they envision some guy who hangs out all day by the park or on a busy sidewalk, with a folding table, selling souvenirs or crafts, or a guy with a hot dog pushcart. That has nothing to do with the "street game", as we knew it in the days before the Knapp-Commission. A real street peddler appears on the streets only during the "RUSH" and disappears when it's over. Depending on the time of year and the item, he might work a morning rush from eight to nine am as people arrive for work. The most important Rush is the noon rush, from noon to two pm. Jerry and I usually worked the First Precinct, that's Wall St's financial district. Giant office buildings where tens of thousands pour out for lunch, covering the sidewalks and filling the deep canyons of lower Manhattan. Normally we worked only the lucrative busy noon rush. But every Friday we would work the "night rush", from four to six pm, selling flowers to homeward bound commuters.

Most days we would meet for coffee and a bagel at a "grab joint" (grab it and go) near the corner of Vesey and Broad St. I always arrived promptly at 10 am so we could eat and ready our pushcarts in plenty of time for the noon rush. Jerry always arrived between 11 and 11:30 am, with the admonition,

Black Tuna Diaries

"Robert, you worry too much. There's plenty of time to get ready. You live in a hurry, you die in a hurry, they bury you in a hurry, and forget about you in a hurry. Relax, or you'll develop an ulcer!"

Of course, I developed an ulcer. Now if you are going to be a peddler on Wall St., you need an office to keep your pushcarts and merchandise. We had one in an office building above the record shop on Vesey St. right off of Broad. We shared the place with Pat, Pauli, and our buddy Joe Fowler, one of the greatest pitchmen in America. Both Jerry and Joe could put Ron Popiel to shame when it came to selling Dial-O-Matics or Ginzu Knives. Joe actually pitched kitchen gadgets during the noon rush. Jerry and I usually worked items that didn't need demonstrating, just a "short pitch and a pass out".

New Yorkers love a bargain and if you are going to peddle in the same area every day, it's got to be a legitimate bargain. Jerry and I spent hours and sometimes days trooping up and down 23rd St., where all the major importers were located, and lower Broadway, where the jobbers and closeout dealers could be found, looking for a hot item for "the street". Jerry had a talent for it. He could spot items I thought would never sell. He always proved me wrong. Tiny radios, pantyhose, cigarette boxes, sweaters, hats, handbags from Morocco, lemon shakes, and decorations. But the most memorable things we ever peddled in Manhattan were Friday flowers, 4th of July sparklers, and Great Music of the Western World.

Every Friday, as soon as the noon rush was over, Jerry and I jumped in our peddler's truck and headed for the wholesale flower market on Broadway near 31st St. Our truck, a 1949 Chevrolet panel truck, bought at the New York City Police auction for a bid of twelve bucks. Formerly a painter's truck, it was hand painted an ugly dark green. The interior still held old canvas throw covers and empty paint cans of all hues. The only ignition key was an old red wooden handled screw driver kept under the driver's seat. Jam the screw driver in the ignition; give it half a turn and we were on our way uptown. Park the truck and walk from wholesaler to wholesaler.

Black Tuna Diaries

"Anything for the street?" We were looking for flowers that were just about to bloom. The wholesalers didn't want to hold on to them over the weekend, and would let them go at bargain prices. Cash!

Roses, of course, are what we always wanted. If we could buy them for twenty-five cents a "head" or less, we could make a killing, selling them at a buck a piece or ten bucks a dozen. But, it wasn't often we scored roses at the right price. Most Fridays we managed to find Daisies or Pompoms at a good price. We'd buy enough of them to take in two or three hundred dollars. Before heading back downtown, we'd stop at the florist supply store for green tissue to wrap the individual bouquets, rubber bands to hold them together on, and cans of pastel floral dye. Red, blue, pink, yellow, green, violet, that was the secret of turning a plain white bunch of Daisies or Pompoms into an irresistible rainbow of color.

It was now three o'clock. We had an hour to get back down to the financial district, wrap and color a hundred bunches of flowers, build a beautiful display, and be ready to sell by four, when the big office buildings broke for the Friday night rush. We usually did our creative preparations by Battery Park at South Ferry on lower Manhattan. One day as we were rushing to color a huge load of Pompoms, when a drunk stumbled up to Jerry and had an epiphany,

"Aha! So that's how come flowers is so many different colors. I always wondered about that"!

Unless the cops chased us away, we always worked flowers in front of the subway "hole" at Broad and Wall. Speaking of the cops, in those Pre-Knapp Commission days, "rent" had to be paid. The beat cop would chase you into an alley and berate you for blocking the sidewalk, while you slipped him a "pound" ($5.00). The "bubble gum machine", the cop car with a flasher on top, would pull up and holler, "hey you, get over here!" You stuck your head in the car and when you heard the words, "how's business?", you opened your fist and dropped a "sawbuck" ($10.00) on the floor of the car. Lastly, when you got back to the office or the truck, the Sergeant, or precinct bag

Black Tuna Diaries

man would be waiting to collect a "double saw" ($20.00) "for the boys in the precinct house".

Lower Manhattan, the financial district, is less than a square mile of tall office buildings and skyscrapers, where more than a million people who live elsewhere, come to work each day. Lawyers, stock brokers, bond dealers, bankers and merchant bankers, secretaries, doctors, food service and maintenance workers, to only mention a few. But no matter how diverse their jobs, at four o'clock on Friday afternoon, they'd pour out of the huge office blocks and into the only viable form of transportation in an area with virtually no parking at all, the subway. And there we were, wearing our newsboy aprons to hold the cash, as we passed out artfully colored bunches of Pompoms, Daisies, or Roses, from a huge display next to the "hole". Women would smile and dig out the two or three bucks as they ran for the train. Men required a bit of New York persuasion.

"Hey.. .big spender.. .bring her home something besides your dirty socks. Maybe you'll get lucky tonight". One way or another, by 6 o'clock, we usually had a couple of hundred bucks in our aprons and few if any flowers left. Jerry and I always saved the two best bunches for our ladies. If we were stuck with a lot of flowers, we would drive up to the Village, and duke them out to tourists, on a date.

"Pretty flowers for your pretty lady". Worked every time! What kind of cheapskate would refuse to spend a couple of bucks to buy his date a Rose or a bunch of pink Daisies.

Indeed the streets of New York are truly paved with gold. Never more so, than right before the Fourth of July. The "sparkler push". One week leading up to 4th of July, when a serious peddler could earn himself between ten or fifteen thousand dollars. I had heard about it, but never worked it. It was 1972. I had the waterfront concessions at The Pier House Hotel in Key West, Florida. Boat rentals, water skiing, fishing, and reef diving. Late June, business was slow, and I needed money for new boats and equipment. The call came from New York. It was Jerry.

Black Tuna Diaries

"Robert...come to New York and work the sparkler push with me". The timing was perfect.

Next morning I got on the big bird for the City. The "sparkler push" was a big operation, maybe the biggest, in the world of street peddlers. First of all, the payoff had to be "top to bottom". That meant everyone from the beat cop to the detectives in City Hall on Center St. That year, the partners that ran the push had paid in advance, $17,000.00 for the privilege of peddling sparklers in three precincts, for five days. Months in advance they had secretly brought into the city, a tractor trailer load of sparklers from New Jersey. This was kept in a secret location. Each morning of the push, a big rental truck would load up with sparklers and deliver a single day's worth of merchandise to a rented van in each of the three precincts. Each van would supply and resupply half dozen peddlers working that precinct. For the 4th of July push, we would all work both a noon rush and a night rush. On each of the four or five days leading up to the 4th, the volume of sales would double. On the last day before the 4th, it would be non-stop duking out sparklers at three boxes for five bucks, and stuffing cash into your apron pockets. Occasionally, you had to stop, just to fold up the bills so that you had room to stuff in another batch of fives and tens. That's the way things were supposed to work. Yeh Right!

In the summer of 72, there was a new wrinkle in the game. The fire department. They wanted an additional ten grand, on top of whatever portion of the original payoff they had already received. No one had ten Gs, nor did any of the original partners want to cut into their profits any deeper after the "top to bottom patch" had been paid. The cops sided with us. They figured the firemen were cutting in on their graft. So, for three days, there was war on Wall St. Promptly at five minutes to noon on the first day, Jerry and I pushed our loaded pushcarts into the elevator of our office building on Vesey St. The jewelers, secretaries, and insurance salesmen that populated the building would always stare in amazement, or sometimes smile and ask, "What are you guys selling today". We pushed the loaded carts up the steep hill to Wall St. and set up for business on opposite street corners.

Black Tuna Diaries

Within ten minutes, a Fire Inspector appeared with a summons book to write us a ticket for illegal sales of class B fireworks. Who cares! Peddlers would save up their summonses and pay them off in walk-in court at the rate of $2.00 each, that is, after a small fee to the detectives on the summons squad. Well just as I was tucking the ticket into my apron, and about to go back to selling sparklers, a big bright candy-apple red hook and ladder fire truck pulls up to the curb. The firemen jump down, throw my pushcart onto the truck and proceed to do the same to Jerry's cart, despite his attempt to disappear into the nearby alley, after seeing my stuff get pinched. This ain't good! The lunch rush is in full swing. It will be over in less than two hours. Missed time on the street can never be made up. We followed the fire trucks, three of them, until they had grabbed every single pushcart in our first precinct crew. There were seven of us working there!

They had us all spotted, ticketed, and our goods scooped up twenty minutes after we hit the street. It was a parade of peddlers trailing the fire engines to the precinct house. Pat, who was the running the operation in the 1st Precinct, was waiting by the police station door.

"Wait till the scumbag firemen leave, den go tru the station to the back door, grab your goods and go back to work".

We hung around while the push carts and boxes of sparklers were unloaded from the back of the fire trucks and pushed in through the front door of the police station. Even before the fire trucks pulled away, one of the precinct cops took me through the station to the back door and helped me get my reloaded cart out the door and down the steps. By the time I had pushed up to the corner, Jerry was wheeling up the street behind me.

"Robert", he shouted, "let's get back on the street and take in what we can before two o'clock". Every peddler knew that at 2 pm sharp, he had to be off the street, or risk immediate arrest. Bribes were only in effect during the rush hours, when the streets were jammed, and the cops could claim they "couldn't find the damn peddlers".

Black Tuna Diaries

We spent the rest of the noon rush trying to sell sparklers and running from the fire trucks. We even worked a night rush. The couple of hundred bucks we took in between us was far short of expectations. The next day was worse. To avoid being busted by the fire department, we took out only one pushcart. One of us would sell, while the other acted as "slough man" or lookout. We got in almost an hour, before the fire inspector was able to sneak up and block our escape before the fire engines pulled up and grabbed our stuff. This time, they left us the pushcart, and only took the merchandise. The reason become apparent when we arrived at the police station to retrieve our goods. It wasn't there! Knowing that the cops would return the goods, the firemen started taking it to the fire station. By the time the noon rush was over, they had grabbed a load of sparklers from every peddler in the precinct. Now we were not only losing the selling time on the street, we were losing merchandise we had already paid for. I still had not made back my plane fare and expenses. Things were getting serious. The cops were encouraging us to go and demand our goods back. The firemen weren't budging. They kept the sparklers under armed guard on the ground floor of the firehouse. It was a standoff. There would be no more work that day.

The bosses, Pat and Pauli, were headed to City Hall on Center St. to ask the police brass to intervene on our behalf. They and been paid and we needed to work. Pauli, who was running a crew up in the 5th Precinct was having the same problems. There was three days left before the weekend of the 4th, and almost an entire tractor trailer load of paid for sparklers, unsold, hidden somewhere in Manhattan.

Wednesday dawned without resolution of the problem. The only place to get funds to pay off the firemen was the loan sharks. This, by the way, was where most of the original payoff money came from.

Pat told us to take small loads of merchandise and try to work the lower end near South Ferry, while someone pulled a fire alarm at the north end of the precinct. None of us liked that idea, but we were getting desperate. In any case, by one

Black Tuna Diaries

o'clock, the fire trucks were again chasing us from pillar to post. That's when it happened! We were hiding in an alleyway.

"Bobby, wait in the alley until you see me go by. I'll be back in fifteen minutes. Once I go by, you'll be able to work for a while undisturbed".

Jerry disappeared and I lit a cigarette and moved deeper into the shadows of the narrow street. I was thinking about taking my loss and getting on a plane back to Key West, when I heard a commotion out on Wall St. Horns, sirens, crowds cheering and clapping. Leaving my meager load of sparklers in a dark alley, I ventured on to the street to see what was going on.

Stuck in traffic a block uptown from me, were three giant hook and ladder fire trucks. Flashers, horns, sirens, and whoop whoops couldn't part the dense traffic. Looking around I couldn't spot a fire. Curious, I climbed up on a fire hydrant to see above the packed lunch hour crowd, just as another loud cheer went up. Passing directly in front of me in the middle of Wall St., leading a parade of cars, trucks, and fire engines, was Jerry. He had made himself a tall red, white and blue Uncle Sam topper, and an absorbent cotton beard. He was pushing Joe Fowler's bright red Dial-O-Matic pushcart piled high with red, white and blue sparkler boxes. Dozens of lit sparklers decorated the cart. Jerry led the parade past thousands of cheering Wall Street workers. Down Wall St. and around to Broad St. then the wrong way up Vesey St. the fire engines chased Jerry, unable to get any closer through the slow dense traffic of lower Manhattan. With the firemen distracted and the crowd in a very patriotic mood, I sold every last sparkler in less than fifteen minutes. New Yorkers love a show. Jerry gave them one for the books.

They screamed at the firemen "Go put out a fire! Leave these guys alone!" And they cheered and clapped as Jerry led the parade three times around the same route.

The rest of the sparkler push was an anti-climax. A deal was struck for a modest payoff to the Fire Dept. The firemen were

Black Tuna Diaries

tired of chasing peddlers around the financial district. We worked unmolested for the last two days and maybe ended up with a couple of grand apiece. I flew back to Key West in time to put on the biggest clambake and beach party the town had ever seen.

Our Swan Song as street peddlers was truly musical. Springtime, maybe 1973, Jerry and I were both broke. Our Home Show season was over, and the summer fairs a couple months away. Why not work the streets? Okay! First we needed an item.

After trooping up and down 23rd St. from importer to importer and finding nothing appealing we could afford, we headed downtown to a jobber we knew, who specialized in perfume and fancy cosmetic closeouts. Those things were really Christmas items, but we were broke and desperate. The owner liked us, so we might be good for a short credit line. As street peddlers, we had a pretty good reputation for paying our bills.

"Boy, do I have something for you guys". He hadn't seen us for a couple of years but thirty seconds after letting us into his showroom was already taking us up on a dark freight elevator. Winding our way through piles of dusty and forgotten closeouts, he led us to a dark corner piled high with record albums. Thousands of record albums! Classical record albums! He grabbed a handful and took them over to a window where sunlight showed us his treasure.

"Great Music of the Western World". Twenty different albums, Bach, Brahms, Beethoven, Stravinsky, Rachmaninoff, Chopin, and more. The London Philharmonic, the Philadelphia Orchestra, Boston Pops, and New York Philharmonic. These were the leftovers from one of those Time/Life TV promotions. "Buy two now and get one each month for the next year and a half for only $9.95 + S&H". If we took them all off his hands, we could have them for fifteen cents apiece. Three thousand albums, $450.00 for the lot! A hell of a bargain! But no one in their right mind was going to buy classical record albums from

Black Tuna Diaries

a street peddler, even at prices too good to be true. Or so I thought.

I pulled Jerry aside. "Forget about it! We don't have $450.00 to begin with, and even if we did, we'd end up eating the damn things. Nobody is gonna buy Bach from a street peddler."

"Robert...relax, trust me. This is a score".

I knew better than to argue with him, we were about to piss away what little money we had. Jerry usually knew what he was doing, but I was convinced he was wrong this time. He turned to the owner,

"Listen; let us take a hundred record albums. If they go, we'll be back tomorrow for the rest of them".

The jobber just smiled and waved away the fifteen bucks I tried to hand him.

"You'll be back tomorrow for the rest of them, you can pay me then. If not, they're on the house". Jerry and I went back to the dust covered stacks to pick out s hundred albums. We tied them in four bundles and schlepped them back downtown on the subway, to our Vesey St. office.

Our "office", a huge dimly lit Aladdin's cave, was shared with Pat, who also owned the record store on the ground floor, Pauli, Yossel (Joey Fowler), Cathy, and one or two other peddlers who could be trusted with the keys. Pushcarts of various descriptions, dollies, slough boxes and tops, mobile sample cases, and the odds and ends of fifty different street promotions. Toys, handbags, pantyhose, men's shirts and ladies sweaters, Christmas decorations, blow-up souvenirs, American Flags left over from a Veteran's Day parade, Dial-O-Matics, Chop-O-Matics, Ginzu Knives, a couple of cases of sparklers, supplies for selling flowers, and boxes of remnants that hadn't been opened in ten years or more. Sitting unused in a dim corner was a large old-fashioned steamer trunk on wheels. Probably had been a salesman's sample case. With both doors

Black Tuna Diaries

fully opened, the old remnant from another era was large enough to hold twenty record racks. There were plenty of record racks from Pat's store, and lots of pegboard we could fit inside to hold the racks.

Using a few tools left over from past projects, we fitted the pegboard, mounted and filled the record racks, closed the 4 ft tall case and pushed it back into the dark corner where it had sat untouched for as long as we could recall.

As we went down the steps of the subway I shook my head and shrugged in doubt. "We have a display, but I still don't see how we can sell these damn things without being able to play them. To do that, we need electricity or maybe a two thousand foot extension cord".

"Relax Robert! You worry too much. I'll see you in the morning".

The next morning, as usual, I arrived at 10 am, waited for Jerry in the coffee shop until after 11, gave up and went up to the office to get ready for the noon rush.

"Didja at least buy me a coffee and a bagel?"

It was Jerry's greeting as he came through the office door at twenty to twelve, with a big box. As a matter of fact, there was a cold coffee and an even colder bagel waiting for him on top of a cardboard box near the door.

"What's in the Box?" I asked. He just smiled as he slugged down cold coffee and bit into the bagel and cream cheese.

"Relax; it's time to hit the street. I'll show you when we set down in front of the Stock Exchange".

Two could play the waiting game. I feigned disinterest, thinking, "at least the New York Stock Exchange might be the right place to sell classical records". We didn't work there often, because it was wide open, no place to hide, when the cops

Black Tuna Diaries

showed up. And they would show up! It would be like working in a huge amphitheater. I envisioned being chased down Wall St. with the heavy steamer trunk, three or four times before the lunch rush was over.

No one was on the elevator when we pushed the trunk and the big box inside and rode down to the street. With Jerry's box on top of our mobile store, we pushed uphill to Wall St. and over to the curb in front of the imposing facade of the Greek columned New York Stock Exchange. I tied on my money apron and opened up the doors of our record display. It was still early, but a few curious passers-by stopped to look and ask the price.

"Two bucks, three for five", I replied, convinced we were wasting our time. Jerry emerged from behind the trunk with a pair of small stereo speakers he had taken from the mystery box.

"Hold these for me Robert". He ducked down again and pulled from the mysterious box a gray plastic portable record player. Now, you have to understand, in the days before tapes, 8 tracks, or CD s, music was in the form of large records that required a turntable, amplifier and speakers. These required more power than the existing batteries could provide for portability. So, there were practically no portable record players. But, Jerry had somehow found one. He looked at me and almost burst out laughing.

"Thirty bucks, my last thirty bucks, down on Canal St. You can find anything on Canal St". He fished eight big "D" cell batteries form his jacket pocket. "I only had enough cash for one set of batteries. I can run up Vesey to the drug store after we take in some bread. These will only last fifteen minutes, if we're lucky. That's why this thing was so cheap. Nobody can afford the batteries."

He put the, stereo together and I picked out a record to test the machine. "Let's rock em with Rachmaninoff."

Black Tuna Diaries

If you know anything about New Yorkers, you can imagine the size of the crowd we had attracted in front of the Exchange. Show Time! I held the album up and made a big deal of breaking the cellophane wrapper, pulling out the large record in its white paper sleeve, handling it like a delicate flower, I slid it from the sleeve and touching only the center and the edges, I put it on the turntable. I found the on/off switch, flipped it on and the record began to spin. The huge crowd was utterly silent, as I lifted the arm from its cradle and gently, oh so gently lowered it to the grooves of the black disc.

Nothing! Not a sound! I searched frantically for the volume control. Found it underneath the turntable case and turned it all the way in both directions. Nothing! The crowd was beginning to turn away.

"Robert", said Jerry as he held up two wires with small jacks on the ends. "I told you don't be in such a hurry". He waved the wires for the crowd to see. "Sorry folks, my partner was never trained on this kind of sophisticated equipment".

I took the wires, jacked them into the speaker inlets and WE HAD MUSIC....BIG MUSIC....even from sixty or seventy feet away, it reverberated and was amplified by the marble portico of the New York Stock Exchange. In seconds the crowd doubled, and doubled again in size. They were rockin to Rachmaninoff. A few brave souls skeptically handed over a deuce and took away a record album. Then a few more!

"Hey...take home some serious sounds", I chanted as I slipped a record into a paper bag. "Each album comes in its own genuine brown paper carrying case."

By 2 pm we had sold most of the records. The slower stuff like Brahms and Handle remained in the racks. Not a bonanza, but a short days pay.

Black Tuna Diaries

Listen Roberto, today they took a shot to see what we were really selling. Once they get home and play them on their home stereo, they'll be back to buy one of everything. Tomorrow we'll sell everything we can carry out here".

We no longer had The Green Monster, our $12.00 peddler's truck, so the following morning I used my Hertz card and rented a van to pick up the balance of the three thousand record albums. When I pulled up in front of the jobber's building, he already had the records loaded on a big cargo dolly, ready to be transferred into my van. "You were expecting me?"

He laughed, "I knew you'd be back for the rest of the records. The only problem is, when these are gone, there are no more".

I handed him a check for $450.00 drawn on my Philadelphia business, "The Ice Cream Factory". "Look, I know you'd rather have cash. Today is Wednesday. Hold the check and I'll be here Friday at 3 o'clock and buy it back from you".

He handed me back my check and said, "Pay me Friday".

I made it down town by 11 and, by some major miracle, Jerry was standing in front of our building on Vesey St. with the biggest dolly in our warehouse. We loaded the records on, and Jerry lugged them up on the elevator, while I stashed the van. By the time I got back to the office, Jerry was loading our steamer trunk with every album he could jam into the racks.

"Robert, load a slough box with extra merchandise and put it on a small dolly. Those stock brokers are gonna grab everything we can carry".

Fully loaded, we could barely manage to push the big trunk and heavy slough box up the steep hill to Wall St. At one minute to noon, we were set up by the curb in front of the imposing columns of the New York Stock Exchange. I reached for the Rachmaninoff.

Black Tuna Diaries

Jerry stopped me. "My turn". He picked out "The 1812 Overture" by the New York Philharmonic. "Put it on the fir cut and but wait till they start coming out the doors before you turn it on."Promptly at high noon they broke through the wide doors of the Exchange. "DIT DIT DIT . . . DAH"! The 1812 Overture...and the pass out was on! They raced down the steps to be first in line to grab one of every album. They were shoving money at us. Jerry had thought to bring out shopping bags so that they could carry off fifteen or twenty records at a time. There wasn't even time to fold the money. Just jam it in the apron pockets. Ones on the right, fives in the center, tens and twenties in the left hand side!

By Friday, we were down to odds and ends. All the good stuff was gone. We sold down to the last thirty of forty records and called it quits by 1:30 pm. We put the trunk back where we found it with the remainder of the records still inside. Jerry took the battery eating stereo for his kids, and we walked uptown to the jobber's place to pay our bill and thank him for his trust. We both left town with two grand in our kick. A nice weeks pay in 1973. Jerry had food and rent money to tide him over for a couple of weeks till the Atlantic City boardwalk would come alive with visitors. I had enough cash to ready my ice cream carts and stock my snack bar concession at Philadelphia's Play House in The Park. The building on Vesey St. where we had our office is gone now. The pushcarts, dollies, slough boxes, and remnants of a hundred street promotions are buried somewhere in a New Jersey landfill. Maybe, if you look up into the sky above the landfill, you just might see a Seagull ... .rocking to Rachmaninoff.

Black Tuna Diaries
Illustrations

With mom in Atlantic City

On my first hit for the South St. Gang

Black Tuna Diaries

The Platshorns of South St. Paula, Annie, Marilyn, Joe, me.

Black Tuna Diaries

The South St. Gang goes to Camp
First row second from left Robby Meinster. Third from left Bobby Platshorn
Second row far right the boss Cookie Baumholtz

Fishing-Miami-1953

Black Tuna Diaries

Actor.."Rep Elliot".Age 15..eighteen hard earned bucks for this resume photo.

Black Tuna Diaries

Lynne 15 & Bob 16-1959-Already on the Rocks

Hot date-H. S. senior-1960

Black Tuna Diaries

University of Miami Years
Miami Beach-1962

My Beehive Beauty-1963-U of M

Black Tuna Diaries

London Years
My Bloomsbury office. Stirred..not shaken.

No its not Austin Powers..Its the original!

Black Tuna Diaries

Astrid shows off her Dynamic Reading skills on the Eamon Andrews Show-London 1968

Black Tuna Diaries

A much needed drink afterwards

Black Tuna Diaries

Back in the USA
Elen with our daughter Hope-1973

With my beautiful daughter Hope

Black Tuna Diaries

Return to Miami
The Platshorns of 9th Ct. Miami...Charlie, Matt & Lynne

Bob & Boob..on Pacifier at Fontainebleau docks

Black Tuna Diaries

The REAL Black Tuna Gang

The Fishing Fools

Black Tuna Diaries

Bobby, Robby, Capt Elm., friends and fish-1978

Our Biggest Distributor and My Pal the Illusive Mr. X

Black Tuna Diaries

A PROMISE KEPT-Lynne, Matt & mom on the Yacht Presidential

Our last photo before prison. 1979

Black Tuna Diaries

FBI and DEA Say They've Broken Nation's Biggest Marijuana Ring

By Charles R. Babcock
Washington Post Staff Writer

Federal authorities announced yesterday that they have broken up what is alleged to be the largest marijuana ring in the country—a paramilitary group charged with smuggling 500 tons of "Colombian Gold" worth $300 million into the United States over the past 16 months.

Fourteen alleged members of the smuggling operation were arrested yesterday on racketeering and drug charges detailed in a 105-page indictment returned by a federal grand jury in Miami.

The indictment charges that the group was run by two businessmen who set up a car dealership to

In April 1978, the indictment charged, Ronald B. Elliott, a former Eastern Air Lines pilot and another of those charged, said he had a plan "to steal an Eastern Airlines Boeing 727-type aircraft, use it to smuggle a load of marijuana into the United States and then ditch the aircraft over the Atlantic Ocean."

In July 1977, Mark S. Phillips, a Fort Lauderdale yacht broker who also was indicted, allegedly walked into the Landmark Bank in Fort Lauderdale and took $223,000 in cash from a suitcase to pay the owner of an 85-foot yacht the group wanted to refit for smuggling. The name of the vessel was

Herald

paper

92 Pages
Copyright 1979 The Miami Herald

Final Edition
20 cents

69th Year — No. 183

Marijuana Cases

Drug Ring Is Busted, Called Giant in Trade

By AL MESSERSCHMIDT And JOE CRANKSHAW
Herald Staff Writers

Like a sophisticated corporation, the Black Tuna Gang smoothly ran its affairs from a Fontainebleau Hotel suite, dispatching an armada of seagoing vessels and a fleet of long-haul trucks, mobilizing a private army, and matter-of-factly banking satchelsful of cash.

But the group's business, a Miami federal grand jury said Tuesday, was drugs — a lot of drugs, even by the jaded standards of South Florida traffic. By the grand jury's reckoning, the Black Tuna Gang realized profits of $12 million during just 16 months of operation in 1976 and 1977.

"This," Attorney General Griffin Bell said in Washington Tuesday, "is the largest case brought by the Department of Justice in the drug trafficking field since I've been

fruits of our policy of combined FBI-DEA investigation into major drug trafficking."

Illegal drug smuggling in the U.S. is a $300-million industry. The Black Tuna Gang's 14 alleged members, Bell said, had a five per cent cut of the trade.

Thirteen of those persons were arrested Tuesday after the jury handed down an exhaustive 105-page indictment that reads like a paperback thriller.

Described by the jury are the $300,000 ransom of a gang member from a Colombian Army colonel who had taken him hostage; the apparent free access to classified Drug Enforcement Administration documents for counter-intelligence purposes; and the private security force equipped with grenades, automatic weapons and

Black Tuna Diaries

UNITED STATES DEPARTMENT OF JUSTICE
DRUG ENFORCEMENT ADMINISTRATION
Washington, D.C. 20537

FOR IMMEDIATE RELEASE
TUESDAY, MAY 1, 1979

DEA
(202) 633-1333

A federal grand jury in Miami, Florida, Monday indicted 14 persons on charges of operating a marihuana smuggling ring that was responsible for bringing in some 500 tons of Colombian marihuana during a 16-month period.

Attorney General Griffin B. Bell said the 40-count indictment, which was unsealed today, was returned in U.S. District Court in Miami. It follows a 12-month investigation conducted by the Drug Enforcement Administration, the Federal Bureau of Investigation and the Criminal Division of the Justice Department.

The indictment alleges that a criminal enterprise organized and headed by Robert Jay Meinster and Robert Elliot Platshorn, both Miami businessmen and co-partners in the South Florida Auto Auction in Miami, began in August of 1974 when Meinster and Platshorn began running ton loads of Colombian marihuana from South Florida to storage facilities in Philadelphia, Pa., which was at that time their base of operation.

-more-

Black Tuna Diaries

8 Men Are Convicted of Operating Drug Ring After a 4½-Month Trial

MIAMI, Feb. 4 (AP) — Eight men accused of running a multimillion-dollar drug smuggling ring known as "Black Tuna" were convicted today after a 4½-month trial.

A six-man, six-woman jury handed down the verdict after deliberating for six days. Among those convicted were three men described as ring leaders, Robert Jay Meinster, 40 years old, and Robert Elliot Platshorn, 37, both of Philadelphia, and Eugene Arter Myers, 40, of Tampa. They were found guilty of conspiracy, racketeering and a Federal charge of running a "continually criminal enterprise" that could result in a life prison term. Sentencing is expected about the end of this month.

The other five were convicted on charges ranging from conspiracy and racketeering to possession of marijuana and perjury. Two of them disappeared after the trial started. One of the 14 persons who were indicted April 30, 1979 by a name assigned to its alleged Colombian supplier, imported $300 million in marijuana into the United States from 1974 to 1978.

Million Pounds Smuggled

The Government said that at one point the ring was responsible for 8 percent of the nation's smuggling total.

Mr. Meinster was found guilty on 10 of 12 counts and could be fined up to $270,000; Mr. Platshorn was convicted on 14 of 17 counts and could be fined a total of $325,000, and Mr. Myers was found guilty on all eight counts against him and could be fined up to $240,000. The others who were convicted were Modesto Echezarreta-Cruz, 43, of Key Biscayne; Randal Gene Fisher, 22, of Fort Lauderdale; Richard Elliott Grant Jr., 24, of Hollywood, Fla., Mark Steven Phillips, 31, and Carl Jerry London, 38, a former Mayor of Clarkesville, Ga.

Drug Smuggling Figure Sentenced to 64 Years

MIAMI, May 24 (AP) — Robert Elliot Platshorn was sentenced to 64 years in prison and fined $325,000 yesterday by Federal District Judge James King for his role in the "black tuna" drug smuggling operation.

Mr. Platshorn was sentenced after five and a half hours of proceedings on 14 counts stemming from his involvement in the elaborate organization.

He was one of eight men convicted in February after a tumultuous, four-and-

Black Tuna Diaries

Doing Time – Growing Old

Lewisburg Pen-1982

FCI Otisville NY-1983

Otisville-1986

FCI Butner-1988

Maxwell AFB-2006

FCI Coleman-2008

© 2009 R. Platshorn   303

Black Tuna Diaries

April 1, 2008 Finally Free
First a day of Fishing

The Old Pitchman is back. Selling cookware at Sam's Club. 2008

Black Tuna Diaries

A video interview for High Times

Tuna Talk-Univ. of Central Fl..2009

Black Tuna Diaries

Weddings & Tattoos   *L. with our granddaughter in limo.*

Lynne and I Commit Matrimony Again
I DO!

A brand new granddaughter

© 2009 R. Platshorn   306

Black Tuna Diaries

Chapter 21
Just like in the Movies

The saddest words in the English language, "Daddy, when are you coming home?"

Sentenced to 64 years in federal prison, most of it under a non-parolable "Kingpin" statute. Kingpin! I'm not even a safety pin, let alone a kingpin. How the hell did I ever get to be a kingpin? Whatever! This sentence will never stick. It will be overturned on appeal. That's what all the lawyers tell us. For pot! Marijuana! Weed! No violence! No way will I have to do all that time. Surely the government will come to their senses. Joke over! "Just hang in until the appeal is decided, then you'll go to some Club Fed camp for a year or two and you'll be back with your family." Of course I believed it! That's how I kept my sanity, not only at the start of my long journey, but all the way up to my last eighteen months in prison. I always believed I was going win an appeal, or a motion for sentence reduction, or would overturn my case with new evidence or a stronger legal argument based on a new case from the Supreme Court. I always had some sort of legal action pending in the courts. Most were written and filed pro se.

But for now we are on our way to the Pen, the Big House, the Joint! Robby with his sixty-one year sentence, to Terre Haute Pen, and me with my sixty-four, to "The Belly of The Beast", Marion Ill., America's only "Supermax"! The place they built to replace Alcatraz "The Rock". Cuffed, shackled, and black-boxed (a very painful device that prevents all movement of the hands and wrists, normally reserved for violent offenders), we began our three month trek north.

First stop the federal prison at Tallahassee. For three weeks we were kept on the top floor of a long unused segregation building. Just Robby, me, and the Colonel, Harold Rosenthal who had recently returned from the dead (his remains had been found in a crashed aircraft several years earlier). Our only other company, a shotgun toting guard stationed at the

Black Tuna Diaries

end of the deserted tier. My only recollection of those weeks isolated in the filthy cobwebbed building was of starving rats and roaches that would swarm onto our face and body whenever we would lie down to sleep. Mostly we slept sitting up with all the lights on. Even then, I'd wake every few minutes to brush off the starving vermin.

Next stop Atlanta, "The Big House". Seven weeks in another segregation unit. This one fully occupied and functioning. Noise, one hell of a lot of noise! Movement? You got to shower three times a week. and go out to the tiny segregation yard every other day. Rats and roaches were only normally troublesome. And "GW", each week they gave us a pouch of George Washington tobacco! Back in those days, they gave you two packs of class B cigarettes on the bus rides and roll-your-own tobacco in the prisons. At "The Big House" you got GW! You could chew it, smoke it in a pipe, or roll it into a cigarette. It was moist and "rough-cut", so it made a very lumpy hard to light cigarette, but it tasted pretty good. The unremitting din of inmates screaming, hollering, banging, and cursing usually went on well past midnight. The relief was palpable when it finally quieted down. And then I heard it! Just like in the old prison movies. Someone was softly playing a mournful spiritual on a harmonica. "Swing low, Sweet Chariot, Coming forth to Carry Me Home". Yeh! This was a real prison. This is where they sent the real tough guys. James Cagney, Edward G. Robinson, George Raft. Those old prison movies, were the only point of reference I had to my present reality.

Last stop before Marion, was Terre Haute Penitentiary. "The Hut"! There, Robby and I were separated. He went to "population", where he would spend the next six years. I was put in "I-Up", the seg unit for all the bad guys headed to Marion Supermax. Except for an occasional shower, I spent the next two weeks in a small single cell where the lights were kept burning brightly twenty-four hours a day.

Each transfer meant a long bus ride in cuffs, shackles, belly chains, and black-boxes. Completely immobilized, I had to contort my entire body to eat, drink or use the toilet. It was a re-

Black Tuna Diaries

lief, after almost three months to finally arrive at my designated hell.

The Supermax penitentiary at Marion Illinois, from the outside looks like a maze of chain link fences, miles of razor wire from the ground to above the top of the fences, and more guard towers than you can easily count. Each one looking like a glass-topped airport control tower. Through the thick maze of razor wire you could just barely make out the long low two story prison building.

Once through the sally port, you step into a small courtyard leading to the entrance to the "Belly of the Beast". On your left, as you hobble along in your shackles and chains, is what looks like a miniature courthouse. And in fact, that is precisely what it is. A Federal Court, within the walls of a federal prison. Nothing could be more emblematic.

There were only four of us delivered up to the beast on that day. Once inside the prison walls you expect your chains, cuffs and shackles to be removed. At Marion that does not happen. We were forced to hobble through three or four sections of corridor, each separated by a metal detector and a heavy barred electric gate, then made to wait on a wooden bench near an elevator. Still chained trussed and hobbled, we were taken, one by one up to the Warden's office for A & 0 , Admittance and Orientation! In any other federal prison, A & 0 is a week long series of lectures by every department head in the prison. It is exhausting, boring and redundant. At Marion the entire process took just five minutes. Still immobilized in my rusty chains and shackles, I was duck-walked to the elevator and delivered in front of the Warden's desk and surrounded by two hacks, two Lieutenants, and the Captain. What took place in the next few minutes was straight out of an old Cagney prison flick.

While the two screws tapped their nightsticks against the palms of their hands, the Warden stood in front of me and gave me the, " we know to handle tough guys" speech. Then the Captain crammed a rulebook down the front of my orange jumpsuit and I was duck walked back to the elevator. Back on

Black Tuna Diaries

the ground floor, it was torture hobbling through several more long corridors divided by more electric gates, until we reached "F" unit. At last the cuffs, chains and shackles were removed. I was admitted to the cell block, and put in a single cell, in the center of the lower tier.

At Marion, because of the extremely high murder rate, everyone gets to live alone in a single cell. In the cell to my right was Nicky Barnes, the heroin king of Harlem. In a few months Nicky would be transferred to Terre Haute and shortly thereafter become an informer for the government To my left was a young white boy who was shortly to become the first corpse I was to see in prison. The reason for his murder, as best as I can recall, was that during the commission of some sort of crime, he had raped an elderly woman and left her tied to a tree to die. I did not witness his demise, but managed to view his corpse strapped to a gurney, handcuffed and chained, despite being obviously quite dead. The body was awaiting an ambulance to take him to a local hospital where he would officially be pronounced "Dead on Arrival". Welcome to federal prison, welcome to Marion!

The prison was on 24/7 lock down when I arrived, and stayed that way for many months. At first our meals were brown-bagged and tossed in through the bars. After a couple of weeks they began marching us, one cell block at a time to the chow hall. That's when the guy in the cell to the left of mine, was eviscerated on his way to lunch. Or was it his way from lunch. I didn't get to see it happen, because I had been told in the strongest of terms, to stay in my cell and not go to lunch. I got to view the corpse on my way to supper five hours later, because it was still "waiting for the ambulance".

The FBI maintained an office in the prison. After each murder, everyone from that cell block was marched in for an interview. Anyone remaining in the FBI office more than thirty seconds, before returning to the cell block, had signed his own death warrant

For a year my lawyer Art Tifford, my friends and family, and my partner Robby's lawyer Dennis Cogan, sued and petitioned

Black Tuna Diaries

the government to have me moved from the Supermax to a Low, where according to Fed's evaluation system, as a non violent first time pot offender, I should have been sent to begin with. My last six months at Marion were spent in the "hole", where I awaited a decision on my removal to a lower level prison.

It was in the seg unit at Marion, I began to learn about the few of the more bazaar sexual aberrations found in federal prison. Three times a week inmates were given two hours of exercise. . You could choose one or two rec partners, if you were willing to sign a release form absolving the prison of any responsibility, if you happened to be murdered by one of your rec partners. In good weather, you could walk out in the small seg yard attached to the unit. Otherwise you could walk up and down the long corridor in front of seg cells, stopping to do sit-ups and push ups at both ends of the corridor. During indoor rec, the first odd thing I noticed was that there was always one or two people standing by their cell doors peering out of the peek-slot, smiling at whoever was in the corridor. According to "One Eyed Joe Deckert", the peepers were masturbating while they "fiended" on whoever was walking by. Male, female, dog, cat, or cockroach, It made no difference! My rec partners were One Eyed Joe, an old pot smuggler and nephew of an old Meyer Lansky associate, and the other, a friend of Joe's called "Footy". Footy was a six foot seven, dark skin black man. Maybe forty-six years old. A New York bank robber.

One cold winter day Footy and I were doing indoor rec. Joe had been removed on writ and Footy and I were walking the corridor in front of the cells, doing push ups, jumping jacks, sit-ups, and running in place at each end of the long passage. During indoor rec, your cell doors remain open so that you can use the toilet or sit down to take a break. Near the end of our two hour rec period, Footy invited me into his cell for a break and a cold drink. After a few minutes, noticing I was tensed and strung out from our workout, Footy offered to help me relax with a foot message.

"Guaranteed to remove all your tension!".

Black Tuna Diaries

I tried to politely demure, but in a few seconds he had my shoes and socks off and my right foot in his lap. His thumbs circled from heel to toe rubbing out the tension. It worked! After a minute or two, I had my eyes closed and was leaning back in the chair in front of Footy's bunk. He was humming as he sat on his bunk working the tension from the bottom of my right foot. Footy , who normally spoke better English than me, started to mumble something that sounded like, "Feets, I loves feets, oh I surely loves feets."

Louder and louder, he kept repeating this litany. I opened my eyes just as I felt his hands tense tightly on my foot and I saw his eyes roll back in his head.

"OH GOD I LOVES FEETS" he yelled as he climaxed.

When he finally let loose of my foot, I grabbed my shoes and socks, and was flying out the cell door as he opened one eye and whispered,

"Now you knows why they calls me Footy "!

Black Tuna Diaries

Chapter 22
Death in the Federal Pen

Everyone knows that a black cat has nine lives, but a Black Tuna has only seven. This is the true story of how I lost my fifth, in the federal penitentiary at Lewisburg Pa.

"We have re-examined Mr. Platshorn's record and agree that he belongs in a lower level institution". That was in a letter to Dennis Cogan and Arthur Tifford, the attorneys who had been trying to spring me from the Supermax at Marion Illinois. It was written by Norman Carlson, the Director of the Federal Bureau of Prisons. It went on to say that considering my lack of a previous criminal record and the fact that I'd never been involved in any sort of violence, I qualified for a low level correctional facility. Using the rational that my crime garnered broad publicity, (generated mostly by government press releases), and involved "sophistication", I had been sent to the most dangerous prison in America, "The Belly of the Beast", Marion penitentiary. The place John Gotti would not survive. Well, despite the ill intent, I survived Marion, for more than a year and a half. Now the Director of Prisons was admitting I should never have been in a place like that and he was having me transferred immediately, "to a lower, level institution". That would have been a real joke, if it hadn't of led to a serious attempt on my life. You see, they didn't transfer me to a camp or even a low level correctional facility. They sent me to the "Pen" at Lewisburg. Maybe, the second toughest joint in the federal system!

After only a few tortuous weeks on the prison express, I landed in the "Burg". But now I was beginning to learn the ropes. My crime and my background did not qualify me for incarceration at a penitentiary, so it was necessary for me to sign a form releasing the Bureau of Prisons from any responsibility in the event I was harmed or murdered. On the advice of my lawyer, I refused to sign the release form. The theory being, that eventually, they would have to send me to a prison commensurate with my classification. In the mean time, since

Black Tuna Diaries

I refused to sign a release, they couldn't put me into the general population. So, they threw me in "The Hole". It's only rival in the Fed system for "Black Hole of Calcutta" title, was another place I had the privilege of spending a few months, the old seg unit in Atlanta, Charlie house.

The seg cells in Lewisburg, ancient narrow affairs, just long enough for a narrow bunk bed, a small sink, and seatless toilet. They were no wider than the space necessary to squeeze past the bunk. Heated year round by huge floor to ceiling ceramic hot water pipes, the cells were so hot, it was necessary to wrap all your bedding around the pipes to insulate against the blazing heat, and lie in bed in no more than your skivvies.

Despite the fact that there were three floors of these tiny torture chambers, it was often so over crowded, that people being held over in transit, were housed four to a cell. Two in the narrow bunks, one on the floor under the bunks and one on the floor half under the sink and partially wrapped around the reeking toilet. Often they would be housed like this for weeks. The stench quickly became overwhelming and those on the floor were constantly fighting off the rats, roaches, spiders and mice, which were endemic to the ancient dungeon. Twice, as a holdover in transit, I spent a week under these conditions.

The eight months I spent in the Lewisburg hole waiting to be assigned to a lower security prison, thankfully were spent in a cell with only one other occupant. Being locked in a cell twenty-four seven, with a stranger rarely engenders an acceptable comfort level. You tend to sleep with one eye open and something sharp within easy reach.

I recall three "cellies" from those months, Benny, Mark, and Stevie. After a month, I became an "Orderly", or as they used to call em in the movies, a "Trustee". That means that I was out of my cell most of the day, helping to feed, clean, hand out laundry, and distribute the vast amounts of contraband that was smuggled into the hole almost every day. But before I got to be an Orderly, I was locked in my overheated dungeon cell with **Benny the Bed Shaker**. Benny, 5ft 6inches tall, maybe a

Black Tuna Diaries

hundred and fifty pounds soaking wet, twenty five years old, with a head barely the size of a softball. He was a pale white guy, with black hair, a scraggly little mustache, and beady pale blue eyes. Benny was raised in DC and thought he was a black man. Not the brightest campfire at the Jamboree, Benny would lie up in the top bunk with his skivvies pulled down to his knees and "choke the chicken" twenty-four seven. Even bolted to the wall, the old steel bunk bed would shake, rattle, and sway uninterrupted, except for meals. He had rubbed his tiny Johnson till it was bright red and worn it down to the size of a peanut. Benny the Bed Shaker, spent the entire day masturbating like a demented monkey.

Finally, on the third day, after begging him to "Give it rest" with no noticeable effect, I couldn't take it anymore. I stood up in the narrow space beside our bunk, and calmly tossed one lit match after another onto his bare, filthy, cum stained mattress.

"Wait! Wait! Just let me finish! Please, just let me finish"! Benny shouted as he frantically fisted his tiny raw organ in a futile effort to climax one more time before the flames reached his skinny unwashed butt. When the guards rushed in to put out the fire, Benny had enough sense to say that he had fallen asleep with a cigarette in his mouth. A mattress fire is always a suspicious occurrence, so Benny the Bed Shaker was moved to another cell.

My next cellie was "Big Cat" Stevie L. Big Cat was a big dark haired, well built Jewish kid in his late twenties. A "homey" from Philly. When it came to throwing fists, Stevie was the second toughest guy I ever met in the federal prison system. Big Cat thought that flag football and basketball were full contact sports. He loved going down to the tiny gym in the seg unit to play "free for all" basketball with five or six of the biggest black guys in the hole. Most times, at the end of the rec period, Big Cat was the only one left standing. There was one other white guy I knew who liked to do the same thing. The man who was considered the toughest fighter in federal prison, Little Ralphie Gambina. Five foot four, with hair down to his butt, Ralphie had a hard time convincing guys twice his

Black Tuna Diaries

size to "play a little ball". Also, a denizen of the "hole" at Lewisburg, I once saw Ralph, who hated prison gangs and bullies, take on and whip four members of a neo-Nazi gang, at one time, and then take on and put down six huge baton wielding members of the prison "Goon Squad". Whenever he was in a fight, you could hear his opponents pleading, "No Ralph! Please Ralph! No more Ralph!"

Once, after a fight, he was confined in a tiny punishment cell. Using nothing but his bare hands, Ralphie tore down the walls to the two adjacent cells, just so he could have room to pace.

But back to my buddy Big Cat. Shortly after he moved in with me, he also made orderly. Now we could both move around the entire three floor seg unit. In no time we found ourselves in charge of distributing the drugs and other contraband that was coming into the unit every day. Given a choice, no one in their right mind would take on that job. But if you were an orderly, and wanted to continue aspirating, you "took care of business". While this activity paid well, in the form of a share of everything that made it in, it was ultimately a suicidal endeavor. Even if the guards never caught you, it was only a matter of time before some homicidal paranoid convict decided that you had helped yourself to his drugs. Fortunately, beside considering us both trustworthy, they were all too shit scared to mess with the "Big Cat".

You may wonder how large quantities of drugs, weapons, and cash could make their way into a high security punishment unit in a high security federal penitentiary. Well, there were a lot of ways. Convicts always find a way! The method in vogue, when Stevie and I worked it, was the beverage container. A twenty-five gallon, four foot high, stainless steel cylinder containing a caustic chemical referred to as "Jim Jones Punch". Three times a day, a huge food cart containing a couple of hundred meals in individual plastic trays and the big juice container would travel from the main kitchen via underground tunnels and emerge in the little seg gym. Big Cat and I would meet the carts at the outer door. We had less than a minute to drag the two hundred pound juice container into the

Black Tuna Diaries

tiny adjacent shower room, remove the sealed top and tip it over spilling almost a third, reach deep inside to retrieve a plastic bag with the contraband, refill the container with water, and drag it back into the gym, before the seg guard opened a door three stories above, to activate the lift gate elevator that would take the carts to the top floor of the seg unit. It was a Chinese Fire drill of heart pounding activity. I hated every second of it, but wasn't given any choice in the matter. I was much relieved when they started sending up the "Jim Jones" in powder form. Right about that time, Steve reached his release date, and I was happy to see him go home to his wife and daughters.

It was just after Big Cat left and before my pal Ralphie Gambina arrived in the hole that the Swede tried to kill me. Had either of my two tough friends been around, I doubt he would have made a move on me. Six foot four, two hundred seventy pounds, blond, ugly, mean, and like most bullies, a physical coward. The Swede was a certified maniac. His favorite past time back in Minnesota, was to go out on one of the many lakes in his speedboat and with a .45 caliber automatic, and shoot big holes in passing boats. He believed there was nothing wrong with shooting boats, as long as he wasn't actually aiming at the occupants. It was easy to imagine the stark terror of a boater out on the lake with his wife and kids, when this giant nut case opened up on them with his .45. I once got up the courage to ask if he ever killed anyone on the lake. His reply was "not deliberately", said as if it absolved him of any responsibility.

My new cellie, Mark "The Magic Man", and I were in the gym waiting for the big stainless steel food cart to make its way slowly up to the third floor, where the Swede was waiting to remove it from the open lift-gate platform that ran on pipes up side of the exposed metal staircase. I was a few feet in front of the jury-rigged lift when it reached the third floor. I was talking to Mark with my back to the lift, when he looked up and turned deathly white. Mark was trying to tell me something, but couldn't get the words out. Just as I took a step closer to hear what he was trying to tell me, there was a sound like thunder. The gym floor shook hard enough to rattle my

Black Tuna Diaries

teeth, and almost a ton of insulated stainless steel, with over a hundred and fifty hot meals, hit the ground exactly where I had been standing. Six foot tall, eight foot long and four foot wide, on six heavy duty wheels, with a heating unit at one end and refrigeration unit at the other, this monster landed upright and exploded open, spewing hot and cold food trays across the gym floor. It took me a couple of seconds to realize how close I had just come to being killed. All the blood must have drained from my head. Mark had to catch me to keep me from passing out as my knees gave way. After a minute, I looked up at the lift gate expecting to see it collapsed or hanging from the heavy pipes. Instead; there it sat, on the third floor landing in perfect condition. Well, maybe the hooks and straps that held the heavy cart on the lift gave-way. But that was extremely unlikely, as Mark and I had secured the cart on the lift gate before sending it three stories up the gym wall. There was no one on the third tier landing, but the door to the Unit was wide open.

"It was the Swede, I saw him unhook the cart, and push it off the lift gate." Mark whispered in my ear, not wanting the Swede to know he had been seen.

I knew I had a serious problem, but needed time to figure out what to do about it. A moment later the guard and the Swede appeared on the third floor landing and started down the skeletal metal stairway to the gym floor. In another minute two more guards appeared from the landings on the first and second floor. The three of us, me Mark and the Swede played dumb.

"No Idea what happened boss." I said, still barely able to speak in a normal voice.

"It just-flew off the lift", Mark told the hacks.

"I wasn't there! I didn't see nuttin", said the Swede.

"Alright, clean this mess up and I'll call the kitchen for another lunch cart". The guards seemed satisfied with our bull-

Black Tuna Diaries

shit denials. Since none of them knew how close I had come to being crushed by the ton of flying food cart, it was unlikely that there would further investigation of the incident. Although it had landed upright, the big food transporter was totaled. The six wheels were driven up into the bottom of the cart. The seams at all four corners were split, and the heating and cooling units were destroyed. Even back in 1981', it cost more than ten grand to replace a cart like that.

That wasn't my problem. My problem was staying alive long enough to figure out what to do about the Swede. Usually when something like that happened, it was for one of five reasons. Someone had hung a snitch label on you. Someone put a contract out on you. The word was out that you were a child molester; your would-be killer thought you had disrespected him or he perceived you to be a potential threat. With a nut job like Swede, it could be almost anything. I either had to confront him, or I had to report the attempt on my life to the segregation lieutenant, and ask for protection. Considering the many years I might have to spend in prison, asking for protection was not a great idea. I had already seen three people murdered who were in "protective custody".

The Swede had gone back upstairs for garbage bags to hold the gigantic mess on the gym floor.

"I need a weapon." I whispered to the Magic Man.

Mark disappeared into the little shower alcove and a few seconds reappeared with a foot long wicked looking shank. That's why they called him the Magic Man. If you wished for something, weapons, drugs, booze, or a t-bone steak, Mark could make it happen, usually in minutes. I slid the shank up the sleeve of my orange jump suite and told Mark to disappear when the Swede returned. To be truthful, I didn't think I could take the big Swede, even with a foot long shank. I was scared shitless, but had no choice but to confront him and get it over with at a place and time of my own choosing. When the choice presented is between catching a murder charge or being murdered, choosing becomes simple.

Black Tuna Diaries

The hulking blond giant came down the steps. Mark vanished into the shower area. Maybe he would help me if I was getting the worst of it, and maybe not. You never know for sure till it's too late to matter.

"Hey Swede, have we got a problem, you and I? Is there some reason you tried to drop that food cart on my head"?

I had a push-broom and was sweeping up peas and carrots that had flown across the gym floor. I tried to look nonchalant, and at the same time kept well out of reach of the giant Scandinavian. He just looked at me for a full thirty seconds trying to figure out if I really knew he had tried to kill me.

"I got nothin against you. You're OK! I just wanted to see what would happen."

That was it! No further conversation! Coming from anyone else, I wouldn't have bought it. But this guy was a certified wacko. He bent down to begin picking up the broken food trays and put them in the big garbage bags. If I was going to use the shank, now would be the perfect time. I couldn't do it! Had he threatened me, maybe it would have been different. Maybe I could have sunk the shiv deep into his neck as he knelt down with the trash bag. Or maybe I'm just not a cold blooded killer. That is as close as I ever came to finding out.

Mark watched my back for the next couple of weeks till the Swede was transferred to a Minnesota state mental institution. A couple of months later I was transferred to FCI Otisville, in upstate New York.

Black Tuna Diaries

Chapter 23
Dead Dentists Don't Lie

FCI Otisville, a Federal Prison in upstate New York! The dentist was about thirty-five years old and looked even younger. I'll call him Mike, to protect his family. He had built a successful practice in South Jersey, had two young kids and a beautiful wife. He was serving a year on some sort of tax beef. I don't remember the exact charge, but it was the kind of thing that usually drew a warning or a fine. Mike was doing time because someone decided to make an example of him.

He lived in the cell next to mine and may have been the most popular guy in the joint. Mike was always willing to help. Health problems, personal problems, or just the need to talk to someone, Mike there for you. He jogged to stay in shape and led an impromptu exercise class in the yard. In federal prison, with generally poor medical care, inmates with medical training are forbidden to help or even discuss health problems with other prisoners. Mike was often willing to risk a trip to "the hole" to advise or help anyone with medical problems that had been misdiagnosed or poorly treated. Even though Mike wasn't a real criminal, he was liked and accepted by the convicts and he was generally respected by the staff.

Like most federal joints, Otisville locked-down at ten pm. You were locked in your cell, counted, and you went to bed. Mike and I had been talking about our kids when we separated for the night. It was almost eleven, when I heard Mike's cellie banging on the door and calling for help. The guard must have been in his office with the door closed. It took forty-five minutes before he showed up.

"My cellie is having a heart attack, he needs his medication" said Mike's roommate.

"I'll call the hospital and ask the PA on duty, what he wants to do", replied the guard. Twenty minutes later he was back.

Black Tuna Diaries

"I spoke to he PA, he says its probably indigestion. He said to take some Pepto if you have any, and to sign up for sick-call in the morning"

The next voice I heard was Mike's. It was weak and seemed to be coming from the. floor of his cell.

"Listen to me, I'm a doctor, I know what's wrong with me. My heart condition is chronic. It's in me medical file. If I don't get my medication, I'll be dead long before morning."

To his credit, the guard left to phone the hospital again. Fifteen minutes later he was back.

"The duty PA is not walking over here with your medication. He said to tell you, you can pick it up at morning pill line, at the infirmary. I'm sorry, I wish I could do something for you" and the guard went back to his office.

The following is a combination of what I heard with my own ears and what Mike's cellie told me the next morning. Mike was lying on the cell floor where he found it easier to breathe the cool air coming under the door. He asked his cellie for pen and paper, calmly wrote out his will and a final letter to his wife and children. He took off his wedding ring, handed it to his cellie, and slowly died. He lay there dead, on the floor of his cell through three "counts".

In the morning he was "rushed to the hospital for treatment" and to the astonishment of no one, his long cold corpse was pronounced dead on arrival. His cell mate was still describing to me the events of the previous night, when a lieutenant and two guards appeared and took him off to "the hole" to prevent him from repeating his tale. Although three years remained on his sentence, Mike's roommate was released from prison three days later. Wardens have the authority to request early release for a prisoner, but it's rarely if ever done. In my twenty-nine years as a federal prisoner, I've only seen it three times. On all three occasions it involved the cover-up of a wrongful death.

Black Tuna Diaries

What happened next, even I found difficult to believe. They Warden decided to hold a memorial service in the prison chapel. They invited Mike's family, the inmates, and the prison staff. I've have never seen or heard of anything like that before or since. In fact I'd never heard of a memorial service held for an inmate, let alone one where civilians were permitted inside the prison compound and allowed to sit with the inmates. One staff member after another, including the Warden, got up in front of Mike's widow and children, and extolled the virtues of a man most had never spoken to. I sat in the back of the auditorium nauseated at the hypocrisy of the staged spectacle. I wanted to go to the grieving widow to tell her the truth about her husband's death.

But I knew that if I left my seat, I'd only cause the family more grief at the wrong time. I felt sure that Mike's roommate who was now out of "the hole", would give the widow a complete account of his death. Two days later, when I saw him walk out a free man; I realized he had been silenced.

Mike was only three weeks from his release when he died on the gray floor of his prison cell.

Surviving in federal prison, under the best of circumstances, is a crapshoot. But if you are seriously ill in the middle of the night, the house lays all the odds, and they ain't good.

To the Bureau of Prison's credit, after who knows how many unnecessary deaths and god only knows how many law suits, "Panic Buttons" were installed in the cells of a few newly constructed prisons. Unfortunately, this solution has proven mostly cosmetic. Inmates needing attention are still often ignored by prison staff. Late night emergencies are still generally trivialized or ignored.

Black Tuna Diaries

Chapter 24
Redd Foxx and Red Dillon

Fred Sanford, the junk man and Dillard Morrison, the "junk dealer"! Redd Foxx and Red Dillon were lifelong friends. Back in the days of the "French Connection", Red Dillon was the Heroin King of Harlem and Redd Foxx was headlining at the Cotton Club. I first met Redd Foxx in Las Vegas, in the late seventies. "Sanford and Son" was still going strong, and Grady and Aunt Ester were part of Redd's entourage. We were in town at the invitation of Big Gene's cousin Scratch. He was trying his best to "mob us up" with a few "nice people" and giving us the VIP tour. He had taken Robby and I back stage at Redd's Sunday morning breakfast show.

Red Dillon was in his late sixties when we met in Otisville federal prison in upstate New York. If today's Hip Hop generation epitomizes the uncool or the anti-cool, Red's generation was the ultra cool. "Never put yourself on front street" according to Red, was "the first rule of cool". If my roommate Woody, a long time friend of Red's, hadn't told me stories about Harlem in the old days, I never would have known anything about Red's past. Red Dillon was so cool, that you had to look twice; just to be sure he was still in the room. According to Woody, Red was so big that Nicky Barns, the later generation heroin king, used to show up every day to wash Red's car and run his errands.

Red never talked about himself. We were good friends. We walked the yard together, listened to jazz on NPR together, and played cards when it was too wet or cold to go to the yard. But, it was more than a year before Red confided to me that he was dying of lung cancer. Just as surprising, was his admission that from wake-up to lock-down, he toked enough good weed to keep a serious buzz going. I never saw it or smelled it. But, as I said, Red was cool! Chemotherapy was making him sicker, without stopping the spread of his cancer. So he took himself off Chemo, and put himself on cannabis therapy. It made him feel good and gave him an appetite. It kept him from falling

Black Tuna Diaries

into the deep depression that inevitably gripped anyone contemplating dying in a lonely prison cell.

Red's greatest fear wasn't death; it was the prospect of waking up one day and not having any herb. To ensure his supply, he had two "bullet-proof" methods of smuggling weed into the joint. He referred to them as "Regular" and "Special".

"Hey Tuna, got any peanut butter man?" Red was standing in my cell with a pair of tattered old jockey shorts in his hand.

"I've got a visit and I'm out of peanut butter". Was he losing his mind? Red was a class act! He'd never be caught dead wearing a pair of raggedy old jockey shorts on a visit or at any other time. And what in hell did peanut butter have to do with anything?

"If you promise not to show this to anyone while I'm still alive, I'll show you how I been getting my weed for the past fifteen years".

Red opened my jar and took a big finger-full of peanut butter. He smeared two wide tracks in the seat of the ratty old skivvies.

"Bobby, I've been doing this on visits for years. My friend brings an ounce of weed pressed flat and wrapped in white tissue paper. I slip it into the crotch panel of my underpants. I guarantee you, when I drop my drawers for the strip search after my visit, ain't no prison guard in the world gonna pickup some old nigger's shitty drawers, to feel the crotch for contraband, once they see those big brown stains".

Red's "Special" stash arrived by an entirely different method. Twice every year, Redd Foxx would fly his entire Las Vegas cast up to Otisville N.Y. to put on one hell of a show for his dying pal and the prison population. He did this for years, until Red finally passed away. Singers, dancers, and a big band with all their props and instruments. They would troop into the prison gym, put on a two hour show, pack up and troop back

Black Tuna Diaries

out. Somehow, something "Special" always remained behind in a forgotten amplifier or guitar. Before they left, Redd and Red always spent a few minutes sitting quietly together saying their goodbyes, perhaps their last.

Red Dillon smoked his herb till the cancer took him. Redd Foxx joined him a few years later. If I close me eyes, I can see them both looking down (or maybe up) at the rest of us and having a good laugh at nothing most of us would understand. They were cool!

Black Tuna Diaries

Chapter 25
Death Under the Expressway

Everyone knows that a black cat has nine lives, but a Black Tuna only Seven. Here is the true story of how I lost number six under an expressway on the Virginia, North Carolina border while being transported between federal prisons.

By a small but fortuitous quirk of fate, I spent three years in what may have been the best prison, if there is such a thing, in America. Before it became a part of one of the Federal Bureau of Prison's monster prison complexes, F.C.I. Butner, was a progressive experimental prison run by psychologists who actually had training in penology. Half the institution, called "Up the Hill", housed people like Jim Baker the famous TV Evangelist, who were there for psychological evaluation and treatment. The other half, "Down the Hill", held the regular prison population.

Normally the only way to be assigned to FCI Butner, was to be a Wackadoodle, and be sent Up the Hill, or be chosen by lottery from the entire national federal prison population, to be housed Down the Hill. The only exceptions that I know of, was when a plane load of us had to be removed immediately from FCI Otisville, so it could become a holding facility to relieve the overcrowding in the Metropolitan Correction Center in Manhattan. FCI Butner was the only place with enough room to take us in.

The aim of the experimental prison at Butner was to remove the prison atmosphere and thereby remove the prison mentality. Inmates could wear their own clothes. Most wore jeans and a nice tee or collar shirt. But you saw inmates wearing three piece suites, bib overalls, and fancy warm-up suits. There was no separation of the two populations. Inmates from Up the Hill and those from Down the Hill, ate, walked, and recced together. Inmates could move about freely all day, instead of being restricted to a "ten minute move" each hour. Everyone was responsible for getting to his job or class at the

Black Tuna Diaries

proper time. At first glance it almost appeared to be a college campus. And it worked! Less violence than any other federal prison! More participation in educational and vocational training and less recidivism! Of course, that was a denial of the way every other federal prison was run, so the experiment was ended a few years later. Get tough, beats effective in the government scheme of things.

My close friends at Butner were Hal Metz, a.k.a. "The Whale", six foot two, three hundred pounds, very loud and very funny. Fox, a trained chef from Miami and charismatic preacher. And the two middle sons of Joe Colombo, Joey and Vinnie, brown haired blue eyed descendants of northern Italians. Bright, interesting and two of the nicest people I met on my long year journey through the federal prison system. Vinnie, on the heavy side, but an exceptional athlete and super quick wit. Joey, the thinker, the schemer, and planner, the natural leader of our small clique. We worked together as a "special volunteer crew" preparing all the special holiday meals. Sometimes we'd pull all-nighters, to prepare Thanksgiving or Christmas meals.

Vinnie was a serious cook who had learned catering in the Colombo family's catering hall in Brooklyn, where the Colombos and their "associates" held their weddings, barmitzvas, christenings, and parties. Fox was a trained chef who could cook or bake almost anything. The Whale did the heavy lifting, I did the fancy garnish work and Joey, well Joey was the boss. Together we turned out some of the best and fanciest meals ever served in any prison any where. In return for working our butts off preparing banquets for a prison population of over eight hundred, we were given carte blanche, to make anything we wanted for ourselves and our friends, and to take back to our dormitories, as much food as we could hide under our coats without getting caught. The Whale, who was also my roommate, taught me to play tennis. With Joey and Vinnie, we played doubles every morning after doing our prep in the kitchen, and we played most of the day on weekends. Vinnie and the Whale were pretty good players. They took turns trying to carry Joey or me, who were not too athletically inclined or in prison parlance, just plain lames.

Black Tuna Diaries

My greatest triumph as a story teller or pitchman came on Passover in the small Officer's Mess, adjacent to the main chow hall at Butner. I was in charge of the kosher food preparation. As a matter of fact, at FCI Butner, because I knew about kosher food and had experience in running food concessions, I was in charge of ordering all the food for the kosher food line. I could order anything I wanted within the budget, with one caveat. There must be no complaints. None! Not one! Ever! If even one Jew complained to even one staff member about the kosher food line, the deal was off. Normally the biggest headache for prison food administrators is the complaining by the Jews, Muslims, and others on special diets. I had no difficulty dealing with this problem. Each new Jew who wanted to eat kosher, first had to meet with me in the dinning room for "orientation". While I explained that I could provide them with anything from "kosher style" to GLATT Kosher, Vinnie or Joey was usually nearby giving the new Jew the "Godfather Stare". The Whale always stood directly behind, with his huge paws on the new guy's shoulders, as I made it very clear that under no circumstances were any complaints to go to anyone but me. Whatever the problem, I'd solve it. No one in the entire federal prison system ate as good as my congregation at Butner. We were not about to let anyone ruin it for us. The final word on the issue was always had by the Whale as he leaned his bulk down on the newcomer and asked,

"You do understand, don't you? I can explain it in much simpler terms if need be." Not a single complaint in three years. That's a record, I'm sure!

Back to the Passover meal. I was in charge of choosing the menu and preparation. Somehow I went brain-dead and let Vinnie and Joey convince me to let them cook and serve the feast. By the time I came out of the ether, the Rigatoni and Chicken Cacciatore were already cooking. Oh crap! Not exactly the traditional Passover fare. At least they used the kosher chicken I had intended to roast. Instead of matzo ball soup, the Colombo brothers served minestrone, and for a vegetable, broccoli cooked in olive oil and garlic. Thank God the matzos didn't turn into Italian bread. There were about a dozen real Jews on the program and two or three Italians with some

Black Tuna Diaries

vague Jewish ancestry, and whose genetic memory was revived by the prospect of good food.

The Seder meal was held in the Officers Mess where we were able to push the tables together like a family Seder. There had to be a Chaplain to supervise and see to the legitimacy of the affair. Since we had no staff Rabbi, it was the Catholic father who joined us.

Everything started out smooth as glass. I presented my abbreviated dramatic reading of the Seder service and passed around the traditional foods from the Seder Plate. Then it was time for our meal, Joey, Vinnie, and the Whale trouped out from the kitchen and began passing out plates heaped with rigatoni and Chicken Cacciatore. Father began clearing his throat. The look in his eye was that of a prison chaplain who didn't like to be fooled with. This entire affair was going to be busted and adjourned to the "hole", if I didn't come up with a plausible explanation for this Italian Seder. That's it! An "Italian Seder!"

Before the priest could say a word, I rose to welcome everyone to our authentic Italian Seder. A perfect recreation of the Seder meal I had eaten in Rome in 1969, when I found myself stuck there during Passover.

The story just seemed to flow from my lips. I was in Rome on business. Staying at the Cavilliere Hilton. When I realized I'd have to remain over Passover, I inquired of the Concierge if the hotel would be hosting a Seder for their Jewish guests. They weren't! But he pointed out a small elderly man circulating among the guests in the lobby asking questions.

"This man", he explained, was "the representative of the Chief Rabbi of Rome. Each year he visits all the major hotels in the city to collect those Jews stranded there without a Seder. He brings them all to home of the Chief Rabbi for a traditional Italian Seder."

Black Tuna Diaries

"Now" I announce, "thanks to Vinnie and Joey Colombo, we can all enjoy the same fabulous traditional Italian Seder meal, prepared for me and all the other visiting Jews by the Rebetzin of the Chief Rabbi of Rome".

How good did I sell that story? Not only were the priest and congregation teary eyed, Joey and Vinnie, who should have known I was just covering their asses, bought it hook line and sinker. Certainly the best off the cuff pitch I ever made.

The problem with a joint like Butner is you get too relaxed. Too comfortable. You don't see the train before it hits you. I should have seen it coming when the new Warden visited me in my dorm room. He claimed he was just passing through and meeting the inmates. Yeah Right! With a supercilious grin, he questioned me for ten minutes, just to hear what he already knew. That I had began serving my 64 year prison term in the super-max penitentiary at Marion Illinois. He smiled, shook my hand, and piled the bullshit a little deeper. "It was nice to meet you." You bet! After a dozen years in prison, that was a new one.

Two or three weeks later the trap was sprung. I just left the kitchen after finishing my morning prep work at about eight in the morning. I went back to my dorm, changed into shorts and tennis shoes, and was heading to the rec yard, when I heard it over the P.A. system.

"Robert Platshorn, inmate Robert Platshorn, report back to food service."

I thought about it for a second. I had finished my prep. The luncheon salad bar was in the coolers and the kosher meal was being cooked. I had already signed the "safety talk" and monthly pay slip. What could be the problem?

As I approached the dinning room door, I didn't notice the two lieutenants flanking the entrance, till they had grabbed me, hand-cuffed me, and propelled me towards the Captain's office. That feeling of ice cold dread that I had almost forgot-

© 2009 R. Platshorn

Black Tuna Diaries

ten, came back with a rush. That terrible fear that hits a prisoner whenever he is reminded of his total vulnerability. After three years at Butner with clear conduct, no problems with anyone, inmates or staff, no "shots"(disciplinary reports), I couldn't fathom what was happening to me . Off balance and dazed, I was prodded into the Captain's office and through a door into the R & D (receiving and departure) area. Sitting in the middle of the floor were six small boxes heaped with personal property, my personal property.

"You have five minutes to inventory your property. There is a van waiting outside with the motor running, to transport you to another institution."

The Captain handed me a sheaf of property forms and a pencil. Still dazed, I wondered how my property could have been collected, boxed and brought here in the five minutes since I left my dorm room. This was not how institutional transfers are done, and it was scaring me. By this time, I had been transferred four times. I had always "packed-out" a few days in advance and been transported with a bus load of other inmates. This time there were no other prisoners. There were only three lieutenants and the Captain supervising my transport. Something was wrong! Still hand-cuffed, I did a perfunctory inventory. My mind racing to figure out what was going on and my adrenal glands drowning my nervous system with freezing fear.

Now shackled at the ankles, as well as handcuffed, I was duck walked by two burly lieutenants past a phalanx of armed guards and pushed into the back of a caged van driven by the same two lieutenants who had grabbed me at the kitchen door. The Captain now toting a shotgun got into a lead chase car and another lieutenant drove a following chase car. I had never seen this kind of security, not even at the super-max in Marion. I was flat out shit-scared. But not as shit-scared as I was going to be an hour later.

After ten or fifteen minutes on the road, I tried to break the icy silence.

Black Tuna Diaries

"Please, what's going on? Where are you taking me?"

The lieutenant riding shotgun in the passenger seat, turned halfway towards me and said, "just shut-up and enjoy the scenery".

Those were the only words spoken in that van until we pulled to the curb under a very high expressway underpass an hour later. The highway above was eight lanes wide and hid the sun, creating an artificial night. I was pulled from my cage, my shackles and cuffs removed. My worst fears returned with a nauseating rush. The chase cars were gone. No witnesses! The lieutenant with the shotgun pressed it to my spine,

"Don't move until your told."

A second later the van and lieutenants were gone. I knew I couldn't be alone in the dark tunnel under the road. My only thought was, I was being set up to be killed while escaping. Just then I heard a voice from the deeper darkness above,

"Put your hands behind you head and slowly come up towards the sound of my voice".

Now frozen with fear and completely disoriented, I looked up into the almost complete blackness of the cave created by the concrete girders, thirty feet overhead.

"Start moving now. Unless you want to be shot!" boomed the deep voice with a gentle southern drawl.

I began making my way up the steep dark cement hill. After about ten feet I could begin to make out the speaker. A very large fat man, sitting on the base of a girder and holding a shotgun pointed directly at me. Now, I once rode a bicycle head long into an oncoming truck. I've been captured in the Colombian jungle and was headed for a firing squad. I've twice piloted a small plane down through thick fog to what I was sure would be a life ending crash landing. On three occasions I've had a loaded gun pointed at me by an angry mal-

Black Tuna Diaries

efactor. And if I thought about it I could probably recall a few other close calls, but I have never, not ever been so completely sure I was about to die. No matter how hard I squeezed my bladder, I could feel a warm trickle wetting the front of the orange jumpsuit I had been forced to wear for the trip. As I climbed higher into the inky gloom I could make-out a second man sitting on a concrete support to my right. In his hand was a genuine Dirty Harry Colt Magnum.

Both men wore cowboy hats, but I knew there were no Texas Rangers in Virginia.

"Keep coming this way" said the fat guy with the shotgun. "Okay, stop there and don't move".

Should I try to run? At least make it harder to kill me? Before I could shake off the paralysis of fear, Dirty Harry came up behind me.

"Put your hands behind your back".

It was almost a relief when the handcuffs snapped shut on my wrists. Surely they wouldn't kill me if I was cuffed up. I still couldn't control the warm flow from my bladder, as the two men led me to a plain brown sedan I hadn't noticed, parked on the dark berm above the road. In the light of the open car door, I could see the badges displayed on in their jacket pockets. U.S. Marshals!

This was some kind of high security prisoner transfer. I guess it was just my unearned reputation that preceded me. Without a single word I was put in the backseat, my ankles chained to a ring in the floor, and driven to FCI Petersburg in Virginia. My only satisfaction was the wet seat and acrid odor I left in the back seat of the Marshal's ride.

My introduction to FCI Petersburg was a week in the second nastiest "hole" in the federal prison system, after Lewisburg Pen.

Black Tuna Diaries

Why, after three problem free years, had been I transferred from the experimental prison at Butner North Carolina? In the Federal Bureau of Prisons, like any branch of government, only more so, whenever a new administrator is installed, he feels compelled to make his mark. Usually by fixing whatever isn't broken. In my case, the new warden wanted to sweep out all the inmates with high profile cases, i.e. those the government had milked for publicity value. His motive? So that no one could claim the Federal Bureau of Prisons was sending us bad guys to nice prisons. My transfer gave the Bureau of Prisons and the U.S. Marshal Service an opportunity to play out their fantasy games. A high security prisoner transfer! Not for the first time had they bravely prevented an escape that was never planned. Not to mention scaring the piss out of me.

Black Tuna Diaries

Chapter 26
The Bare Butt Witness

I know this story is true, because Zev and I ended up with the money. We were working in the prison laundry at FCI Petersburg. My good buddy Zev and I had to load and unload the huge commercials washers and dryers. Each morning we got a big cart full of dirty clothes from the segregation unit. Inmates going into the "hole" would be strip searched, made to wear a special jump suit, and their clothes sent to the laundry. On the top of pile, was a pair of khaki pants and a jacket rolled together. I lifted them out to toss them in the washer, when I realized, they must have weighed twenty-five or thirty pounds. I checked to be sure no one was watching and ducked behind the huge washing machine to investigate. Four hundred bucks! Forty rolls of quarters were hidden in the pockets and lining of the jacket. Was this a trap, a test of some sort? Could the seg guards possibly have missed forty rolls of quarters during the strip search.

I hid the garments. Two days later, when no one had come looking for the cash, I gave Zev and a few other laundry workers a split and took the rest out of the building. We were permitted to have two rolls of quarters to spend in the vending machines. So I buried most of my score, and brought it out when I wanted to spend it in the machines or to buy things on the "black market". It was many months before we learned how the coins came to be in the clothes.

Once upon a time there were four Mexican convicts who peddled pot on the "pound" (compound). They were pretty cool about their business, so it was a couple years before two of them were caught in the act. The investigating lieutenant gave them a choice, tell on their source or face prosecution and a long sentence. They "gave it up!" They "got down!" They named an old time prison guard as their source, and claimed that he had brought them an ounce of pot every week for over three years. They paid him four hundred an ounce and sold it in tiny lids (Chap Stick tops) for ten dollars a piece. For

Black Tuna Diaries

a profit of about a grand and ounce! When they were busted, the cash in their clothes was to pay for the next delivery.

Fast forward six months to the officer's trial. The guard pleads not guilty and hires the best dope lawyer in Virginia. One of the Mexicans is on the stand describing to jury, how he would load the coins into his pockets and meet the guard under the bleachers in the rec yard to make the exchange.

No further questions your Honor". The prosecutor takes-his seat.

The high priced defense counsel rises., "May I approach the witness, your Honor?"

He slowly walks to the witness box and places his expensive attaché case on the railing in front of the witness. He pops open the lid to dramatically reveal forty rolls of quarters.

"Is this what you claim to have carried to the yard to pay my client?"

"Yes sir".

The lawyer has to take a deep breath to suppress his elation, before he springs his trap.

"With the Court's permission, I'd like you to stand up and show the jury how you were able to smuggle forty rolls of quarters out to the rec yard to pay for the marijuana you claim you bought from my client".

The skinny convict looked into the briefcase. After a minute, he began picking up the rolls. Two rolls in each sock, and his socks were falling. Then, three rolls disappear into his jockey shorts. Three rolls in his left hand pants pocket, three into his right. His pants begin to slip down. He tightens his belt until his belly presses against his backbone, and loads two of the heavy rolls into his right back pocket, but as he reaches for two more rolls, his pants head south, followed closely by his

Black Tuna Diaries

over loaded skivvies. The jury is treated to a view of the Mexican convict's skinny butt, tattooed with the words "La Raza" on one cheek and "Maria" on the other. Tattooed on his lower belly with an arrow pointing down to his small flaccid organ, was the pretentious misnomer, "EL Grande".

Not Guilty! The following week the guard was back on the job.

Black Tuna Diaries

Chapter 27
Six More Federal Prisons-Can I go Home Now?

After six years at FCI Petersburg, I guess I was getting too comfortable again. I was working with old time mobsters like Sonny Francaise. Running the Officers Mess in the mornings, playing tennis every afternoon, and hanging out in Delaware cell house with Joey and Vinnie Colombo's older brother Anthony. Later, when half the kitchen larder was found in my cell, at the request of management, I changed my job to morning laundry detail. That's where I met my buddy Zev and found the four hundred bucks in quarters.

In any case, I was again dragged off, kicking, screaming, chained, cuffed, shackled, and flown to the worst, most inhumane joint in the federal system. FCI Elkton Ohio! A stark and forbidding concrete hell where people were stored in huge gray cinder block warehouses. A low level prison where it was harder to do time, than in the "Belly of The Beast" super-max at Marion. Triple bunked on steel shelves reminiscent of Auschwitz, brightly lit twenty-four hours a day to insure sleep deprivation, FCI Elkton was designed to be the ultimate politically correct prison. Nothing that hinted of human comfort was permitted. Cold steel bleachers were the only seating in the freezing little TV rooms. Any attempt to take a blanket or pillow into the bare cement TV rooms would result a "shot" and a trip to the "hole".

There were many more inmates than there were jobs. A hundred and twenty of us were assigned to work in the tiny gym building that passed as a rec department for a population of over two thousand men. No assigned job took more than five or ten minutes, but instead of being released to rec or study on our own, we were forced to sit jammed onto the small gym bleachers, in full work uniform, with steel toed work boots, no books, no radios for eight torturous hours. For me the back pain of sitting without back support past that first hour was excruciating. Of all things instituted by Elkton's wacko warden, maybe the nuttiest, were the inmate badges. Identical

Black Tuna Diaries

to those clear plastic ridiculous name badges worn by conventioniers. "Hi. I'm Inmate Robert Platshorn, 00603-004". All I could think of when told we would have to wear them at all times, was, "Badges, Badges, we don't need no stinking Badges!"

In an effort to get shipped out of that joint, I refused to wear the badge. But instead of reacting, they ignored me. Totally committed to running the most politically correct prison in America, a place that could never be accused of being soft on criminals, the warden instituted some of the most bazaar practices ever seen in a federal prison.

Five foot two in his elevator shoes, the warden was never seen on the compound without his cartoon trench coat with the huge collar always raised to hide his face. He looked like Boris Badinoff from the Rocky and Bullwinkle toons. And he was never, absolutely never, never seen without his two huge bodyguards. Even in the pen, I had never seen a warden who was so clearly afraid to walk the "pound" on his own. To act this way in a Low level FCI was seriously strange.

How badly did I want out of FCI Elkton? Well on my third day there, the inmates called a food strike to demand better living conditions and decent food in larger than child size portions. Food strikes are rarely successful! Mainly because inmates that don't have a locker crammed with food purchased from the commissary, get hungry and are back in the chow hall within two days.

Whenever there is a food strike or demonstration of any sort, the S.I.S. (Security Investigation Specialist) interviews every inmate in the prison. They try to break the solidarity, find the inmate leaders and ship them out. As soon as I was dragged into the office of the chubby Latino S.I.S. Lieutenant, I immediately confessed to being the leader and organizer of all the Jews in FCI Elkton.

"Ship me out! Put me on the next bus to anywhere! I'm the one who organized all the Jews."

Black Tuna Diaries

He looked at me and just laughed.

"One, you just got here and didn't have time to organize anything. And number two, there is only one other Jew on this compound, and he never heard of you. I interviewed him ten minutes ago. And number three, no one, absolutely no one will leave here in the next eighteen months. You can take that to the bank!"

Well, that sounds like a challenge, and no matter how much it might hurt, I've never been smart enough to pass up a challenge. After more than fifteen years in federal prison, if I did not know how to be transferred in less than eighteen months, shame on me. I knew for certain that the prisoners would soon be so desperate for decent living conditions, that there would be another mass action of some sort.

Bingo! A few weeks later and now there is talk of a work strike. Now a work strike is the next scariest thing to a riot. It requires that the entire joint be on lockdown for weeks and sometimes for months. It is extremely costly! Extra guards are needed to watch the cell houses and to do all the jobs normally done by the convicts. Food Service, plumbing, electrical maintenance, heat and air, etc, etc. The budget overruns quickly reach into the millions. All I had to do was stay close to the action.

Sure enough. I was in the Arts and Crafts room trying to read a book and watching out of the corner of my eye as several inmates prepared posters to be put up in the cell houses calling for a work strike and laying out their demands for better living conditions. Uh oh! The Assistant Warden and the Captain appear in the doorway looking for me. They were there to ask me if I knew where to find my Lebanese cell mate. They intended to throw him in the hole for having a name that sounded Arab. During the first Gulf War that happened frequently.

Standing near the door, was a tall hulking Puerto Rican inmate, I'll call Jose. Jose was president of his local chapter of the powerful "Latin Kings". He had just picked up four copies

Black Tuna Diaries

of the strike poster, in Spanish. Jose panicked! He busted through the doorway, pushing the Captain and A.W. out of the way. Not the brightest thing to do. He than proceeded to try eating the evidence. He ran through: the building and out onto the bare concrete compound, stuffing the four posters into his mouth, but of course not able to swallow. The Captain tackled him and the A.W. extracted the Spanish strike posters from his mouth. Jose didn't even wait to be questioned, before he gave me up.

"I was only holding these for that Jewish guy in the Art room. The guy whose name you were calling. Plat something."

Next thing I knew, I was in the hole, sharing a cell with my Lebanese roommate, who they mistakenly thought was an Arab. Shortly thereafter, I was sitting in the interrogation cell getting the third degree from the fat Chicano S.I.S. lieutenant.

"Come on. You're an old timer. A real convict. I know you're not going to let Jose take the rap for this by himself." He spread the wrinkled poster on the table in front of me.

"Do you know anything about this? Jose said that you gave it him to put up in his unit."

I looked at him as if he were nuts.

"What does it say, I don't read Spanish!" That was all the conversation he ever got from me. When he asked me for my version of the incident, all he got was, "no comment". They dicked around, keeping me in the hole for several months, trying various ploys to get me to confess. In the end although they couldn't convict me of having anything to do with the Spanish poster. They were afraid to send me back to "population" for fear I would organize another strike. So, guess what? They shipped me out. Just about seven months after my arrival at FCI Elkton Ohio, I was on my way to FCI Milan Michigan.

Like FCI Petersburg, Milan was an older joint where they shipped people they considered problematic. Like many older

Black Tuna Diaries

joints, it was the kind of place where they let you alone to do your job, get your rec, and do your time without being harassed. It was an uneventful few years. I worked in the kitchen as a garnish chef in the mornings, played tennis in the afternoons, and tried to remain invisible. Invisible is the safest way to do your time. Once at a disciplinary hearing at FCI Otisville, my Unit Manager asked me if I had just arrived in his unit. I thought his teeth would fall out when I told him I had been in his unit for over four years.

The best thing that happened to me at FCI Milan or any place else in the federal prison system, was my Case Worker. He worked his butt off calling in favors, to get me sent to a camp. Normally the transfer process, once initiated, takes a couple of weeks. In my case it was seven months before my Case Manager could secure the permissions needed from the Institution, the Region Offices, and the Central Office in Washington D.C. No one wanted to take a chance on me! He worked hard to convince everyone that I had been getting a raw deal for the past twenty-two years and deserved to be in a camp.

Against all odds, he succeeded, and in July of 1999, I actually traveled by furlough, from FCI Milan Michigan, to FPC Eglin (Air force Base) Fla. There was no way I believed that this was actually going to happen. Right up until I walked into the Greyhound station in Detroit to buy my ticket, I was sure this particular rug was about to be pulled from under my feet.

Traveling from one inner city slum to another, where most bus terminals are now located, was not my idea of an interesting trip after twenty-two years of prison. On the other hand, Lynne picked me up when the bus reached Florida, and we spent a few very nice hours together, before I had to report to the prison camp.

Eglin, which no longer exists, was the original place the press dubbed "Club Fed". It may have been a nice place to do time, but let me disabuse you of the idea of a "Club Fed". There just ain't no such thing! Most of the inmates at Eglin go out to work on the Air force Base five or six days a week. Cut-

Black Tuna Diaries

ting grass, pruning trees, picking up papers, doing laundry or hauling trash. They provided these essential labors for the grand sum of twenty-two cents an hour. Imagine what it cost the taxpayers to replace five hundred and eighty convict laborers, with high paid civilian employees.

It was called Club Fed mainly because it had four old beat-up tennis courts. For some reason any prison with a tennis court is thought to be coddling prisoners. Basketball courts? Every prison has a dozen or more, one or two softball fields, at least one soccer field, and a football field. No problem! Convicts need to rec, to workout their frustrations and aggressions. But tennis, no way, that's a genteel sport. No fights, no injuries! What is really funny was there were tennis courts in the super-max at Marion, and at most of the old time pens like Lewisburg or the Big House at Atlanta. No one ever called those places a Club Fed. But most of the lower security joints were forced to remove their tennis courts because of the Bureau of Prison's fear of public perception. For what its worth, for fourteen years, from when I learned to play at FCI Butner, until they closed the courts at FPC Eglin, I played an average of two hours a day. It kept me healthy. Kept my weight down, my cholesterol down, and probably saved the taxpayers a ton on my medical care. I am now on three "old guy" medications that I did not need when I could get on the tennis courts everyday.

At FPC Eglin, I again worked as a garnish chef, creating food displays from fruits and vegetables. Besides garnishing the meals in our chow hall, I did dozens of banquets on the Air Force Base, where my fancy creations were always the main topic of conversation at the parties given by the commanding general . For pocket money and funds for the family, I hustled sandwiches. I'd help the butcher cut meats and help my pal and Master Baker, Dan Levitan, bake all sorts of excellent breads, then take the leftovers and make a half a dozen sandwiches at two bucks per. I always had a couple of hundred bucks to send my son or Lynne for family emergencies. Finally a hurricane in 2004 gave the BOP the excuse they wanted, to shut down Club Fed. The storm hadn't caused much damage,

Black Tuna Diaries

but it provided a convenient excuse. The Air Force had to spend millions to replace the cheap convict labor.

I was shipped, along with fifty other Eglin inmates to another good Camp, FPC Maxwell (Air Force Base). There I worked as a garnish chef, taught fancy food prep, and even got to play tennis again. The tennis courts at Maxwell were where the public couldn't see them, so they remained open. Eglin's courts had been near the visitor's parking lot, where the public and press might spot them. So they had been closed and painted over.

If I had been more observant, I could have seen the train before it hit me. But I don't know if I could have stopped it. It doesn't take a genius to figure out that the Bureau of Prisons doesn't much care for anyone audacious enough to try filing Administrative Remedies. In my case, I was helping a few not very literate inmates, to file their remedies and legal briefs. In the blink of an eye, I found myself in Alabama's infamous Elmore County Jail. No heat, no air, no TV, no radios, no newspapers, no coffee, no tea, no cigarettes, no exercise yard, very little food, and most of that, worthless starch. For those few of us that showered, it was in the middle of a cold concrete common area, with a hundred prisoners for an audience. The high point at Elmore was the four nights a week they served us two thin peanut butter and jelly sandwiches on stale Wonder Bread for dinner. It was the only meal anyone looked forward to eating. I spent three months sitting in the freezing concrete common area wrapped in a tissue thin blanket, trying to keep warm and reading and rereading the few torn paperbacks, mostly westerns. That's not to say there was nothing to read. There must have been fifty Christian bibles stacked on a window ledge next to the iron cell door. And don't think that because we had no TV, radio, newspapers, or books, that we were deprived of entertainment. Because it didn't matter if we were Christian, Catholic, Muslim, Jew or Atheist, we were herded out of our cells into the cold common area and forced to listen to every wanna be evangelical preacher in the state of Alabama. One week I counted eleven different Christian preachers, most of them ranted for four hours or more, often till two in the morning.

Black Tuna Diaries

It was a huge relief when after three miserable months, to finally be cuffed, chained, shackled and sent off to the Medium/High prison at Marianna Florida. Medium/High? How did I end up at a Medium /High? It had taken me twenty two years in the federal prison system to earn my way down from penitentiary status to camp status. It took me just twenty-two days at Maxwell Camp in Montgomery Alabama, to make it back up to just below penitentiary status. What happened? There are very few things that truly lend themselves to a simple explanation. Over the next three years, as I worked my way back down to an FCI Low before my release, I was given in confidence, three different explanations of my loss of camp status. It's likely that all three reasons played a part in people on the staff at FPC Maxwell! Warden Smallbrooks, a "recreation specialist", who had been made a Warden, due to the explosive growth of the federal prisons and the lack of qualified people willing to work in them. Captain Farley, a racist, sadistic, steroidal black man who did the dirty work for Warden Smallbrooks. Lastly, the Case manager Coordinator, who at the behest of Smallbrooks and Farley, simply changed the numbers of my custody evaluation to raise my security two levels. And she did this, despite my Case manager's insistence that I had earned a drop to Community Custody. It was such an egregious falsification of records that my Case Manager felt compelled to phone my son and disclaim any responsibility for this injustice.

The three explanations given to me in confidence were as follows . One, the fact that I had granted High Times Magazine an interview, concerning a ten year error in my sentence computation. The interview had been approved by the Bureau of Prisons, but it still pissed them off. Two, I was one of the very few people at Maxwell Camp, who was willing and able to help inmates file grievances and legal actions. Prison rules allow for inmate legal assistance. But at FPC Maxwell Alabama the "old boys" who ran things didn't much care for the idea of a Yankee Jew helping the illiterate locals. Lastly, and most sadly, was the "Jewish problem". As a result of the hurricane that closed the camp at Eglin, twenty six Jews were sent to an Alabama prison Camp that had never before had more than two Jews at any one time. Eglin had had the largest Jewish population of any prison in the federal system aside from Otis-

© 2009 R. Platshorn

Black Tuna Diaries

ville, N.Y. Due to religious needs like kosher food and holiday observances, the BOP decided it would be best if the entire Jewish population of Eglin Camp were sent to one place. Now that is truly proof that even a blind squirrel can occasionally find an acorn. Or perhaps in this case, half an acorn. Maxwell Alabama wasn't the greatest place to send a bus load of Jewish convicts. Not only did they inherit an instant Jewish congregation. But included in that group were two different Hassidic sects. Lubavitchers and Satmar. The Satmar wouldn't even go into the chow hall, let alone eat the federal "Common Fare" version of kosher food. They barricaded themselves in a tiny room in the chapel and refused to eat anything but raw fruit and food shipped in by the Satmar Reb.

The simple solution for the red neck warden was to get rid of every last Jew. One at a time. And that is pretty much what they accomplished.

Now I have to backtrack a bit. It's no small thing calling a prison official racist, sadistic, and steroidal. I explain! At a prison where the vast majority of inmates are black, and the Captain, who is also black, takes disciplinary actions mainly against white inmates, for infractions that are committed in equal or greater measure by black inmates, it is not inappropriate to consider that the Captain just might possibly be a tad racist. Sadist? Well, that's an easy one. Just seeing the joy that radiated from his smile every time he got to stick it to an inmate, is fairly conclusive. In my case he got off big time. I was standing next to the jailer at the Elmore County jail when the officer who had transported me, handed me over, verbally confirmed Captain Farley's orders. I was to be kept for the first four days to "soften me up", in a tiny interrogation cell. No bed, no toilet, no sink or shower, no way to turn off the lights. Both the jailer and the transporting officer showed me the "captain's request" in order to absolve themselves of any responsibility for what was about to happen to me. Farley wanted to force me to confess that I had helped and encouraged other inmates to break the rules. That way he could take away my camp status without having to falsify my records. After four days in the tiny glass walled box, Farley appeared and couldn't even keep the supercilious smile off his face, as

Black Tuna Diaries

he expressed his great surprise at terrible treatment I had received at the hands of the county's jailer. Of course I didn't confess, and so paid the price. Three months in one of America's most vile county jails, before Warden Smallbrooks and Captain Farley could get someone to dummy-up my paperwork and ship me off to the medium/high prison at Marianna Florida. Steroidal! Look at the guy and draw your own conclusions. Built like a truck stuffed into a suit. Rational?

A year later Smallbrooks turned up as the new warden at Marianna. Scared the crap out of me! I stayed out of his line of sight until I was sent to the low at Coleman Florida in May of 2002. The good news? Smallbrooks career had hit the wall. Marianna was his last two year assignment before having to take early retirement. What happened? Be patient, it gets better. When when I was transferred to FCI Coleman, my last stop in the BOP, who do I see guarding bananas in the chow hall ? Farley, Lieutenant Farley! Not Captain Farley! Now getting demoted in the BOP is only slightly more difficult than getting Hanna Montana tickets. What happened? Smallbrooks and Farley duked it out, they had a fist fight at FPC Maxwell Alabama. Despite the bullshit rumors that Farley was a changed man, I was determined to stay out of his line of sight for my ten months remaining at Coleman.

So far, so good. After almost twenty-nine years of incarceration, in seven weeks, four days, and a wake-up, on April 1st (not a good omen) barring any further catastrophes, I will be picked up at the gate by my nephew Jon and driven to a Salvation Army "Residential Re-Entry Center". There for six months, I will be sent out to work each morning. As a senior citizens maybe I'll get to work in the thrift shop or perhaps they will send me out to Mickey D's to flip burgers. With any luck I'll get weekend passes and eventually be put on home confinement. Mostly, I'm hoping to see my son , my daughter-in-law, and get to meet my beautiful three year old granddaughter Maddison. OH! Home confinement means home with Lynne, and that makes me luckier than most.

I'll leave prison with nothing. No money. No clothes. No car. And almost no Social Security. I worked and paid into the sys-

Black Tuna Diaries

tem from when I was fourteen years old till I was arrested, but because I couldn't pay in during my long incarceration. I'll get just six hundred dollars a month. Old guys coming out of prison are up the creek without a paddle. I'll try to find work as a copywriter, promoter, producer, or pitchman. That is, if I can scrounge up enough dough for a few false teeth. Three decades of Federal Prison dental care, have left me looking like the biker who lost the bar fight. No front teeth!

Black Tuna Diaries

Chapter 28
April Fool!

I actually slept pretty well the night before my release. It was April 1$^{st.}$ Not a good omen for someone who had spent his last twenty-nine years in federal prisons. Up at 5am, I dressed and made what I hoped was my last trip to a prison chow hall. I tried to stay invisible, avoiding prolonged good-byes with the dozens of inmates who wanted to make a big deal of the occasion. To be honest, I was afraid of the embarrassment. If something went wrong I could end up right back on the compound before the end of the day.

What could go wrong? Well, I was headed to a halfway house for the final six months of my prison term. That is supposed to be a privilege, not a right. They can pull the rug out for any reason, or no reason. It wouldn't be the first time I was denied what other inmates were routinely given. My greatest fear was the reporter and film crew I knew would be waiting to escort me to the Salvation Army halfway house in West Palm Beach. I had originally decided to try to avoid any publicity about my release. But the need to generate interest in "Black Tuna Diaries", overcame my good sense and fear of the Federal Bureau of Prisons pathological hatred of publicity. At the last moment, I agreed to let my nephew Jon Udell, an audio mixer who's worked on dozens of feature films and TV series, bring along an award winning documentary maker and a reporter who would do an in depth story for later release. My case manager had twice warned me, "no cameras". I told Jon that discretion was imperative. No cameras in evidence!

I was scheduled to present myself at R&D at eight, for a nine am release. Things began going hinky as soon as I arrived at the Receiving and Discharge door. There were four of us scheduled for release that day. Me at nine, two guys at nine-thirty and one at ten! We were all refused admittance and ordered to wait outside. There were seventy undocumented inmates inside. They were being processed for repatriation to their home countries. The Bushies were sweeping tens of thou-

Black Tuna Diaries

sands of them out of the prison system. Even those who still had long sentences to serve! It normally took hours to process that many inmates for travel. Fingerprints, handcuffs, chains, shackles and dress out clothes! All four of us were afraid we'd be sent back to our cell houses and told to try again in a day or two. I could picture Jon, the reporter and the filmmaker who had all traveled up from Miami the night before, being sent away.

After an interminable thirty minutes, we were admitted to R&D and put in a holding cell, separated from the deportees. Fortunately there were four extra officers prepping the chain gang. Shortly before nine the two bus loads of aliens were on their way to the immigration pens to be sorted out and trans-shipped like so many cattle. Now it was my turn, but instead of calling me to dress out, the officer in charge took the two nine-thirty guys out the cell and began to dress and process them out.

"HEY! What about me? I'm supposed to leave before them"! I screamed silently to myself. OH crap, I know my ride is here. Something's wrong. Shit, maybe they spotted the cameraman with his sixty pound Panasonic Pro on his shoulder. I had twice told them " no cameras in view on prison property". I jumped up and down like a monkey on a stick until the guard came over to the door.

"What's happening? I was supposed to leave at nine; it's almost nine-thirty." He just shrugged and said. "I haven't heard anything. Your people must not be here yet."

Now I knew he was lying. I had seen him answer the phone a few minutes earlier and look over at me. Something was wrong.

After he escorted the two nine-thirty guys out to the front lobby, my hopes rose when he slipped the key in the cell door. Nope! It was the ten o'clock inmate he called for dress out. Now I was really shitting myself. I was sure I wouldn't be leaving on this day or maybe any other, before my final six months were up.

Black Tuna Diaries

After the last inmate had gone and I was alone in the holding cell, the guard come and told me there was a problem. S.I.S., the prison security squad, had found a man with the biggest TV camera they had ever seen. They were investigating! I would be called when and if things were explained to the satisfaction of the Chief S.I.S officer.

The next half hour was heart pounding, gut freezing agony. This was the day I had dreamed about for twenty-nine long years, now it was quickly swirling down the vortex of an industrial strength prison crapper. I found myself pacing the seven step length of the narrow holding cell. I've never had a panic attack, but one was on the way. My breathing was shallow. I feared if I couldn't get myself under control, I'd have a heart attack before I walked out the front door.

The phone at the officer's station rang. He picked it up, listened for a minute, looked over at me nodding. Good news? Bad news? He took his time walking over. It took him a minute to sort out the right key from the dozen big brass lock levers on his belt.

"Let's go"!

We walked the ten feet to the long counter where for the last time he pressed my thumb in an ink pad, then held my hand in both of his as he rolled my thumb on a fingerprint card. While I used a paper towel to try to wipe the black ink from my thumb, he put my few personal effects on the counter and counted out the sixty one dollars that had remained in my commissary account. My legacy of twenty nine years! A comb, a handful of pictures, a prison ID card, a small leather ID case with a Black Tuna on it that a friend had made as a going-away gift, and sixty one bucks.

They say the "longest walk" is from your cell on death row, to the death chamber. For me, it was the walk from R&D to the front lobby where I waited for the word I could leave, then out the door to the parking lot, and finally driving out through the gates and away from the forbidding gray barbed wired vista of the prison.

Black Tuna Diaries

But the shades of April Fools Day weren't done with me. As the guard escorted me into the big cold marble lobby with its long counters, x-ray machines, and metal detectors I looked for my nephew Jon. Aside from four guards and the SIS lieutenant, the only occupants were two strangers. A taller version of Jimmy Olsen, cub reporter and a dark haired fortyish, hairy legged, chubby dude, in a wide pair of abbreviated cargo shorts and a tee shirt. Chubby at the counter was clutching a long lens Panasonic video camera that was bigger than a ghetto blaster and must have weighed half a hundred. As we passed through the last metal detector and approached the counter, my keeper nodded toward Mr. Hairy Legs and asked,

"These guys picking you up"?

You have to understand, the rules about who can to pick you up and drive you on furlough to the halfway house, are very strict. They must be investigated and pre-approved weeks in advance. I had listed my son and my nephew. My son was stuck at home two thousand miles away, and Jon was nowhere to be seen. The wrong answer would put me back in my cell. Decide! Quick! No hesitation!

"You bet!" I walked right over to the big guy, grabbed his hand, pulled him close for a hug, and whispered,

"Are you Scott, the documentary guy"? He gave me a nervous smile. Jimmy Olsen cub reporter was fading back toward the exit trying for total invisibility. Just then Scott turned his head to the left, as my nephew Jon, a strikingly handsome, blond six footer, who at thirty-seven still looked like a college quarterback, emerged from a curtained room, usually reserved for private interrogations.

Relief or Panic? Was I out the door or caught in a lie? I grabbed on to Jon, gave him a serious hug and a couple of man kisses on both his cheeks.

"Okay!" I whispered "Now head for the front door and hope no one stops us". Relief began as I stepped out into the Florida

Black Tuna Diaries

sun. Trailed by Scott with the huge Panasonic hanging by his side and Jimmy Olsen still trying to look invisible, I followed Jon across the lot to a big green SUV. Me in the front with Jon, Scott in the left rear with the Panasonic already on his shoulder, and Brantley Hargrove alias Jimmy Olsen, a reporter for The New Times, in the right rear seat with note book in hand.

Let's stop directly across the street so I can start the interview with the entire prison complex in the background". Scott was pointing to the narrow shoulder on the busy two lane highway opposite the prison entrance. Jon pulled across the road and we all piled out again. With almost no room on the dirt strip, Scott was backed up against the trees, and I was standing on the edge of the blacktop with passing cars almost kissing my butt. Behind me, across the road, the camera saw the federal monstrosity. Five prisons! Two penitentiaries, a medium security, a low security, and a prison camp! Grey, ugly, miles of chain link fences, and tons of vicious razor wire! A billboard size sign at the entrance, warned of the consequences of a hundred different violations of conduct on federal property.

Scott taped, and I talked about how it felt to be on the other side of the road after twenty nine years. All the time dodging the speeding cars by jerking my hips forward and sucking in my fat butt.

At last after twenty minutes he lowered the camera. We piled back in the green monster for the three hour drive to the Salvation Army halfway house in West Palm Beach. The questions didn't stop. I was half turned in my seat talking to the camera lens for the entire ride. Prison stories, smuggling stories, tales of my years in the pitch business, and my years in Europe running the Dynamic Reading Institutes! My nephew Jon checking the sound levels as he drove. **The End.**

Black Tuna Diaries

Afterward

My partner and life long friend Robby is alive and well. We talk frequently. My partner Gene Myers passed away just before I left prison. I heard second hand that Chip died, I hope it isn't so. Capt. Crunch died a few years ago. I found Capt. Randy. He lives nearby and we fish together whenever possible. The Fishing Fools are fishing together again. Barry the Stoner has disappeared without a trace. Mark Phillips is still "out of the country" as far as I know. Rumor has it that Capt. Beercan (Brooks Moore) went down with a load on the side of a mountain in Colombia. Bo (El Gigante), last I heard, was selling airplanes out west. Dr Moe, is in Belize giving enemas to tourists.

George Purvis Jr., was the government's principle informer and witness against us. A few years ago, according to the Fayetteville area newspapers, after speaking to his minister, he went aboard his yacht and blew his brains out. It seems the cops were on their way.

My pal Zev is battling cancer and Woody is gone.

Lynne and I live in a small rental apartment in a South Florida retirement community. I am again working as a Pitchman, selling cookware in big box stores and doing TV commercials with my old business partner Jerry Crowley. I speak at university meetings and criminal justice classes. In my spare time I fish and help to promote legalization of medical marijuana so that others don't suffer long lost years in prison for no rational reason.

Join The Gang
Wear the Infamous Golden Medallion
The Black Tuna Gang

In 1979, a joint DEA/FBI task force in Miami immobilized the Black Tuna Gang, a major marijuana smuggling ring responsible for bringing 500 tons of marijuana into the United States over a 16-month period.
. <u>Many of the gang members wore solid-gold medallions bearing a black tuna emblem. The medallions served as a talisman and symbol of their membership in this smuggling group.</u> It was a highly organized ring, with gang members maintaining security and eavesdropping on radio frequencies used by police and U.S. Customs officials.

The Black Tuna Gang ran an elaborate operation, complete with electronically equipped trucks used to maintain contact with the freighters and to monitor law enforcement channels.

**18 Karat Gold Finish
Free Chain**

**Order Now
$19.95**

www.blacktunadiaries.com